Lecture Notes in Computer Science 15947

Founding Editors

Gerhard Goos
Juris Hartmanis

Editorial Board Members

Elisa Bertino, *Purdue University, West Lafayette, IN, USA*
Wen Gao, *Peking University, Beijing, China*
Bernhard Steffen, *TU Dortmund University, Dortmund, Germany*
Moti Yung, *Columbia University, New York, NY, USA*

The series Lecture Notes in Computer Science (LNCS), including its subseries Lecture Notes in Artificial Intelligence (LNAI) and Lecture Notes in Bioinformatics (LNBI), has established itself as a medium for the publication of new developments in computer science and information technology research, teaching, and education.

LNCS enjoys close cooperation with the computer science R & D community, the series counts many renowned academics among its volume editors and paper authors, and collaborates with prestigious societies. Its mission is to serve this international community by providing an invaluable service, mainly focused on the publication of conference and workshop proceedings and postproceedings. LNCS commenced publication in 1973.

Mirco Giacobbe · Anna Lukina
Editors

AI Verification

Second International Symposium, SAIV 2025
Zagreb, Croatia, July 21–22, 2025
Proceedings

Editors
Mirco Giacobbe 󠀂
University of Birmingham
Birmingham, UK

Anna Lukina 󠀂
Delft University of Technology
Delft, The Netherlands

ISSN 0302-9743　　　　　　　ISSN 1611-3349 (electronic)
Lecture Notes in Computer Science
ISBN 978-3-031-99990-1　　　ISBN 978-3-031-99991-8 (eBook)
https://doi.org/10.1007/978-3-031-99991-8

© The Editor(s) (if applicable) and The Author(s), under exclusive license to Springer Nature Switzerland AG 2026

This work is subject to copyright. All rights are solely and exclusively licensed by the Publisher, whether the whole or part of the material is concerned, specifically the rights of translation, reprinting, reuse of illustrations, recitation, broadcasting, reproduction on microfilms or in any other physical way, and transmission or information storage and retrieval, electronic adaptation, computer software, or by similar or dissimilar methodology now known or hereafter developed.
The use of general descriptive names, registered names, trademarks, service marks, etc. in this publication does not imply, even in the absence of a specific statement, that such names are exempt from the relevant protective laws and regulations and therefore free for general use.
The publisher, the authors and the editors are safe to assume that the advice and information in this book are believed to be true and accurate at the date of publication. Neither the publisher nor the authors or the editors give a warranty, expressed or implied, with respect to the material contained herein or for any errors or omissions that may have been made. The publisher remains neutral with regard to jurisdictional claims in published maps and institutional affiliations.

This Springer imprint is published by the registered company Springer Nature Switzerland AG
The registered company address is: Gewerbestrasse 11, 6330 Cham, Switzerland

If disposing of this product, please recycle the paper.

Preface

This volume contains the proceedings of the 8th International Symposium on AI Verification (SAIV), co-located with the 37th International Conference on Computer Aided Verification (CAV) in Zagreb, Croatia, on July 21–22, 2025. SAIV 2025 built on an 8-year legacy as the successor to the *FoMLAS* and *WOLVERINE* workshops, and the previous edition of SAIV. Dedicated to addressing the grand challenge of verifying the safety of AI systems, SAIV brings together researchers from the formal methods and artificial intelligence communities, serving as a platform for exchanging ideas and driving innovation at the intersection of these critical fields. SAIV 2025 hosted the 6th International Verification of Neural Networks Competition (VNN-COMP).

The symposium solicited four categories of submissions: regular papers presenting original research; presentation-only papers featuring recently published or submitted work; extended abstracts describing preliminary or in-progress research; and benchmarks or case studies showcasing practical evaluations, real-world applications, or lessons learned in deploying safety-critical AI systems. The scope of the symposium was organized into two broad thematic areas. The first, formal methods for artificial intelligence, included topics such as formal specifications, analysis, synthesis, testing, statistical analysis, and explainability for systems with AI components. The second, artificial intelligence for formal methods, focused on AI techniques applied to formal verification, synthesis, safe control, and falsification. This structure encouraged a wide range of contributions, supporting both theoretical developments and applied research relevant to the safe deployment of AI technologies.

The symposium attracted 28 submissions for original contributions, extended abstracts, and case studies, each of which was carefully reviewed by three PC members in a single-blind process. As a result, 13 papers were accepted for publication in these proceedings, including 8 regular papers, one case study, and 4 extended abstracts. The present proceedings also include four VNN-COMP contributions.

The program included six invited talks by Nora Ammann (Advanced Research + Invention Agency), Luca Arnaboldi (University of Birmingham), Andreea Costea (TU Delft), Eleonora Giunchiglia (Imperial College London), Guillermo Perez (University of Antwerp), and Masaki Waga (Kyoto University). The invited talks were followed by round-table discussions. As part of the programme, the symposium featured over 20 posters presenting peer-reviewed results as well as ongoing unpublished work.

We thank all authors who submitted papers, the programme committee members, the invited speakers, the participants, the organisers of the VNN-COMP, and the hosting organizers of CAV for making SAIV 2025 a successful event.

July 2025   Mirco Giacobbe

                                                                                                                                                    Anna Lukina

Organization

Program Committee Chairs

Mirco Giacobbe   University of Birmingham, UK
Anna Lukina   Delft University of Technology, The Netherlands

Program Committee

Alessandro Abate	University of Oxford, UK
Luca Arnaboldi	University of Birmingham, UK
Guy Avni	University of Haifa, Israel
Stanley Bak	Stony Brook University, USA
Clark Barrett	Stanford University, USA
Elena Botoeva	University of Kent, UK
Dana Drachsler Cohen	Technion, Israel
Hoang Dung Tran	University of Nebraska, USA
Vijay Ganesh	Georgia Tech, USA
Thomas A. Henzinger	Institute of Science and Technology Austria, Austria
Taylor T. Johnson	Vanderbilt University, USA
Guy Katz	Hebrew University of Jerusalem, Israel
Bettina Könighofer	TU Graz, Austria
Ekaterina Komendantskaya	University of Southampton, UK
Jan Křetínský	Masaryk University, Czechia
Linyi Li	Simon Fraser University, Canada
Alessio Lomuscio	Imperial College London, UK
Kaushik Mallik	IMDEA, Spain
Ravi Mangal	Colorado State University, USA
Edoardo Manino	University of Manchester, UK
Daniel Neider	TU Dortmund University, Germany
Corina Pasareanu	Carnegie Mellon University, USA
Guillermo Perez	University of Antwerp, Belgium
Luca Pulina	University of Sassari, Italy
Chelsea Sidrane	KTH Royal Institute of Technology, Sweden
Gagandeep Singh	University of Illinois Urbana-Champaign, USA
Christian Schilling	Aalborg University, Denmark
Armando Tacchella	University of Genoa, Italy

Shufang Zhu University of Liverpool, UK
Đorđe Žikelić Singapore Management University, Singapore

Contents

Technical Program

Scenario-Based Compositional Verification of Autonomous Systems
with Neural Perception 3
   *Christopher Watson, Rajeev Alur, Divya Gopinath, Ravi Mangal,
and Corina S. Păsăreanu*

Robustness Margin: A New Measure for the Robustness of Neural Networks ... 29
   *Lionel Kielhöfer, Annelot W. Bosman, Holger H. Hoos,
and Jan N. van Rijn*

GRENA: GPU-Aided Abstract Refinement for Neural Network Verification 49
   Yuyi Zhong, Shaun Tan Zong Zhi, Hanping Xu, and Siau-Cheng Khoo

ClassInvGen: Class Invariant Synthesis Using Large Language Models 64
   *Chuyue Sun, Viraj Agashe, Saikat Chakraborty, Jubi Taneja,
Clark Barrett, David Dill, Xiaokang Qiu, and Shuvendu K. Lahiri*

Bridging Neural ODE and ResNet: A Formal Error Bound for Safety
Verification 97
   Abdelrahman Sayed Sayed, Pierre-Jean Meyer, and Mohamed Ghazel

Probabilistic Verification of Neural Networks with Sampling-Based
Probability Box Propagation 115
   Marcel Chwiałkowski, Eric Goubault, and Sylvie Putot

How to Verify Generalization Capability of a Neural Network with Formal
Methods 136
   Arthur Clavière, Dmitrii Kirov, and Darren Cofer

Certified Error Analysis of Homomorphically Encrypted Neural Networks 156
   Philipp Kern, Edoardo Manino, and Carsten Sinz

Neural Network Verification for Gliding Drone Control: A Case Study 180
   *Colin Kessler, Ekaterina Komendantskaya, Marco Casadio,
Ignazio Maria Viola, Thomas Flinkow, Albaraa Ammar Othman,
Alistair Malhotra, and Robbie McPherson*

Extended Abstracts

Abstraction-Based Proof Production in Formal Verification of Neural
Networks (Extended Abstract) 203
   *Yizhak Yisrael Elboher, Omri Isac, Guy Katz, Tobias Ladner,
and Haoze Wu*

On the Complexity of Formal Reasoning in State Space Models (Extended
Abstract) 221
   Eric Alsmann and Martin Lange

Quantifiers for Differentiable Logics in Rocq (Extended Abstract) 227
   *Jairo Miguel Marulanda-Giraldo, Ekaterina Komendantskaya,
Alessandro Bruni, Reynald Affeldt, Matteo Capucci,
and Enrico Marchioni*

CTRAIN - A Training Library for Certifiably Robust Neural Networks
(Extended Abstract) 238
   Konstantin Kaulen and Holger H. Hoos

Competition Contributions

NeuralSAT: Scaling Constraint Solving for DNN Verification
(Competition Contribution) 253
   Hai Duong and ThanhVu Nguyen

NNV: A Star Set Reachability Approach (Competition Contribution) 260
   Diego Manzanas Lopez, Samuel Sasaki, and Taylor T. Johnson

PyRAT: Verifying Neural Networks with Abstract Interpretation
(Competition Contribution) 266
   Augustin Lemesle, Julien Lehmann, Tristan Le Gall, and Zakaria Chihani

SobolBox: Boxed Refinement of Sobol Sequence Samples for Neural
Network Verification (Competition Contribution) 272
   Sarthak Das

Author Index 279

Technical Program

Scenario-Based Compositional Verification of Autonomous Systems with Neural Perception

Christopher Watson[1](✉), Rajeev Alur[1], Divya Gopinath[2], Ravi Mangal[3], and Corina S. Păsăreanu[2,4]

[1] University of Pennsylvania, Philadelphia, USA
ccwatson@seas.upenn.edu
[2] KBR Inc., NASA Ames, Mountain View, USA
[3] Colorado State University, Fort Collins, USA
[4] Carnegie Melon University, Pittsburgh, USA

Abstract. Recent advances in deep learning have enabled the development of autonomous systems that use deep neural networks for perception. Formal verification of these systems is challenging due to the size and complexity of the perception DNNs as well as hard-to-quantify, changing environment conditions. To address these challenges, we propose a probabilistic verification framework for autonomous systems based on the following key concepts: (1) *Scenario-based Modeling:* We decompose the task (e.g., car navigation) into a composition of *scenarios*, each representing a different environment condition. (2) *Probabilistic Abstractions:* For each scenario, we build a compact *abstraction of perception* based on the DNN's performance on an offline dataset that represents the scenario's environment condition. (3) *Symbolic Reasoning and Acceleration:* The abstractions enable efficient compositional verification of the autonomous system via symbolic reasoning and a novel *acceleration proof rule* that bounds the error probability of the system under arbitrary variations of environment conditions. We illustrate our approach on two case studies: an experimental autonomous system that guides airplanes on taxiways using high-dimensional perception DNNs and a simulation model of an F1Tenth autonomous car using LiDAR observations.

1 Introduction

Recent advances in deep learning have enabled the development of autonomous systems that use deep neural networks (DNNs) for perception [10–12,19,21,32] Formal verification of these systems is uniquely challenging due to the complexity of formal reasoning about the DNNs. The perception DNNs are massive (with millions or billions of parameters) and are also known to be very sensitive to input perturbations. For instance, changing the light conditions in an image can lead to very different DNN outputs and this can adversely affect the safety of the overall system. Furthermore, real-world autonomous systems typically operate in an environment whose configuration is a priori unknown (e.g., the car is navigating in a location with an unknown layout of tracks). In this work, we propose a probabilistic verification framework to address these challenges.

System Description. Consider the autonomous system from Fig. 1; it consists of four interacting components: *Sensor*, *Perception DNN*, *Controller*, and *Dynamics*. The *Sensor* (e.g., a camera or LiDAR system) observes the current underlying system state (potentially subject to hard-to-model environmental conditions) and produces sensor readings (e.g., images or LiDAR readings).

The *Perception DNN* takes inputs from the *Sensor* and produces *state estimates* that are used by the *Controller* to output control commands for the system. In response to these commands, the system state is updated as described by the *Dynamics* and the cycle repeats. This forms a closed-loop system where the *Perception DNN* repeatedly receives *Sensor* inputs as the system operates in its environment. Note that such systems

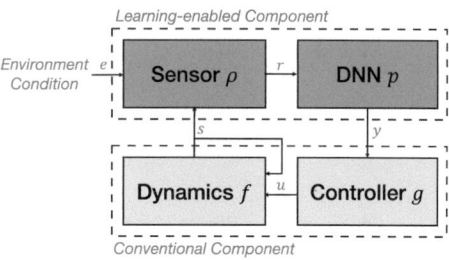

Fig. 1. Components of an autonomous system with DNN-based perception.

tend to be stochastic, even when *Dynamics* and *Controller* are deterministic, due to the uncertainty in the *Sensor* readings.

Safety Properties. We analyze such systems with respect to critical safety properties that can be framed as reachability queries. We focus on two questions: (1) given a set of initial conditions, what is the probability of reaching an error state? and (2) given a user-specified bound on the probability of reaching an error state, what is the corresponding set of most permissive initial conditions? The specific notion of error depends on the system being analyzed. In our first case study, we analyze an autonomous airplane taxiing system that relies on Boeing's *TaxiNet* perception DNN and define error as excessive deviation from the runway's centerline. In our simulated F1Tenth case study, we define error to be collision with the edge of the race track or failure to navigate a track segment within a predetermined time limit.

Modeling the Learning-enabled Components. The conventional components (*Controller* and *Dynamics*) can be modeled using well-known techniques [29], for instance, they can be modeled as transition systems or Discrete-time Markov Chains (DTMCs). However, the learning-enabled components (*Perception DNN* and *Sensor*) are difficult to model due to enormous sizes of modern DNNs and the complex nature of the sensors as well as the changing environmental conditions in which these systems operate. The key challenge is to analyze the learning enabled components in a way that can be composed with traditional systems verification techniques to obtain a guarantee for the entire closed loop system. Approaches to this challenge form three groups: (1) those that apply neural network verification to the *Perception DNN* and precisely model the *Sensor* mathematically [8,14,15,30] or with a learned model [1,5,22,33] (2) those that build *contracts* [2,17,18,24,25,29,31] around the learning enabled components, and (3) those that build *probabilistic abstractions* [3,4,6,7,28] around the learning enabled component.

In general, neural network verification only scales to DNNs of modest size, and realistic sensors are hard to model, especially when subject to environmental disturbances. Contract-based approaches provide obligations for the learning-enabled components that ensure system safety, but cannot quantify system safety if the contracts are not met. To provide a scalable, quantitative analysis of sytem-level safety, our current work extends the technique of *probabilistic abstraction*, which models the learning-enabled components' behavior as an explicit map from each system state to a distribution over *Perception DNN* outputs. The probabilities in this map are computed from the *confusion matrix* that measures the performance of the *Perception DNN* on a representative dataset obtained from simulations or real-world setting. With this abstraction, the resulting system can be modeled as a DTMC and is amenable to verification using off-the-shelf tools such as PRISM [23] and Storm [16].

While the compact abstraction of the learning-enabled components allows the analysis to scale to arbitrarily large DNNs and does not require modeling the *Sensor*, if the offline dataset pools data from multiple distinct environment conditions the abstraction may be too coarse, resulting in an imprecise analysis.

Our Proposal. In this work, we structure the analysis of the autonomous system as a composition of *scenarios*, each of which represents the behavior of the system under a different *environment condition* for a fixed duration. In the context of our autonomous taxiing case study, we observe that the *TaxiNet* perception system has dramatically different performance in *bright* versus *dark* lighting conditions (see Fig. 2). To perform an analysis of system level safety that accounts for changes in lighting conditions, we define the scenarios `bright` and `dark`. Within the `bright` scenario,

Fig. 2. TaxiNet achieves 91.25% accuracy when estimating heading for a *bright* image dataset but only 53.87% accuracy for a *dark* image dataset.

we can accurately model the behavior of the closed loop system by incorporating a probabilistic of abstraction constructed using a dataset collected in *bright* light. A separate dataset lets us accurately model the system's behavior in the `dark` scenario. Similarly, to analyze an autonomous race car, we define a separate scenario for each kind of track segment (*straight*, *left turn*, or *right turn*) to efficiently analyze safety for a diverse set of track configurations. While scenario-based decomposition is inspired by the non-probabilistic analysis of [20], our probabilistic abstraction of the learning-enabled component of each scenario allows our analysis to scale to arbitrarily complex sensor and perception systems. Scenario-based decomposition also allows our approach to efficiently compute safety guarantees for long time horizons.

Contributions. Overall, we make the following contributions: (1) we present an approach for compactly modeling autonomous systems that accounts for changing environment conditions via decomposition into environment-specific scenarios; (2) we extend prior work [28] by allowing a system designer to define separate probabilistic abstractions, representing DNN performance in different environment conditions; we further generalize the confusion matrices to account for arbitrary state estimate definitions, not just the underlying system state as in previous work; (3) we describe an efficient symbolic approach for analyzing finite sequences of scenarios with respect to initial conditions specified as a set of distributions over the system states; (4) we also give a novel family of compositional proof rules for accelerated analysis of finite sequences with arbitrary interleavings of scenarios; these rules enable developers to compute a bound on error probability even when the precise configuration of the environment is not known a priori; (5) we illustrate our approach on two case studies: a model of an experimental autonomous system that guides airplanes on taxiways using high-dimensional perception DNNs and a model of an F1Tenth autonomous car using LiDAR observations.

Related Work. We have already discussed closely related work on formal analysis of learning-enabled systems. Other related work includes approaches based on statistical simulation [35] that require less computation but provide a different type of guarantee than probabilistic model checking. Moreover, statistical model checking is not suitable for models that include nondeterminism, thus cannot be compared with the guarantees we obtain for arbitrary interleavings of scenarios. Another related line of work is compositional probabilistic model checking [34], which, however does not address the central challenge of incorporating machine-learning components.

Also related is the work on probabilistic predicate transformers [26]. Each of our scenarios can be seen as a probabilistic assignment, and the backward analysis of Sect. 3.1 is a special case of the weakest precondition computation. Much work on predicate transformers concerns general loops, which are not immediately relevant to modeling autonomous systems over bounded horizons. To our knowledge, no analogue of our acceleration rules exists in the literature.

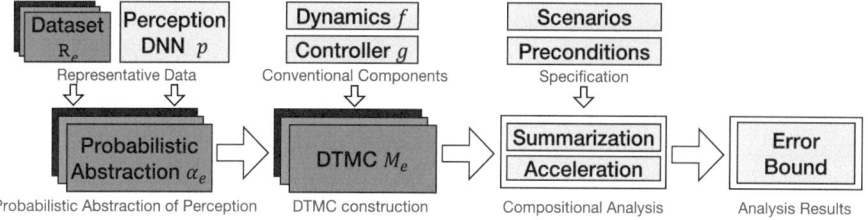

Fig. 3. Scenario-based compositional analysis of autonomous systems.

2 Scenario-Based Probabilistic Abstractions of Perception

Figure 3 illustrates our approach. The goal is to analyze safety properties of autonomous systems, subject to changing environment conditions. We assume that a domain expert can identify a finite set E of environment conditions, e.g. *bright* vs *dark* lighting. For each environment condition $e \in E$, the domain expert provides a dataset R_e that represents the behavior of the *Sensor* subject to that environment condition. This, combined with black-box access to the *Perception DNN*, allows us to construct a *probabilistic abstraction of perception* α_e for each environment condition, which can in turn be composed with a model of the conventional components to yield a DTMC model M_e of the closed-loop system subject to each environment condition. For simplicity of presentation, we assume that only the behavior of learning-enabled components changes with the environment conditions, more generally, the conventional components may also change. Our techniques are applicable to this more general setting, and in Sect. 4 we consider such a case.

A scenario represents the behavior of the autonomous system subject to a particular environment condition for a fixed finite time horizon. The inputs to our compositional analysis are a sequence of scenarios and a precondition that constrains the set of initial state distributions. A *summarization* procedure allows us to efficiently compute a worst-case error bound for a fixed scenario sequence, and our *acceleration* proof rules allow us to derive a bound on error probability that is parametric with respect to the length of a scenario sequence of unbounded length. We make these notions precise in the following sections.

2.1 Modeling the Closed-Loop Autonomous System

A discrete-time closed-loop autonomous system is composed of conventional components *Controller* and *Dynamics* as well learning-enabled components *Sensor* and *Perception DNN*. Given a fixed environment condition $e \in E$, at each timestep t, the *Sensor* $\rho_e : S \to \mathbf{Dist}(R)$[1] (which may be a camera or LiDAR

---

[1] We write $\mathbf{Dist}(X)$ for the set of probability distributions over a finite set X and identify each $x \in \mathbf{Dist}(X)$ with its representation as a row vector in $\mathbb{R}^{|X|}$.

system) observes the current underlying system state $s_t \in S$ and probabilistically produces a sensor reading $r_t \in R$ sampled from the distribution $\rho_e(s_t)$ (where r_t is an image, LiDAR reading, etc.). The *Perception DNN* $p: R \to Y$ processes r_t to yield an estimate $y_t \in Y$ of the system state. The *Controller* $g: Y \to U$ receives this state estimate and outputs a control signal $u_t \in U$. At the start of the next timestep $t+1$, the *Dynamics* $f: S \times U \to S$ produces a new system state $s_{t+1} \in S$ in response to the control input u_t and the cycle continues. The sets S, Y, and U are assumed to be finite.

Probabilistic Abstraction of Perception. Constructing models of the *Sensor* and the *Perception DNN* is a central challenge given their complexity. We extend past work [28] and build compact abstractions $\alpha_e : S \to \mathbf{Dist}(Y)$ of the learning-enabled components.

The key idea is that the input-output behavior of the learning-enabled components (as a function of type $S \to \mathbf{Dist}(Y)$) can be estimated using an offline dataset of sensor readings gathered using the *Sensor* onboard the autonomous system. A limitation of previous work was that they built a single abstraction, regardless of environment conditions, leading to overly imprecise results, as illustrated in Fig. 2.

In this work, we address this important limitation by building a separate probabilistic abstraction of perception α_e for each environment condition e. For each pair of environment condition e and state s, we assume access to an offline dataset $R_{e,s}$ of sensor readings collected while the autonomous system was in state s and subject to condition e.

Another limitation of previous work was that the probabilistic abstraction was based on computing confusion matrices under the restricted assumption that the DNN outputs correspond precisely to the state definition. In practice, DNNs can be used to estimate only some aspects of the underlying state. Thus, we generalize confusion matrices to account for arbitrary state estimate definitions, not just the underlying system state as in previous work.

The construction of probabilistic abstraction α_e for condition e proceeds as follows. First, for each $s \in S$, we apply the *Perception DNN* function $p : R \to Y$ to each r_s in $R_{e,s}$ to obtain the pair $(s, p(r_s))$; here, r_s is a sensor reading gathered in state s because it is from $R_{e,s}$. We combine all of these pairs to form a labeled dataset of $S \times Y$ pairs that describes the behavior of the learning-enabled components subject to e. From this dataset we can build a contingency matrix[2] $\boldsymbol{C}_e$. For any $s \in S$ and $y \in Y$, we write $\boldsymbol{C}_e(s,y)$ for the frequency of the pair (s,y) in the labeled dataset. We define the probabilistic abstraction of perception $\alpha_e : S \to \mathbf{Dist}(Y)$ as

$$\alpha_e(s)(y) := \frac{\boldsymbol{C}_e(s,y)}{\sum_{y' \in Y} (\boldsymbol{C}_e(s,y'))}$$

---

[2] This is a *confusion matrix* when $S = Y$.

System Model. The probabilistic abstraction α_e of the learning-enabled component in environment condition e can be composed with the discrete models of the conventional components to yield a discrete-time Markov chain (DTMC) that models the closed-loop system as in [3,7,28]. We denote this DTMC as $\mathcal{M}_e = (S, \boldsymbol{P}_e)$ in which S is a finite set of states (in particular, the set of states of the autonomous system) and $\boldsymbol{P}_e$ is a $|S| \times |S|$ right-stochastic matrix. At each timestep, the probability of a transition from some $s \in S$ to some $s' \in S$ is:

$$\boldsymbol{P}_e(s, s') := \sum_{y \in Y} \alpha_e(s)(y)[f(g(y)) = s']$$

where $[f(g(y)) = s']$ evaluates to 1 whenever $f(g(y)) = s'$ and 0 otherwise. For our case studies, we follow the procedure of [28] to represent this DTMC using PRISM, see Sect. 4.1 for details.

Without loss of generality, we assume that the autonomous system has a distinguished *error state*, which we denote s_{err}. We assume that the conventional dynamics ensure that the error state is *absorbing*, i.e., once the system reaches s_{err}, it stays there. This modeling assumption both reflects the natural meaning of an "error state" and facilitates the compositional analysis.

2.2 Scenarios

We are interested in modeling the behavior of autonomous systems under changing environmental conditions. For this purpose, we introduce the notion of *scenarios*. Consider an autonomous system with states S and environment conditions E. For each $e \in E$, let $\mathcal{M}_e = (S, \boldsymbol{P}_e)$ be the DTMC that models execution of the autonomous system subject to environment condition e.

A *scenario* is a pair $(e, H) \in E \times \mathbb{N}$ that comprises an environment condition and a time horizon. Semantically, each scenario induces a map $[\![(e, H)]\!] : \mathbf{Dist}(S) \to \mathbf{Dist}(S)$ defined as

$$[\![(e, H)]\!](\boldsymbol{x}) := \boldsymbol{x} \boldsymbol{P}_e^H$$

that maps a distribution $\boldsymbol{x} \in \mathbf{Dist}(S)$ to the transient distribution reached after taking H steps in $\mathcal{M}_e$.

To model transitions between environment conditions, we consider nonempty sequences of scenarios. Each scenario is also a *scenario sequence*. Given two scenario sequences w_1 and w_2, the sequential composition $w_1; w_2$ is also a scenario sequence. Sequential composition is associative. Semantically, we define $[\![w_1; w_2]\!] : \mathbf{Dist}(S) \to \mathbf{Dist}(S)$ inductively as:

$$[\![w; w']\!] := [\![w']\!] \circ [\![w]\!]$$

Scenario Summary. When representing the semantics $[\![w]\!]$ of a scenario $w = (e, H)$, we find it useful to treat the error state s_{err} in a special manner as this facilitates the compositional analysis presented in Sect. 3.2. To treat the error state separately, we first partition the state space S of M_e as $S = \underline{S} \sqcup \{s_{err}\}$. Then, our explicit representation of $[\![(e,H)]\!]$ takes the form of the *summary* $(\boldsymbol{A}, \boldsymbol{b})$, such that for any initial distribution $\boldsymbol{x} \in \mathbf{Dist}(\underline{S})$ (we assume here that the initial distribution places no weight on s_{err}), executing the scenario (e, H) causes the autonomous system to transition to the error state with probability $\boldsymbol{x} \cdot \boldsymbol{b}$ and induces the subdistribution[3] $\boldsymbol{xA} \in \mathbf{SDist}(\underline{S})$ over the non-error states. Since we assume that the error state is absorbing, the error probability $\boldsymbol{x} \cdot \boldsymbol{b}$ is the probability that the system reaches the error state at any timestep during the scenario. The summary $(\boldsymbol{A}, \boldsymbol{b})$ of an atomic scenario $w = (e, H)$ is related to the stochastic matrix $\boldsymbol{P}_e$ as follows:

$$\begin{bmatrix} \boldsymbol{A} & \boldsymbol{b} \\ \boldsymbol{0} & 1 \end{bmatrix} = \boldsymbol{P}_e^H$$

We lift the definition of summary to scenario sequences inductively. If a scenario w has summary C, then the singleton scenario sequence w also has summary C. If the scenario sequences w_1 and w_2 have summaries $C_1 = (\boldsymbol{A}_1, \boldsymbol{b}_1)$ and $C_2 = (\boldsymbol{A}_2, \boldsymbol{b}_2)$, respectively, then the scenario sequence $w_1; w_2$ has the summary $C_1 C_2 = (\boldsymbol{A}_1 \boldsymbol{A}_2, \boldsymbol{b}_1 + \boldsymbol{A}_1 \boldsymbol{b}_2)$. This composition is well-defined because each summary is defined with respect to the set of system states S, which is common to all scenarios.

3 Compositional Analysis with Scenario Summaries

We analyze the probability that the autonomous system will reach the distinguished error state s_{err} during the execution of a scenario sequence. We propose two types of analysis: (1) a symbolic analysis that provides a tight analysis of the error probability of a fixed scenario sequence with respect to a symbolic precondition and (2) a novel *acceleration rule* that can be used to derive an upper bound on error probability that is parametric with respect to the length of an arbitrary interleaving of a set of scenarios.

3.1 Symbolic Analysis of Fixed Scenarios

For a fixed scenario sequence w with summary $(\boldsymbol{A}, \boldsymbol{b})$, the expression $\boldsymbol{x} \cdot \boldsymbol{b}$ represents the probability that the autonomous system will reach the error state when started from an initial state distribution $\boldsymbol{x}$. This linear expression allows us to efficiently perform *forward* and *backward* analyses that relate preconditions over initial distributions with bounds on error probability.

Forward Analysis. A domain expert may identify a precondition ϕ over the set of initial state distributions and wish to compute the worst-case probability of reaching the error state during the execution of the scenario sequence from an

---
[3] A subdistribution $\boldsymbol{x} \in \mathbf{SDist}(\underline{S})$ may have $|\boldsymbol{x}| < 1$.

initial distribution $x \in \mathbf{Dist}(\underline{S})$ that satisfies ϕ. Recall that we represent each distribution as a vector in $\mathbb{R}^{|\underline{S}|}$. We consider preconditions that can be expressed as an intersection of affine constraints, i.e. of the form $xa_1 \leq \theta_1 \wedge \ldots \wedge xa_d \leq \theta_d$ for some coefficient vectors $a_1, \ldots, a_d \in \mathbb{R}^{|\underline{S}|}$ and offset scalars $\theta_1, \ldots, \theta_d \in \mathbb{R}$.

The worst-case error probability is given by the following linear program:

$$\begin{aligned}
\max_{x} \quad & x \cdot b \\
\text{subject to} \quad & x \cdot a_i \leq \theta_i, \quad \forall i, \in \{1, \ldots, d\} \\
& x \geq 0, \\
& \|x\|_1 = 1.
\end{aligned}$$

where the first d constraints encode ϕ and the last two constraints enforce that x represents a probability distribution. This linear program can be solved using optimization software such as Gurobi [13].

Backward Analysis. If a domain expert provides a maximum allowable error probability ϵ for the execution of the scenario sequence, the precondition $\phi := x \cdot b \leq \epsilon$ is the weakest precondition over initial state distributions that ensures the error probability does not exceed ϵ.

Comparison with PRISM. The symbolic analyses allow the domain expert to reason about the error probability of the autonomous system with respect to a set of initial distributions. This complements the analyses supported by the probabilistic model checker PRISM, which permits forward analysis from a single initial state (or finite set of initial states).

3.2 Acceleration Rules

The aforementioned analyses are useful when the domain expert fixes a particular scenario sequence to consider. However, such foresight is not always possible. To address this, we introduce novel *acceleration* rules that allow us to bound the probability of error without fixing the length of the scenario sequence or the order in which the scenarios appear *a priori*. with respect to an unpredictable sequence of environment conditions.

Hoare-Style Assertions. We reason about scenario sequences using Hoare-style assertions with special treatment of error states. An assertion is a quadruple of the form $\{\phi\}C\{\psi\}\{\epsilon\}$ where $C \equiv (A, b)$ denotes the summary of a scenario sequence, the precondition ϕ and postcondition ψ are predicates over $\mathbf{Dist}(\underline{S})$ expressed as intersections of affine constraints over $\mathbb{R}^{|\underline{S}|}$ and $0 \leq \epsilon \leq 1$ is the required bound on error probability. We write $\phi(x)$ when x satisfies ϕ. The assertion $\{\phi\}C\{\psi\}\{\epsilon\}$ holds exactly when

$$\forall x \in \mathbf{Dist}(\underline{S}), \phi(x) \Rightarrow x \cdot b \leq \epsilon \wedge \psi(\mathit{norm}(xA))$$

Here *norm* is an operation that (L1) *normalizes* a subdistribution to make it a proper distribution, i.e., $norm(\boldsymbol{x}) = \frac{\boldsymbol{x}}{|\boldsymbol{x}|}$. We normalize the output subdistribution $\boldsymbol{x}\boldsymbol{A}$ of C as ψ is defined with respect to $\textbf{Dist}(\underline{S})$. Given the explicit summary of the scenario, such assertions can be checked efficiently using an off-the shelf solver, such as Z3 [9] as we will show in the following example.

Example. Consider the scenario with summary $C \equiv (\boldsymbol{A}, \boldsymbol{b})$ shown below:

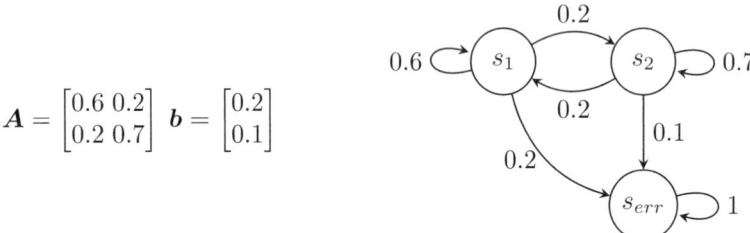

$$A = \begin{bmatrix} 0.6 & 0.2 \\ 0.2 & 0.7 \end{bmatrix} \quad b = \begin{bmatrix} 0.2 \\ 0.1 \end{bmatrix}$$

Let $\boldsymbol{x} = [x_1, x_2]$ denote an initial distribution over the system states s_1 and s_2. Upon executing the scenario, the probability of transitioning to error state is $\boldsymbol{x} \cdot \boldsymbol{b} = 0.2x_1 + 0.1x_2$ and the resulting distribution over the system states (conditioned on not reaching s_{err}) will be:

$$\boldsymbol{x}' = norm(\boldsymbol{x}\boldsymbol{A}) = \frac{\boldsymbol{x}\boldsymbol{A}}{1 - \boldsymbol{x} \cdot \boldsymbol{b}} = \frac{[0.6x_1 + 0.2x_2, 0.2x_1 + 0.7x_2]}{(1 - (0.2x_1 + 0.1x_2))}$$

Let us consider the precondition $\phi := x_1 \leq 0.7 \wedge x_2 \leq 0.7$. We will show how to check the assertion $\{\phi\}C\{\phi\}\{0.15\}$ using Z3.

We can encode the set of distributions that satisfy ϕ as a polyhedron in $\mathbb{R}^{|\underline{S}|}$ with H-representation $\boldsymbol{M}_\phi \boldsymbol{x}^\top \leq \boldsymbol{\theta}_\phi$ for some 6×2 matrix $\boldsymbol{M}_\phi$ and 6-dimensional vector $\boldsymbol{\theta}_\phi$ of offsets. The H-representation comprises 6 inequalities since four inequalities define the subset of $\mathbb{R}^{|\underline{S}|}$ that represents $\textbf{Dist}(\underline{S})$ and the predicate ϕ contains two additional constraints. In order to check whether $\phi(\boldsymbol{x}) \Rightarrow \boldsymbol{x} \cdot \boldsymbol{b} \leq \epsilon \wedge \psi(norm(\boldsymbol{x}\boldsymbol{A}))$ we can ask Z3 whether $\boldsymbol{M}_\phi \boldsymbol{x}^\top \leq \boldsymbol{\theta}_\phi \wedge \neg(\boldsymbol{x} \cdot \boldsymbol{b} \leq 0.15)$ and $\boldsymbol{M}_\phi \boldsymbol{x}^\top \leq \boldsymbol{\theta}_\phi \wedge \neg(\boldsymbol{M}(norm(\boldsymbol{x}\boldsymbol{A}))^\top \leq \boldsymbol{\theta}_X)$ are both unsatisfiable. If both are unsatisfiable (as they are for this example), then we can conclude $\{\phi\}C\{\phi\}\{0.15\}$.

Rule for Sequential Composition. The building block for our acceleration rules is the following compositional rule which bounds the error probability for the sequential composition of two scenarios.

$$\frac{\{\phi\}C\{\psi\}\{\epsilon\}, \{\phi'\}C'\{\psi'\}\{\epsilon'\}, \psi \implies \phi'}{\{\phi\}CC'\{\psi'\}\{1 - (1-\epsilon)(1-\epsilon')\}} \quad \text{Rule 1}$$

Rule 1 generalizes to our first *acceleration rule*, where C^k is shorthand for sequential composition of C applied $k \in \mathbb{N}$ times

$$\frac{\{\phi\}C\{\phi\}\{\epsilon\}}{\{\phi\}C^k\{\phi\}\{1-(1-\epsilon)^k\}} \text{ RULE 2}$$

Rule 2 can be seen as a family of rules (parameterized by k) that provides a *recipe* for bounding the error probability of a k-ary sequential composition. A user only needs to prove the premise of the rule once (using constraint solving as described above) and can then apply the rule to obtain a bound on error probability for any desired k. We are now ready to present our main *acceleration rule* that generalizes the preceding rules:

$$\frac{\{\phi\}C\{\phi\}\{\epsilon\}}{\{\phi\}C^k\{\phi\}\{1-(1-\epsilon)^k\}} \text{ RULE 2}$$

Using Rule 3, we can estimate the error probability for scenarios formed through arbitrary sequential compositions of C_1, C_2, C_m up to length k (here we use '|' to represent choice). Like Rule 2, Rule 3 can be seen as a family of rules; it provides a *recipe* for bounding the error probability for sequences of scenarios of length k that can be generated from the regular expression $(C_1 \mid \ldots \mid C_m)^k$.

Note also that while the above rules are sound (see Appendix A for proofs) the error bound is not *tight*. Nevertheless, the acceleration rules give a domain expert the flexibility to efficiently bound the error probability for scenario sequences, without *a priori* knowing the sequence length or the order of scenarios.

Choice of ϕ and ϵ. To apply Rule 3, we must find a precondition ϕ and $\epsilon \in \mathbb{R}$ that satisfy the rule's premise. This ϕ needs to be "invariant" in the sense that ϕ serves as both a pre- and post-condition. We can use Z3 to check whether a particular ϕ satisfies the rule's premise as described in the context of our example above. Before introducing our heuristic search to find an invariant ϕ, we note that the vacuous precondition $\phi = \top$ satisfies Rule 3's premise $\{\phi\}C_1\{\phi\}\{\epsilon\}, \ldots, \{\phi\}C_m\{\phi\}\{\epsilon\}$ when ϵ is chosen as:

$$\epsilon = \max_{i \in \{1,\ldots,m\}} (||\boldsymbol{b}_i||_\infty)$$

where $C_i \equiv (\boldsymbol{A}_i, \boldsymbol{b}_i)$ for each i. This ϵ is the worst-case *local* error probability achieved from any initial distribution by any C_i. In practice, this ϵ may be too high to provide a useful safety guarantee.

We describe our heuristic search for an invariant ϕ that allows us to apply Rule 3 to bound the error probability of arbitrary sequential compositions of a finite set of scenario sequences with summaries $(\boldsymbol{A}_1, \boldsymbol{b}_1), \ldots, (\boldsymbol{A}_m, \boldsymbol{b}_m)$. We use the same procedure in the context of Rule 2, which is equivalent to Rule 3 when $m = 1$. Our search considers only the preconditions that are *weakest preconditions* with respect to a particular value of ϵ.

1. Choose desired local error probability $0 \leq \epsilon \leq 1$ and define $\phi := \wedge_{i \in \{1,\ldots,m\}} \boldsymbol{x} \cdot \boldsymbol{b}_i \leq \epsilon$.

Table 1. Excerpted rows and columns from the TaxiNet *bright* (left) and *dark* (right) confusion matrices. The rows and columns are labeled by states, expressed as (cte,he) pairs.

TaxiNet Accuracy (Bright)

	(0,0)	(0,1)	(0,2)	(1,0)
(0,0)	964	44	30	18
(0,1)	4	233	0	2
(0,2)	3	1	258	0
(1,0)	45	39	3	475

TaxiNet Accuracy (Bright)

	(0,0)	(0,1)	(0,2)	(1,0)
(0,0)	499	621	14	13
(0,1)	1	473	0	3
(0,2)	188	23	84	0
(1,0)	203	765	1	125

2. Check whether $\forall i \in \{1,\ldots,m\}, \forall x \in \mathbf{Dist}(\underline{S}), \phi(x) \Rightarrow \phi(\frac{xA_i}{1-x \cdot b_i})$ using a numerical solver such as Z3.
3. If the check from the previous step succeeds, then ϕ is an invariant precondition and we are done. Otherwise, we return to step 1 and choose a different, higher value of ϵ.

4 Experimental Evaluation

We apply our analysis techniques to two case studies, one based on the real-world TaxiNet perception system and another based on a simulated F1Tenth race car.

TaxiNet. TaxiNet is a neural network used for perception in an experimental system developed by Boeing for autonomous centerline tracking on airport taxiways. It takes as input a picture of taxiway and estimates the plane's position with respect to the centerline in terms of two outputs: *cross track error* (*cte*), which is the distance in meters of the plane from the centerline and *heading error* (*he*), which is the angle of the plane with respect to the centerline. This regression is performed by a DNN containing 24 layers including five convolution layers and three dense layers (with 100/50/10 ELU neurons) before the output layer. The resulting state estimates are fed to a controller, which maneuvers the plane to follow the centerline. Error is defined as excessive deviation from the centerline. We analyze a discretized version of the system, for details see Appendix B.1.

Prior work [28] builds a probabilistic abstraction of perception based on the performance of TaxiNet on a dataset provided by Boeing, and performs an analysis of the closed-loop system to estimate the probability of error In our current work, we refine this analysis by first partitioning the dataset into a *bright* dataset and a *dark* dataset, then building a separate probabilistic abstraction of perception for each condition.

Table 1 shows excerpts from the confusion matrices made from the *bright* and *dark* partitions. Interestingly, the frequency and kind of misclassifications is markedly different between lighting conditions. To investigate how different lighting conditions (and transitions between lighting conditions) affect system level safety, we construct two scenarios bright $= (bright, 20)$ and dark $= (dark, 20)$ that represent execution of the autonomous system for 20 timesteps in *bright* or *dark* lighting, respectively and apply the compositional analysis techniques introduced in Sect. 3. To provide a point of comparison with prior work that builds a single probabilistic abstraction, [28], we also consider a *pooled* environment condition, which corresponds to the lighting condition being identically distributed at each timestep, proportionately to the frequency of light vs. dark images in the original, unpartitioned dataset. We define the scenario pooled $= (pooled, 20)$ to demonstrate that our bright and dark scenarios permit a refined analysis.

F1Tenth. Our second case study is inspired by the F1Tenth autonomous racing competition [27], in which a model race car navigates a track. In particular, we analyze an idealized discrete-state model of driving dynamics. The car's *Sensor* produces 21-dimensional LiDAR observations, which are processed by a multilayer perceptron with ReLU activations, two hidden layers, and 128 neurons per hidden layer, to produce state estimates. We trained the MLP using 1000 simulated observations gathered from each system state in each track segment and evaluated its performance using a separate, identically constructed dataset. Each simulated LiDAR observation was constructed from a position sampled uniformly within a small L1 radius of the discrete state's canonical position.

Inspired by [20], we consider the set of environment conditions to be the set of track segments, i.e. $E = \{left, right, straight\}$ and define the scenarios left $= (left, 30)$, right $= (right, 30)$, and straight $= (straight, 30)$. We allow the *Dynamics* $f : E \times S \times U \to S$ and *Controller* $g : E \times Y \to U$ to condition their behavior on the current environment condition. The dependency of f on the current track segment is necessary to model the track configuration; the dependency of g on the current track segment corresponds to a controller equipped with a perfect mode predictor that identifies the current scenario.

The meaning of a state $(pos_{side}, pos_{front}, heading, \tau) \in S \setminus \{s_{err}\}$ is defined with respect to the current scenario and diagrammed in Fig. 4. The components are:

- $pos_{side} \in \{-7, \ldots, 7\}$, which denotes sideways position.
- $pos_{front} \in \{0, \ldots, 16\}$, which denotes front/back position.
- $heading \in \{0, \ldots 7\}$ which denotes the car's heading, measured in increments of $\pi/4$ radians where $heading = 0$ denotes facing towards the front wall.
- $\tau \in \{1, \ldots, 30\}$ which denotes the timesteps spent in the current scenario.

The set of control inputs are $U = \{-1, 0, 1\}$ which represent adjustments to the current heading. At each timestep, the car's heading is updated based on the control input u. Then, the car moves one grid-position in the direction of the updated heading.

To model walls and the final goal of each track segment, we define the subsets of the car positions as shown in Fig. 4. During the left scenario, the car's goal is to reach the final region F_{left}. Failure to reach the final region F_{left} in 30 timesteps triggers a transition to s_{err}, as does attempting to enter any position not in $Track \cup Track_{left}$. This is defined similarly for the other track segments, for complete details, including technical treatment of the transitions between track segments, see Appendix B.2.

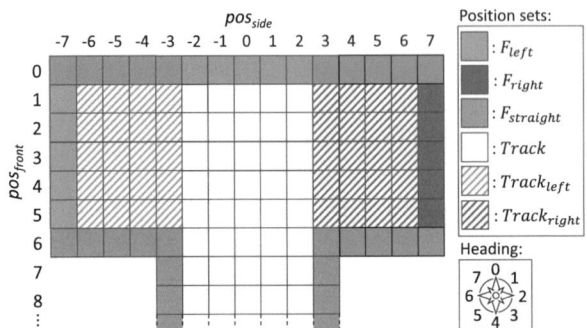

Fig. 4. Each F1Tenth scenario corresponds to a track segment.

4.1 Implementation

We adapt the PRISM model construction of [28] to allow us to compute a *summary* for each atomic scenario. The PRISM construction reflects the system decomposition illustrated in Fig. 1. In particular, the PRISM model takes three timesteps (one for the learning-enabled components, one for the *Controller*, and one for the *Dynamics*) to model one timestep of the autonomous system. This coordination is mediated by bookkeeping variables, for details, see Appendix B.

Consider an autonomous system with state set S and the atomic scenarios $(e_1, H_1), \ldots, (e_m, H_m)$. Our PRISM model contains a set of variables V_S such that each valuation to V_S uniquely determines a system state $s \in \underline{S}$. Our model also contains a variable scenario that maintains the index $i \in \{1, \ldots, m\}$ of the current scenario and a variable timer that maintains the timestep of the original autonomous system. To model the horizon of each scenario we define the PRISM formula exit_condition as ! error & ((scenario = 0 & timer = H_i) | ... | (scenario = m & timer = H_m)) and ensure that each PRISM state that satisfies exit_condition has no outgoing transitions. To compute the summary $(\boldsymbol{A}_i, \boldsymbol{b}_i)$ of scenario (e_i, H_i), we do the following for each $s \in \underline{S}$:

1. Modify the PRISM model so that initially scenario $= i$, timer $= 1$ and the valuation to V_S determines s.
2. For each $s' \in S$, execute the PRISM query P=? F[exit_condition & s'] and fill this value into $\boldsymbol{A}_i(s, s')$. In the preceding PRISM query, s' stands for the state predicate that holds iff the valuation to V_S determines s'.
3. Execute the PRISM query P=? F[error] and fill this value into $\boldsymbol{b}_i(s)$.

4.2 Fixed Scenario Analysis

We apply the analysis techniques described in Sect. 3.1 to fixed sequences of the scenarios bright and dark from the TaxiNet case study to explore how a shift in lighting conditions affects system level safety. For the F1Tenth case study, we consider sequences of the scenarios straight, left, and right that represent different track configurations.

Table 2. Forward analysis for TaxiNet (left) and F1Tenth (right). For each scenario sequence, we report the worst-case error probability given a precondition over the initial state distribution. In F1Tenth, l, r, and s abbreviate left, right, and straight, respectively.

TaxiNet	$\phi_{nominal}^{taxi}$	ϕ_{center}^{taxi}	ϕ_{right}^{taxi}	F1Tenth	$\phi_{nominal}^{f1tenth}$	$\phi_{center}^{f1tenth}$	$\phi_{right}^{f1tenth}$
bright;bright	0.030	0.099	0.215	l;l;l;l	0.338	0.586	0.804
bright;dark	0.323	0.371	0.452	r;r;r;r	0.069	0.118	0.213
dark;bright	0.368	0.570	0.455	s;s;s;s	0.00	0.00	0.00
dark;dark	0.551	0.694	0.613	r;s;s;l	0.514	0.522	0.513
pooled;pooled	0.307	0.462	0.399	r;s;s;r	0.060	0.110	0.203

Forward Analysis. For the *forward analysis*, we define preconditions over the initial state distribution and report the worst-case error probability in Table 2. For TaxiNet, we consider the precondition $\phi_{nominal}^{taxi}$ that requires the airplane to start with *heading error* and *cross track error* both equal to 0 with probability > 0.9, the more lax precondition ϕ_{center}^{taxi} that merely requires the airplane to start close to the center of the runway with probability > 0.9, and the precondition ϕ_{right}^{taxi} that requires the airplane to start on the far right side of the runway with probability > 0.9. We encode these preconditions as affine constraints. For some boolean-valued expression ψ over the variables *cte* and *he* we let $\boldsymbol{a}_\psi$ denote the *indicator vector* such that $\boldsymbol{a}_\psi(s) = 1$ iff a valuation to PRISM variables that determines s satisfies ψ.

$$\phi_{nominal}^{taxi} = \boldsymbol{x}\boldsymbol{a}_{cte \neq 0 \vee he \neq 0} \leq 0.1$$
$$\phi_{center}^{taxi} = \boldsymbol{x}\boldsymbol{a}_{cte > 2} \leq 0.1$$
$$\phi_{right}^{taxi} = \boldsymbol{x}\boldsymbol{a}_{cte \neq 4} \leq 0.1$$

We define the analogous preconditions $\phi_{nominal}^{f1tenth}$, $\phi_{center}^{f1tenth}$, and $\phi_{right}^{f1tenth}$ for the F1Tenth case study. As a technical detail, each F1Tenth precondition refines the precondition $\phi_{forward}^{f1tenth}$, which ensures the car at the beginning of the track segment and facing within $\pi/4$ radians of straight forward with probability 1.

$$\phi_{forward}^{f1tenth} = xa_{|pos_{side}|>2 \vee 1<heading<7 \vee \tau \neq 0 \vee pos_{front} \neq 15} \leq 0$$
$$\phi_{nominal}^{f1tenth} = \phi_{forward}^{f1tenth} \wedge xa_{pos_{side} \neq 0 \vee heading \neq 0} \leq 0.1,$$
$$\phi_{center}^{f1tenth} = \phi_{forward}^{f1tenth} \wedge xa_{|pos_{side}|>1} \leq 0.1,$$
$$\phi_{right}^{f1tenth} = \phi_{forward}^{f1tenth} \wedge xa_{pos_{side} \neq 2} \leq 0.1.$$

Environment Conditions. In the TaxiNet case study, the sequence bright;bright has low error probability, which shows that the learning-enabled component and controller work well in well-lit conditions. On the other hand, each sequence that includes the dark scenario has extremely high error probability. This dependence on light conditions would not have been detectable if we had not built separate probabilistic abstractions of perception for light and dark operating conditions. We include hypothetical results based on the naive probabilistic abstraction of perception that pools data collected in both bright and dark conditions as the scenario sequence pooled;pooled.

Similarly, we observe that when started from an initial state distribution that satisfies $\phi_{nominal}^{f1tenth}$, the F1Tenth car achieves low worst case error probability (0.069) for the track configuration r;r;r;r but a relatively high worst case error probability (0.338) for l;l;l;l. A system designer could use this information to understand that it may be acceptable to deploy the car on a track that loops clockwise, but the system should be retooled before deployment on a counterclockwise loop.

Initial Distributions. Our forward analysis also shows how the initial state distribution affects system-level safety. This effect is best illustrated in the F1Tenth case study. Returning to Table 2, we observe that the precondition $\phi_{nominal}^{f1tenth}$ ensures the lowest error probability of any of the considered preconditions for each scenario that we consider. Some scenarios, namely namely s;s;s;s and r;s;s;l are relatively robust to less-than-ideal initial distributions and exhibit a similar worst-case error probability for the more lax precondition $\phi_{center}^{f1tenth}$ as they do for the strict $\phi_{nominal}^{f1tenth}$. Interestingly, we also observe that $\phi_{right}^{f1tenth}$, which requires the car to start on the right side of the track with probability > 0.9 leads to extremely high error probability for the scenario l;l;l;l in which the car must navigate a counterclockwise loop. Our forward analysis can help a system designer discover which combinations of track segments and initial state distributions will permit safe deployment of the autonomous system. The results from our F1Tenth case study would cause a system designer to focus on improving performance on track configurations that include left turn segments.

Backward Analysis. For the *backward analysis*, we assume that the domain expert provides a scenario sequence along with a maximum allowable error probability ϵ for the entire execution of the scenario sequence. We then compute the summary $(\boldsymbol{A}, \boldsymbol{b})$ of the scenario sequence and observe that the weakest precondition that ensures the error probability does not exceed ϵ is $\phi_\epsilon := \boldsymbol{x} \cdot \boldsymbol{b} \leq \epsilon$. We visualize these preconditions in Fig. 5 by highlighting the set of point distributions that ensure error probabilities less than 0.305, 0.05, and 0.01 for the scenario sequence bright;bright and the (singleton) scenario sequence dark.

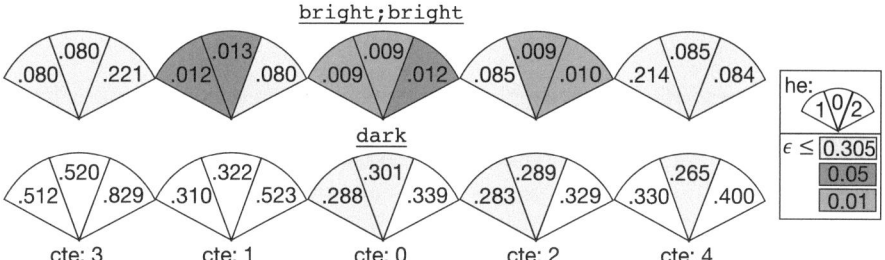

Fig. 5. Error probability by initial point distribution for bright;bright and dark scenarios. Initial point distributions that ensure error probability at most 0.305, 0.05 and 0.01 are highlighted in gray, blue, and green, respectively.

Computational Overhead. Both the *forward* and *backward* analyses are very computationally efficient, assuming that the summary of each atomic scenario has already been computed. The linear programs generated during our forward analysis can be quickly solved by Gurobi; it took less than 0.2 seconds to compute all the values in Table 2. The backward analysis requires no computation beyond the construction of $\boldsymbol{b}$. The upfront summary computation only needs to be performed once per atomic scenario. Generating all summaries for the TaxiNet and F1Tenth case studies took 79.56 s and 360.86 s, respectively.[4]

Our analyses consider *sets* of initial distributions, which are not naturally expressible in PRISM, so a direct comparison of computational efficiency vs. PRISM is not possible. However, one could use PRISM compute the error probability coefficients $\boldsymbol{b}$ by first building a monolithic DTMC that represents the execution of a particular scenario, then using either (1) PRISM's parametric model checking feature or (2) PRISM's experiments feature. Neither method scales gracefully: for our TaxiNet case study using parametric model checking to compute $\boldsymbol{b}$ for the scenario bright takes 6.912 s and exceeds PRISM's default 1GB of allocated RAM for bright; bright. PRISM's experiments feature can calculate $\boldsymbol{b}$ for bright;bright in 7.027 s, however computing $\boldsymbol{b}$ for the long scenario bright^{64} takes 481.692 s much more than the $\sim$ 79.56 s needed by our approach. We visualize the computational scalability in Fig. 6.

---

[4] All durations are reported based on single-threaded execution using a commodity laptop with a 2 GHZ processor.

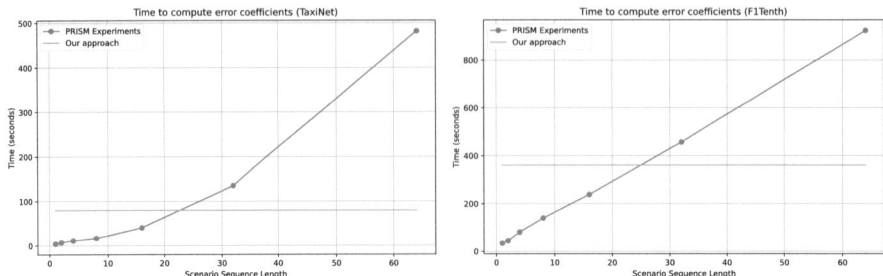

Fig. 6. Time needed to construct the error coefficients vector b using our compositional approach vs. a non-compositional application of PRISM's Experiments feature. For our approach, we report the time needed for the one-time summary generation, which can then be composed with minimal overhead for any sequence of scenarios. For PRISM experiments, we report the time needed to compute b for fixed scenario sequences of varying length. For TaxiNet we chose scenario sequences containing only bright, for F1Tenth we chose scenario sequences containing only right.

4.3 Using the Acceleration Rule

The acceleration rules introduced in Sect. 3.2 allow us to bound error probability of sequence scenarios, without putting an *a priori* bound on sequence length. Empirically, we find that our procedure to guess invariant preconditions works well for our case studies. Out of all of our singleton scenario sequences (bright, dark, straight, left, and right) and the ϵ values $\{0, 0.01, 0.02, \ldots 0.99\}$, the only instances where our guessed ϕ_ϵ did not satisfy the premise of Rule 2 were:

- TaxiNet's dark scenario with the ϵ values 0.27, 0.28, 0.29, and 0.30.
- F1Tenths's left scenario with $0.02 \leq \epsilon \leq 0.13$.
- F1Tenth's right scenario with ϵ values 0.00, 0.01, and 0.02.

Acceleration. Practically, the procedure yields an upper bound on the error probability of an unbounded sequential iteration of a single scenario. For example, for a desired *local* error probability of $\epsilon = 0.01$, we apply Rule 2 to TaxiNet's bright scenario with $\phi = \boldsymbol{x} \cdot \boldsymbol{b}_{\text{bright}} \leq 0.01$ to prove:

$$\{\phi\}(\text{bright})^k\{\phi\}\{1 - (1 - 0.01)^k\}$$

for any $k \in \mathbb{N}$. This bound on error probability is parametric in the number of iterated executions of the bright scenario. Though not necessarily tight, such a parametric upper bound can help a system designer reason about how the cumulative probability of error increases during the execution of the autonomous system.

Rule 2 is particularly useful for autonomous systems that can maintain perfect safety. In our F1Tenth case study, we found that for the `straight` scenario, the precondition $\phi = \boldsymbol{x} \cdot \boldsymbol{b}_{\text{straight}} \leq 0$ is invariant, so we can prove:

$$\{\phi\}(\texttt{straight})^k\{\phi\}\{0\}$$

for any k. The precondition ϕ is actually quite permissive, in particular, it is more permissive than any of $\phi_{\text{nominal}}^{f1tenth}$, $\phi_{\text{center}}^{f1tenth}$, and $\phi_{\text{right}}^{f1tenth}$ introduced in Sect. 3.1.

Acceleration with Choice. For the more complex Rule 3, once again, we found that our proposed procedure successfully finds recurrent preconditions in the context of our case studies. For the TaxiNet case study, applying this procedure for $\epsilon = 0.306$ and $\phi_{0.306} := \boldsymbol{x} \cdot \boldsymbol{b}_{\text{bright}} \leq 0.306 \wedge \boldsymbol{x} \cdot \boldsymbol{b}_{\text{dark}} \leq 0.306$ allows us to prove:

$$\{\phi_{0.306}\}(\texttt{bright} \,|\, \texttt{dark})^k\{\phi_{0.306}\}\{1 - (1 - 0.306)^k\}$$

this form of error bound is useful to a system designer who cannot predict the sequence of atomic scenarios the autonomous system will encounter during operation. We plot this upper bound on error probability against the true error probability of an adversarially chosen scenario sequence in Fig. 7.

In the context of the F1Tenth case study, Rule 3 lets us derive an error bound for arbitrary track configurations. Importantly, we only need to collect datasets for each atomic scenario and our compositional reasoning allows us to generalize our guarantee to any track configuration formed from these atomic scenarios. Trying our procedure to guess an invariant precondition that satisfies the premise of Rule 3 for the scenarios `left`, `right`, and `straight`, we found that for $\epsilon \in \{0.74, 0.75, \ldots, 0.99\}$ the precondition $\phi_\epsilon := \boldsymbol{x} \cdot \boldsymbol{b}_{\text{left}} \leq \epsilon \wedge \boldsymbol{x} \cdot \boldsymbol{b}_{\text{right}} \leq \epsilon \wedge \boldsymbol{x} \cdot \boldsymbol{b}_{\text{straight}} \leq \epsilon$ is invariant and nontrivial. We can thus conclude:

$$\{\phi_{0.74}\}(\texttt{left} \,|\, \texttt{right} \,|\, \texttt{straight})^k\{\phi_{0.74}\}\{1 - (1 - 0.74)^k\}$$

This bound allows extremely high error probability. A domain expert might restrict the deployment of the autonomous car to tracks formed from `right` and `straight` segments. Here, we find that $\phi_\epsilon := \boldsymbol{x} \cdot \boldsymbol{b}_{\text{right}} \leq \epsilon \wedge \boldsymbol{x} \cdot \boldsymbol{b}_{\text{straight}} \leq \epsilon$ is nontrivial and invariant for $\epsilon \in \{0.13, 0.14, \ldots, 0.99\}$. In particular, we can conclude

$$\{\phi_{0.13}\}(\texttt{right} \,|\, \texttt{straight})^k\{\phi_{0.13}\}\{1 - (1 - 0.13)^k\}$$

Concerning the relatively high error probabilities, we currently work with high-level abstractions of actual systems so computed error probabilities should be taken with a grain of salt. Still, our acceleration rules can reveal useful trends to system developers. Moreover, we expect lower error probabilities when applied to more accurate models of real-world systems; the analysis of fixed scenario sequences (Sect. 3.1) is tight.

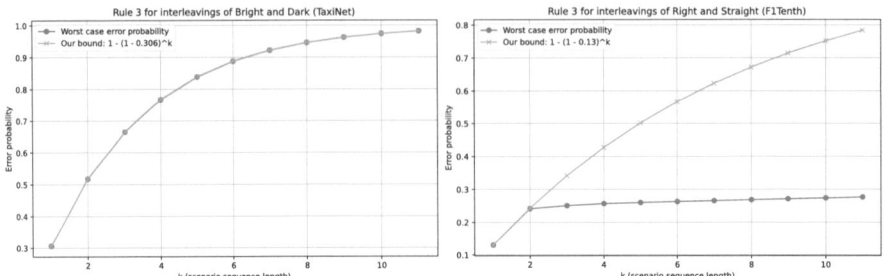

Fig. 7. The error bounds found by applications of Rule 3 vs. true worst-case error probability. For the worst case error probabilities, we consider all possible scensario interleavings and all starting distributions that satisfy the precondition ϕ_ϵ used in our application of Rule 3..

5 Conclusion

Our verification framework decomposes the autonomous system and its operating conditions into scenarios to enable efficient probabilistic analysis. Our compositional proof rules enable system designers to obtain a bound on error probability that is parametric with respect to the length of an arbitrary interleaving of scenarios, which is useful for reasoning about the system under unpredictable changes in operating conditions. In future work, we plan to investigate more nuanced approaches to discover the invariant preconditions that enable application of our acceleration rule.

Building a probabilistic abstraction of perception with respect to a discretized state space can introduce inaccuracies. In our work, we avoid this concern by assuming that the distribution of state estimates yielded by the learning-enabled component is uniquely determined by the current environment condition and (discrete) state. In future work we plan to develop (possibly symbolic) abstractions of perception for continuous-state system models and to account for distribution shifts that are continuous, instead of discrete as we do here.

Acknowledgments. This research was conducted during the first author's internship at the NASA Ames Research Center. This research was partially supported by NSF award SLES 2331783 and by a gift from AWS AI to Penn Engineering's ASSET Center for research in Trustworthy AI.

A Soundness Proofs

We prove soundness of the rules introduced in Sect. 3.2 with respect to the definition of sequential composition of *summaries* found at the end of Sect. 2.2.

$$\frac{\{\phi\}C\{\psi\}\{\epsilon\}, \{\phi'\}C'\{\psi'\}\{\epsilon'\}, \psi \implies \phi'}{\{\phi\}CC'\{\psi'\}\{1-(1-\epsilon)(1-\epsilon')\}} \text{ Rule 1}$$

Proof. Let $C \equiv (\boldsymbol{A}, \boldsymbol{b})$ and $C' \equiv (\boldsymbol{A'}, \boldsymbol{b'})$.

By the definition of sequential composition of scenarios, we know $CC' \equiv (\boldsymbol{AA'}, \boldsymbol{b} + \boldsymbol{Ab})$.

We prove the two obligations:

- To show that $\phi(\boldsymbol{x}) \Rightarrow \psi'(norm(\boldsymbol{x}\boldsymbol{AA'}))$ we fix $\boldsymbol{x}$ w.l.o.g. and apply the first premise to obtain $\psi(norm(\boldsymbol{xA}))$. We then apply the third premise to obtain $\phi(norm(\boldsymbol{xA}))$ and the second premise to obtain $\psi'(norm(norm(\boldsymbol{xA})\boldsymbol{A'}))$. Expansion of the definition of $norm$ and algebraic manipulation completes this branch of the proof.
- To show that $\phi(\boldsymbol{x}) \to \boldsymbol{xb} + \boldsymbol{xAb'} \leq 1 - (1-\epsilon)(1-\epsilon')$ we fix $\boldsymbol{x}$ w.l.o.g. Next we observe that $\boldsymbol{xb} + \boldsymbol{xAb'} = \boldsymbol{xb} + (1 - \boldsymbol{xb})\boldsymbol{xAb'}$ by the definition of norm and of a summary. We can rewrite this as $1 - (1 - \boldsymbol{xb})(1 - norm(\boldsymbol{xA})\boldsymbol{b'})$. So it suffices to show $1 - (1 - \boldsymbol{xb})(1 - norm(\boldsymbol{xA})\boldsymbol{b'}) \leq 1 - (1-\epsilon)(1-\epsilon')$. Premise 1 lets us bound $\boldsymbol{xb} \leq \epsilon$ and premise 2 lets us bound $norm(\boldsymbol{xA})\boldsymbol{b'} \leq \epsilon'$ so we can bound $(1 - \boldsymbol{xb}) \geq 1 - \epsilon$ and $1 - norm(\boldsymbol{xA})\boldsymbol{b'} \geq 1 - \epsilon'$. Together these imply the desired bound.

$$\frac{\{\phi\}C\{\phi\}\{\epsilon\}}{\{\phi\}C^k\{\phi\}\{1-(1-\epsilon)^k\}} \text{ Rule 2}$$

Proof. Direct application of Rule 3, which we prove below.

$$\frac{\{\phi\}C_1\{\phi\}\{\epsilon\}, \ldots, \{\phi\}C_\ell\{\phi\}\{\epsilon\}}{\{\phi\}(C_1 \mid \ldots \mid C_m)^k\{\phi\}\{\epsilon\}\}} \text{ Rule 3}$$

Proof. By induction over k. The case $k = 1$ is immediate and the case $k = 2$ follows by Rule 1. For the inductive step, assume w.l.o.g. that the conclusion of this instance of Rule 3 is $\{\phi\}C_{i_1} \ldots C_{i_{k-1}}C_{i_k}\{\phi\}\{1-(1-\epsilon)^k\}$. By the inductive hypothesis, we know $\{\phi\}C_{i_1} \ldots C_{i_{k-1}}\{\phi\}\{1-(1-\epsilon)^{(k-1)}\}$, so we can apply Rule 1 to complete the proof.

B PRISM Model Construction

We provide additional details about the our PRISM model construction introduced in Sect. 4.1 and adapted from [28]. Assume that we are modeling an autonomous system in which the dynamics uses state set S, the perception model outputs state estimates from Y, the controller issues commands from U, and there are m distinct scenarios which we will refer to by the counting numbers $\{1, \ldots, m\}$. For each scenario i, we denote the probabilistic abstraction of perception as $\alpha_i : S \to \mathbf{Dist}(Y)$ the time horizon as $H_i \in \mathbb{N}$. Let H_{max} denote $\max_{i \in \{1,\ldots,m\}}(H_i)$.

Our PRISM model has a set of state variables V which can be partitioned as $V = V_S \sqcup V_Y \sqcup V_U \sqcup \{\texttt{pc}, \texttt{scenario}, \texttt{timer}\}$. Each valuation V_S, V_Y, or V_U uniquely determines an element of S, Y, or U, respectively. For each $s \in S$, we write s as shorthand for the PRISM state predicate that evaluates to true exactly when the current valuation of V_S determines s.

Our construction introduces a *program counter* variable $\texttt{pc}$ with range $\{0, 1, 2\}$, a variable $\texttt{scenario}$ with range $\{1, \ldots, m\}$, and a variable $\texttt{timer}$ with range $\{1, \ldots, H_{max}\}$. PRISM indexes timesteps starting at 0. We maintain $\texttt{pc}$ and $\texttt{timer}$ such that at PRISM timestep t, we have $\texttt{pc} = mod(t, 3)$ and $\texttt{timer} = \min(quotient(t,3) + 1, H_{max})$. The other variables are updated as follows:

- **Perception:** When $pc = 0$, the valuation of V_Y will be updated according to the valuation of V_S and on the next step. This update's transition probabilities are given by the *probabilistic abstraction* for the current scenario, which we represent using the value of $\texttt{scenario}$. The value of $\texttt{scenario}$ is never updated, later on we will explain how we initialize the value of scenario to compute each summary.
- **Controller:** When $pc = 1$, the valuation of V_U is updated according to the valuation of V_Y.
- **Dynamics:** When $pc = 2$, the valuation of V_S is updated according to the valuation of V_U and the current valuation of V_S.

We can now apply the summary generation technique detailed in Sect. 4.1 to this model.

B.1 Additional TaxiNet Details

For the purpose of our analysis, we discretize TaxiNet's outputs and treat it as a classifier. cte $\in [-8.0\,\text{m},\, 8.0\,\text{m}]$ and he $\in [-35.0\circ,\, 35.0\circ]$ are translated into cte $\in 0, 1, 2, 3, 4$ and he $\in 0, 1, 2$ as shown below.

$$cte = \begin{cases} 3 \text{ if } -8.0\text{ m } <= cte < -4.8\text{ m} \\ 1 \text{ if } -4.8\text{ m } <= cte < -1.6\text{ m} \\ 0 \text{ if } -1.6\text{ m } <= cte <= 1.6\text{ m} \\ 2 \text{ if } 1.6\text{ m } < cte <= 4.8\text{ m} \\ 4 \text{ if } 4.8\text{ m } < cte <= 8.0\text{ m} \end{cases} \qquad he = \begin{cases} 1 \text{ if } -35.0\text{ deg } <= he < -11.67\text{ deg} \\ 0 \text{ if } -11.67\text{ deg } <= he <= 11.66\text{ deg} \\ 2 \text{ if } 11.66\text{ deg } < he <= 35.0\text{ deg} \end{cases}$$

Yielding the discretized set of system states $\underline{S} := [0..4] \times [0..2]$. Any airplane position with in which the magnitude of the cross-track error exceeds 8 m or the magnitude of the heading error exceeds 35° represents the error state s_{err}.

B.2 Additional F1Tenth Details

We provide additional details about the F1Tenth case study. At each timestep, the car's heading *heading* is updated based on the control input u. Then, the car

Algorithm 1: F1Tenth Dynamics

Input: Track segment $e \in E$; Current state $s \in S$; control input $u \in U$
Output: Next state $s' \in S$

1. **if** $s = s_{err}$ **then**
2.   **return** s_{err}
3. **else**
4. $(pos_{side}, pos_{front}, heading, \tau) \leftarrow s$;
5.   **if** $\tau < 30$ **then**
6. $heading' \leftarrow mod(heading + u, 8)$;
7. $pos'_{side} \leftarrow pos_{side} - \mathbb{1}_{\{1,2,3\}}(heading) + \mathbb{1}_{\{5,6,7\}}(heading)$;
8. $pos'_{front} \leftarrow pos_{front} - \mathbb{1}_{\{0,1,7\}}(heading) + \mathbb{1}_{\{3,4,5\}}(heading)$;
9. $(pos'_{side}, pos'_{front}) \leftarrow f^{pos}((pos_{side}, pos_{front}, heading), u)$;
10.   **else if** $(pos'_{side}, pos'_{front}) \in Track \cup Track_e \cup F_e$ **then**
11.   **return** $(pos'_{side}, pos'_{front}, heading', \tau + 1)$;
12.   **else**
13.   **return** s_{err};
14.   **else if** $(pos_{side}, pos_{front}) \in F_e$ **then**
15.   **if** $e = \texttt{left}$ **then**
16.   **return** $(3 - pos_{front}, 15, mod(heading - 2, 8), 1)$;
17.   **else if** $e = \texttt{right}$ **then**
18.   **return** $(pos_{front} - 3, 15, mod(heading + 2, 8), 1)$;
19.   **else**
20.   **return** $(pos_{side}, 15, heading, 1)$;
21.   **else**
22.   **return** s_{err}

moves one grid-position in the direction of the updated heading. The dynamics function $f : E \times S \times U$ also accounts for walls and transitions between track segments.

We define one scenario $(e, 30)$ for each track segment e. We wish for the scenario $(e, 30)$ to end when the car reaches the end of the current track segment, which we represent as F_e. This requires careful definition of the dynamics function, since the car may take more or less than the horizon value of 30 timesteps to reach F_e. We present pseudocode for the dynamics function in f. At a high level, we introduce a time limit 30 and transition to s_{err} if the car does not reach F_e in fewer than 30 steps. To address cars that reach F_e in less than 30 timesteps, we stop updating the position and heading of the car until the start of the next scenario.

We built a *Controller* $g : E \times Y \to U$. The dependence on Y corresponds to the autonomous system being equipped with an oracle that detects which track segment is being navigated currently. This controller can navigate each track segment safely when it recieves the ground-truth state estimate at each timestep and begins from an initial state with heading $heading = 0$. When operating under these conditions, the controller completes each track segment with its heading such that it starts the next segment with $heading = 0$. This implies that the controller can safely navigate any sequence of track segments assuming perfect behavior of the learning-enabled component.

References

1. Arjomand Bigdeli, A., Mata, A., Bak, S.: Verification of neural network control systems in continuous time. In: 7th Symposium on AI Verification (SAIV) (2024)
2. Astorga, A., Hsieh, C., Madhusudan, P., Mitra, S.: Perception contracts for safety of ml-enabled systems. Proc. ACM Program. Lang. **7**(OOPSLA2), 2196–2223 (2023). https://doi.org/10.1145/3622875
3. Badithela, A., Wongpiromsarn, T., Murray, R.M.: Leveraging classification metrics for quantitative system-level analysis with temporal logic specifications. In: 2021 60th IEEE Conference on Decision and Control (CDC), pp. 564–571. IEEE (2021)
4. Badithela, A., Wongpiromsarn, T., Murray, R.M.: Evaluation metrics of object detection for quantitative system-level analysis of safety-critical autonomous systems. In: 2023 IEEE/RSJ International Conference on Intelligent Robots and Systems (IROS), pp. 8651–8658. IEEE (2023)
5. Cai, F., Fan, C., Bak, S.: Scalable surrogate verification of image-based neural network control systems using composition and unrolling (2024)
6. Calinescu, R., Imrie, C., Mangal, R., Pasareanu, C.S., Santana, M.A., Vázquez, G.: Discrete-event controller synthesis for autonomous systems with deep-learning perception components. CoRR arxiv:2202.03360 (2022)
7. Calinescu, R., et al.: Controller synthesis for autonomous systems with deep-learning perception components. IEEE Trans. Softw. Eng. 1–22 (2024). https://doi.org/10.1109/TSE.2024.3385378
8. Cruz, U.S., Shoukry, Y.: Certified vision-based state estimation for autonomous landing systems using reachability analysis. In: 2023 62nd IEEE Conference on Decision and Control (CDC), pp. 6052–6057 (2023). https://doi.org/10.1109/CDC49753.2023.10384107
9. De Moura, L., Bjørner, N.: Z3: an efficient SMT solver. In: Proceedings of the Theory and Practice of Software, 14th International Conference on Tools and Algorithms for the Construction and Analysis of Systems, TACAS'08/ETAPS'08, pp. 337–340. Springer-Verlag, Heidelberg (2008). http://dl.acm.org/citation.cfm?id=1792734.1792766
10. Fremont, D.J., Chiu, J., Margineantu, D.D., Osipychev, D., Seshia, S.A.: Formal analysis and redesign of a neural network-based aircraft taxiing system with VerifAI. In: 32nd International Conference on Computer Aided Verification (CAV) (2020)
11. Fremont, D.J., et al.: Formal scenario-based testing of autonomous vehicles: from simulation to the real world. In: 23rd IEEE International Conference on Intelligent Transportation Systems (ITSC) (2020)
12. Grigorescu, S.M., Trasnea, B., Cocias, T.T., Macesanu, G.: A survey of deep learning techniques for autonomous driving. CoRR arxiv:1910.07738 (2019)
13. Gurobi Optimization, LLC: Gurobi Optimizer Reference Manual (2024). https://www.gurobi.com
14. Habeeb, P., Deka, N., D'Souza, D., Lodaya, K., Prabhakar, P.: Verification of camera-based autonomous systems. IEEE Trans. Comput. Aided Des. Integr. Circuits Syst. **42**(10), 3450–3463 (2023). https://doi.org/10.1109/TCAD.2023.3240131

15. Habeeb, P., D'Souza, D., Lodaya, K., Prabhakar, P.: Interval image abstraction for verification of camera-based autonomous systems. IEEE Trans. Comput. Aided Des. Integr. Circuits Syst. (2024)
16. Hensel, C., Junges, S., Katoen, J.P., Quatmann, T., Volk, M.: The probabilistic model checker Storm. Int. J. Softw. Tools Technol. Transfer **24**(4), 589–610 (2022)
17. Hsieh, C., Koh, Y., Li, Y., Mitra, S.: Assuring safety of vision-based swarm formation control. In: American Control Conference (ACC) (2024)
18. Hsieh, C., Li, Y., Sun, D., Joshi, K., Misailovic, S., Mitra, S.: Verifying controllers with vision-based perception using safe approximate abstractions. IEEE Trans. Comput. Aided Des. Integr. Circuits Syst. **41**(11), 4205–4216 (2022). https://doi.org/10.1109/TCAD.2022.3197508
19. Huang, X., et al.: A survey of safety and trustworthiness of deep neural networks: verification, testing, adversarial attack and defence, and interpretability. Comput. Sci. Rev. **37**, 100270 (2020)
20. Ivanov, R., Jothimurugan, K., Hsu, S., Vaidya, S., Alur, R., Bastani, O.: Compositional learning and verification of neural network controllers. ACM Trans. Embed. Comput. Syst. **20**(5s) (2021). https://doi.org/10.1145/3477023
21. Kadron, I.B., Gopinath, D., Pasareanu, C.S., Yu, H.: Case study: analysis of autonomous center line tracking neural networks. In: Bloem, R., Dimitrova, R., Fan, C., Sharygina, N. (eds.) Software Verification - 13th International Conference, VSTTE 2021, New Haven, CT, USA, 18–19 October 2021, and 14th International Workshop, NSV 2021, Los Angeles, CA, USA, 18–19 July 2021, Revised Selected Papers, Lecture Notes in Computer Science, pp. 104–121. Springer, Heidelberg (2021). https://doi.org/10.1007/978-3-030-95561-8_7
22. Katz, S.M., Corso, A.L., Strong, C.A., Kochenderfer, M.J.: Verification of image-based neural network controllers using generative models. J. Aeros. Inf. Syst. **19**(9), 574–584 (2022)
23. Kwiatkowska, M., Norman, G., Parker, D.: PRISM 4.0: verification of probabilistic real-time systems. In: Gopalakrishnan, G., Qadeer, S. (eds.) CAV 2011. LNCS, vol. 6806, pp. 585–591. Springer, Heidelberg (2011). https://doi.org/10.1007/978-3-642-22110-1_47
24. Li, J., Nuzzo, P., Sangiovanni-Vincentelli, A., Xi, Y., Li, D.: Stochastic assume-guarantee contracts for cyber-physical system design under probabilistic requirements (2017). https://arxiv.org/abs/1705.09316
25. Li, Y., Yang, B.C., Jia, Y., Zhuang, D., Mitra, S.: Refining perception contracts: case studies in vision-based safe auto-landing (2023)
26. Morgan, C., McIver, A., Seidel, K.: Probabilistic predicate transformers. ACM Trans. Program. Lang. Syst. **18**(3), 325–353 (1996). https://doi.org/10.1145/229542.229547
27. O'Kelly, M., Zheng, H., Karthik, D., Mangharam, R.: F1tenth: an open-source evaluation environment for continuous control and reinforcement learning. In: Escalante, H.J., Hadsell, R. (eds.) Proceedings of the NeurIPS 2019 Competition and Demonstration Track. Proceedings of Machine Learning Research, vol. 123, pp. 77–89. PMLR (2020). https://proceedings.mlr.press/v123/o-kelly20a.html
28. Păsăreanu, C.S., et al.: Closed-loop analysis of vision-based autonomous systems: a case study. In: Enea, C., Lal, A. (eds.) Computer Aided Verification, pp. 289–303. Springer, Cham (2023). https://doi.org/10.1007/978-3-031-37706-8_15
29. Pasareanu, C.S., Mangal, R., Gopinath, D., Yu, H.: Assumption generation for learning-enabled autonomous systems. In: Katsaros, P., Nenzi, L. (eds.) Runtime Verification - 23rd International Conference, RV 2023, Thessaloniki, Greece, 3–6

October 2023, Proceedings. Lecture Notes in Computer Science, vol. 14245, pp. 3–22. Springer, Heidelberg (2023). https://doi.org/10.1007/978-3-031-44267-4_1
30. Santa Cruz, U., Shoukry, Y.: Nnlander-verif: A neural network formal verification framework for vision-based autonomous aircraft landing. In: Deshmukh, J.V., Havelund, K., Perez, I. (eds.) NASA Formal Methods, pp. 213–230. Springer, Cham (2022). https://doi.org/10.1007/978-3-031-06773-0_11
31. Sun, D., Yang, B., Mitra, S.: Learning-based inverse perception contracts and applications. In: International Conference on Robotics and Automation (2024)
32. Tabernik, D., Skocaj, D.: Deep learning for large-scale traffic-sign detection and recognition. CoRR arxiv:1904.00649 (2019)
33. Waite, T., Robey, A., Hamed, H., Pappas, G.J., Ivanov, R.: Data-driven modeling and verification of perception-based autonomous systems (2023)
34. Watanabe, K., Eberhart, C., Asada, K., Hasuo, I.: Compositional probabilistic model checking with string diagrams of mdps. In: Enea, C., Lal, A. (eds.) Computer Aided Verification, pp. 40–61. Springer, Cham (2023). https://doi.org/10.1007/978-3-031-37709-9_3
35. Yalcinkaya, B., Torfah, H., Fremont, D.J., Seshia, S.A.: Compositional simulation-based analysis of AI-based autonomous systems for Markovian specifications. In: Katsaros, P., Nenzi, L. (eds.) Runtime Verification, pp. 191–212. Springer, Cham (2023). https://doi.org/10.1007/978-3-031-44267-4_10

Robustness Margin: A New Measure for the Robustness of Neural Networks

Lionel Kielhöfer[1,2(✉)], Annelot W. Bosman[2], Holger H. Hoos[2,3], and Jan N. van Rijn[2]

[1] Intelligence in Quality Sensing, Laboratory for Machine Tools and Production Engineering, RWTH Aachen, Campus-Boulevard 30, 52074 Aachen, Germany
lionel.kielhoefer@wzl-iqs.rwth-aachen.de
[2] Leiden Institute of Advanced Computer Science, Leiden University, Leiden, The Netherlands
{a.w.bosman,j.n.van.rijn}@liacs.leidenuniv.nl
[3] Chair for AI Methodology, RWTH Aachen University, Aachen, Germany
hh@aim.rwth-aachen.de

Abstract. Neural networks are vulnerable to small input perturbations, which can cause misclassifications to instances that would be correctly classified otherwise. Therefore, assessing the robustness of a neural network is essential in safety-critical applications. Existing robustness measures, such as robust accuracy, fail to capture the robustness of individual inputs to the network and are not easy to interpret, making them unsuitable for comparing different networks. This work introduces a novel robustness measure that addresses these issues by using a probabilistic model of robustness and evaluating its quantiles. Furthermore, we propose both a parametric and a non-parametric estimator to compute confidence bounds for this measure. We evaluate both estimators based on their accuracy and precision over the amount of data used. Both perform reliably given sufficient data; however, the parametric estimator achieves comparable performance with about half as much data, rendering it computationally more efficient.

Keywords: robustness measure · neural network verification · distributions · adversarial robustness

1 Introduction

Knowing whether a neural network is robust and under what conditions is crucial for many use cases, especially as it is known that neural networks can be deceived by slightly altered data during inference. These deviations can occur naturally, as a result of noisy input data, or be induced maliciously when attackers intentionally attempt to cause errors in the network [14,27]. Measuring the robustness is especially important for safety-critical systems [16], where misclassifications could lead to harmful outcomes. In these situations, a network that is less sensitive to deviations might be preferred over a slightly more accurate one [20].

For image classification, the robustness of a neural network is commonly measured on a per-instance level. Multiple input images are selected, and the robustness of the network against small perturbations on these images is verified. For each image, all deviations within a chosen perturbation size ϵ are considered. If it is not possible to alter the image classification within this ϵ range, the neural network is deemed ϵ-robust on the respective image [2,4,5,10,28], this is also called the local robustness. The largest perturbation size ϵ for which the network maintains ϵ-robustness on the image is called the critical epsilon [2]. Once the ϵ-robustness or critical epsilon is measured across multiple images, various robustness measures can be employed to gauge the overall global robustness of a given network [1,6,7,12,14,15,17,22,24,25,27–29]. A commonly used measure is *robust accuracy*, calculated as the percentage of images on which the network demonstrates ϵ-robustness [1,12,14,15,17,22,25,27–29]. While approaches that involve altering the model or its training process do exist [9,21], in this work, we consider only robustness measures that evaluate neural networks without requiring any modifications to their architecture or training procedure.

Robust accuracy has several notable drawbacks [2]:

- It is highly dependent on the selected perturbation size ϵ, which requires input from a domain expert to be set to an appropriate value.
- It does not properly capture the local robustness of a network for an individual image, as it requires a predefined perturbation size ϵ and measures the percentage of images that are ϵ-robust.
- These limitations make it difficult to compare the robustness of different networks, as important nuances in their robustness behaviour are not always captured.

Other robustness measures exist that partially address these drawbacks [6,7,13,24,27,28]. However, they still do not enable the effective comparison of robustness between different networks, which is important for neural architecture search [20].

Bosman *et al.* [2] aim to address these drawbacks by introducing robustness distributions. These distributions show how the critical epsilon values are distributed across images for various neural networks. By using the distribution of critical epsilon values, this approach offers a better indication of the robustness of individual images and removes the dependence on a fixed parameter. However, computing these distributions incurs significant computational costs. While they provide valuable statistical insights that can be analysed using standard statistical tools (e.g., the Kolmogorov–Smirnov test [2,18,26]), it is often preferable to summarise robustness with a single representative value to simplify direct network comparisons and interpretation.

In this work, we introduce a robustness measure called the *robustness margin*, which also uses robustness distributions to address several of the limitations of robust accuracy. The robustness margin calculates a predetermined σ-quantile of the robustness distribution, allowing for a small probability σ that an arbitrary reference image will not be ϵ-robust. It determines the largest perturbation size ϵ consistent with this probability. The parameter σ is task-specific and reflects the desired level of permissible error.

A key advantage of our approach is that it reduces the reliance on a domain expert. Selecting an appropriate ϵ-value typically requires both domain-specific knowledge and expertise in robustness verification. In contrast, the σ-parameter in our method directly corresponds to the acceptable quality threshold, a concept already familiar to experts and routinely used in practice. Since the determination of such thresholds is a well-established task, extensive guidance from existing literature is available, making it straightforward for practitioners to select meaningful σ-values for a wide range of applications.

Additionally, our statistical approach inherently supports the construction of confidence intervals. Rather than relying solely on singular queries to a verification engine, these confidence intervals provide an explicit indication of whether the available data (in terms of samples for which a critical epsilon value has been determined) is sufficient to draw meaningful conclusions about the robustness of the network or if additional verification queries are necessary, saving computational resources. When more samples are being processed, the estimators become more reliable in determining the robustness margin, and the confidence bounds become smaller.

Here, the robustness margin is measured on neural networks trained for image classification tasks. However, the measure and our contributions are not task-specific and are broadly applicable to any task where evaluating the adherence of a given network to an acceptable quality threshold is relevant. Specifically, we make the following contributions:

– **Robustness margin:** We introduce the robustness margin, a novel robustness measure, and provide its formal mathematical definition.
– **Estimation methods:** We propose two distinct estimators for calculating the confidence interval of the robustness margin, providing statistical accuracy in the measure:
  • The *non-parametric estimator* serves as a ground truth of the robustness margin.
  • The *parametric estimator* leverages the findings of Bosman *et al.* [2], which highlight similarities between robustness distributions and log-normal distributions, to increase the computational efficiency.
– **Evaluation of estimators:** We assess both estimators in terms of computational efficiency by examining their accuracy, precision, and effectiveness in selecting the network with the highest robustness margin as the number of samples used for the estimation increases. The samples used for the estimators are the calculated critical epsilon values for different images, which provide insight into the underlying robustness distribution.

We find that the non-parametric estimator exhibits significantly higher variance than the parametric estimator, particularly when fewer than 20 samples are used, at which point the variance becomes too large for it to be an effective estimator. Beyond this, the parametric estimator is more precise on average, and with around 100 samples, it consistently outperforms the non-parametric estimator in terms of precision.

Table 1. Overview of the most important notation used in this paper

Notation	Meaning
$x \in \mathbb{R}^n$	**Input.** For example, if this were an image, it would consists of n pixels, each taking a value in the set of real numbers. Correctly classified inputs and perturbations are denoted x_0 and x, respectively
$f : \mathbb{R}^n \to \mathbb{N}$	**Neural Network.** Various types of neural networks exist, but our notation describes neural networks as functions whose output is a natural number indicating the class of the input
ϵ	**Perturbation size.** Given a correctly classified reference input x_0, the perturbation size ϵ defines the neighbourhood of perturbations x around the reference input that is considered. The set of perturbations is expressed as $\{x : \|x - x_0\| < \epsilon\}$, where $\| \cdot \|$ is a specific norm

Additionally, both estimators are accurate across any number of samples, as their confidence intervals tend to overlap with the ground truth. For comparing the robustness margin of two networks, we observe that both estimators are conservative, typically indicating overlap of the confidence intervals rather than incorrectly suggesting that the wrong network is strictly more robust.

In our experiments, the non-parametric estimator requires at least 200 samples to reliably indicate the more robust network, while the parametric estimator achieves this with only 100 samples. Furthermore, when two networks are equally robust, the non-parametric estimator tends to incorrectly suggest a more robust network when fewer than 20 samples are used, highlighting its ineffectiveness at these lower sample numbers. In contrast, the parametric estimator does not suffer from this issue and consistently indicates an overlap, even at lower sample numbers.

2 Background

In this section, we present the formal definitions relevant to the robustness of neural networks. With these definitions, we formalised different robustness measures.

2.1 Local Robustness

One of the most prominent robustness properties is local robustness, which means that a neural network is robust against small input perturbations in a given input. To maintain generality, the norm is not specified in the definitions, as it varies across the literature. Commonly used norms include the l_1, l_2 and l_∞ norms. For the results presented in this paper, the l_∞-norm is used, as most verifiers are compatible with this norm [19]. Table 1 provides a summary of the mathematical notation used in the definitions.

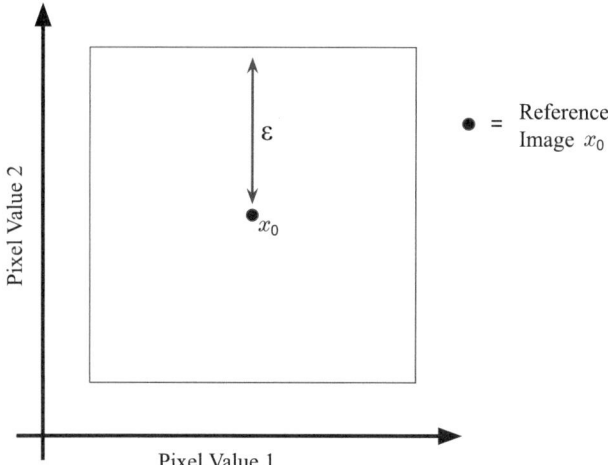

Fig. 1. A 2-dimensional example of verifying whether a correctly classified reference input x_0 is ϵ-robust using the l_∞ norm. For example, if the input were an image, each axis would represent the value of a different pixel, meaning we are examining the space of images composed of only two pixels. The ϵ-square around x_0 is displayed in grey, and x_0 is considered ϵ-robust if each x within the square is assigned the same class as x_0.

The local robustness property of a neural network for an input can formally be expressed as follows:

Definition 1 (ϵ-robustness). *Consider a neural network $f : \mathbb{R}^n \to \mathbb{N}$ that classifies inputs, a correctly classified reference input $x_0 \in \mathbb{R}^n$, and a perturbation size ϵ. The network is ϵ-robust, or locally robust, on x_0 if $\forall x \in \mathbb{R}^n : ||x - x_0|| < \epsilon \Rightarrow f(x) = f(x_0)$.*

The idea of ϵ-robustness is to analyse all potential perturbations within a distance ϵ from the reference input to determine whether any of them cause the neural network to misclassify. A visual example can be seen in Fig. 1. We note that robustness is only considered for originally correctly classified inputs, whilst the robustness of misclassified inputs is not considered in this paper. However, we retain the general notation for generality. In our case, $f(x_0)$ is the ground truth label of x_0.

We adopt the critical robustness framework used by Bosman *et al.* [2], according to which the critical robustness property of a neural network for a correctly classified reference input can formally be defined as follows:

Definition 2 (Critical epsilon ϵ^*). *Consider a neural network $f : \mathbb{R}^n \to \mathbb{N}$ that classifies inputs and a correctly classified reference input $x_0 \in \mathbb{R}^n$. The critical epsilon, or critical robustness, of the network on that input is the perturbation size ϵ^* such that the network is ϵ-robust on x_0 for all $\epsilon \leq \epsilon^*$, but not ϵ-robust for any $\epsilon > \epsilon^*$.*

The critical epsilon represents the maximum perturbation size ϵ for which the network retains ϵ-robustness; it is denoted ϵ^*, or $\epsilon^*_{x_0}$ when the reference input x_0 is not explicitly clear from the context. Note that the critical epsilon ϵ^* is hard to determine exactly; for that reason, we often resort to finding a lower bound on the critical epsilon. Additionally, Bosman et al. [2] introduced robustness distributions, which can formally be defined as follows:

Definition 3 (Robustness distribution). *Consider a neural network $f : \mathbb{R}^n \to \mathbb{N}$ that classifies inputs. A robustness distribution represents the probability that the network achieves a critical epsilon ϵ^* for an arbitrary correctly classified reference input x_0. It is typically represented by its cumulative distribution function (CDF):*

$$P(\epsilon^* < \epsilon) := \mathbb{P}(\{x_0 : \epsilon^*_{x_0} < \epsilon\}) \tag{1}$$

where $\epsilon^*_{x_0}$ is the critical epsilon of the reference input x_0. Note that the set of correctly classified reference inputs x_0 is not specified. This is intentional, as it is task-dependent and usually unknown. When necessary, this set will be denoted $\mathcal{X}_0 \subset \mathbb{R}^n$.

2.2 Robust Accuracy

These definitions offer a framework to formally define the commonly used robustness measure: robust accuracy.[1] Reviewing the literature [1,12,14,15,17,22,25, 27–29], this measure can formally be expressed as follows:

Definition 4 (Robust accuracy). *Consider a neural network $f : \mathbb{R}^n \to \mathbb{N}$ and a perturbation size ϵ. Robust accuracy indicates the probability that the network is ϵ-robust for an arbitrary classified reference input x_0. This will be denoted by:*

$$P(\epsilon) := \mathbb{P}(\{x_0 : ||x - x_0|| < \epsilon \Rightarrow f(x) = y_{x_0}\}) \tag{2}$$

where y_{x_0} is the ground truth label of a reference input x_0. In practice, the following estimator is used to calculate the robust accuracy [1,12,15,17,22,25, 27–29]:

Estimator 1 (Robust accuracy). *Given a set of test data D, which was not used to train the neural network $f : \mathbb{R}^n \to \mathbb{N}$, an estimator for its robust accuracy is obtained by taking the mean over the classified test data D, as follows:*

$$\widehat{P(\epsilon)} := \frac{|\{x_0 \in D : \forall x \in \mathbb{R}^n \text{ it holds that } ||x - x_0|| < \epsilon \Rightarrow f(x) = y_{x_0}\}|}{|D|} \tag{3}$$

---

[1] It is also referred to as the astuteness [29], adversarial error rate [12], adversarial accuracy [28] and certified accuracy [22]. It is also equivalent to 1 minus the adversarial frequency [1].

2.3 Average Minimum Distortion

A less common robustness measure is the average minimum distortion.[2] Reviewing the literature [6,7,13,24,27,28], this measure can formally be expressed as follows:

Definition 5 (Average minimum distortion). *Consider a neural network $f : \mathbb{R}^n \to \mathbb{N}$. The average minimum distortion represents the expected critical epsilon for an arbitrary correctly classified reference input x_0, denoted as $E(\epsilon^*) := \mathbb{E}(\{\epsilon^*_{x_0} : x_0 \in \mathcal{X}_0\})$, where $\mathcal{X}_0$ is the set of all possible correctly classified reference inputs in the given task.*

To calculate the average minimum distortion, the following estimator is used in practice [6,7,13,24,27,28]:

Estimator 2 (Average minimum distortion). Given a set of correctly classified test data D, which was not used to train the neural network $f : \mathbb{R}^n \to \mathbb{N}$, an estimator for its average minimum distortion is obtained by taking the mean over D, as follows:

$$\widehat{E(\epsilon^*)} := \frac{1}{|D|} \cdot \sum_{x_0 \in D} \epsilon^*_{x_0} \quad (4)$$

The average minimum distortion addresses the first limitation of robust accuracy by not being dependent on a parameter. This eliminates the need for expert domain knowledge. However, the second limitation persists, as it does not provide a reliable indication of the robustness of an individual input. Especially when dealing with robustness distributions with high variance or outliers, the mean can fail to reflect the robustness of individual inputs. Bastani et al. [1] address this issue by introducing the concept of adversarial severity. This measure is similar to the average minimum distortion but only takes into account critical epsilons that are below a specific perturbation size ϵ, so $E(\epsilon^* < \epsilon) := \mathbb{E}(\{\epsilon^*_{x_0} < \epsilon : x_0 \in \mathcal{X}_0\})$. However, this reintroduces the need for expert domain knowledge for selecting an appropriate perturbation size ϵ. Just like robust accuracy, these limitations make it challenging to compare the robustness of two networks using the average minimum distortion.

3 Robustness Margin and Estimators

To address the limitations of robust accuracy, we introduce a new robustness measure that is based on robust accuracy and incorporates elements inspired by statistical hypothesis testing. We call this measure the robustness margin. After, we introduce two estimators that determine the robustness margin for a given network.

---

[2] It is also referred to as the average verified bound [13] and the mean minimum adversarial distortion [28].

3.1 Robustness Margin

The robustness margin allows for a small probability σ that an arbitrary correctly classified reference input will not be ϵ-robust and determines the largest ϵ consistent with this probability. The value of σ should be chosen to be very small. A common choice, often used in statistical hypothesis testing, is $\sigma = 0.05$, which can also be adopted in this context. However, the selection of σ is task-dependent, as some tasks may require a significantly lower permissible error.

Definition 6 (Robustness margin). *Consider a neural network $f : \mathbb{R}^n \to \mathbb{N}$ and a permitted error of $\sigma \in (0,1)$. The robustness margin indicates the maximum perturbation size ϵ such that the network is ϵ-robust on an arbitrary correctly classified reference input, provided that we allow an error of σ:*

$$\epsilon_\sigma : P(\epsilon_\sigma) = 1 - \sigma \tag{5}$$

Where $P(\epsilon) = \mathbb{P}(\{x_0 : ||x - x_0|| < \epsilon \Rightarrow f(x) = f(x_0)\})$ is the robust accuracy.

The robustness margin returns a value of ϵ for a given permitted error σ, thus removing the dependence on ϵ. With the critical robustness framework from Definitions 2 and 3, this can be reformulated. The following observation can be made about $P(\epsilon)$ from Definition 4:

$$P(\epsilon) = \mathbb{P}(\{x_0 : \epsilon^*_{x_0} \geq \epsilon\}) = 1 - \mathbb{P}(\{x_0 : \epsilon^*_{x_0} < \epsilon\}) = 1 - P(\epsilon^* < \epsilon) \tag{6}$$

This is because a correctly classified reference input that is ϵ-robust is also ϵ-robust for all perturbation sizes smaller than ϵ. Therefore, its critical epsilon is guaranteed to be at least ϵ.

Therefore, the robustness margin can be reformulated as follows:

$$\epsilon_\sigma : P(\epsilon^* < \epsilon_\sigma) = \sigma \tag{7}$$

Therefore, determining the robustness margin corresponds to a quantile estimation problem for the underlying robustness distribution. Figure 2 provides a visual example of how the robustness margin and robust accuracy can be determined from a given robustness distribution.

The robustness margin addresses the disadvantages of robust accuracy as follows:

a. The parameter σ is more intuitive for someone without expertise in safety margins and neural network verification; it is rooted in statistics and directly reflects the tolerance for mistakes. Also known as the acceptable quality threshold, a concept routinely used in practice. This parameter is task-specific and is chosen to reflect the desired level of permissible error. Because it is a widely used concept, extensive task-specific literature already provides guidance on appropriate values of σ.

b. The robustness margin provides a perturbation size ϵ for which an arbitrary input has a probability of $1 - \sigma$ to remain robust, offering a reliable indication of the robustness of individual inputs.

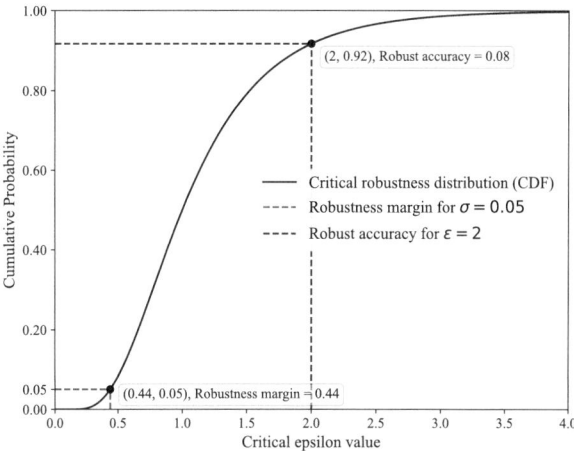

Fig. 2. Illustration of how the robustness margin and robust accuracy can be read of a robustness distribution, whose (hypothetical) CDF is shown in blue. The dashed red lines indicate how the robustness margin for $\sigma = 0.05$ can be read off the plot. The dashed green lines indicate how the robust accuracy for $\epsilon = 2$ can be read from the plot, where the robust accuracy is given by $1 - P(\epsilon^* < \epsilon)$, as shown in Eq. 6 (Color figure online).

c. By addressing the first two issues, the robustness margin provides a more reliable indicator of a network's robustness behaviour, making it better suited than robust accuracy for comparing the robustness of two networks.

Determining the robustness margin of a neural network for a given σ is equivalent to identifying the σ-quantile of its robustness distribution, as visually represented in Fig. 2. In the following, we will present two different methods for empirically determining this value. The first method is a non-parametric approach, which does not make any assumptions about the robustness distribution. The second method is parametric, relying on an assumption about the family of the robustness distribution. The non-parametric approach makes no assumptions about the distribution; however, it requires a significant amount of data to converge to a precise estimate. For the parametric approach to be accurate, a good understanding of the underlying functional family of the distribution is required. For this approach, the robustness distribution is assumed to belong to a functional family, and its parameters are fitted to the data.

This approach requires significantly less data to converge to a precise estimate when compared to the non-parametric approach, provided the distributional assumption holds.

In Sect. 4, the non-parametric method is used as a baseline to evaluate the reliability of the parametric method. Furthermore, both methods are compared in terms of data efficiency.

3.2 Order Statistics

Order statistics are essential to the non-parametric method and are formally defined as follows:

Definition 7 (Order statistics). *Given a dataset $\{x_1, \cdots, x_n\}$, the values are arranged in ascending order to form the ordered set $\{x_{(1)}, \cdots, x_{(n)}\}$, where $x_{(i)}$ denotes the i-th order statistic.*

The following three properties of order statistics, as derived by Meeker et al. [23], are relevant:

a. Given a continuous random variable X with CDF P, it follows that $P(X) \sim U(0, 1)$, meaning $P(X)$ is uniformly distributed on the interval $[0, 1]$.
b. Given that $X_{(i)}$ is the i-th order statistic sampled from $U(0, 1)$ with a sample size of n, it follows that $X_{(i)} \sim \text{Beta}(i, n - i + 1)$. That is, $X_{(i)}$ has a Beta distribution with parameters i and $n - i + 1$.
c. Given the CDF of the Beta distribution with parameters α and $n - \alpha + 1$ at a point x, denoted as $\text{Beta}(x; \alpha, n - \alpha + 1)$, it holds that $\text{Beta}(x; \alpha, n - \alpha + 1) = 1 - \text{Binom}(\alpha - 1; n, x)$, where $\text{Binom}(\alpha - 1; n, x)$ denotes the CDF of a Binomial distribution with parameters n (number of trials) and x (probability of success in each trial), evaluated at $\alpha - 1$.

Using the first two, the i-th order statistic $X_{(i)}$ sampled from a distribution with CDF P and a sample size of n satisfies

$$P(X_{(i)}) \sim \text{Beta}(i, n - i + 1). \tag{8}$$

3.3 Non-parametric Estimator

For the non-parametric estimator, our method follows Meeker et al. [23]. Given a dataset of critical epsilons $\{\epsilon_1^*, \epsilon_2^*, \ldots, \epsilon_n^*\}$, the order statistics are given by the ordered set $\{\epsilon_{(1)}^*, \epsilon_{(2)}^*, \ldots, \epsilon_{(n)}^*\}$ and the σ-quantile by $P^{-1}(\sigma)$. A non-parametric confidence interval (CI) for this quantile, with a confidence level of $1 - \alpha$, is constructed by selecting appropriate l and u, such that the interval $[\epsilon_{(l)}^*, \epsilon_{(u)}^*]$ has a probability of $1 - \alpha$ to contain the σ-quantile. Mathematically, this requires solving the following:

$$\mathbb{P}(\epsilon_{(l)}^* \leq P^{-1}(\sigma) \leq \epsilon_{(u)}^*) = 1 - \alpha,$$
$$\mathbb{P}(\epsilon_{(l)}^* \leq P^{-1}(\sigma)) - \mathbb{P}(\epsilon_{(u)}^* \leq P^{-1}(\sigma)) = 1 - \alpha,$$
$$\mathbb{P}(P(\epsilon_{(l)}^*) \leq \sigma) - \mathbb{P}(P(\epsilon_{(u)}^*) \leq \sigma) = 1 - \alpha,$$
$$\text{Beta}(\sigma; l, n - l + 1) - \text{Beta}(\sigma; u, n - u + 1) = 1 - \alpha,$$
$$\text{Binom}(u - 1; n, \sigma) - \text{Binom}(l - 1; n, \sigma) = 1 - \alpha,$$

where the relevant properties related to order statistics have been used. To simplify this even further, only two-sided intervals are considered, meaning that $\mathbb{P}(\epsilon_{(l)}^* \geq P^{-1}(\sigma)) = \mathbb{P}(\epsilon_{(u)}^* \leq P^{-1}(\sigma)) = \alpha/2$. Consequently, the non-parametric estimator is given as follows:

Estimator 3 (Non-parametric confidence interval for the robustness margin). Given a set of test data not used in training the neural network $f : \mathbb{R}^n \to \mathbb{N}$, with corresponding critical epsilons $\{\epsilon_1^*, \epsilon_2^*, \ldots, \epsilon_n^*\}$, we define the non-parametric confidence interval, of at least $1 - \alpha$ level, for the robustness margin at σ as $[\epsilon_{(l)}^*, \epsilon_{(u)}^*]$, where:

$$l = \text{Binom}^{-1}(\alpha/2; n, \sigma) + 1 \qquad (9)$$

$$u = \text{Binom}^{-1}(1 - \alpha/2; n, \sigma) + 1 \qquad (10)$$

To find a confidence interval for the robustness margin non-parametrically, we order all critical epsilon values from lowest to highest and determine which two indices in this ordered set form a $1-\alpha$ level confidence interval. These indices are given by l and u.

3.4 Parametric Estimator

A key observation by Bosman et al. [2] is the similarity between robustness distributions and log-normal distributions. If $\{\epsilon_1^*, \epsilon_2^*, \ldots, \epsilon_n^*\}$ follow a log-normal distribution, then $\{\ln(\epsilon_1^*), \ln(\epsilon_2^*), \ldots, \ln(\epsilon_n^*)\}$ follow a normal distribution. The following two distributions are introduced for the parametric estimator:

a. The standard normal distribution at a point x is denoted $Z(x)$; Z has a mean of 0 and a variance of 1.
b. The noncentral t distribution at a point x is denoted $t(x; n - 1, \delta)$, with n-1 degrees of freedom and noncentrality parameter δ.

To estimate the confidence interval for the σ-quantile, with a confidence level of $1 - \alpha$, under the assumption of a log-normal distribution, we use the method described by Meeker et al. [23]:

Estimator 4 (Parametric confidence interval for the robustness margin). Given a set of test data not used in training the neural network $f : \mathbb{R}^n \to \mathbb{N}$, with corresponding critical epsilons $\{\epsilon_1^*, \epsilon_2^*, \ldots, \epsilon_n^*\}$ assumed to be log-normally distributed, we define the $1-\alpha$ level confidence interval for its robustness margin at σ as $[\epsilon_a^*, \epsilon_b^*]$, where:

$$\ln \epsilon_a^* = \mu - t^{-1}(1 - \alpha/2; n - 1, \delta) \cdot \frac{s}{\sqrt{n}} \qquad (11)$$

$$\ln \epsilon_b^* = \mu - t^{-1}(\alpha/2; n - 1, \delta) \cdot \frac{s}{\sqrt{n}} \qquad (12)$$

with $\mu = \frac{1}{n}\sum_i \epsilon_i^*$, $s = \sqrt{\frac{1}{n}\sum_i (\epsilon_i^* - \mu)^2}$ and $\delta = -\sqrt{n}Z^{-1}(\sigma)$.

Assuming a log-normal distribution of the critical epsilon values, we transform the data into a normal distribution by taking their logarithm. The $1 - \alpha$ level confidence interval of the robustness margin can then be computed using the mean μ, standard deviation s, and non-centrality parameter δ of the resulting normal distribution.

4 Results

The parametric and non-parametric estimators are evaluated in the following three ways, with each evaluation conducted over an increasing number of samples used for the estimator:[3]

- Amount of uncertainty.
- The ability to identify the network with better robustness between the two options.
- The accuracy of the parametric estimator.

4.1 Experimental Setup

For the results, we pre-computed[4] critical epsilon values for 1000 instances of 3 networks trained on MNIST [11]. The MNIST dataset consists of handwritten digits along with their corresponding labels, containing 60 000 training instances and 10 000 testing instances. All train instances are used for training the network, and we selected the first 100 test and 100 train instances for each class, leading to 1000 test and 1000 train instances in total, to measure critical epsilons across the selected networks as in [3].

Bosman *et al.* [3] utilise a recent version of the Branch-and-Bound-based neural network verification framework (BaB) [5,10] for verification. For each of the selected instances, for each network, they iteratively make use of k-binary search [2,8] for finding the critical epsilon value. Note that they discretise the search space and investigate a range of ϵ values from 0.001 to 0.4 in intervals of 0.002. Only correctly classified instances for each network were considered for evaluation, potentially resulting in different images selected for each network.

We selected three networks based on the critical epsilon distributions reported by Bosman *et al.* [2]: mnist relu 4 1024, mnist-net 256x4 and mnist-net. mnist relu 4 1024 has the largest average critical epsilon, mnist-net 256x4 has a more typical distribution, and mnist-net has the largest minimal critical epsilon in their study. This way, the three networks form a representative set.

The estimators are evaluated over varying sample sizes, ranging from 10 to 850. For each sample size n, the pre-computed critical epsilon values are used to draw n critical epsilons with replacement. This process is repeated 1000 times, resulting in 1000 different orderings of n instances, and consequently $n \cdot 1000$ critical epsilons. This provides insight into the distribution and performance of the estimators for each sample size, where the sample size represents the number of critical epsilon values available to the estimator.

4.2 Amount of Uncertainty

For both estimators, we calculated the mean and quantile information of the estimator to show the uncertainty in the estimation of the robustness margin. Naturally, the uncertainty decreases as the critical epsilon of more reference images

---

[3] All code is available on: https://github.com/ADA-research/Robustness-Metric.
[4] For exact computation see: https://github.com/ADA-research/VERONA.

is determined. Note that these uncertainty calculations are purely intended to display the variability of the estimators over multiple repeated measurements of the robustness margin, while the predictive consequences of these results are discussed in later sections.

In the following, we determine the number of critical epsilon values needed to obtain a certain amount of uncertainty.

Figure 3 illustrates the mean confidence interval size of the robustness margin over the number of samples, along with the 0.025 and 0.975 quantiles. The samples used for the estimators are the calculated critical epsilon values of different reference images. For each sample size n, 1000 different subsets of size n are drawn from the set of critical epsilons, and their intervals are computed. The difference between the upper and lower bounds of each interval is calculated, and the mean, as well as the 0.025 and 0.975 quantiles of these differences, are determined across the 1000 subsets.

For all three networks, the parametric estimator quickly becomes more precise than the non-parametric estimator as the number of samples increases. With fewer than 20 samples, the non-parametric estimator has a smaller uncertainty on average. However, at these low sample sizes, the quantiles of the non-parametric estimator range from near 0 to 0.04, indicating that the estimator is uncertain at this point. In contrast, the quantiles of the parametric estimator remain much closer together, indicating that it is more certain as it produces a smaller range of values. As the number of samples increases, this trend persists, and by around 100 samples, there is very little overlap between the quantiles of the two estimators. Beyond this point, the parametric estimator can be considered statistically more precise as the amount of uncertainty remains smaller.

Some artefacts can be seen in the plots for the non-parametric estimator; this is due to the discrete nature of the binomial distribution. This discreteness can be seen in Eqs. 9 and 10, which are used to calculate the indices of the non-parametric interval. To improve smoothness in the curve, a normal approximation of the binomial distribution can be used.

4.3 Identifying the More Robust of Two Given Networks

We evaluate the number of samples required for the estimators to reliably determine which of two given networks has a higher robustness margin at $\sigma = 0.05$. Specifically, we assess the chance that each estimator correctly identifies the network with the greater robustness margin as the number of samples increases. As we saw in Fig. 3, as the number of samples increases, the estimators become more confident about the robustness margin of the networks. Using a low number of samples, the confidence intervals of the robustness margin for different neural networks will typically still overlap. Note that this is not revealed by this figure, as it merely shows the amount of uncertainty (averaged over all repetitions), and not the predicted mean of the estimators. However, at some point, the uncertainty will be so small that the confidence intervals no longer overlap, and the estimators can determine one of the networks to be most robust. This experiment can be repeated various times with various subsets of the data. In

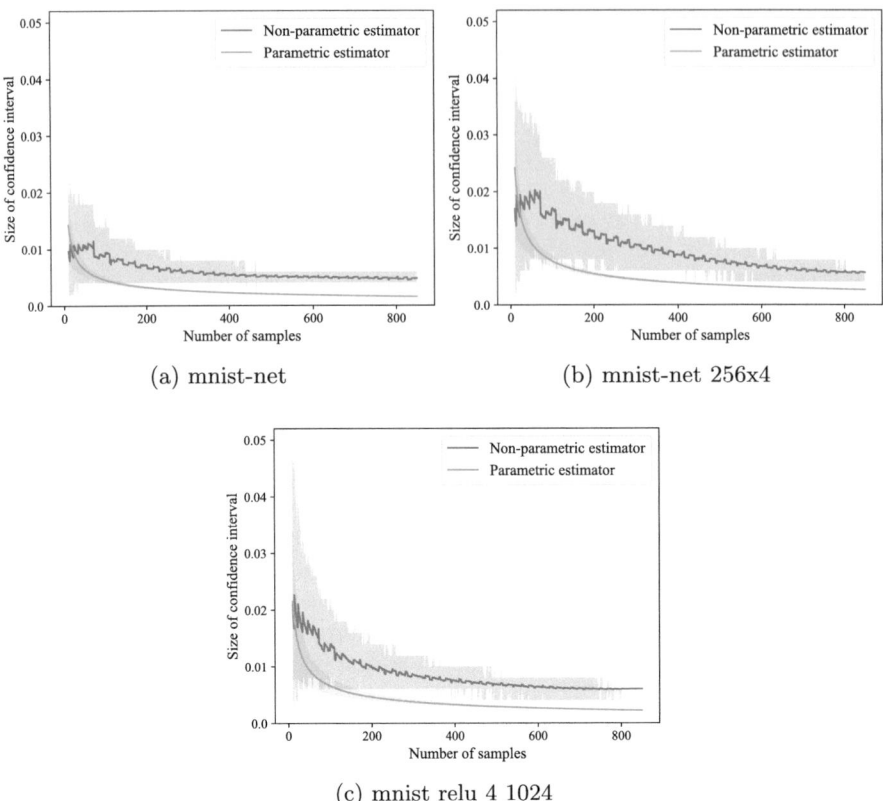

Fig. 3. Size of the confidence interval as a function of the number of samples for both estimators. For each sample size, 1000 sets were drawn from the dataset of critical epsilons. The darker line indicates the mean confidence interval size of these sets, while the shaded region represents the range between the 0.025 and 0.975 quantiles for the confidence interval size.

the following, we will report for any number of samples the ratio of experiments in which a given estimator selects the most robust network or whether it is not able to select one yet because there is still overlap in the confidence intervals. We expect that, as the number of samples increases, both estimators will be more likely to correctly identify the network with the greater robustness margin. Furthermore, if the parametric estimator is based on an appropriate parametric model, logically, it should reach this conclusion faster than the non-parametric estimator, as it leverages additional information about the distribution.

Figure 4 illustrates the evolution of uncertainty in a single binary comparison, showing both the non-parametric and parametric estimators separately, while Fig. 5 summarises the results across all comparisons combining the outcomes of both estimators in each plot. In this case, mnist-net is more robust than mnist-net 256×4, and mnist relu 4 1024 is also more robust than mnist-net 256×4. Additionally, mnist-net and mnist relu 4 1024 are equally robust. Note that these results are specific to the chosen σ value. For different values of σ, the relative robustness between networks may change. The optimal outcome, given enough samples, would show no overlap between the confidence intervals and all experiments correctly identifying the more robust network.

The same artefacts mentioned in the previous section can also be seen in these plots. For each sample size n, 1000 different subsets of size n are drawn from the set of critical epsilons, and their intervals are computed. The ratios are calculated based on these intervals.

Both estimators are conservative in their predictions, as they are more likely to indicate overlap rather than incorrectly identifying the more robust network. Figures 5a and 5c illustrate that the parametric estimator correctly identifies the more robust network with fewer samples compared to the non-parametric estimator. The parametric estimator requires approximately 100 samples to, on average, reliably indicate the more robust network, whereas the non-parametric estimator needs at least 200 samples. Additionally, Fig. 5b shows that with fewer than 20 samples, the non-parametric estimator struggles to consistently indicate overlap when that is the ground truth. In contrast, the parametric estimator performs consistently in such cases.

From this, a recommended approach for comparing networks is to progressively gather critical epsilon values and recompute the robustness margin until a conclusion can be drawn about which network is more robust, avoiding any unnecessary additional computations. The robustness margin is very unlikely to indicate the wrong, more robust network and will show overlap when more critical epsilon values are needed. Thus, when no overlap is present, the identified network is very likely the more robust one.

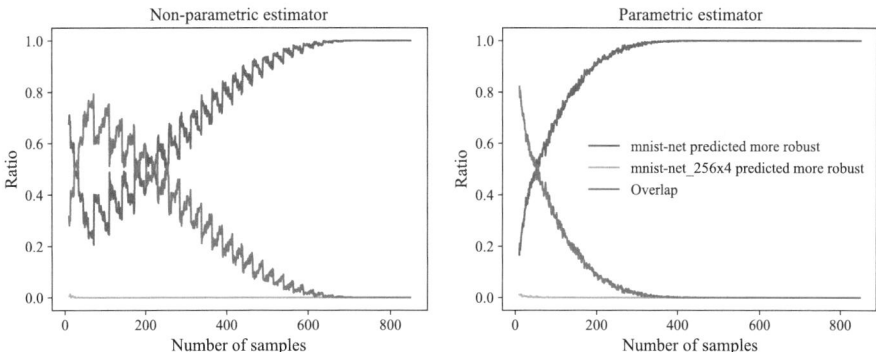

Fig. 4. Evolution of uncertainty for the binary comparison between mnist-net and mnist-net 256x4. The plots show how the proportion of predicted more robust network and overlaps changes as the number of samples increases for the non-parametric estimator (left) and parametric estimator (right).

4.4 Accuracy of Parametric Estimator

For both estimators, we calculate the mean and quantile information of the robustness margin to assess their accuracy. An estimator is considered accurate if the calculated quantiles overlap with the ground truth. The ground truth is defined as the robustness margin measured by the non-parametric estimator after 850 samples. We expect the non-parametric estimator to be accurate regardless of the number of samples, as it makes no assumptions about the underlying distribution. Additionally, if the parametric estimator is based on an appropriate parametric model, it should also maintain accuracy for any number of samples.

Figure 6 shows the 0.025 quantile of the lower bound and the 0.975 quantile of the upper bound for the estimated interval of the robustness margin over the number of samples. For each sample size n, 1000 different subsets of size n are drawn from the set of critical epsilons, and their intervals are computed. The

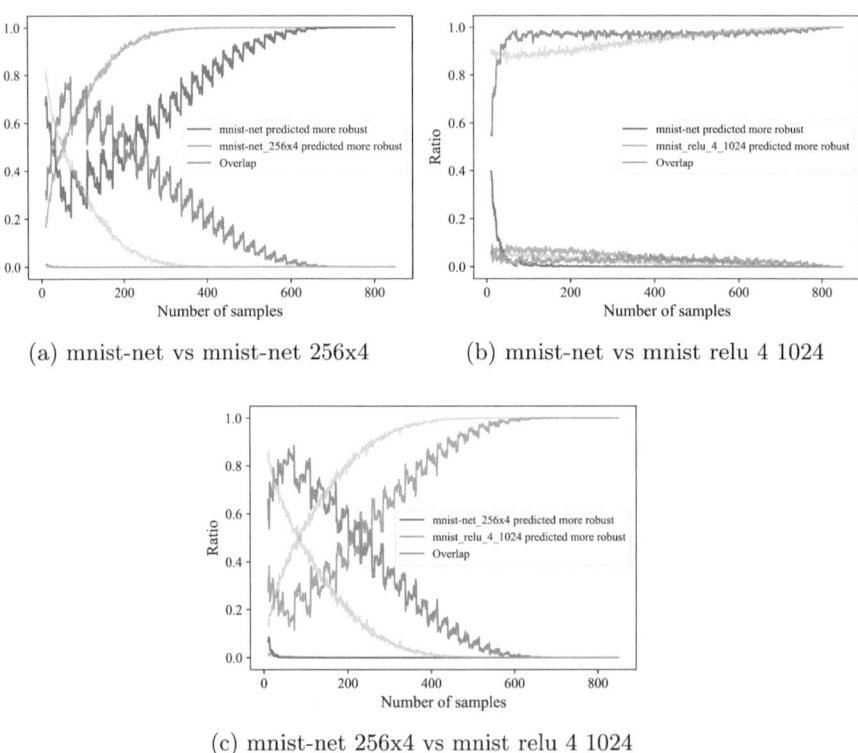

Fig. 5. The ratio of network 1 predicted more robust, network 2 predicted more robust, and number of times there is still overlap for each comparison between two networks over a range of sample sizes. We repeated the experiment 1000 times with a different order of instances to account for random effects. Based on these repetitions, we can calculate the ratios. Solid lines represent the non-parametric estimator, and transparent lines represent the parametric estimator.

0.025 quantile of the lower bound and the 0.975 quantile of the upper bound for each interval are taken across those 1000 intervals. The result of the non-parametric estimator at 850 samples is used as a ground truth to assess the accuracy of both estimators.

The distribution of intervals for the parametric estimator consistently overlaps with the ground truth, indicating that the parametric estimator provides an accurate estimation of the robustness margin.

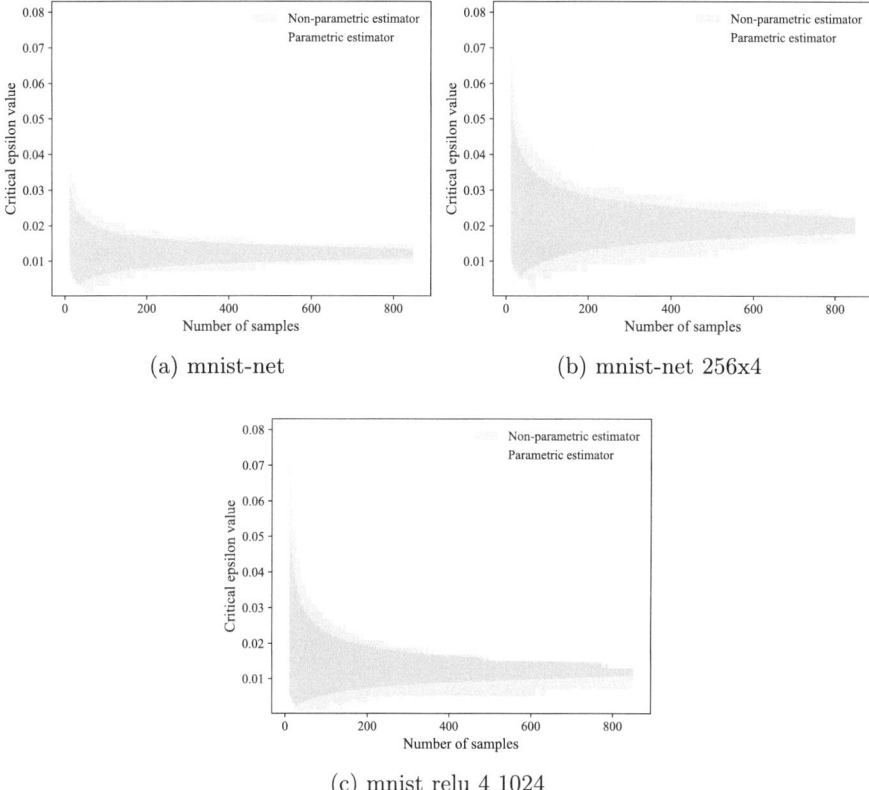

Fig. 6. Distribution of intervals generated by both estimators over several samples. For each sample size, 1000 sets were drawn from the dataset of critical epsilons. The bottom of the shaded region indicates the 0.025 quantile of the lower bounds, while the top indicates the 0.975 quantile of the upper bounds over the 1000 sets.

5 Conclusion

In this paper, we have introduced a new robustness measure, the robustness margin. Our new measure addresses the limitations of robust accuracy by providing a more intuitive control parameter σ and by offering an interpretable indication of robustness for individual images. It thus provides a solid basis for comparing the robustness of networks. To estimate its confidence bounds in practice, we derived both a parametric and a non-parametric estimator. We evaluated these estimators based on their efficiency in terms of the required number of instances for (i) the ability to identify the more robust of two given networks, (ii) estimator precision, and (iii) estimator accuracy.

We find that both estimators tend to be accurate for 10 instances. The parametric estimator surpasses the precision of the non-parametric estimator at around 20 instances. However, before reaching this point, the variance of the non-parametric estimator becomes too high for the estimator to be reliable, suggesting that the parametric estimator should be preferred even before 20 instances.

When comparing the robustness of two networks, both estimators are quite conservative, being more likely to indicate a possible tie rather than incorrectly favouring the wrong network. In the scenarios we studied, when one network is more robust, the non-parametric estimator requires at least 200 instances to reliably identify the correct winner, whereas the parametric estimator achieves this with only 100 instances.

In cases where the networks have a similar robustness margin, the non-parametric estimator has a high chance of incorrectly favouring one network when fewer than 20 instances are used, reinforcing that it is not reliable in this range. The parametric estimator seems to not suffer from this problem with at least 10 instances.

To further validate the reliability and efficiency of the parametric estimator, the same experiments should be conducted on a larger set of networks. Due to computational constraints, evaluations have only been performed on three networks. Expanding the analysis would provide a more comprehensive assessment of its performance across different architectures.

While in this study, we have only employed complete verification methods, it would be interesting to evaluate our estimators with incomplete verification methods. Using these for estimating critical epsilon values, it may be possible to achieve significant gains in terms of computational efficiency.

References

1. Bastani, O., Ioannou, Y., Lampropoulos, L., Vytiniotis, D., Nori, A., Criminisi, A.: Measuring neural net robustness with constraints. In: Advances in Neural Information Processing Systems 29 (NeurIPS 2016), vol. 29, pp. 2613–2621 (2016)
2. Bosman, A.W., Berger, A., Hoos, H.H., van Rijn, J.N.: Robustness distributions in neural network verification. J. Artif. Intell. Res. (2025, to appear)
3. Bosman, A.W., Münz, A.L., Hoos, H.H., van Rijn, J.N.: A preliminary study to examining per-class performance bias via robustness distributions. In: International Symposium on AI Verification (SAIV) co-located with the 36th International Conference on Computer Aided Verification (CAV 2024), pp. 116–133. Springer (2024)

4. Botoeva, E., Kouvaros, P., Kronqvist, J., Lomuscio, A., Misener, R.: Efficient verification of ReLU-based neural networks via dependency analysis. In: Proceedings of the 34th AAAI Conference on Artificial Intelligence (AAAI 2020), pp. 3291–3299 (2020)
5. Bunel, R., Turkaslan, I., Torr, P., Kohli, P., Mudigonda, P.K.: A unified view of piecewise linear neural network verification. In: Advances in Neural Information Processing Systems 31 (NeurIPS 2018), pp. 1–10 (2018)
6. Carlini, N., Katz, G., Barrett, C., Dill, D.L.: Ground-Truth Adversarial Examples. arXiv preprint arXiv:1709.10207 (2017)
7. Carlini, N., Wagner, D.: Towards evaluating the robustness of neural networks. In: 2017 IEEE Symposium on Security and Privac (SP), pp. 39–57. IEEE (2017)
8. Cicalese, F., Gargano, L., Vaccaro, U.: On searching strategies, parallel questions, and delayed answers. Discret. Appl. Math. **144**(3), 247–262 (2004)
9. Cohen, J., Rosenfeld, E., Kolter, Z.: Certified adversarial robustness via randomized smoothing. In: Chaudhuri, K., Salakhutdinov, R. (eds.) Proceedings of the 36th International Conference on Machine Learning. Proceedings of Machine Learning Research, vol. 97, pp. 1310–1320. PMLR (2019)
10. De Palma, A., et al.: Improved Branch and Bound for Neural Network Verification via Lagrangian Decomposition. arXiv preprint arXiv:2104.06718 (2021)
11. Deng, L.: The MNIST database of handwritten digit images for machine learning research [best of the web]. IEEE Signal Process. Mag. **29**(6), 141–142 (2012)
12. Dvijotham, K., Stanforth, R., Gowal, S., Mann, T.A., Kohli, P.: A dual approach to scalable verification of deep networks. In: Proceedings of the 38th Conference on Uncertainty in Artificial Intelligence (UAI 2018), pp. 550–559 (2018)
13. Gehr, T., Mirman, M., Drachsler-Cohen, D., Tsankov, P., Chaudhuri, S., Vechev, M.: Safety and robustness certification of neural networks with abstract interpretation. In: 2018 IEEE Symposium on Security and Privacy (SP), pp. 3–18. IEEE (2018)
14. Goodfellow, I.J., Shlens, J., Szegedy, C.: Explaining and harnessing adversarial examples. arXiv preprint arXiv:1412.6572 (2014)
15. Huang, R., Xu, B., Schuurmans, D., Szepesvari, C.: Learning with a Strong Adversary. arXiv e-prints pp. arXiv–1511 (2015)
16. Julian, K.D., Kochenderfer, M.J., Owen, M.P.: Deep neural network compression for aircraft collision avoidance systems. J. Guid. Control Dyn. **42**(3), 598–608 (2019)
17. Katz, G., Barrett, C., Dill, D.L., Julian, K., Kochenderfer, M.J.: Reluplex: an efficient SMT solver for verifying deep neural networks. In: Proceedings of the 29th International Conference on Computer Aided Verification (CAV 2022), pp. 97–117. Springer (2017)
18. Kolmogorov, A.: Sulla determinazione empirica di una legge didistribuzione. Giorn Dell'inst Ital Degli Att **4**, 89–91 (1933)
19. König, M., Bosman, A.W., Hoos, H.H., Rijn, J.N.: Critically assessing the state of the art in neural network verification. J. Mach. Learn. Res. **25**(12), 1–53 (2024)
20. König, M., Hoos, H.H., van Rijn, J.N.: Accelerating adversarially robust model selection for deep neural networks via racing. In: Thirty-Eighth AAAI Conference on Artificial Intelligence (AAAI 2024), pp. 21267–21275. AAAI Press (2024)
21. Leino, K., Wang, Z., Fredrikson, M.: Globally-robust neural networks. In: Meila, M., Zhang, T. (eds.) Proceedings of the 38th International Conference on Machine Learning. Proceedings of Machine Learning Research, vol. 139, pp. 6212–6222. PMLR (2021)

22. Li, L., Xie, T., Li, B.: SoK: certified robustness for deep neural networks. In: 2023 IEEE Symposium on Security and Privacy (SP 2023), pp. 94–115. IEEE Computer Society (2023)
23. Meeker, W.Q., Hahn, G.J., Escobar, L.A.: Distribution-Free Statistical Intervals, chap. 5, pp. 73–98. Wiley (2017)
24. Papernot, N., McDaniel, P., Wu, X., Jha, S., Swami, A.: Distillation as a defense to adversarial perturbations against deep neural networks. In: 2016 IEEE Symposium on Security and Privacy (SP), pp. 582–597. IEEE (2016)
25. Shaham, U., Yamada, Y., Negahban, S.: Understanding Adversarial Training: Increasing Local Stability of Neural Nets through Robust Optimization. arXiv preprint arXiv:1511.05432 (2015)
26. Smirnov, N.V.: Approximate laws of distribution of random variables from empirical data. Uspekhi Matematicheskikh Nauk **10**, 179–206 (1944)
27. Szegedy, C., et al.: Intriguing properties of neural networks. In: Proceedings of the 2nd International Conference on Learning Representations (ICLR 2014), pp. 1–10 (2014)
28. Tjeng, V., Xiao, K., Tedrake, R.: Evaluating robustness of neural networks with mixed integer programming. In: Proceedings of the 7th International Conference on Learning Representations (ICLR 2019), pp. 1–21 (2019)
29. Yang, Y.Y., Rashtchian, C., Zhang, H., Salakhutdinov, R.R., Chaudhuri, K.: A closer look at accuracy vs. robustness. In: Advances in Neural Information Processing Systems 33 (NeurIPS 2020), pp. 8588–8601 (2020)

GRENA: GPU-Aided Abstract Refinement for Neural Network Verification

Yuyi Zhong[✉], Shaun Zong Zhi Tan, Hanping Xu, and Siau-Cheng Khoo

National University of Singapore, Singapore, Singapore
{yuyizhong,shauntanzongzhi,xuhanping}@u.nus.edu, khoosc@nus.edu.sg

Abstract. Since neural network verification problems can be formulated as optimization problems, linear programming (LP) solvers have been deployed as off-the-shelf tools in such processes. However, existing LP solvers running on CPU scale poorly on large networks. To expedite the process, we propose an LP-solving *theorem* tailored to neural network verification. In practice, we transform the constrained solving problem into an unconstrained problem that can be executed on GPUs, significantly speeding up the solving process. We explicitly include constraints on layers that take more than one predecessor instead of handling multiple predecessors by inefficient concatenation. Our theorem applies to widely used networks, such as fully connected, convolutional, and residual networks. From our evaluation, our GPU-aided solver achieves comparable precision to the state-of-the-art (SOTA) solver GUROBI with significant speed improvements and helps acquire competitive verification precision compared to advanced verification methods.

Keywords: Abstract Refinement · Linear Programming · Neural Network Verification

1 Introduction

Researchers have investigated the verification of neural networks due to their wide application [18,25,28]. Throughout the evolution of verification techniques, abstract interpretation-based techniques [6,15,20,22–24,27,32] continue to play an important role. However, due to the nature of over-approximation, the methods could suffer from severe precision loss for deeper networks. Theoretically, such abstraction can be refined with the help of (mixed integer) linear programming (MILP or LP) [21,31,34] where GUROBI [11] solver is commonly used despite the scalability concern that it executes on the CPU.

Therefore, we propose a tailored theorem to accelerate LP solving for abstract-refinement-based methods. Notably, our theorem could handle three types of constraints: output constraints, intermediate neuron constraints and constraints of layers that take more than one predecessor, which enhances the scientific rigor of the verification of residual networks. Our paper offers a methodical transformation from the stage of verification specification to the stage of effective implementation as an analyzer named GRENA (<u>G</u>PU-aided abstract <u>RE</u>finement for <u>N</u>eural network verific<u>A</u>tion), and we assess it against the state-of-the-art tools to empirically support its strong solving and verification capacities. Our dockerized system, data, usage documentation and experiment scripts are available at https://github.com/Grena-verifier/Grena-verifier. We summarize our contributions below:

- We propose a novel, formal and rigorous theorem to solve constrained optimization problems that include output constraints, multi-ReLU constraints, and complex constraints of residual network layers. Specifically, to the best of our knowledge, this is the first work that uses Lagrangian dual on spurious-adversarial-label guided refinement process to enhance the scientific rigor of the verification of residual networks.
- We utilize the multi-ReLU abstraction in WraLU [12] to further tighten our constraint set for precision improvement.
- We provide strong and effective implementations and demonstrate the verification efficiency of our system through empirical experiments, and deliver a video showcase[1] of our analyzer.

2 Overview

To provide an intuitive understanding, we use an example in Fig. 1 to show how the approach works given the network and the input space $I = [-1, 1] \times [-1, 1]$ of 2 input neurons x_1, x_2. This network has 2 output neurons y_1, y_2, corresponding to two labels L_1, L_2 that an input can be classified as, and we aim to verify that $y_1 - y_2 > 0$ for all inputs in I.

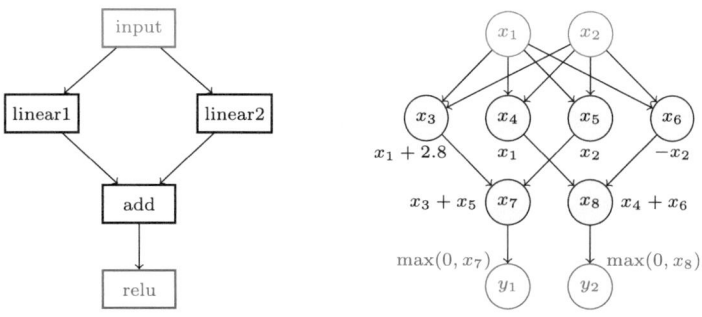

(a) The network with an add layer   (b) Neuron connections

Fig. 1. The example network to be verified with $y_1 - y_2 > 0$ with input space $I = [-1, 1] \times [-1, 1]$.

---

[1] https://drive.google.com/file/d/17v1WnabNrzC-ZwJzJ4dLTQmm9JvDYfj5/view?usp=sharing.

We first apply the abstract interpretation technique, as deployed by DeepPoly [20], to compute the reachable statuses for each neuron at Fig. 1b and represent them by four elements (l_i, u_i, l_i^s, u_i^s). The *concrete* lower and upper bounds l_i, u_i form an interval $[l_i, u_i]$ that over-approximates all the values that neuron x_i could take. The *symbolic* constraints l_i^s, u_i^s are linear expressions of x_i defined over preceding neurons while satisfying $l_i^s \leq x_i \leq u_i^s$. The abstract values are displayed near the corresponding nodes at Fig. 2.

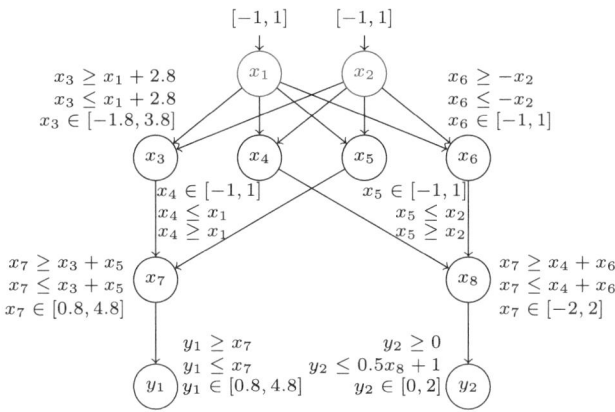

Fig. 2. The network to perform abstract interpretation.

Based on the abstraction, the computed value for the lower bound of $y_1 - y_2$ is -0.2 ($y_1 - y_2$ will be treated as an auxiliary neuron in order to compute its lower bound, the details can be found in [20]), failing to assert that $y_1 - y_2 > 0$. However, this failure is due to the over-approximation error, and there is no such instance that leads to $y_1 - y_2 < 0$. To prove $y_1 - y_2 < 0$ to be infeasible, we will construct a constraint set that encodes the existence of spurious counterexamples together with the network constraints (conjunction of all linear inequities including the *concrete* bounds and *symbolic* constraints of all neurons). Based on the constraint set, we send it to our tailored LP solver (details of our solving theorem at Subsect. 3.1) to resolve the concrete bounds of input neurons (x_1, x_2) and those linear neurons (x_8) that are followed by ReLU and take both negative and positive values. The returned bounds will be tighter, as shown in Fig. 3, and diminish the inconclusiveness produced by the previous abstract interpretation.

Based on the updated bounds, we rerun abstract interpretation and update the abstract values of all neurons accordingly, as shown in Fig. 4. Based on the new abstraction, the lower bound of $y_1 - y_2$ is 0.7, making $y_1 - y_2 \leq 0$ actually infeasible, which means that y_1 dominates over y_2 and we could conclude that $y_1 - y_2 > 0$.

In summary, our system uses LP solving and abstract interpretation to eliminate adversarial labels that are actually infeasible. Note that in our constraint set, we explicitly encode an Add layer that takes two predecessors as

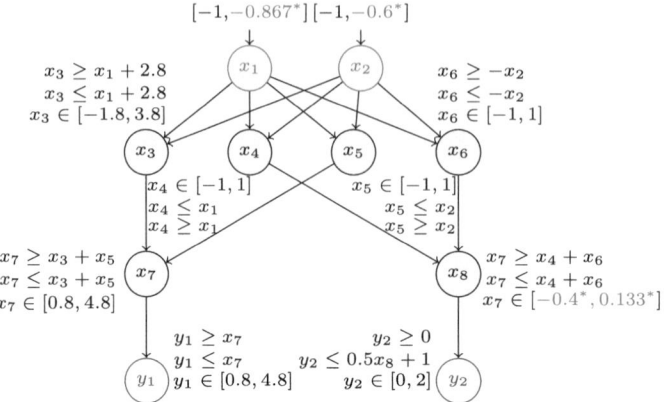

Fig. 3. The result of resolving bounds (in red marked by *) (Color figure online)

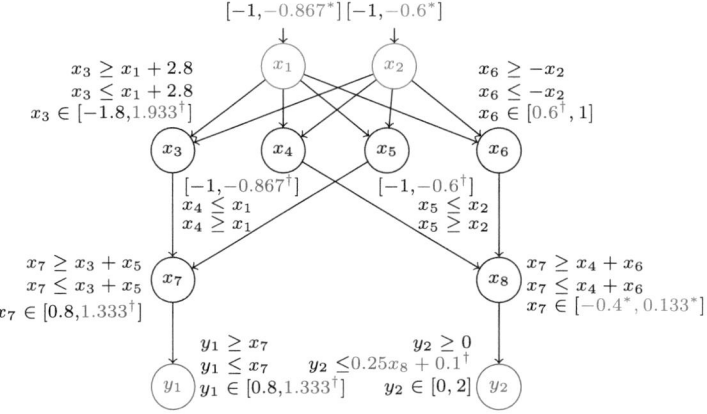

Fig. 4. The updated abstract values (in blue marked by †) (Color figure online)

$[x_7, x_8] = [x_3, x_4] + [x_5, x_6]$, and we will elaborate on how our theorem handles two predecessors at Theorem 1 instead of simply concatenating two predecessors into one in an engineering manner.

3 Methodologies

We provide a simplified case that only contains one adversarial label y_2 in the previous section. But in general, the verification process repeatedly selects multiple adversarial labels and attempts to eliminate them through iterations of refinements as illustrated in Fig. 5. In each iteration, we take the encoding of multiple adversarial labels (the disjunction is handled by following the convention in [34]), the current network abstraction, plus the SOTA WraLU *multi-neuron constraints* as the constraint set. We eliminate δ spurious adversarial labels if

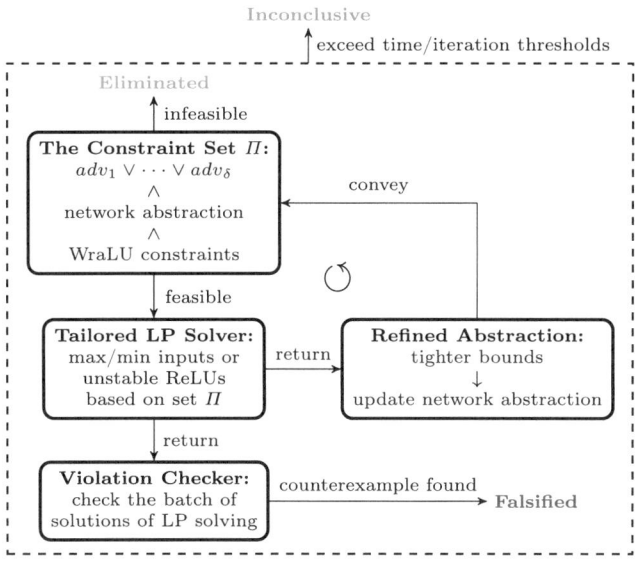

Fig. 5. The iterative process of abstract refinement.

the constraint set is infeasible, and eliminating all adversarial labels results in successful verification. If the constraint set is feasible, we send it to our *tailored LP solver on GPU* (details deferred till Subsect. 3.1) and resolve neuron bounds to obtain a refined abstraction, where the refined abstraction is used in the next iteration. Furthermore, as a feasible constraint set indicates the possibility of a property violation, we collect *the batch of input neuron assignments* during each solving substep and pass them to the model to check if they constitute an adversarial example which falsifies the property. We repeat this process until a conclusive result is obtained; or until the time/iteration threshold has exceeded, indicating inconclusive result.

3.1 GPU-Aided Linear Programming Solver

This subsection presents our theorem of transforming a constrained linear programming problem into an unconstrained solving problem *amenable to GPU acceleration*.

Preliminaries. Given a network with $L+1$ layers and each layer corresponds to a layer index, the *input layer* is at index 0 and the output layer is at index L. We denote the set of all ReLU layer indexes as $[R]$, the set of all linear layer indexes with one connected preceding layer as $[L_1]$, the set of all indexes of linear layers that take two preceding layers as $[L_2]$. We assume that $[R] \cup [L_1] \cup [L_2] = [1, \ldots, L]$ and both $1, L \in [L_1]$. The output and input/preceding layer of a ReLU layer are respectively represented by $\hat{x}^{(i)}$ and $\hat{x}_p^{(i)}$, for $i \in [R]$. Given a neuron index j and a layer index i, $\hat{x}^{(i)j}$ represents the j-th neuron at i-th layer and $\hat{x}_p^{(i)j}$ refers to its input neuron. Symbol $x^{(i)}, i \in [L_1] \cup [L_2]$ represents the output of a linear layer; symbols $\hat{x}^{(0)}, x^{(0)}$ both denote the input layer. Symbol $x_p^{(i)}, i \in [L_1]$ refers to the predecessor of layer $x^{(i)}$ for $i \in [L_1]$; whereas $x_{p_1}^{(i)}, x_{p_2}^{(i)}$ are the two preceding layers of layer $x^{(i)}$ for $i \in [L_2]$. Finally, we designate $S(i)$ as a set that includes the indexes of all connected succeeding layers of layer i and $i_s \in S(i)$; the set $S^2(i) = \cup_{i_s \in S(i)} S(i_s)$, which includes the successors' indexes of succeeding layers of layer i and $i_{s^2} \in S^2(i)$.

Theorem 1. *The constrained optimization problem in neural network verification (as shown in Eq. 1) can be transformed into an unconstrained problem in Eq. 2 by using Lagrangian dual.*

Proof. The derivation can be found at this appendix[2].

In detail, the constrained problem formulation is given as:

$$\min_{x,\hat{x}} c^{(0)} \hat{x}^{(0)} + \sum_{i \in [R]} c^{(i)T} \hat{x}_p^{(i)}$$

$$\text{s.t. } l^{(0)} \leq \hat{x}^{(0)} \leq u^{(0)}; Hx^{(L)} + d \leq 0$$

$$x^{(i)} = W^{(i)} x_p^{(i)} + b^{(i)}, \text{ for } i \in [L_1]$$

$$x^{(i)} = x_{p_1}^{(i)} + x_{p_2}^{(i)}, \text{ for } i \in [L_2]$$

$$\hat{x}^{(i)j} = \hat{x}_p^{(i)j}, \text{ for } i \in [R], j \in I^{+(i)} \quad (1)$$

$$\hat{x}^{(i)j} = 0, \text{ for } i \in [R], j \in I^{-(i)}$$

$$\hat{x}^{(i)j} \geq 0, \hat{x}^{(i)j} \geq \hat{x}_p^{(i)j}, \text{ for } i \in [R], j \in I^{\pm(i)}$$

$$\hat{x}^{(i)j} \leq \frac{u^{(i)j}}{u^{(i)j} - l^{(i)j}} (\hat{x}_p^{(i)j} - l^{(i)j}), \text{ for } i \in [R], j \in I^{\pm(i)}$$

$$P^{(i)} \hat{x}_p^{(i)} + \hat{P}^{(i)} \hat{x}^{(i)} - p^{(i)} \leq 0, \text{ for } i \in [R]$$

In detail, $l^{(0)}, u^{(0)}$ record the lower and upper bounds of input neurons; $Hx^{(L)} + d \leq 0$ represents the output constraints that encode the existence of multiple adversarial examples. For ReLU neurons, their functionalities depend on the stability statuses. For example, suppose a linear layer i is followed by a ReLU layer i_s. A ReLU neuron is stably activated if it takes a non-negative input interval, in which case it equals the input neuron, and we collect the indexes of those non-negative input neurons at layer i as $I^{+(i)}$. Stably deactivated ReLU neurons have non-positive inputs, with outputs that are always evaluated to 0, and we denote the indexes of those non-positive input neurons as a set $I^{-(i)}$. Unstable ReLU neurons take both positive and negative input values, their corresponding input neuron indexes are recorded in $I^{\pm(i)}$. In particular, the unstable ReLU neuron is approximated by an orange-colored triangle shape as Fig. 6 illustrates, where $l^{(i)j}, u^{(i)j}$ record its input interval and $\frac{u^{(i)j}}{u^{(i)j} - l^{(i)j}}$ is abbreviated as $s^{(i)j}$.

---

[2] https://github.com/Grena-verifier/misc-files/blob/master/theorem_proof.pdf.

Constraints $P^{(i)} \hat{x}_p^{(i)} + \hat{P}^{(i)} \hat{x}^{(i)} - p^{(i)} \leq 0$ capture the dependencies of multiple ReLU neurons in the same layer, which is obtained from the WraLU [12] method to improve solving precision. The coefficients $c^{(0)}$ and $c^{(i)}, i \in [R]$ are used to control the objective function. As we aim to resolve the input neurons as well as the input lower and upper bounds of unstable ReLU neurons to refine the abstraction, we only set one element among $c^{(0)}, c^{(i)}, i \in [R]$ as 1 (for lower bound computation) or -1 (for upper bound) for the respective neuron, the rest of the elements are set as 0.

Eventually, we transform the constrained solving problem into an unconstrained one using Lagrangian variables as shown below, where we annotate $[x]_+ = \max(x, 0), [x]_- = -\min(x, 0)$:

$$\max_{\gamma, \upsilon, \pi, \alpha} l^{(0)} [c^{(0)T} - v^{(1)T} w^{(1)}]_+ - u^{(0)} [v^{(1)T} w^{(1)} - c^{(0)T}]_+ + \gamma^T d$$
$$+ \sum_{i \in [R]} \sum_{j \in I^{\pm(i)}} [\hat{v}^{(i)j}]_+ \cdot s^{(i)j} \cdot l^{(i)j} - \sum_{i \in [R]} \pi^{(i)T} p^{(i)} - \sum_{i \in [L_1]} v^{(i)T} b^{(i)}$$

$$\text{s.t. } v^{(L)} = -H^T \gamma; \ \gamma, \pi \geq 0; \ \alpha \in [0, 1]$$

for $i \in [L_1] \cup [L_2], i_s \in [R] \cap S(i), i_s \notin [L_2]$:

$$v^{(i)j} = -c^{(i_s)j}, j \in I^{-(i)}$$

$$v^{(i)j} = \sum_{i_{s2} \in S(i_s) \cap [L_1]} v^{(i_{s2})T} W_{:,j}^{(i_{s2})} - c^{(i_s)j}, j \in I^{+(i)} \quad (2)$$

for $j \in I^{\pm(i)}: v^{(i)j} = s^{(i_s)j} [\hat{v}^{(i_s)j}]_+ - c^{(i_s)j} - \pi^{(i_s)T} P_{:,j}^{(i_s)} - \alpha^{(i_s)j} [\hat{v}^{(i_s)j}]_-$

$$\hat{v}^{(i)j} = \sum_{i_{s2} \in S(i_s) \cap [L_1]} v^{(i_{s2})T} W_{:,j}^{(i_{s2})} - \pi^{(i_s)T} \hat{P}_{:,j}^{(i_s)}$$

for $i \in [L_1]$ and $i_s \in [L_2] \cap S(i)$ and $i_s \notin [R]$:

$$v^{(i)} = v^{(i_s)}$$

Any valid setting of $\gamma, \pi \geq 0; \alpha \in [0, 1]$ leads to a safe lower bound of the original problem. Based on the values of γ, π, α, we compute the values of $v^{(i)}$ and $\hat{v}^{(i)}$ in reverse order from $v^{(L)}$ to $v^{(0)}$. Using all assignments of variables, we could compute the objective value. In practice, the solving process starts with a valid initialization of γ, π, α, then we optimize these variables using gradient information.

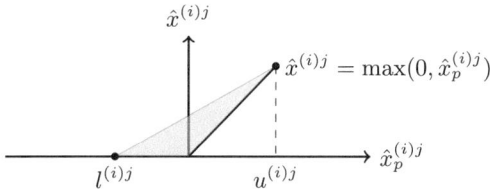

Fig. 6. The approximation of a ReLU neuron. (Color figure online)

Algorithm 1. Bounds tightening procedure
___
Input:
- M: neural network model
- $\mathcal{L}_L$: list of old lower bounds for all ReLU and input layers
- $\mathcal{L}_U$: list of old upper bounds for all ReLU and input layers
- Π: output constraints
- Θ: WraLU constraints

Output: improved lower and upper bounds

1: $\mathcal{S} \leftarrow \text{CREATE\_SOLVER\_MODEL}(M, \mathcal{L}_L, \mathcal{L}_U, \Pi, \Theta)$
2: $list\_new\_L, list\_new\_U \leftarrow [\,], [\,]$ ▷ initialization
3: **for** i **in** $\text{RANGE}(\text{len}(\mathcal{L}_L))$ **do** ▷ solve for each layer
4: $\quad \mathcal{S}.\text{SET\_LAYER}(i)$ ▷ reset to solve for this layer
5: $\quad \mathcal{S}.\text{INITALIZE\_LAGRANGIAN\_VARS}()$
6: $\quad max\_obj \leftarrow \text{TRAIN\_UNTIL\_CONVERGENCE}(\mathcal{S})$
7: $\quad N_L, N_U \leftarrow \text{GET\_NEW\_BOUNDS}(\mathcal{L}_L[i], \mathcal{L}_U[i], max\_obj)$
$\quad\quad$ ▷ improve old bounds based on solved values
8: $\quad list\_new\_L.\text{APPEND}(N_L)$ ▷ record updated bounds
9: $\quad list\_new\_U.\text{APPEND}(N_U)$
10: **return** $list\_new\_L, list\_new\_U$
___

Algorithm 1 shows the process of solving tighter bounds for each layer by training Lagrangian variables. While Lagrangian multipliers are commonly used in prior works [5,9,28,30], to the best of our knowledge, our method is the first to apply them to spurious-adversarial-label-guided refinement. Furthermore, we incorporate multi-neuron constraints, output constraints and L_2 layer constraints that explicitly consider two preceding layers, which enhances the theoretical rigor of residual network verification.

4 Experiments

We compare the performance of our prototypical verifier GRENA with SOTA verifiers including the incomplete tool WraLU [12] and the complete tool α,β-CROWN [3] - the winner of VNNCOMP (International Verification of Neural Networks Competition). In addition, we compare our tailored LP solver with SOTA GUROBI with respect to returned bound tightness and execution time.

4.1 Experiment Setup

The dataset includes MNIST (denoted as 'M') [2] and CIFAR10 (shortened as 'C') [10]. We test fully-connected (denoted as 'FC'), convolutional ('Conv') and residual ('Res') networks with various sizes, that are obtained from the ERAN system [4] and VNNCOMP [1]. The number of intermediate layers (#Layers), the number of intermediate neurons (#Neurons), and the trained defense are enumerated in Table 1 (a trained defense is a defense method against adversarial examples to improve robustness of networks).

Table 1. Detailed information of the experimental networks

Network	Type	ϵ	#Layers	#Neurons	Defense
M_6x256	FC	0.033	6	1,010	None
M_ConvSmall	Conv	0.11	3	3,604	None
M_ConvMed	Conv	0.1	3	5,704	None
M_ConvBig	Conv	0.313	6	48,064	DiffAI [14]
C_ConvMed	Conv	0.006	3	7,144	PGD [13]
C_ConvBig	Conv	0.0078	6	62,464	DiffAI
C_Resnet4b	Res	0.0042	10	14,436	None
C_ResnetA	Res	0.0033	8	11,364	None
C_ResnetB	Res	0.012	8	11,364	None

4.2 Comparison with SoTA Verifiers

To test the verification performance of GRENA, we select 30 images from the datasets for each network to verify robustness and compare the results and time costs. To verify robustness, we choose a perturbation parameter ϵ for each tested network as indicated in Table 1 and apply the perturbation to each image. We check if all the "perturbed" images within ϵ will be classified the same as the original image by the networks as the perturbation is imperceptible to human eyes. If so, we conclude the robustness to be verified. Otherwise, if a counterexample with a different label is detected, we falsify the robustness property. If the analysis is inconclusive, we return *unknown* (abbreviated as '#Unk') to the user.

The verification results of each tool and average execution time per image are shown in Table 2. We can observe that we *outperforms both* WraLU *and* α, β-CROWN with respect to precision as we return more conclusive results (either verified or falsified). In particular, we return **50.7%** more conclusive images than WraLU while WraLU fails to handle two residual networks. Even compared with the complete tool α, β-CROWN, our tool produces **13** more conclusive images in total and achieve **better or the same** verification/falsification precision on most networks. The empirical results demonstrate *the strong verification efficiency of our system*.

4.3 Comparison with GUROBI

We now compare the bound-solving abilities of our tailored solver to those of GUROBI in the context of neural network encoding. We select one image for each network and collect all the constraints where we use the constraint set to solve all unstable neuron bounds and input bounds by our solver and GUROBI, later we compare the tightness of the solved bounds as visualized in Fig. 7.

Table 2. The verification results of WraLU, α,β-CROWN and our system GRENA with average execution time per image

Network	Methods	Verification results			
		#Unk	#Verify	#Falsify	Time(s)
M_6x256	WraLU	27	3	0	26.6
	α,β-CROWN	8	**12**	**10**	87.9
	GRENA	15	7	8	195.5
M_ConvSmall	WraLU	17	13	0	7.2
	α,β-CROWN	0	**26**	**4**	5.8
	GRENA	0	**26**	**4**	35.7
M_ConvMed	WraLU	15	15	0	18.0
	α,β-CROWN	2	22	**6**	28.6
	GRENA	0	**24**	**6**	42.9
M_ConvBig	WraLU	10	**20**	0	35.6
	α,β-CROWN	3	**20**	7	31.8
	GRENA	2	**20**	**8**	77.0
C_ConvMed	WraLU	19	11	0	60.8
	α,β-CROWN	8	17	5	84.8
	GRENA	0	**23**	**7**	119.9
C_ConvBig	WraLU	0	**30**	0	32.7
	α,β-CROWN	2	28	0	25.1
	GRENA	0	**30**	0	58.0
C_Resnet4b	WraLU	7	23	0	49.7
	α,β-CROWN	0	**26**	**4**	6.3
	GRENA	0	**26**	**4**	87.8
C_ResnetA	WraLU	-	-	-	-
	α,β-CROWN	0	**27**	**3**	10.2
	GRENA	0	**27**	**3**	77.6
C_ResnetB	WraLU	-	-	-	-
	α,β-CROWN	8	16	**6**	100.2
	GRENA	1	**23**	**6**	191.5

Figure 7 depicts log-scale histograms of bound improvements for both GUROBI and our tailored solver, where "improvement" is defined as the original neuron bound minus the new neuron interval returned by the two solvers. The bar heights represent the number of neurons with improvements at the magnitude indicated on the x-axis. Figure 7a, 7d, 7e and 7f show significant overlap between the orange and blue bars, meaning our tailored solver achieved **comparable** improvements to GUROBI. It is noteworthy that the average solving time for GUROBI was 35503.32 s, while our GPU-accelerated solver took only

47.38 s, achieving an impressive **749×** speedup. More results and details can be found in our Github repo.

In conclusion, our tailored LP solver *obtained comparable bound improvements* compared to GUROBI while *significantly reducing* the solving time.

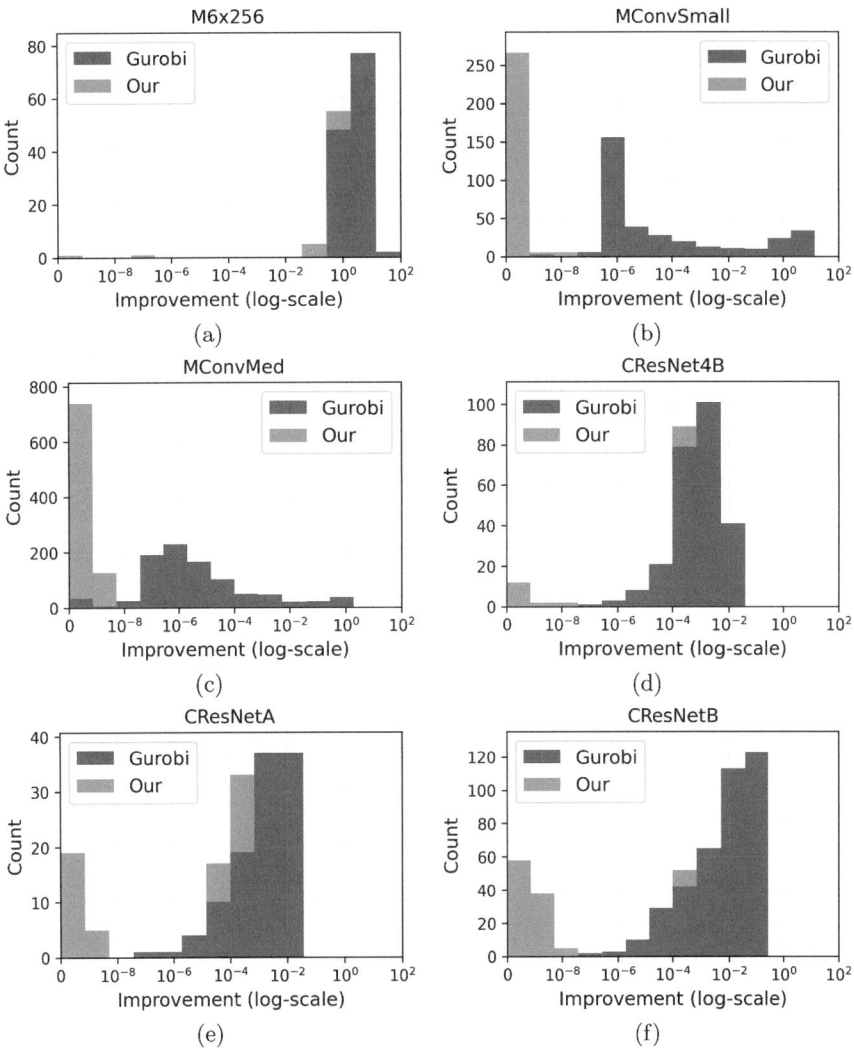

Fig. 7. Bound improvement comparison between our solver and GUROBI (Color figure online)

5 Related Works

Generally speaking, verification of deep neural networks is an NP-hard problem [8]. Therefore, there are a series of incomplete verification methods that sacrifice completeness. Representative works include those abstract interpretation based [6,14,19,20] or bound propagation based [7,16,26,29,33], etc. To mitigate the precision loss of incomplete methods, researchers have been relying on LP or MILP to encode the network more tightly. For example, DeepSRGR [31] or ARENA [34] or PRIMA [17] systems would invoke the GUROBI solver to resolve LP and obtain tighter neuron intervals. However, the usage of an off-the-shelf solver on the CPU fails to leverage the nature of neural network encoding.

Inspired by works aiming to migrate the verification of neural networks to GPUs with the help of Lagrangian dual problems [5,9,28], we propose our tailored LP solver on GPU that benefits our LP formulation. Note that previous works [5,9,28] only encode one-predecessor cases where the multiple predecessors would be concatenated into one. Although this could be handled by other engineering approaches, it lacks rigorous theoretical derivation. On the contrary, we explicitly encode multi-predecessor cases in our formulation. Furthermore, [5,28] only considers intermediate neuron constraints and [9] only includes output constraints in their constraint set, while our formulation captures both intermediate and output constraints. Lastly, to our knowledge, our method is the first to effectively deploy the Lagrangian dual problem to spurious-adversarial-label-guided refinement process.

6 Conclusion

In this paper, we propose a theorem to solve LP problem on GPU in the context of neural network verification. To the best of our knowledge, our work is the first to use Lagrangian dual on spurious-adversarial-label guided refinement process and encode complex network constraints that take more than one predecessor, which enhances the scientific rigor of the verification of residual networks. We implemented our solving theorem in a GPU-based tailored solver; our empirical study strongly indicates that our tailored solver could return comparable solved values compared to GUROBI while obtaining significant speed gains. Furthermore, it enables our verifier GRENA to return more conclusive results than SOTA verifiers within a reasonable amount of time, demonstrating the strong efficacy of our system.

Acknowledgments. This research is supported by a Singapore Ministry of Education Academic Research Fund Tier 1 T1-251RES2103.

Disclosure of Interests. The authors have no competing interests to declare that are relevant to the content of this article.

References

1. 3rd International Verification of Neural Networks Competition (VNN-COMP'22) (2022). https://sites.google.com/view/vnn2022
2. Deng, L.: The MNIST database of handwritten digit images for machine learning research [best of the web]. IEEE Signal Process. Mag. **29**(6), 141–142 (2012)
3. Alpha-beta-crown: A fast and scalable neural network verifier using the bound propagation framework (2025). https://github.com/Verified-Intelligence/alpha-beta-CROWN. Accessed 4 Jan 2025
4. ETH: ETH Robustness Analyzer for Neural Networks (ERAN) (2025). https://github.com/eth-sri/eran. Accessed 2 Jan 2025
5. Ferrari, C., Müller, M.N., Jovanovic, N., Vechev, M.T.: Complete verification via multi-neuron relaxation guided branch-and-bound. In: The Tenth International Conference on Learning Representations, ICLR 2022, Virtual Event, 25–29 April 2022. OpenReview.net (2022). https://openreview.net/forum?id=l_amHf1oaK
6. Gehr, T., Mirman, M., Drachsler-Cohen, D., Tsankov, P., Chaudhuri, S., Vechev, M.T.: AI2: safety and robustness certification of neural networks with abstract interpretation. In: 2018 IEEE Symposium on Security and Privacy, SP 2018, Proceedings, 21–23 May 2018, San Francisco, California, USA, pp. 3–18. IEEE Computer Society (2018). https://doi.org/10.1109/SP.2018.00058
7. Gowal, S., et al.: Scalable verified training for provably robust image classification. In: 2019 IEEE/CVF International Conference on Computer Vision, ICCV 2019, Seoul, Korea (South), 27 October–2 November 2019, pp. 4841–4850. IEEE (2019). https://doi.org/10.1109/ICCV.2019.00494
8. Katz, G., Barrett, C.W., Dill, D.L., Julian, K., Kochenderfer, M.J.: Reluplex: an efficient SMT solver for verifying deep neural networks. CoRR abs/1702.01135 (2017). http://arxiv.org/abs/1702.01135
9. Kotha, S., Brix, C., Kolter, J.Z., Dvijotham, K., Zhang, H.: Provably bounding neural network preimages. In: Oh, A., Naumann, T., Globerson, A., Saenko, K., Hardt, M., Levine, S. (eds.) Advances in Neural Information Processing Systems 36: Annual Conference on Neural Information Processing Systems 2023, NeurIPS 2023, New Orleans, LA, USA, 10–16 December 2023 (2023). http://papers.nips.cc/paper_files/paper/2023/hash/fe061ec0ae03c5cf5b5323a2b9121bfd-Abstract-Conference.html
10. Krizhevsky, A., Nair, V., Hinton, G.: CIFAR-10/100 (Canadian institute for advanced research). http://www.cs.toronto.edu/~kriz/cifar.html
11. Gurobi Optimizer (2025). https://www.gurobi.com/. Accessed 1 Jan 2025
12. Ma, Z., Li, J., Bai, G.: Relu hull approximation. Proc. ACM Program. Lang. **8**(POPL), 2260–2287 (2024). https://doi.org/10.1145/3632917
13. Madry, A., Makelov, A., Schmidt, L., Tsipras, D., Vladu, A.: Towards deep learning models resistant to adversarial attacks. In: 6th International Conference on Learning Representations, ICLR 2018, Vancouver, BC, Canada, 30 April–3 May 2018, Conference Track Proceedings. OpenReview.net (2018). https://openreview.net/forum?id=rJzIBfZAb
14. Mirman, M., Gehr, T., Vechev, M.T.: Differentiable abstract interpretation for provably robust neural networks. In: Dy, J.G., Krause, A. (eds.) Proceedings of the 35th International Conference on Machine Learning, ICML 2018, Stockholmsmässan, Stockholm, Sweden, 10–15 July 2018. Proceedings of Machine Learning Research, vol. 80, pp. 3575–3583. PMLR (2018). http://proceedings.mlr.press/v80/mirman18b.html

15. Müller, C., Serre, F., Singh, G., Püschel, M., Vechev, M.T.: Scaling polyhedral neural network verification on GPUs. In: MLSys. mlsys.org (2021)
16. Müller, C., Singh, G., Püschel, M., Vechev, M.T.: Neural network robustness verification on GPUs. CoRR abs/2007.10868 (2020). https://arxiv.org/abs/2007.10868
17. Müller, M.N., Makarchuk, G., Singh, G., Püschel, M., Vechev, M.T.: PRIMA: general and precise neural network certification via scalable convex hull approximations. Proc. ACM Program. Lang. **6**(POPL), 1–33 (2022). https://doi.org/10.1145/3498704
18. Paulsen, B., Wang, J., Wang, C.: Reludiff: differential verification of deep neural networks. In: Rothermel, G., Bae, D. (eds.) ICSE 2020: 42nd International Conference on Software Engineering, Seoul, South Korea, 2020, pp. 714–726. ACM (2020). https://doi.org/10.1145/3377811.3380337
19. Singh, G., Gehr, T., Mirman, M., Püschel, M., Vechev, M.T.: Fast and effective robustness certification. In: Bengio, S., Wallach, H.M., Larochelle, H., Grauman, K., Cesa-Bianchi, N., Garnett, R. (eds.) Advances in Neural Information Processing Systems 31: Annual Conference on Neural Information Processing Systems 2018, NeurIPS 2018, 3–8 December 2018, Montréal, Canada, pp. 10825–10836 (2018). https://proceedings.neurips.cc/paper/2018/hash/f2f446980d8e971ef3da97af089481c3-Abstract.html
20. Singh, G., Gehr, T., Püschel, M., Vechev, M.T.: An abstract domain for certifying neural networks. Proc. ACM Program. Lang. **3**(POPL), 41:1–41:30 (2019). https://doi.org/10.1145/3290354
21. Singh, G., Gehr, T., Püschel, M., Vechev, M.T.: Boosting robustness certification of neural networks. In: 7th International Conference on Learning Representations, ICLR 2019, New Orleans, LA, USA, 6–9 May 2019. OpenReview.net (2019). https://openreview.net/forum?id=HJgeEh09KQ
22. Tjandraatmadja, C., Anderson, R., Huchette, J., Ma, W., Patel, K.K., Vielma, J.P.: The convex relaxation barrier, revisited: Tightened single-neuron relaxations for neural network verification. Adv. Neural. Inf. Process. Syst. **33**, 21675–21686 (2020)
23. Ugare, S., Banerjee, D., Misailovic, S., Singh, G.: Incremental verification of neural networks. Proc. ACM Program. Lang. **7**(PLDI), 1920–1945 (2023). https://doi.org/10.1145/3591299
24. Ugare, S., Singh, G., Misailovic, S.: Proof transfer for fast certification of multiple approximate neural networks. Proc. ACM Program. Lang. **6**(OOPSLA1), 1–29 (2022)
25. Urban, C., Christakis, M., Wüstholz, V., Zhang, F.: Perfectly parallel fairness certification of neural networks. Proc. ACM Program. Lang. **4**(OOPSLA), 185:1–185:30 (2020). https://doi.org/10.1145/3428253
26. Wang, S., Pei, K., Whitehouse, J., Yang, J., Jana, S.: Efficient formal safety analysis of neural networks. In: Bengio, S., Wallach, H.M., Larochelle, H., Grauman, K., Cesa-Bianchi, N., Garnett, R. (eds.) Advances in Neural Information Processing Systems 31: Annual Conference on Neural Information Processing Systems 2018, NeurIPS 2018, 3–8 December 2018, Montréal, Canada, pp. 6369–6379 (2018). https://proceedings.neurips.cc/paper/2018/hash/2ecd2bd94734e5dd392d8678bc64cdab-Abstract.html
27. Wang, S., Pei, K., Whitehouse, J., Yang, J., Jana, S.: Formal security analysis of neural networks using symbolic intervals. In: Enck, W., Felt, A.P. (eds.) 27th USENIX Security Symposium, USENIX Security 2018, Baltimore, MD, USA, 15–17 August 2018. USENIX Association (2018). https://www.usenix.org/conference/usenixsecurity18/presentation/wang-shiqi

28. Wang, S., et al.: Beta-crown: efficient bound propagation with per-neuron split constraints for complete and incomplete neural network verification. CoRR abs/2103.06624 (2021). https://arxiv.org/abs/2103.06624
29. Weng, T., et al.: Towards fast computation of certified robustness for relu networks. In: Dy, J.G., Krause, A. (eds.) Proceedings of the 35th International Conference on Machine Learning, ICML 2018, Stockholmsmässan, Stockholm, Sweden, 10–15 July 2018. Proceedings of Machine Learning Research, vol. 80, pp. 5273–5282. PMLR (2018). http://proceedings.mlr.press/v80/weng18a.html
30. Xu, K., et al.: Automatic perturbation analysis for scalable certified robustness and beyond. In: Larochelle, H., Ranzato, M., Hadsell, R., Balcan, M., Lin, H. (eds.) Advances in Neural Information Processing Systems 33: Annual Conference on Neural Information Processing Systems 2020, NeurIPS 2020, 6–12 December 2020, virtual (2020). https://proceedings.neurips.cc/paper/2020/hash/0cbc5671ae26f67871cb914d81ef8fc1-Abstract.html
31. Yang, P., et al.: Improving neural network verification through spurious region guided refinement. In: Groote, J.F., Larsen, K.G. (eds.) TACAS 2021. LNCS, vol. 12651, pp. 389–408. Springer, Cham (2021). https://doi.org/10.1007/978-3-030-72016-2_21
32. Zelazny, T., Wu, H., Barrett, C.W., Katz, G.: On optimizing back-substitution methods for neural network verification. In: Griggio, A., Rungta, N. (eds.) 22nd Formal Methods in Computer-Aided Design, FMCAD 2022, Trento, Italy, 17–21 October 2022, pp. 17–26. IEEE (2022). https://doi.org/10.34727/2022/ISBN.978-3-85448-053-2_7
33. Zhang, H., Weng, T., Chen, P., Hsieh, C., Daniel, L.: Efficient neural network robustness certification with general activation functions. In: Bengio, S., Wallach, H.M., Larochelle, H., Grauman, K., Cesa-Bianchi, N., Garnett, R. (eds.) Advances in Neural Information Processing Systems 31: Annual Conference on Neural Information Processing Systems 2018, NeurIPS 2018, 3–8 December 2018, Montréal, Canada, pp. 4944–4953 (2018). https://proceedings.neurips.cc/paper/2018/hash/d04863f100d59b3eb688a11f95b0ae60-Abstract.html
34. Zhong, Y., Ta, Q., Khoo, S.: ARENA: enhancing abstract refinement for neural network verification. In: Dragoi, C., Emmi, M., Wang, J. (eds.) Verification, Model Checking, and Abstract Interpretation - 24th International Conference, VMCAI 2023, Boston, MA, USA, 16–17 January 2023, Proceedings. Lecture Notes in Computer Science, vol. 13881, pp. 366–388. Springer (2023). https://doi.org/10.1007/978-3-031-24950-1_17

ClassInvGen: Class Invariant Synthesis Using Large Language Models

Chuyue Sun[1(✉)], Viraj Agashe[2], Saikat Chakraborty[2], Jubi Taneja[2], Clark Barrett[1], David Dill[1], Xiaokang Qiu[3], and Shuvendu K. Lahiri[2]

[1] Stanford University, Stanford, USA
chuyues@stanford.edu
[2] Microsoft Research, Redmond, USA
[3] Purdue University, West Lafayette, USA

Abstract. Formal program specifications in the form of preconditions, postconditions, and class invariants have several benefits for the construction and maintenance of programs. They not only aid in program understanding due to their unambiguous semantics but can also be enforced dynamically (or even statically when the language supports a formal verifier). However, synthesizing high-quality specifications in an underlying programming language is limited by the expressivity of the specifications or the need to express them in a declarative manner. Prior work has demonstrated the potential of large language models (LLMs) for synthesizing high-quality method pre/postconditions for Python and Java, but does not consider class invariants.

In this work, we describe ClassInvGen, a method for co-generating executable class invariants and test inputs to produce high-quality class invariants for a mainstream language such as C++, leveraging LLMs' ability to synthesize pure functions. We demonstrate that ClassInvGen outperforms a pure LLM-based technique for generating specifications (from code) as well as prior data-driven invariant inference techniques such as Daikon. We contribute a benchmark of standard C++ data structures along with a harness that can help measure both the correctness and completeness of generated specifications using tests and mutants. We also demonstrate its applicability to real-world code by performing a case study on several classes within a widely used and high-integrity C++ codebase.

Keywords: Program Synthesis · Large Language Models · Class Invariants · Formal Verification

1 Introduction

Invariants are predicates that hold on the program state for all executions of the program. Many invariants hold only at specific code locations. For sequential imperative programs, it is useful to associate invariants with entry to a method (preconditions), exit from a method (postconditions), and loop headers (loop invariants). Further, for stateful classes, class invariants are facts that hold as both preconditions and postconditions of the public methods of the class, in addition to serving as a postcondition for the class constructors for the class.

These program invariants help make explicit the assumptions on the rest of the code, helping modular review, reasoning, and analysis. Program invariants are useful for several aspects of software construction and maintenance during the lifetime of a program. First, executable program invariants can be enforced at runtime, where they provide an early indicator of state corruption, help with root causing, and allow a program to halt with an error instead of producing unexpected values. Runtime invariants serve as additional test oracles to amplify testing efforts to catch subtle bugs related to state corruption; this, in turn, helps with regression testing as the program evolves to satisfy new requirements. The utility of program invariants has led to design-by-contract in languages such as Eiffel [31], as well as support in other languages such as Java (JML [4]) and .NET (Code Contracts [11]). Furthermore, for languages that support static formal verification (e.g., Dafny [25], Verus [23], F* [40], Frama-C [19]), invariants can serve as a part of the specification, helping make formal verification modular and scalable. Unfortunately, invariants are underutilized because they require additional work and are sometimes difficult to write, so it would be useful to find a way to generate them automatically.

We focus specifically on automating the creation of class invariants for mainstream languages without first-class specification language support (e.g., C++) for several reasons:

- Class invariants are crucial for maintaining the integrity of data structures and help point to state corruption that may manifest much later within the class or in the clients. Documenting such implicit contracts can greatly aid the understanding for maintainers of the class.
- Class invariants often form important parts of preconditions and postconditions for high-integrity data structures. Encapsulating such invariants and asserting them in preconditions and postconditions helps reduce bloat in the specifications.
- Class invariants are challenging for users to write, as writing them requires global reasoning across all the public methods for the class.

For example, consider the class in Fig. 1 for a doubly-linked list, as implemented in the Z3 SMT solver.[1]

We see that the invariant is repeated four times: as a precondition and postcondition for the object instance `this` and for `other`. The invariant is also nontrivial, requiring local variables and a loop.

Synthesizing program invariants has been an active line of research, with both static and dynamic analysis-based approaches. Static analysis approaches based on variants of *abstract interpretation* [6] and *interpolation* [17] create invariants that are sound by construction. However, such techniques do not readily apply to mainstream programming languages with complex language constructs

---
[1] https://github.com/Z3Prover/z3/blob/master/src/util/dlist.h.

```
1   void insert_before(T* other) {
2       ...
3       SASSERT(invariant());
4       SASSERT(other->invariant());
5       ...
6       T* prev = this->m_prev;
7       T* other_end = other->m_prev;
8       prev->m_next = other;
9       other->m_prev = prev;
10      other_end->m_next = static_cast<T*>(
        this);
11      this->m_prev = other_end;
12      ...
13      SASSERT(invariant());
14      SASSERT(other->invariant());
15      ...
16  }

17  bool invariant() const {
18      auto* e = this;
19      do {
20          if (e->m_next->m_prev
            != e)
21              return false;
22          e = e->m_next;
23      }
24      while (e != this);
25      return true;
26  }
```

Fig. 1. An invariant in the doubly linked list class in Z3.

or require highly specialized methods that do not scale to large modules, since the invariants need to be additionally *provably inductive* to be retained. On the other hand, Daikon [10] and successors learn invariants dynamically by instantiating a set of templates and retaining the predicates that hold on concrete test cases. While applicable to any mainstream language, it is well known that Daikon-generated invariants overfit the test cases and are not sound for all test cases [38]. Recent works have studied fine-tuning large language models (LLMs), to learn program invariants [37] but these methods inherit the limitations of Daikon because their training data consists of Daikon-generated invariants. More importantly, the approach has not been evaluated on stateful classes to construct class invariants.

Recent work on *prompting* LLMs such as GPT-4 to generate program invariants for mainstream languages [9,15,29] has been used to generate preconditions, postconditions, and loop invariants, but these methods do not readily extend to generating class invariants. These pipelines work at single-loop or single-method scope and validate only scalar, intraprocedural predicates, so they lack the heap-aware, cross-method perspective required to state class invariants. Further, these methods cannot construct expressive invariants that require iterating over complex data structures (such as in Fig. 1) other than simple arrays.

In this work, we introduce ClassInvGen, a novel method for generating high-quality object invariants for C++ classes through *co-generation* of invariants and test inputs using LLMs such as GPT-4o. We leverage LLMs' ability to generate code to construct invariants that can express properties over complex data structures. The ability to consume not only the code of a class but also the surrounding comments and variable names helps establish relationships difficult for purely symbolic methods. Since an LLM can generate incorrect invariants, the method also generates test inputs to *heuristically* prune incorrect candidate invariants.

We leverage the framework proposed by Endres et al. [9] to evaluate the test-set correctness and completeness given a set of hidden validation tests and mutants. We contribute a new benchmark comprising standard C++ data structures along with a harness that can help measure both the correctness and completeness of generated invariants (Sect. 4.1). We demonstrate that ClassInvGen outperforms a pure LLM-based technique for generating program invariants from code (Sects. 4.3–4.4) as well as prior data-driven invariant inference techniques such as Daikon (Sect. 4.5). We also demonstrate its applicability for real-world code by performing a case study on a set of classes in the Z3 SMT solver codebase, including the relatively complex `bdd_manager` class; the developers of the codebase confirmed most of the new invariants proposed by ClassInvGen for these modules (Sect. 5).

Our contributions are summarized below:

- We introduce a new technique for invariant-test co-generation by combining simple static analysis with LLMs and implement an end-to-end prototype (Sect. 3).
- We introduce a high-quality ClassInvGen-instrumented benchmark for evaluating object invariants (Sect. 4.1).
- We investigate LLM-assisted class invariant synthesis (Sects. 4.3–4.5).
- We conduct a case study on Z3 class modules using ClassInvGen (Sect. 5).

ClassInvGen is conceived as a *specification-drafting aid*: it produces candidate invariants that a developer can accept, refine, or discard, thereby following the long-advocated "human-in-the-loop" paradigm in specification mining [34]. Our aim is not to replace expert judgement, but to accelerate it.

2 Running Example: AVL Tree

Throughout this paper, `AvlTree` [8,42] from our benchmark (Sect. 4.1) will be used as a running example to illustrate the workflow. An AVL tree is a self-balancing binary search tree (BST) where the difference in heights between the left and right subtrees of any node (called the balance factor) is at most 1. This ensures that the tree remains approximately balanced. In this implementation shown in Fig. 3 in Sect. 3.1, the `AvlTree` class contains several public methods: `insert`, `remove`, `contains`, `clear`, `height`, `size`, `empty`, `in_order_traversal`, `pre_order_traversal`, `post_order_traversal`. `AvlTree` maintains several class invariants determined by the authors of this paper:

- BST Property: Left child values are less than the node's value, and right child values are greater.
- Balance Factor: For each node, the difference in the heights of the left and right subtrees is between –1 and 1.
- Correct Heights: The height of each node is 1 plus the maximum height of its children.

Each of these invariants should hold true before and after every public method call, and be established after the constructor method. The task is to infer these high-quality invariants from the source code.

3 Approach

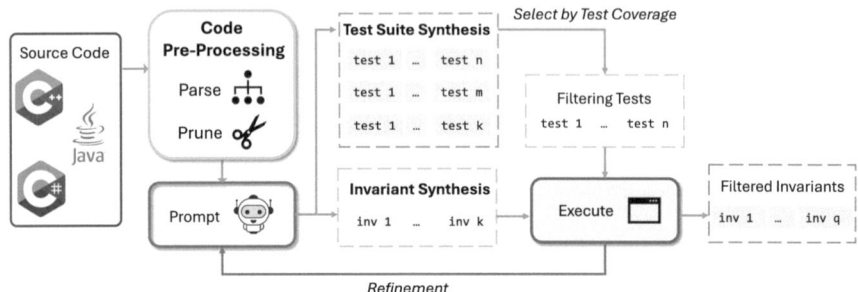

Fig. 2. Overview of ClassInvGen.

An overview of the ClassInvGen framework is shown in Fig. 2. It outlines an automated pipeline for inferring class invariants from source code. ClassInvGen takes a complete source program as input and outputs invariant candidates it has identified with high confidence (called *filtered invariants*). ClassInvGen starts with a preprocessing step which performs static analysis on the program (Sect. 3.1). Next, an LLM is used to generate candidate invariants and filtering test suites (Sect. 3.1). Then, the code is instrumented to facilitate checking candidate invariants (Sect. 3.1). Finally, ClassInvGen uses generated tests to prune invariant candidates (Sect. 3.2), and a refinement loop is used to iteratively improve the results (Sect. 3.3).

3.1 Generation

Preprocessing. As illustrated in Fig. 2, the generation phase begins with a static analysis of the source program. ClassInvGen uses a Tree-Sitter-based parser for program preprocessing; Tree-Sitter [3] is a parser generator tool that constructs a syntax tree from source files.

ClassInvGen parses the entire source program into an abstract syntax tree (AST) to extract class members and their recursive dependencies. It then identifies the target class and gathers details (e.g., method declarations, field declarations, and subclass definitions) relevant to forming correct class invariants. ClassInvGen recursively analyzes all identified classes (i.e., the target class and its subclasses) and performs a topological sort to prepare generation from the leaf class upward as shown in Algorithm 1.

Generation by LLM. After building the source program AST, ClassInvGen uses LLMs to analyze the class module and infers both invariants for the target class and tests that exercise the class's implementation as thoroughly as possible. ClassInvGen uses a fixed system prompt that defines class invariants and outlines

Algorithm 1: Function to generate invariants for target class AST

```
 1  Function GenerateInvariant(target_class):
 2      if target_class.id ∈ invariants_dict then
 3          return invariants_dict[target_class.id]
 4      dep_classes ← getClassRecursively(target_class)
 5      rev_topsorted_classes ← reverseTopologicalSort(dep_classes)
 6      foreach class ∈ rev_topsorted_classes do
 7          class_code ← getCodeForClass(class, invariants_dict)
 8          foreach dep ∈ getClassDependencies(class) do
 9              // Invariant: dep has been generated invariants for
10              dep_code ← getCodeForClass(dep, invariants_dict)
11              class_code ← class_code + dep_code
12          invariants_dict[class.id] ← generateInvariantWithLLM(class_code)
13      return invariants_dict[target_class.id]
14  Function getCodeForClass(class, invariants_dict,
        include_method_bodies=False):
15      class_text ← class.get_declaration_text()          // Header
16      if class.id ∈ invariants_dict and invariants_dict[class.id] then
17          class_text ← invariants_dict[class.id] + class_text   // Get
              generated invariants
18      if include_method_bodies then
19          // Add method bodies if context allows
20      return class_text
```

two main tasks: (1) generating class invariants from the source code, and (2) creating a test suite of valid API calls without specifying expected outputs (see prompt details in Appendix). Next, ClassInvGen instantiates a user prompt template with the actual target class.

From the source program AST, ClassInvGen identifies program dependencies and populates the prompt template with the leaf struct/class. Starting from the leaf nodes, ClassInvGen leverages previously generated invariants by including them in the prompt for later classes. To accommodate the LLM's context window limit, only the relevant child classes of the current target class are included in the prompt, with method implementations and private fields/methods hidden when necessary. An algorithm for this process is presented in Algorithm 1.

Algorithm 1 presents the invariant generation process for a source program AST. The main function GenerateInvariant takes a `target_class` and leverages a caching mechanism through `invariants_dict` to avoid redundant computations (Line 3). The algorithm first collects dependent classes via getClassRecursively (Line 4) and sorts them using reverseTopologicalSort to ensure dependency-aware processing (Line 5). For each `class` in the sorted order, it constructs the necessary context by obtaining the class code through getCodeForClass (Line 7). For each dependency `dep` of the current `class`, it retrieves the dep_code and concatenates it with class_code (Lines 10–11). The algorithm then generates invariants using GENERATEINVARIANTWITHLLM and stores them in invariants_dict (Line 12). The helper function GETCODEFORCLASS constructs class representations by combining the declaration text with any existing invariants from invariants_dict (Lines 15–17). It optionally includes method bodies based on context window constraints. This approach ensures efficient invariant generation while maintaining all necessary context and dependencies (Line 19). The algorithm concludes by returning final_invariants for the target class, effectively managing the invariant generation process while respecting LLM context limitations.

ClassInvGen accommodates large codebases by dividing the source program into smaller modules that fit within the LLM's context window. It then iteratively generates invariants and test cases, starting from leaf classes and working up towards the root class. At each step, ClassInvGen leverages previous invariants generated for child classes to inform the invariants for parent classes.

For the AvlTree example, we begin by instantiating the prompt with Node for annotation, followed by AvlTree, since Node is a subclass of AvlTree, as illustrated in Fig. 3. In this specific case, however, Algorithm 1 does not make a difference due to the small size of the source program; the entire AvlTree code fits within the LLM's context window easily.

```
1  class AvlTree {
2  public:
3    AvlTree();
4    AvlTree(const AvlTree &t);
5    AvlTree &operator=(const AvlTree &t);
6    ~AvlTree();
7
8    void insert(const T &v);
9    void remove(const T &v);
10   bool contains(const T &v);
11   void clear();
12   int height();
13   int size();
14   bool empty();
15   std::vector<T> in_order_traversal() const;
16   std::vector<T> pre_order_traversal() const;
17   std::vector<T> post_order_traversal() const;
18 private:
19   struct Node {
20     T data;
21     std::unique_ptr<Node> left;
22     std::unique_ptr<Node> right;
23     int balance_factor();
24   };
25   // rest of the file
26 }
```

Fig. 3. Header file of AvlTree.

In contrast, when working with the bdd_manager class in Z3 (around 1700 lines of code), ClassInvGen begins generation with bdd, a subclass of bdd_manager. Algorithm 1 enables ClassInvGen to partition bdd_manager class and outputs meaningful class invariants (see Sect. 5).

Instrumentation. To check candidate invariants, each public method is automatically instrumented with a `check_invariant` call at both the start and end of its implementation. This allows us to verify that invariants hold both before and after method execution. Each invariant is implemented as a method call to prevent conflicts with local variables.

When a specific invariant is being checked, its code is plugged into the `check_invariant` function with assertions. This ensures that during pruning, whenever a public API call is made, each invariant candidate is automatically verified.

Additional examples of instrumentation and invariant checking are provided in Appendix C.

3.2 Heuristic Pruning

The LLM generates test suites that serve as filters for invariant candidates. To select the most effective test suite, we use line coverage as a metric, as it provides a straightforward proxy for test suite completeness. The test suite with the highest coverage becomes our set of *filtering tests*.

When generating tests, ClassInvGen creates valid sequences of API calls without asserting expected behavior, since our goal is to filter invariant candidates rather than test the source program directly. Among all generated test suites, we compile and run each one with the source program, selecting the one with the highest line coverage as the *filtering tests*.

ClassInvGen dynamically expands the *filtering tests* only if coverage falls below a specified threshold (default 80%). In our experiments, each benchmark task's *filtering tests* includes 5 to 15 individual tests, with each test comprising 5 to 20 lines of code (see example in Appendix C).

If an invariant candidate successfully compiles and runs with the *filtering tests*, it is designated a *filtered invariant* and included in the final output of ClassInvGen.

3.3 Refinement

For invariants that fail during compilation or runtime, ClassInvGen implements a feedback-driven refinement process. The system collects compiler output, error messages, and test results, then feeds this information back to the LLM using a dedicated prompt template.

This feedback loop allows ClassInvGen to repair failing invariants by providing the LLM with specific error information and the context in which the error occurred. We set a default threshold of 3 refinement attempts per invariant, balancing the cost of LLM calls with the benefit of repairs.

Refinement allows ClassInvGen to fix common issues such as type errors, undefined references, and logical inconsistencies. More detailed examples of the refinement process are provided in Appendix C.

4 Results

4.1 Benchmark

Table 1. Characteristics of the benchmark data structures. # LoC represents lines of code, # methods indicates the number of implemented methods, and # dep. shows the number of dependent classes for each data structure.

	avl_tree	binary_search_tree	hash_table	heap	linked_list	queue	red_black_tree	stack	vector
# LoC	249	229	176	135	172	117	282	96	117
# methods	25	22	11	14	14	12	25	11	18
# dep.	1	1	0	0	0	0	1	0	0

We use a C++ implementation of classical data structures for our microbenchmarks [8], which include 9 data structures with associated unit tests: `AvlTree`, `BinarySearchTree`, `HashTable`, `Heap`, `LinkedList`, `Queue`, `RedBlackTree`, `Stack`, and `Vector`. Table 1 shows the statistics of these benchmark data structures. To ensure correctness, we thoroughly examined each benchmark example and corrected a few implementation bugs, treating this refined benchmark as the ground truth. All subsequent experiments are based on this benchmark setup.

In addition to textbook examples, we also conducted experiments on utility classes [45] from Z3 [33], including `ema`, `dlist`, `heap`, `hashtable`, `permutation`, `scoped_vector`, and the most complex class, `bdd_manager`. The latter will be discussed in detail as a case study, including an evaluation with one of the authors of Z3.

4.2 Evaluation

In this section, we evaluate the quality of ClassInvGen invariants. Specifically, we explore the following research questions:

1. How many of these invariants are **correct** (with respect to the user-provided test cases) and do they capture essential properties of the source code (Sect. 4.3)?
2. How **complete** are the invariants in their ability to distinguish the correct program from buggy counterparts (Sect. 4.4)?
3. How does ClassInvGen compare to a state-of-the-art technique in invariant generation (namely Daikon, the most widely adopted tool for dynamic invariant synthesis) (Sect. 4.5)?

Our experiments were conducted on a machine with 24 CPU cores and 64 GB of RAM. We implemented ClassInvGen using GPT-4o as the underlying LLM, with its default temperature setting of 1.

4.3 Correctness

ClassInvGen produces *filtered invariants*, which we evaluate using an automated pipeline (Fig. 4) against our benchmark (Sect. 4.1). A *filtered invariant* is considered correct if it reports no errors for any tests that successfully compile and run. Our manual review confirmed that all validated *filtered invariants* are indeed correct, capturing essential properties of the data structures.

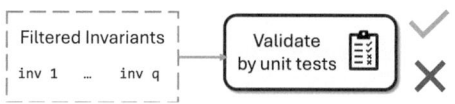

Fig. 4. Evaluation of ClassInvGen generated invariants

Benefits of Co-Generation. When generating invariants in isolation, ClassInvGen produces an average of 25 unique invariants per benchmark with a 77% pass rate against unit tests. With test co-generation, ClassInvGen successfully eliminates all incorrect invariants, achieving perfect accuracy.

Refinement Effectiveness. After refinement, the number of *filtered invariants* grows from 17 to 22 per example, representing a 29% increase. This demonstrates ClassInvGen's ability to transform potentially buggy invariants into valid ones through feedback-guided refinement.

Summary. ClassInvGen's invariant-test co-generation approach improves correctness from 77% to 100%. The *filtering tests* effectively identify valid invariants, while the refinement process successfully expands the set of correct invariants (Tables 2 and 3).

Table 2. Invariant-only results from 8 completions show that 25 invariants per benchmark and 77% pass unit tests.

Example	# inv.	# compiles	# pass tests	pass rate
avl_tree	30	28	17	56.7%
queue	30	30	30	100.0%
linked_list	32	32	24	75.0%
binary_search_tree	25	25	24	96.0%
hash_table	29	29	26	89.7%
heap	22	22	12	54.5%
red_black_tree	26	26	15	57.7%
stack	15	15	11	73.3%
vector	18	18	16	88.9%
Average	25.22	24.56	19.44	77.0%

Table 3. For each example, the table shows the number and line coverage of *filtering tests*, the number of *filtered invariants* without refinement, and with 1 refinement, as well as the unit test pass rate after 1 refinement. With *filtering tests* and 1 refinement, ClassInvGen achieves a perfect unit test pass rate.

Example	# filter tests (coverage)	# filtered inv.	# good inv. (1 refine)	pass rate (1 refine)
avl_tree	10 (91.7%)	15	20	100.0%
queue	8 (100.0%)	20	29	100.0%
linked_list	8 (92.3%)	22	36	100.0%
binary_search_tree	12 (95.6%)	16	19	100.0%
hash_table	9 (90.3%)	25	27	100.0%
heap	7 (96.0%)	10	11	100.0%
red_black_tree	13 (85.4%)	11	18	100.0%
stack	8 (100.0%)	14	14	100.0%
vector	10 (94.6%)	22	22	100.0%
Average	9.44 (94.0%)	17.22	21.78	100.0%

4.4 Completeness

Table 4. Performance Over Baseline for Previously Survived Mutants. The table shows additional mutants killed by ClassInvGen compared to the baseline and percentage improvement.

Data Structure	Unsolved Base (#(%))	Add. by ClassInvGen (#)	Impr. (%)
binary_search_tree	107(23.67)	7	6.54
hash_table	258(37.83)	38	14.73
heap	108(32.24)	12	11.11
linked_list	57(13.54)	2	3.51
red_black_tree	184(27.10)	9	4.89
stack	67(28.39)	6	8.96
vector	101(29.79)	33	32.67
avl_tree	84(17.57)	0	0.00
queue	91(26.30)	11	12.09
Total	**1057**	**118**	**11.16**

To evaluate completeness, we use mutation testing. This independent mutant-killing oracle mitigates the co-adaptation risk discussed in Sect. 7. We generate mutants using mutate_cpp [28], producing between 236 and 682 mutants per program. We focus on mutants that either compile successfully but crash during execution or survive execution without errors.

We conducted experiments to evaluate three configurations: unit tests only, ClassInvGen only, and unit tests with ClassInvGen (strongest test oracles). As shown in Table 4, ClassInvGen's invariants kill an additional 11.2% of mutants on average compared to unit tests alone, with improvements reaching up to 32.67% for specific data structures.

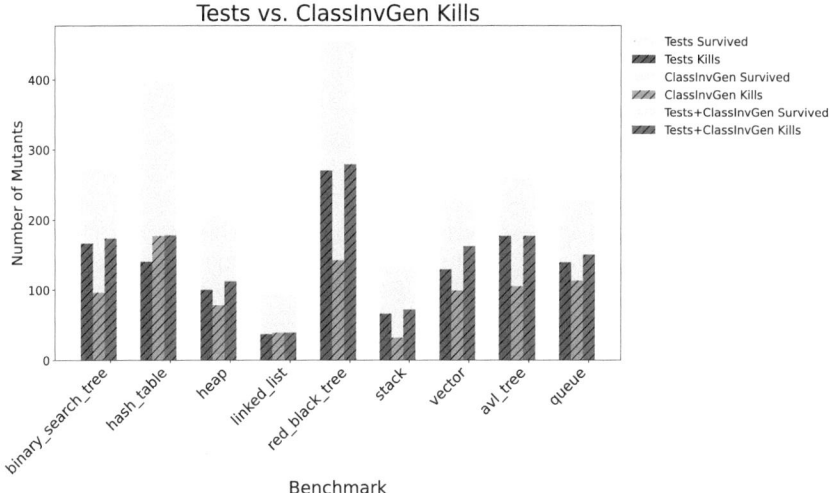

Fig. 5. Completeness Experiment Result. The 3 bars from left to right are Tests, ClassInvGen, Tests+ClassInvGen. Tests+ClassInvGen kills the most mutants.

Fig. 5 shows tests with ClassInvGen kill the most mutants. Figures 6 and 7 show examples of mutants that survived unit tests but were killed by ClassInvGen invariants.

```
1   void HashTable::clear_table() {
2     this->table.clear();
3     this->_num_elements = 0;
4 -   this->_size = 0;
5 +   this->_size += 0;
6   }
7   }
```

Fig. 6. Mutant that survived unit tests but killed by ClassInvGen

4.5 Comparison of ClassInvGen v.s. Daikon

We compared ClassInvGen with Daikon [10], using *filtering tests* to generate program traces for Daikon's invariant detector. On average, each benchmark example has around 5 Daikon invariants, with some being incorrect (Table 5).

Through manual review, we identified 7 incorrect Daikon invariants that pass unit test validation. These invariants pass because both the *filtering tests* and unit tests coincidentally constructed similar data structures.

Most Daikon invariants simply indicate that class pointers are not null (27 of 40 correct invariants) or that element counts are non-negative (6 invariants).

```
1    this->hash_function = hash_function;
2    this->_num_elements = 0;
3    this->_size = size;
4  - this->load_factor = 0.75;
5  + this->load_factor = -0.75;
6    this->table =
7        std::vector<std::shared_ptr<std::vector<std::pair<Key, Value>>>>(size);
8  }
```

Fig. 7. Another Mutant that survived unit tests but was killed by ClassInvGen

Table 5. Daikon Incorrect Invariants per Benchmark

Data Structure	Total # Invariants	Incorrect Invariants
hash_table	8	1
binary_search_tree	3	0
heap	10	1
red_black_tree	2	0
avl_tree	4	0
vector	3	1
stack	6	2
queue	7	1
linked_list	4	1
Average	**5.2**	**0.78**

The most valuable invariants, like `this->n < this->maxSize` in `Stack`, have more impact on identifying mutants (Fig. 8).

This shows a key weakness of Daikon: it cannot differentiate between universally true invariants and those that hold only in specific test contexts. LLMs are better at capturing true "class" invariants that are inherent to the data structure rather than incidental to the tests.

5 Case Study: Z3 `bdd_manager` class

Table 6. Statistics of the studied data structures in Z3

	ema	dlist	heap	hashtable	permutation	scoped_vector	bdd_manager
# LoC	57	243	309	761	177	220	1635
# dependencies	0	2	1	9	2	2	13

As a real-world case study, we apply ClassInvGen to synthesize invariants for 7 core data structures from Z3 [33], ranging from the simple 57-line `ema`

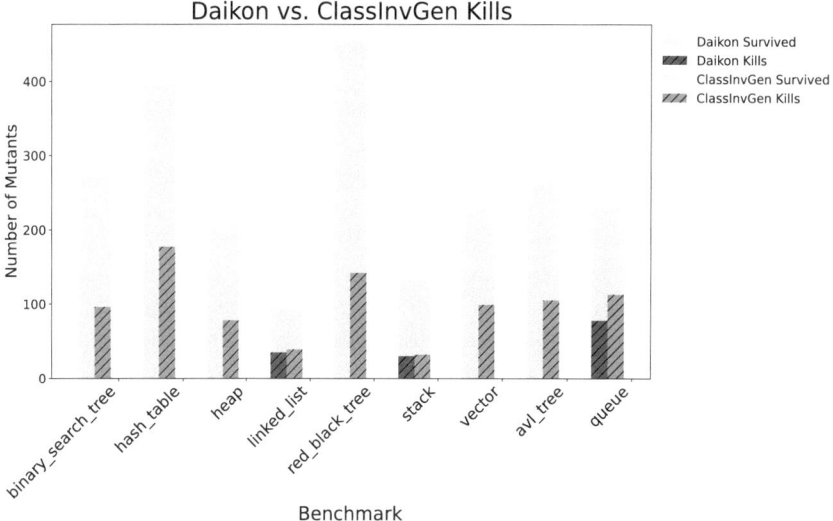

Fig. 8. Daikon vs. ClassInvGen Kills

class to the complex 1635-line `bdd_manager`. The complete set includes `dlist`, `heap`, `hashtable`, `permutation`, and `scoped_vector`, with varying implementation complexity and the number of dependent classes as shown in Table 6. Our results were validated by one of the Z3 authors, who confirmed at least one *correct and useful* invariant for each studied class, with the `bdd_manager` class yielding 11 valuable invariants including the 2 already written by Z3 authors.

Z3 is a widely adopted SMT solver used in a variety of high-stakes applications requiring rigorous correctness, such as formal verification, program analysis, and automated reasoning. It is integrated into tools like LLVM [22], KLEE [5], Dafny [25] and Frama-C [19]. We selected the Z3 codebase due to its stringent correctness requirements; as an SMT solver, Z3 is employed in applications demanding high reliability. This high-stakes environment makes Z3 an ideal testbed for assessing the effectiveness of synthesized invariants.

The `bdd_manager` class[2] is particularly noteworthy. It was chosen because it is a self-contained example with developer-written unit tests for validation, presenting a realistic yet manageable challenge. Note that the existing developer tests were used after invariants were generated, not as input to the LLM. The `bdd_manager` class in Z3 is a utility for managing Binary Decision Diagrams (BDDs), which are data structures used to represent Boolean functions efficiently. In BDDs, Boolean functions are represented as directed acyclic graphs, where each non-terminal node corresponds to a Boolean variable, and edges represent the truth values of these variables (*true* or *false*). This representation simplifies complex Boolean expressions and enables efficient operations on Boolean functions.

---

[2] https://github.com/Z3Prover/z3/blob/master/src/math/dd/dd_bdd.h

With 382 lines of code in its header and 1253 lines in the implementation file, bdd_manager surpasses standard data structure complexity, offering an opportunity to evaluate ClassInvGen's capability to generate meaningful invariants relevant to real-world scenarios. ClassInvGen achieves this by compositional generation, recursively traversing the source program's AST (Sect. 20). Recursive generation became crucial when handling large classes like bdd_manager, which exceeded the LLM's context window. Decomposing and processing its components separately allowed us to fit relevant parts into the model's input, demonstrating the utility of recursive invariant generation for large codebases. This supports its relevance in real-world applications beyond the benchmarks.

The bdd_manager class includes a developer-written member function for checking its well-formedness, as shown in Fig. 9, which we removed during ClassInvGen generation. Of the 56 invariants generated by ClassInvGen, one of Z3 main authors identified 11 distinct *correct and useful* invariants (e.g., Fig. 10) including the 2 developer-written invariants; these invariants could potentially be integrated into the codebase. An additional 5 distinct *ok* invariants (e.g., Fig. 11) are labeled correct but have limited utility, 16 distinct *correct but useless* invariants (e.g., those already checked during compilation, such as type checks and constants, Fig. 12), and 2 *incorrect* invariants (e.g., Fig. 13). The remaining invariants were repetitions within these categories. This evaluation aligns with ClassInvGen's validation results, as our validation pipeline also identified 2 incorrect invariants that failed bdd_manager unit tests.

Overall, the Z3 authors' evaluation results further confirm ClassInvGen's potential utility in real-world, large-scale codebases.

6 Related Work

In this section, we discuss how ClassInvGen relates to previous works on synthesizing program invariants statically, dynamically and neurally.

6.1 Static Approaches

Static techniques, such as interpolation [30] or abstract interpretation [6] perform a symbolic analysis of source code to compute static over-approximations of runtime behavior and represent them as program invariants over suitable domains. These techniques are often used to prove the safety properties of the code. They focus on synthesizing loop invariants and method pre/postconditions, and a few around module-level specifications [21]. Given the undecidability of program verification, these techniques scale poorly for real-world programs, especially in the presence of complex data structures and frameworks. In contrast, ClassInvGen can be applied to large codebases to synthesize high-quality class invariants but does not guarantee soundness by construction.

```
bool bdd_manager::well_formed() {
    bool ok = true;
    for (unsigned n : m_free_nodes) {
        ok &= (lo(n) == 0 && hi(n) == 0 && m_nodes[n].m_refcount == 0);
        if (!ok) {
            IF_VERBOSE(0, verbose_stream() << "free node is not internal " << n <<
   " " << lo(n) << " " << hi(n) << " " << m_nodes[n].m_refcount << "\n";
            display(verbose_stream()););
            UNREACHABLE();
            return false;
        }
    }

    for (bdd_node const& n : m_nodes) {
        if (n.is_internal()) continue;
        unsigned lvl = n.m_level;
        BDD lo = n.m_lo;
        BDD hi = n.m_hi;
        ok &= is_const(lo) || level(lo) < lvl;
        ok &= is_const(hi) || level(hi) < lvl;
        ok &= is_const(lo) || !m_nodes[lo].is_internal();
        ok &= is_const(hi) || !m_nodes[hi].is_internal();
        if (!ok) {
            IF_VERBOSE(0, display(verbose_stream() << n.m_index << " lo " << lo <<
   " hi " << hi << "\n"););
            UNREACHABLE();
            return false;
        }
    }
    return ok;
}
```

Fig. 9. Z3 developer-written class invariants for bdd_manager class

```
// Node consistency: Each node's index should match its position in m_nodes
for (unsigned i = 0; i < m_nodes.size(); ++i) {
    assert(m_nodes[i].m_index == i);
}
```

Fig. 10. *Correct and useful* invariant for bdd_manager class

```
// Cache consistency: Entries in the operation cache should be valid
for (const auto* e : m_op_cache) {
    assert(e != nullptr);
    assert(e->m_result != null_bdd);
}
```

Fig. 11. *Ok* invariant for bdd_manager class

```
// m_is_new_node is a boolean
assert(m_is_new_node == true || m_is_new_node == false);
```

Fig. 12. *Correct and useless* invariant for bdd_manager class

```
// The number of nodes should not exceed the maximum number of BDD nodes
assert(m_nodes.size() <= m_max_num_bdd_nodes);
```

Fig. 13. *Incorrect* invariant for bdd_manager class

6.2 Dynamic Approaches

Dynamic synthesis techniques, such as Daikon [10], DIG [35], SLING [24], and specification mining [1], learn invariants by observing the dynamic behaviors of programs over a set of concrete execution traces. One advantage of these dynamic techniques is that they can be agnostic to the code and generally applicable to different languages. However, these approaches are limited by the templates or patterns over which the invariants can be expressed. DySy [7] employs dynamic symbolic execution to alleviate the problem of fixed templates for bounded executions but resorts to ad-hoc abstraction for loops or recursion. [16] trained models to predict the quality of invariants generated by tools such as Daikon, but do not generate new invariants. SpecFuzzer [32] generates numerous candidate assertions via fuzzing to construct templates and filters them using Daikon and mutation testing. Finally, Geminus [2] aims at synthesizing sound and complete class invariants representing the set of reachable states, guiding their search using random test cases termed Random Walk.

Unlike these approaches, ClassInvGen can generate a much larger class of invariants, leveraging multimodal inputs, including source code, test cases, comments, and even the naming convention learned from training data, to enhance invariant synthesis. Further, unlike prior dynamic approaches, LLM-based test generation (an active area of research [26,39,44]) reduces the need to have a high-quality test suite to obtain the invariants.

For the use case of static verification, learning-based approaches have been used to iteratively improve the quality of the synthesized inductive invariants [13, 14,36] from dynamic traces. However, these approaches have not been evaluated in real-world programs due to the need for symbolic reasoning.

6.3 Neural Approaches

LLM-based invariant synthesis is an emerging area of research with some noteworthy recent contributions. [37] trained a model for zero-shot invariant synthesis, which incurs high training costs and lacks feedback-driven repair. Their approach uses Daikon-generated invariants as both training data and ground truth, which can lead to spurious invariants.

Prior work on nl2postcond [9] prompts LLMs to generate pre and postcondition of Python and Java benchmarks, illustrating LLMs' ability to generate high-quality specifications. However, they do not prune incorrect invariants and do not generate class invariants that ClassInvGen does. It is an interesting future work to combine this work with ClassInvGen to generate complete class-level specifications including pre and postconditions for the public methods of the class.

Two very recent neurosymbolic pipelines extend LLM prompting to *other* kinds of specifications. [43] combine GPT-4 with bounded-model checking to infer *loop invariants*: the LLM enumerates candidate predicates, a BMC oracle filters them, and the surviving predicates are re-assembled into provable invariants, yielding a 97% success rate on 316 numeric-loop benchmarks. [41]

(AUTOSPEC) weave static slicing and an off-the-shelf program verifier with LLM generation to synthesise *function-level contracts*; AutoSpec verifies 79 % of heterogeneous benchmarks plus an X.509 parser case study. Both systems rely on *static* or SMT-based oracles and target scalar loops or procedure specifications, whereas ClassInvGen tackles *pointer-rich class/object invariants* in idiomatic C++ and validates them chiefly through *dynamic* test-suite execution plus mutation testing. The different oracle allows our approach to scale to data-structure code bases where precise SMT models are hard to obtain.

For static verification, recent works include the use of LLM for intent-formalization from natural language [20], and inferring specifications and inductive program invariants [18,29]. None of these techniques scale to real-world programs due to the need for complex symbolic reasoning.

7 Limitation

At present, ClassInvGen judges an invariant's correctness with the same test suite that the LLM co-generates alongside that invariant. This design keeps the pipeline fully automated, but it also risks co-adaptation: the model can drift toward invariants that merely fit the behaviours exercised by its own tests, overstating their generality.

ClassInvGen uses generated tests for invariant pruning, but the test suite may include spurious tests that can incorrectly prune valid invariants. The generated tests might not represent valid sequences of method calls; for example, invoking a `pop()` method before a `push()` method could fail certain assertions, leading to improper pruning.

Another limitation is the LLM's context window, which restricts the amount of code that can be processed in a single call. This limitation makes it challenging to handle large codebases. ClassInvGen partially addresses this issue through compositional generation, breaking down the code into manageable parts. Ongoing advancements in LLMs, as highlighted in recent work [12,27], are also expected to mitigate this limitation.

For future work, we plan to integrate invariant generation with the generation of formal specifications for member functions, enabling LLM a more comprehensive understanding of program behavior. Additionally, we aim to evaluate ClassInvGen on larger and more complex systems beyond Z3, demonstrating its scalability to diverse codebases.

8 Conclusion

In this paper, we describe an approach to leverage LLMs and a lightweight mixed static/dynamic approach to synthesize class invariants. Our experiments on standard C++ data structures as well as a popular and high-assurance codebase demonstrate the feasibility of our approach. Our technique is currently limited by an automated way to integrate the generated tests into the build system of the underlying repo, and the need for developers to validate the invariants. We envision that integrating ClassInvGen with the continuous integration (CI) and pull requests (PR) can aid in scaling the approach to more developers. In future work, we also plan to investigate incorporating developer feedback to repair or strengthen generated invariants.

A Prompt

```
 1 You are an expert in creating program invariants from code and natural language.
 2 Invariants are assertions on the variables in scope that hold true at different
   program points
 3 We are interested in finding invariants that hold at both start and end of a
   function within a data structure. Such an invariant is commonly known as an object
   invariant.
 4
 5 The invariants can usually be expressed as a check on the state at the particular
   program point. The check should be expressed as a check in the same underlying
   programming language which evaluates to true or false. To express these, you can
   use:
 6 - An assertion in the programming language
 7 - A pure method (which does not have any side effect on the variables in scope)
   that checks one or more assertion
 8 - For a collection, you can use a loop to iterate over elements of the collection
   and assert something on each element or a pair of elements.
 9
10 Task Description:
11 Task 1: Given a module, in the form of a class definition, your task is to infer
   object invariants about the class. For doing so, you may examine how the methods
   of the class read and modify the various fields of the class.
12 For coming up with invariants, you may use the provided code and any comments in
   the code. You may also use world knowledge to guide the search for invariants.
13
14 Task 2: Generate unit tests for the class based on the class definition and public
   API methods. The test cases should simulate a series of public method calls to
   verify the behavior of the class, but do not use any testing framework like gtest.
   Do not add 'assert' or any form of assertions.
```

Fig. 14. ClassInvGen Generation system prompt: instruction and task description. Lines 3–7 give the formal definition of a class invariant (must hold before and after every public method).

Figure 14 and Fig. 15 show the system prompt used by ClassInvGen for invariant-test co-generation. The former presents the instruction and task description, while the latter illustrates the input-output format (Figs. 16, 17, 18 and Tables 7, 8, 9, 10, 11, 12, 13, 14, 15).

```
Input Format:
You will be given the name of a class or typedef, and a section of code containing
   the definition of the class. You will also be given the definitions of functions
   that read and modify the fields of the class.

Output Format:
The output should be in the following format:

The first paragraph should begin with "REASONING:". From the next line onwards, it
   should contain the detailed reasoning and analysis used for the inference of the
   object invariants. The entire text should be enclosed in $$$. For example,
'''$$$
REASONING:
explanation
$$$

The next paragraph should begin with "INVARIANTS:". From the next line onwards, it
   should contain a list of the various invariants inferred. The invariants should
   be in the form of code in the same underlying programming language, enclosed by
   '''. Each invariant should start from a new line, and be separated by "---". Use
   lambda if necessary. If lambda is recursive, explicitly specify the type of the
   lambda function and use 'std::function' for recursion. Do not use helper functions
   . For example,
INVARIANTS:
'''/* Invariant 1 */'''
---
'''/* Multi line Invariant 2 */
   assert(...); '''
---
'''/* Invariant 3 */'''

The next paragraph should begin with "TESTS:". From the next line onwards, it
   should contain a list of a API call sequence in the form of code enclosed by '''.
   Each test should start from a new line, and be separated by "---". For example,
TESTS:
'''/* Test 1 */
   this->method1();
   this->method2();'''
---
'''/* Test 2 */
   this.method3(...); '''
---
'''/* Test 3 */'''

Important:
1. Follow the output format strictly, particularly enclosing each invariant in
   triple-ticks ('''), and enclosing the reasoning in $$$.
2. Only find object invariants for the target class provided to you, do not infer
   invariants for any other class.
3. Make sure the invariant is a statement in the same underlying programming
   language as the source program.
4. If you can decompose a single invariant into smaller ones, try to output
   multiple invariants.
```

Fig. 15. ClassInvGen Generation system prompt: input-output format.

```
Name of Data Structure to Annotate: {struct}
Code:
'''
{code}
'''
```

Fig. 16. ClassInvGen Generation user prompt template.

```
You are an expert in repairing program invariants from code and natural language.
Invariants are assertions on the variables in scope that hold true at different
    program points.

We are interested in finding invariants that hold at both start and end of a
    function within a data structure. Such an invariant is commonly known as an object
    invariant.

The invariants can usually be expressed as a check on the state at the particular
    program point. The check should be expressed as a check in the same underlying
    programming language which evaluates to true or false. To express these, you can
    use:
- An assertion in the programming language
- A pure method (which does not have any side effect on the variables in scope)
    that checks one or more assertion
- For a collection, you can use a loop to iterate over elements of the collection
    and assert something on each element or a pair of elements.

Task Description:
Given a module, in the form of a class definition, your task is to infer object
    invariants about the class. For doing so, you may examine how the methods of the
    class read and modify the various fields of the class.

For coming up with invariants, you may use the provided code and any comments in
    the code. You may also use world knowledge to guide the search for invariants.

Input Format:
You will be given the name of a class or typedef, and a section of code containing
    the definition of the class. You will also be given the definitions of functions
    which read and modify the fields of the class.

Output Format:
The output should be in the following format:

The first paragraph should begin with "REASONING:". From the next line onwards, it
    should contain the detailed reasoning and analysis used for the inference of the
    object invariants. The entire text should be enclosed in $$$. For example,
'''$$$
REASONING:
explanation
$$$'''

The next paragraph should begin with "INVARIANTS:". From the next line onwards, it
    should contain a list of the various invariants inferred. The invariants should
    be in the form of code in the same underlying programming language, enclosed by
    '''. Each invariant should start from a new line, and be separated by "---". For
    example,
INVARIANTS:
'''/* Invariant 1 */'''
---
'''/* Multi line Invariant 2 */
    assert(...);'''
---
'''/* Invariant 3 */'''

Important:
1. Follow the output format strictly, particularly enclosing each invariant in
    triple-ticks ('''), and enclosing the reasoning in $$$.
2. Only find object invariants for the target class provided to you, do not infer
    invariants for any other class.
3. Make sure the invariant is a statement in the same underlying programming
    language as the source program.
4. If you can decompose a single invariant into smaller ones, try to output
    multiple invariants.
```

Fig. 17. ClassInvGen Refinement system prompt: instruction and task description.

```
1 Please fix the failed invariants given the feedback, tests and the original source
    code.
2
3 Failed Invariant:
4 '''
5 {invariant}
6 '''
7
8 Error message for the failed invariant:
9 '''
10 {feedback}
11 '''
12
13 Name of Data Structure to Annotate: {struct}
14
15 Original Code:
16 '''
17 {code}
18 '''
19
20 Gold Tests that Fail the Invariant:
21 {tests}
```

Fig. 18. ClassInvGen Refinement user prompt template.

B Daikon Invariants Frequency Tables

Table 7. Invariants for avl_tree, 11 public methods.

Invariant	Count
this->root has only one value	4
this->root._M_t has only one value	4
this->root._M_t.__uniq_ptr_impl<AvlTree::Node, std::default_delete<AvlTree::Node> >._M_t has only one value	4
this[0] has only one value	3
this->n one of { 3, 4 }	3
this[0] != null	2
this->root != null	2
this->root._M_t != null	2
this->root._M_t.__uniq_ptr_impl<AvlTree::Node, std::default_delete<AvlTree::Node> >._M_t != null	2
this->n one of { 1, 2, 3 }	1
this->n one of { 0, 3 }	1
this->n >= 1	1
this->n == 3	1
t.root has only one value	1
t.root._M_t has only one value	1
t.root._M_t.__uniq_ptr_impl<AvlTree::Node, std::default_delete<AvlTree::Node> >._M_t has only one value	1
t.n == 3	1
this->n == return	1

Table 8. Invariants for red_black_tree, 11 public methods.

Invariant	Count
this[0] != null	3
this->root != null	3
this->root._M_t != null	3
this->root._M_t.__uniq_ptr_impl<RedBlackTree::Node, std::default_delete<RedBlackTree::Node> >._M_t != null	3
this->n one of { 3, 4, 6 }	3
this->root has only one value	3
this->root._M_t has only one value	3
this->root._M_t.__uniq_ptr_impl<RedBlackTree::Node, std::default_delete<RedBlackTree::Node> >._M_t has only one value	3
this[0] has only one value	2
this->n >= 0	1
(No intersection exists)	1
t.root has only one value	1
t.root._M_t has only one value	1
t.root._M_t.__uniq_ptr_impl<RedBlackTree::Node, std::default_delete<RedBlackTree::Node> >._M_t has only one value	1
t.n == 3	1
No intersection	1

Table 9. Invariants for linked_list, 8 public methods.

Invariant	Count
this[0] has only one value	5
this->head has only one value	5
this->head._M_t has only one value	5
this->head._M_t.__uniq_ptr_impl<LinkedList::Node, std::default_delete<LinkedList::Node> >._M_t has only one value	5
this[0] != null	4
this->head != null	4
this->head._M_t != null	4
this->head._M_t.__uniq_ptr_impl<LinkedList::Node, std::default_delete<LinkedList::Node> >._M_t != null	4
this->tail[].elements != null	2
this->tail[].next elements != null	2
this->tail[].next._M_t elements != null	2
this->n >= 0	2
this->n == 0	1
this->tail[].data elements one of { 1 }	1
this->tail[].data one of { [1] }	1
this->n one of { 1 }	1
this->n one of { 1, 2 }	1
this->tail[].data elements >= 1	1
this->tail[].data elements <= this->n	1
this->tail[].data elements one of { 1, 2, 4 }	1
this->tail[].data one of { [1], [2], [4] }	1
this->n one of { 2, 3 }	1
this->tail[].data == [3]	1
this->tail[].data elements == 3	1

Table 10. Invariants for binary_search_tree, 11 public methods.

Invariant	Count
this->root has only one value	4
this->root._M_t has only one value	4
this->root._M_t.__uniq_ptr_impl<BinarySearchTree::Node, std::default_delete<BinarySearchTree::Node> >._M_t has only one value	4
this->n one of { 0, 2, 3 }	3
this->n one of { 0, 3 }	3
this[0] has only one value	3
this[0] != null	2
this->root != null	2
this->root._M_t != null	2
this->root._M_t.__uniq_ptr_impl<BinarySearchTree::Node, std::default_delete<BinarySearchTree::Node> >._M_t != null	2
t.root has only one value	1
t.root._M_t has only one value	1
t.root._M_t.__uniq_ptr_impl<BinarySearchTree::Node, std::default_delete<BinarySearchTree::Node> >._M_t has only one value	1
t.n == 3	1
(this->n == return) == (return == orig(this->n))	1

Table 11. Invariants for heap, 7 public methods.

Invariant	Count
this->comp._M_invoker has only one value	7
this->comp._Function_base._M_manager has only one value	7
this[0] has only one value	6
this->data has only one value	6
this->data._Vector_base<int, std::allocator<int> >._M_impl has only one value	6
this->comp has only one value	6
this->comp._Function_base._M_functor has only one value	6
this->comp._Function_base._M_functor._M_unused has only one value	6
this[0] != null	3
this->data != null	3
this->data._Vector_base<int, std::allocator<int> >._M_impl != null	3
this->comp != null	3
this->comp._M_invoker != null	3
this->comp._Function_base._M_functor != null	3
this->comp._Function_base._M_functor._M_unused != null	3
this->comp._Function_base._M_manager != null	3
this->data._Vector_base<int, std::allocator<int> >._M_impl._Vector_impl_data._M_start[] elements >= 1	2
this->data._Vector_base<int, std::allocator<int> >._M_impl._Vector_impl_data._M_start != null	1
this->data._Vector_base<int, std::allocator<int> >._M_impl._Vector_impl_data._M_finish != null	1
this->data._Vector_base<int, std::allocator<int> >._M_impl._Vector_impl_data._M_end_of_storage != null	1

Table 12. Invariants for hash_table, 7 public methods.

Invariant	Count
::__digits == "000102...6979899"	3
::__tag == ""	3
this[0] has only one value	3
this->hash_function has only one value	3
this->hash_function._Function_base._M_functor has only one value	3
this->hash_function._Function_base._M_functor._M_unused has only one value	3
this->hash_function._Function_base._M_functor._M_pod_data == ""	3
this->load_factor == 0.75	3
this->table has only one value	3
this->table._Vector_base<...>._M_impl has only one value	2
this->table._Vector_base<...>._M_impl has only one value	1
this->_num_elements one of { 0, 1 }	1
this->_size == 10	1
this->table._Vector_base<...>>>>>._M_impl._Vector_impl_data._M_end_of_storage	1
key._M_dataplus has only one value	1
key._M_dataplus._M_p one of { "key1", "key2" }	1
key._M_string_length == 4	1
this->_num_elements >= 0	1
this->_size >= 0	1
this->_num_elements <= this->_size	1

Table 13. Invariants for vector, 11 public methods.

Invariant	Count
this[0] has only one value	9
this->capacity == 5	7
this->data has only one value	5
this->data[] elements one of { 1, 2 }	5
this->n == 2	4
this->data[] == [1, 2]	4
this->n in this->data[]	4
this->data[] == [1]	3
this->n == 0	2
this->n one of { 1 }	2
this->n in return[]	1
return[] == [1, 2]	1
return[] elements one of { 1, 2 }	1
this->capacity == 0	1
this->data == null	1
this->n == 1	1
this->n == v.n	1
this->capacity == v.capacity	1
v.data has only one value	1
v one of { 1, 2 }	1
this->capacity one of { 5 }	1
this->data[] sorted by <	1
this->n <= this->capacity	1
this->n < this->capacity	1
this->n one of { 2, 5 }	1
this->data[] elements == 1	1
this->data[] one of { [1], [1, 2] }	1
return one of { 1, 2 }	1

Table 14. Invariants for queue, 7 public methods.

Invariant	Count
this->data has only one value	5
this->maxSize == 10	5
this[0] has only one value	4
this->data[] == [10, 20, 30]	2
this->data[] elements one of { 10, 20, 30 }	2
this->head one of { 0, 1 }	2
this->tail == 3	2
this->n one of { 2, 3 }	2
this->maxSize in this->data[]	2
this[0] != null	2
this->data != null	2
this->data[] elements >= 0	2
this->data[] sorted by <	2
this->head < this->maxSize	2
this->tail < this->maxSize	2
this->data[] elements one of { 1, 2 }	2
this->data[] one of { [1], [1, 2] }	2
this->tail one of { 0, 1, 2 }	2
this->tail in this->data[]	2
this->head - this->tail + this->n == 0	1
this->tail one of { 2, 3, 100 }	1
this->maxSize one of { 10, 160 }	1
this->n < this->maxSize	1
this->head one of { 0, 50 }	1
this->tail >= 0	1
this->n <= this->maxSize	1
this->head <= this->tail	1
this->head one of { 0, 2 }	1
this->n one of { 0, 1 }	1
this->head == other.head	1
this->maxSize == other.maxSize	1
this->data[] == [7, 14]	1
this->data[] elements one of { 7, 14 }	1
this->head == 0	1
other.data has only one value	1
other.tail == 2	1
this->head one of { 0, 1, 2 }	1
this->head - this->tail + return == 0	1
return one of { 0, 1, 2 }	1

Table 15. Invariants for stack, 6 public methods.

Invariant	Count
this->maxSize one of { 10, 160, 1280 }	4
this->data[] sorted by <	4
this->data[] elements < this->maxSize	4
this->n < this->maxSize	3
this[0] != null	3
this->data != null	3
this[0] has only one value	2
this->data[] elements >= 0	2
this->n one of { 0, 1, 2 }	1
this->maxSize == other.maxSize	1
this has only one value	1
this->data has only one value	1
this->n == 2	1
this->maxSize == 10	1
other.data has only one value	1
other.data[] == [1, 2]	1
other.data[] elements one of { 1, 2 }	1
this->n <= this->maxSize	1

C Additional Implementation Details

This appendix provides additional details and examples for the implementation of ClassInvGen.

C.1 Code Instrumentation and Invariant Examples

Figure 19 shows how a public method is instrumented with invariant checks, and Fig. 20 shows an example of an incorrect invariant.

```
1  bool AvlTree::empty() {
2      check_invariant();
3      auto ret = empty_original();
4      check_invariant();
5      return ret;
6  }
7
8  bool AvlTree::empty_original() {
9      return n == 0;
10 }
```

(a) AvlTree instrumented with invariants

```
1  void AvlTree::check_invariant() {
2      std::function<bool(const std::unique_ptr<
             Node>&)>
3      is_balanced = [&](const std::unique_ptr<
             Node>& node) -> bool {
4          if (!node) return true;
5          int left_height = height(node->left);
6          int right_height = height(node->right);
7          if (std::abs(left_height - right_height
                ) > 1)
8              return false;
9          return is_balanced(node->left) &&
                     is_balanced(node->right);
10     };
11     };
12     assert(is_balanced(root));
13 }
```

(b) Example of a correct AvlTree class invariant

Fig. 19. AvlTree instrumentation and invariant example

```
1  void AvlTree::check_invariant() {
2      assert(height(root) == get_height(root));
3  }
```

Fig. 20. Example of an incorrect invariant of AvlTree because there is no get_height method

C.2 Test Generation Examples

Figure 21 shows an example of a generated test suite used for filtering invariants.

```
1  int main() {
2      // Test Case 1: Basic insertions and traversals
3      {
4          AvlTree tree;
5          tree.insert(10); tree.insert(20); tree.insert(5);
6          tree.in_order_traversal();
7          tree.pre_order_traversal();
8      }
9      // Test Case 2: Size, height, empty checks
10     {
11         AvlTree tree;
12         tree.insert(10); tree.insert(20);
13         tree.size(); tree.height(); tree.empty();
14     }
15     // ... more test cases ...
16 }
```

Fig. 21. A test suite generated for AvlTree

C.3 Refinement Details

ClassInvGen implements a feedback loop for refining failing invariants. Figure 23a shows an error message, while Figs. 23b and 23 show the BST invariant before and after refinement (Fig. 22).

```
1  avl_tree.cpp: In lambda function:
2  avl_tree.cpp:21:16: error: use of
3  'is_balanced' before deduction of '
       auto'
```

(a) gcc compiler error messages

```
1  void AvlTree::check_invariant() {
2    auto is_bst = [&](const std::unique_ptr
          <Node>& node,
3      const T& min, const T& max) -> bool {
4      if (!node) return true;
5      if (node->data <= min ||
6          node->data >= max) return false;
7      return is_bst(node->left, min, node->
          data) &&
8            is_bst(node->right, node->data,
           max);
9    };
10   assert(is_bst(root, std::numeric_limits<
          T>::min(),
11          std::numeric_limits<T>::max()));
12 }
```

(b) BST property before refinement

Fig. 22. (a) gcc compiler error messages. (b) BST property before refinement

```
1  void AvlTree::check_invariant() {
2    std::function<bool(const std::unique_ptr<Node>&, const T&, const T&)>
3    is_bst = [&](const std::unique_ptr<Node>& node, const T& min, const T& max) ->
         bool {
4      if (!node) return true;
5      if (node->data <= min || node->data >= max) return false;
6      return is_bst(node->left, min, node->data) &&
7             is_bst(node->right, node->data, max);
8    };
9    assert(is_bst(root, std::numeric_limits<T>::min(), std::numeric_limits<T>::max()
         ));
10 }
```

Fig. 23. BST property after refinement: auto is changed to explicit declarations

References

1. Ammons, G., Bodík, R., Larus, J.R.: Mining specifications. In: Proceedings of the 29th ACM SIGPLAN-SIGACT Symposium on Principles of Programming Languages, POPL '02, pp. 4–16. Association for Computing Machinery, New York (2002). https://doi.org/10.1145/503272.503275
2. Boockmann, J.H., Lüttgen, G.: Comprehending object state via dynamic class invariant learning. In: Beyer, D., Cavalcanti, A. (eds.) Fundamental Approaches to Software Engineering, pp. 143–164. Springer, Cham (2024). https://doi.org/10.1007/978-3-031-57259-3_7
3. Brunsfeld, M., et al.: Kolja: tree-sitter/tree-sitter: v0.24.4 (2024). https://doi.org/10.5281/zenodo.14061403
4. Burdy, L., et al.: An overview of jml tools and applications. Int. J. Softw. Tools Technol. Transfer **7**, 212–232 (2005)
5. Cadar, C., Dunbar, D., Engler, D.: Klee: unassisted and automatic generation of high-coverage tests for complex systems programs. In: Proceedings of the 8th USENIX Conference on Operating Systems Design and Implementation, OSDI'08, pp. 209–224. USENIX Association (2008)
6. Cousot, P., Cousot, R.: Abstract interpretation: a unified lattice model for static analysis of programs by construction or approximation of fixpoints. In: Proceedings

of the 4th ACM SIGACT-SIGPLAN Symposium on Principles of Programming Languages, pp. 238–252 (1977)
7. Csallner, C., Tillmann, N., Smaragdakis, Y.: Dysy: dynamic symbolic execution for invariant inference. In: Proceedings of the 30th International Conference on Software Engineering, ICSE '08, pp. 281–290. Association for Computing Machinery, New York (2008). https://doi.org/10.1145/1368088.1368127
8. Dimitrios, A.: Algorithms and data structures (2023). https://github.com/djeada/Algorithms-And-Data-Structures/tree/master/src/collections_and_containers/cpp
9. Endres, M., Fakhoury, S., Chakraborty, S., Lahiri, S.K.: Can large language models transform natural language intent into formal method postconditions? Proc. ACM Softw. Eng. **1**(FSE) (2024). https://doi.org/10.1145/3660791
10. Ernst, M.D., et al.: The Daikon system for dynamic detection of likely invariants. Sci. Comput. Program. **69**(1–3), 35–45 (2007)
11. Fähndrich, M.: Static verification for code contracts. In: Cousot, R., Martel, M. (eds.) SAS 2010. LNCS, vol. 6337, pp. 2–5. Springer, Heidelberg (2010). https://doi.org/10.1007/978-3-642-15769-1_2
12. Gao, Y., et al.: Retrieval-augmented generation for large language models: a survey. arXiv preprint arXiv:2312.10997 (2023)
13. Garg, P., Löding, C., Madhusudan, P., Neider, D.: ICE: a robust framework for learning invariants. In: Biere, A., Bloem, R. (eds.) CAV 2014. LNCS, vol. 8559, pp. 69–87. Springer, Cham (2014). https://doi.org/10.1007/978-3-319-08867-9_5
14. Garg, P., Neider, D., Madhusudan, P., Roth, D.: Learning invariants using decision trees and implication counterexamples. In: Proceedings of the 43rd Annual ACM SIGPLAN-SIGACT Symposium on Principles of Programming Languages, POPL '16, pp. 499–512. Association for Computing Machinery, New York (2016). https://doi.org/10.1145/2837614.2837664
15. Greiner, S., Bühlmann, N., Ohrndorf, M., Tsigkanos, C., Nierstrasz, O., Kehrer, T.: Automated generation of code contracts: Generative ai to the rescue? In: Proceedings of the 23rd ACM SIGPLAN International Conference on Generative Programming: Concepts and Experiences, pp. 1–14 (2024)
16. Hellendoorn, V.J., Devanbu, P.T., Polozov, A., Marron, M.: Are my invariants valid? a learning approach. arXiv preprint (2019). https://www.microsoft.com/en-us/research/publication/are-my-invariants-valid-a-learning-approach/
17. Henzinger, T.A., Jhala, R., Majumdar, R., McMillan, K.L.: Abstractions from proofs. In: Proceedings of the 31st ACM SIGPLAN-SIGACT Symposium on Principles of Programming Languages, pp. 232–244 (2004)
18. Kamath, A., et al.: Finding inductive loop invariants using large language models (2023). https://arxiv.org/abs/2311.07948
19. Kirchner, F., Kosmatov, N., Prevosto, V., Signoles, J., Yakobowski, B.: Frama-c: a software analysis perspective. Formal Aspects Comput. **27**(3), 573–609 (2015)
20. Lahiri, S.: Evaluating llm-driven user-intent formalization for verification-aware languages. In: Formal Methods in Computer-Aided Design (FMCAD'24) (2024). https://www.microsoft.com/en-us/research/publication/evaluating-llm-driven-user-intent-formalization-for-verification-aware-languages/
21. Lahiri, S.K., Qadeer, S., Galeotti, J.P., Voung, J.W., Wies, T.: Intra-module inference. In: Bouajjani, A., Maler, O. (eds.) CAV 2009. LNCS, vol. 5643, pp. 493–508. Springer, Heidelberg (2009). https://doi.org/10.1007/978-3-642-02658-4_37

22. Lattner, C., Adve, V.: Llvm: a compilation framework for lifelong program analysis & transformation. In: International Symposium on Code Generation and Optimization, 2004, CGO 2004, pp. 75–86 (2004). https://doi.org/10.1109/CGO.2004.1281665
23. Lattuada, A., et al.: Verus: verifying rust programs using linear ghost types. Proc. ACM Program. Lang. **7**(OOPSLA1), 286–315 (2023)
24. Le, T.C., Zheng, G., Nguyen, T.: Sling: using dynamic analysis to infer program invariants in separation logic. In: Proceedings of the 40th ACM SIGPLAN Conference on Programming Language Design and Implementation, PLDI 2019, pp. 788–801. Association for Computing Machinery, New York (2019). https://doi.org/10.1145/3314221.3314634
25. Leino, K.R.M.: Dafny: an automatic program verifier for functional correctness. In: Clarke, E.M., Voronkov, A. (eds.) LPAR 2010. LNCS (LNAI), vol. 6355, pp. 348–370. Springer, Heidelberg (2010). https://doi.org/10.1007/978-3-642-17511-4_20
26. Lemieux, C., Inala, J.P., Lahiri, S.K., Sen, S.: Codamosa: escaping coverage plateaus in test generation with pre-trained large language models. In: Proceedings of the 45th International Conference on Software Engineering, ICSE '23, pp. 919–931. IEEE Press (2023). https://doi.org/10.1109/ICSE48619.2023.00085
27. Liu, N.F., et al.: Lost in the middle: how language models use long contexts. Trans. Assoc. Comput. Linguist. **12**, 157–173 (2024)
28. Lohmann, N., et al.: mutate_cpp - mutation testing tool for c++ (2017). https://github.com/nlohmann/mutate_cpp
29. Ma, L., Liu, S., Li, Y., Xie, X., Bu, L.: Specgen: automated generation of formal program specifications via large language models. CoRR arxiv:2401.08807 (2024). https://doi.org/10.48550/ARXIV.2401.08807
30. McMillan, K.L.: An interpolating theorem prover. In: Jensen, K., Podelski, A. (eds.) TACAS 2004. LNCS, vol. 2988, pp. 16–30. Springer, Heidelberg (2004). https://doi.org/10.1007/978-3-540-24730-2_2
31. Meyer, B.: The eiffel programming language (1992). http://www.eiffel.com
32. Molina, F., d'Amorim, M., Aguirre, N.: Fuzzing class specifications. In: Proceedings of the 44th International Conference on Software Engineering, ICSE '22, pp. 1008–1020. Association for Computing Machinery, New York (2022). https://doi.org/10.1145/3510003.3510120
33. de Moura, L., Bjørner, N.: Z3: an efficient smt solver. In: 2008 Tools and Algorithms for Construction and Analysis of Systems, pp. 337–340. Springer, Heidelberg (2008). https://www.microsoft.com/en-us/research/publication/z3-an-efficient-smt-solver/
34. Newcomb, J.L., Bodik, R.: Using human-in-the-loop synthesis to author functional reactive programs (2019). https://arxiv.org/abs/1909.11206
35. Nguyen, T., Kapur, D., Weimer, W., Forrest, S.: Using dynamic analysis to discover polynomial and array invariants. In: 2012 34th International Conference on Software Engineering (ICSE), pp. 683–693 (2012). https://doi.org/10.1109/ICSE.2012.6227149
36. Padhi, S., Sharma, R., Millstein, T.D.: Data-driven precondition inference with learned features. In: Proceedings of the 37th ACM SIGPLAN Conference on Programming Language Design and Implementation, PLDI 2016, Santa Barbara, CA, USA, 13–17 June 2016, pp. 42–56 (2016). https://doi.org/10.1145/2908080.2908099

37. Pei, K., Bieber, D., Shi, K., Sutton, C., Yin, P.: Can large language models reason about program invariants? In: Krause, A., Brunskill, E., Cho, K., Engelhardt, B., Sabato, S., Scarlett, J. (eds.) Proceedings of the 40th International Conference on Machine Learning. Proceedings of Machine Learning Research, vol. 202, pp. 27496–27520. PMLR (2023). https://proceedings.mlr.press/v202/pei23a.html
38. Polikarpova, N., Ciupa, I., Meyer, B.: A comparative study of programmer-written and automatically inferred contracts. In: Proceedings of the Eighteenth International Symposium on Software Testing and Analysis, pp. 93–104 (2009)
39. Schäfer, M., Nadi, S., Eghbali, A., Tip, F.: An empirical evaluation of using large language models for automated unit test generation (2023). https://arxiv.org/abs/2302.06527
40. Swamy, N., Chen, J., Fournet, C., Strub, P.Y., Bhargavan, K., Yang, J.: Secure distributed programming with value-dependent types. ACM SIGPLAN Not. **46**(9), 266–278 (2011)
41. Wen, C., et al.: Enchanting program specification synthesis by large language models using static analysis and program verification. In: Gurfinkel, A., Ganesh, V. (eds.) Computer Aided Verification, pp. 302–328. Springer, Cham (2024). https://doi.org/10.1007/978-3-031-65630-9_16
42. Wikipedia contributors: Avl tree—Wikipedia, the free encyclopedia (2024). https://en.wikipedia.org/w/index.php?title=AVL_tree&oldid=1255561501. Accessed 15 Nov 2024
43. Wu, G., Cao, W., Yao, Y., Wei, H., Chen, T., Ma, X.: Llm meets bounded model checking: Neuro-symbolic loop invariant inference. In: Proceedings of the 39th IEEE/ACM International Conference on Automated Software Engineering, ASE '24, pp. 406–417. Association for Computing Machinery, New York (2024). https://doi.org/10.1145/3691620.3695014
44. Yang, C., et al.: Whitefox: white-box compiler fuzzing empowered by large language models. Proc. ACM Program. Lang. **8**(OOPSLA2), 709–735 (2024)
45. z3Prover: z3prover util classes (2024). https://github.com/Z3Prover/z3/tree/master/src/util

Bridging Neural ODE and ResNet: A Formal Error Bound for Safety Verification

Abdelrahman Sayed Sayed(✉)[id], Pierre-Jean Meyer[id], and Mohamed Ghazel[id]

Univ Gustave Eiffel, COSYS-ESTAS, 59657 Villeneuve d'Ascq, France
{abdelrahman.ibrahim,pierre-jean.meyer,mohamed.ghazel}@univ-eiffel.fr

Abstract. A neural ordinary differential equation (neural ODE) is a machine learning model that is commonly described as a continuous-depth generalization of a residual network (ResNet) with a single residual block, or conversely, the ResNet can be seen as the Euler discretization of the neural ODE. These two models are therefore strongly related in a way that the behaviors of either model are considered to be an approximation of the behaviors of the other. In this work, we establish a more formal relationship between these two models by bounding the approximation error between two such related models. The obtained error bound then allows us to use one of the models as a verification proxy for the other, without running the verification tools twice: if the reachable output set expanded by the error bound satisfies a safety property on one of the models, this safety property is then guaranteed to be also satisfied on the other model. This feature is fully reversible, and the initial safety verification can be run indifferently on either of the two models. This novel approach is illustrated on a numerical example of a fixed-point attractor system modeled as a neural ODE.

Keywords: Neural ODE · ResNet · Formal relationship · Safety verification · Reachability analysis

1 Introduction

Neural ordinary differential equations (neural ODE) are gaining prominence in continuous-time modeling, offering distinct advantages over traditional neural networks, such as memory efficiency, continuous-time modeling, adaptive computation balancing speed and accuracy [5,14,23]. This surge in interest stems from recent advancements in differential programming, which have enhanced the ability to model complex dynamics with greater flexibility and precision [24].

Neural ODE can be viewed as a continuous-depth generalization of residual networks (ResNet) [10], and conversely a ResNet represents an Euler discretization of the continuous transformations modeled by a neural ODE [9,18]. Unlike ResNet, neural ODE enable smooth and robust representations through continuous dynamics, leading to improved modeling of time-evolving systems [5,9]. By interpreting ResNet as discretized neural ODE, we can leverage advanced ODE solvers to enhance computational efficiency and reduce the number of required parameters [5]. Furthermore, the continuous formulation of neural ODE supports flexible handling of varying input resolutions and scales, making them adaptable to diverse data modalities. This perspective also facilitates theoretical analysis using tools from differential equations, providing insights into network stability and convergence [14].

Despite the growing interest in neural ODE for continuous-time modeling, formal analysis techniques for these models remain underdeveloped [17]. Current verification methods for neural ODE are still maturing, with existing reachability approaches primarily focusing on stochastic methods [7,8]. Other works include the NNVODE tool [17] which is an extension of the Neural Network Verification (NNV) framework [16,28] that investigates reachability for a general class of neural ODE. Additionally, another line of verification based on topological properties was introduced in [15] through a set-boundary method for safety verification of neural ODE and invertible residual networks (i-ResNet) [3].

The similarity between the neural ODE and ResNet models enables bidirectional safety verification, where the properties verified for one model can be used to deduce safety guarantees for the other one. This motivates our work, which investigates how verification results from one model can serve as a proxy for the other, addressing practical scenarios where only one model or compatible verification tools are available. The main contributions of this work are as follows:

- We derive a rigorous bound on the approximation error between the neural ODE and ResNet models for a given input set.
- We use the derived error bound in conjunction with the reachable set of one model as a proxy to verify safety properties of the other model, without applying any verification tools to the other model as illustrated in Fig. 1.

Related Work. Although the similarity between the ResNet and neural ODE models is well established [5,14], to the best of our knowledge, very few works have tried connecting these models through some more formal relationships. These include various theoretical perspectives, such as quantifying the deviation between the hidden state trajectory of a ResNet and its corresponding neural ODE, focusing on approximation error [26], while [20] derives generalization bounds for neural ODE and ResNet using a Lipschitz-based argument, emphasizing the impact of successive weight matrix differences on generalization capability. On the other hand, [21] investigates implicit regularization effects in deep ResNet and its impact on training outcomes. While these studies focus on theoretical analyses of approximation error, generalization, and regularization to understand model behavior and performance, our work leverages this relationship for formal safety verification. We propose a verification proxy approach that uses the reachable set of one model to verify the safety properties of the other, incorporating an error bound to ensure conservative over-approximations, which enables practical verification of nonlinear systems.

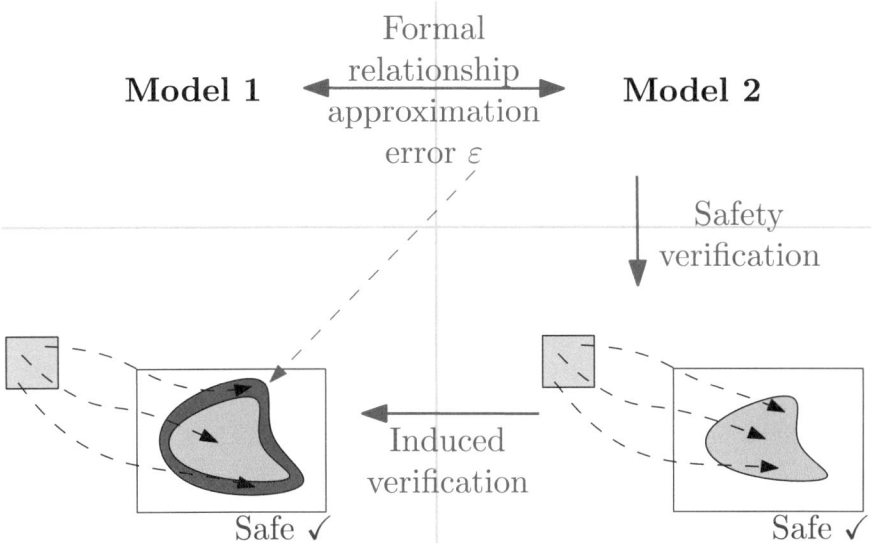

Fig. 1. Illustration of the proposed framework to verify Model 1 based on the outcome of the verification of Model 2 and a bound ε on the maximal error between the models.

Abstraction-based verification (i.e., verifying properties of one model by working on an abstraction of its behaviors into a simpler model) has been a popular topic in the past decades outside of the AI field [27]. Within the field of AI verification, its primary application has been on abstracting specific model components rather than the whole model itself, as in approaches based on convex relaxation of nonlinear ReLU activation functions [11,13]. On the other hand, full-model abstraction has been mostly unexplored for AI verification, except on the topic of neural network model reduction, where the verification of a neural network is achieved at a lower computational cost on a reduced network with less neurons, see e.g. [4] for unidirectional relationships, or [29] for bidirectional ones through the use of approximate bisimulation relations. Although the overall principle of the proposed approach in our paper is similar (abstracting a model by one that over-approximates the set of all its behaviors), the main difference with the above works between two discrete neural networks is that our paper considers the formal relationships between a continuous neural ODE model and a discrete ResNet one.

Organization of the Paper. The remainder of the paper is structured as follows. First, we formulate the safety verification problem of interest and provide some preliminaries in Sect. 2. In Sect. 3, we describe our proposed approach to bound the approximation error between the ResNet and neural ODE models, and use this error bound to verify the safety of one model based on the reachability analysis of the other. Following this, we provide numerical illustrations of our error bounding and verification proxy results (in both directions: from ResNet to neural ODE, and from neural ODE to ResNet) on an academic example in Sect. 4. Finally, we summarize the main findings of the paper and discuss potential future work in Sect. 5.

2 Preliminaries

2.1 Neural ODE and ResNet Models

We consider the following neural ODE:

$$\dot{x}(t) = \frac{dx(t)}{dt} = f(x(t)), \tag{1}$$

with state $x \in \mathbb{R}^n$, initial state $x(0) = u$, and vector field $f : \mathbb{R}^n \to \mathbb{R}^n$ defined as a finite sequence of classical neural network layers (such as fully connected layers, convolutional layers, activation functions, batch normalization). The state trajectories of (1) are defined based on the solution $\Phi : \mathbb{R} \times \mathbb{R}^n \to \mathbb{R}^n$ of the corresponding initial value problem:

$$x(t) = \Phi(t, x(0)) = \Phi(t, u).$$

In [5], such a neural ODE is described as a continuous-depth generalization of a residual neural network constituted of a single residual block. Conversely, this ResNet can be seen as the Euler discretization of the neural ODE (1):

$$y = u + f(u), \tag{2}$$

where $u \in \mathbb{R}^n$ is the input, $y \in \mathbb{R}^n$ is the output, and the residual function $f : \mathbb{R}^n \to \mathbb{R}^n$ is identical to the vector field of the neural ODE (1).

Since the approach proposed in this paper relies on the Taylor expansion of the trajectories of (1) up to the second order, we assume here for simplicity that the neural network described by the vector field f is continuously differentiable.

Remark 1. The case where f contains piecewise-affine activation functions such as ReLU can theoretically be handled as well, since our approach only really requires their derivatives to be bounded (but not necessarily continuous). But for the sake of clarity of presentation (to avoid the case decompositions of each ReLU activation), this case is kept out of the scope of the present paper.

2.2 Problem Definition

As mentioned above and in [5], both the neural ODE and ResNet models describe a very similar behavior, and either model could be seen as an approximation of the other. Our goal in this paper is to provide a formal comparison of these models in the context of safety verification, by evaluating the approximation error between them. For such comparison to be meaningful, we consider the outputs y of the ResNet (2) on one side, and the outputs $\Phi(1, u)$ of the neural ODE (1) at continuous depth $t = 1$ on the other side, since other values $t \neq 1$ of this continuous depth have no elements of comparison in the discrete architecture of the ResNet.

Given an initial set $\mathcal{X}_{in} \subseteq \mathbb{R}^n$ for the neural ODE (or equivalently referred to as *input set* for the ResNet), we first define the sets of reachable outputs for either model:

$$\mathcal{R}_{\text{neural ODE}}(\mathcal{X}_{in}) = \{y \in \mathbb{R}^n \mid y = \Phi(1, u), \ u \in \mathcal{X}_{in}\},$$

$$\mathcal{R}_{\text{ResNet}}(\mathcal{X}_{in}) = \{y \in \mathbb{R}^n \mid y = u + f(u), \ u \in \mathcal{X}_{in}\}.$$

Since we usually cannot compute these output reachable sets exactly, we will often rely on computing an over-approximation denoted as $\Omega(\mathcal{X}_{in})$ such that $\mathcal{R}(\mathcal{X}_{in}) \subseteq \Omega(\mathcal{X}_{in})$.

Our first objective is to bound the approximation error between the two models, as formalized below.

Problem 1 (Error Bounding). Given an input set $\mathcal{X}_{in} \subseteq \mathbb{R}^n$, we want to over-approximate the set $\mathcal{R}_\varepsilon(\mathcal{X}_{in})$ of errors between the ResNet (2) and neural ODE (1) models, defined as:

$$\mathcal{R}_\varepsilon(\mathcal{X}_{in}) = \{\Phi(1, u) - (u + f(u)) \mid u \in \mathcal{X}_{in}\}.$$

Our second problem of interest is to use one of our models as a verification proxy for the other. In other words, we want to combine this error bound with the reachable set of one model to verify the satisfaction of a safety property on the other model, without having to compute the reachable output set of this second model.

Problem 2 (Verification Proxy). Given an input-output safety property defined by an input set $\mathcal{X}_{in} \subseteq \mathbb{R}^n$ and a safe output set $\mathcal{X}_s \subseteq \mathbb{R}^n$, the verification problem consists in checking whether the reachable output set of a model is fully contained in the targeted safe set: $\mathcal{R}(\mathcal{X}_{in}) \subseteq \mathcal{X}_s$. In this paper, we want to verify this safety property on one model by relying only on the error set $\mathcal{R}_\varepsilon(\mathcal{X}_{in})$ from Problem 1 and the reachability analysis of the other model.

3 Proposed Approach

As mentioned in Sect. 2.2, the ResNet model in (2) can be seen as the Euler discretization of the neural ODE (1) evaluated at continuous depth $t = 1$:

$$x(1) = \Phi(1, u) \approx u + f(u) = y. \tag{3}$$

Our initial goal, related to Problem 1, is to evaluate this approximation error for a given set of inputs $u \in \mathcal{X}_{in}$. This is done below through the use of a Taylor expansion and its Lagrange-remainder form, combined later with some tools dedicated for reachability analysis.

3.1 Lagrange Remainder

The Taylor expansion of the state trajectory $x(t)$ of the neural ODE (1) at $t = 0$ is given by the infinite sum:

$$x(t) = x(0) + t\frac{dx(0)}{dt} + \frac{t^2}{2!}\frac{d^2x(0)}{dt^2} + \frac{t^3}{3!}\frac{d^3x(0)}{dt^3} + \ldots \tag{4}$$

The Lagrange remainder theorem offers the possibility to truncate (4) without approximation error, hence preserving the above equality. We only state below the result in the case of a truncation at the Taylor order 2 corresponding to the case of interest in our work.

Proposition 1 (Lagrange remainder [25]). *There exists $t^* \in [0, t]$ such that*

$$x(t) = x(0) + t\frac{dx(0)}{dt} + \frac{t^2}{2!}\frac{d^2x(t^*)}{dt^2} \tag{5}$$

Notice that in (5), the second order derivative $\frac{d^2x}{dt^2}$ is evaluated at $t^* \in [0, t]$ instead of t as in the Taylor series (4). Although the truncation in Proposition 1 provides a much more manageable expression than the infinite sum in (4), the main difficulty is that this result only states the existence of a $t^* \in [0, t]$ satisfying the equality in (5), but its actual value is unknown.

3.2 Error Function

To compare the continuous state $x(t)$ with the discrete output of the ResNet, the state of the neural ODE (1) should be evaluated at depth $t = 1$.

The first term of the right-hand side in (5) is the known initial condition of the neural ODE (1): $x(0) = u$.

The second term is provided by the definition of the vector field of the neural ODE (1), and thus reduces to:

$$t\frac{dx(0)}{dt} = 1 \cdot f(x(0)) = f(u).$$

The second derivative appearing in the third term of (5) can be computed using the chain rule as follows:

$$\begin{aligned}\frac{d^2x(t)}{dt^2} &= \frac{df(x(t))}{dt} \\ &= \frac{\partial f(x(t))}{\partial t} + \frac{\partial f(x(t))}{\partial x}\frac{dx(t)}{dt} \\ &= \frac{\partial f(x(t))}{\partial t} + f'(x(t))f(x(t)).\end{aligned}$$

In our context of Sect. 2, the function f is assumed not to be explicitly dependent on the depth t due to its definition as a single residual block with classical layers. Therefore, the partial derivative $\frac{\partial f(x(t))}{\partial t}$ is equal to 0, and the third term of (5) thus reduces to:

$$\frac{t^2}{2!}\frac{d^2 x(t^*)}{dt^2} = \frac{1}{2}f'(x(t^*))f(x(t^*)).$$

We can thus re-write (5) as an equation defining the output of the neural ODE based on the output of the ResNet (for the same initial state/input u) and an error term:

$$\Phi(1, u) = (u + f(u)) + \varepsilon(u), \quad (6)$$

where the approximation error between our models for this particular input u is expressed by the Lagrange remainder of Taylor order 2:

$$\varepsilon(u) = \frac{1}{2}f'(x(t^*))f(x(t^*)), \quad (7)$$

with $x(t^*) = \Phi(t^*, u)$ for a fixed but unknown $t^* \in [0, 1]$.

Equation (6) can also be modified to rather express the outputs of the ResNet based on those of the neural ODE:

$$u + f(u) = \Phi(1, u) - \varepsilon(u). \quad (8)$$

The error function $\varepsilon : \mathbb{R}^n \to \mathbb{R}^n$ appearing positively in (6) and negatively in (8) is defined in (7) only for a specific input u. However, in the context of our Problem 1, we are interested in analyzing the approximation error between both models over an input set $\mathcal{X}_{in} \subseteq \mathbb{R}^n$. In addition, since the specific value of t^* is unknown, we need to bound (7) for any possible value of $t^* \in [0, 1]$. Therefore in the next sections, we focus on converting the equalities (6)-(8) to set inclusions over all $u \in \mathcal{X}_{in}$ and $t^* \in [0, 1]$.

3.3 Bounding the Error Set

The reachable error set $\mathcal{R}_\varepsilon(\mathcal{X}_{in})$ introduced in Problem 1, can be redefined based on the error function (7) as follows:

$$\mathcal{R}_\varepsilon(\mathcal{X}_{in}) = \{\Phi(1, u) - (u + f(u)) \mid u \in \mathcal{X}_{in}\}$$
$$= \left\{\frac{1}{2}f'(\Phi(t^*, u))f(\Phi(t^*, u)) \,\bigg|\, t^* \in [0, 1],\, u \in \mathcal{X}_{in}\right\}. \quad (9)$$

To solve Problem 1, our objective is thus to compute an over-approximation $\Omega_\varepsilon(\mathcal{X}_{in})$ bounding the error set: $\mathcal{R}_\varepsilon(\mathcal{X}_{in}) \subseteq \Omega_\varepsilon(\mathcal{X}_{in})$.

The first step (corresponding to line 1 in Algorithm 1) is to compute the reachable tube of all possible states that can be reached by the neural ODE (1) over the whole range $t \in [0, 1]$ and for any initial state $x(0) = u \in \mathcal{X}_{in}$. This reachable tube can be defined similarly to $\mathcal{R}_{\text{neural ODE}}(\mathcal{X}_{in})$ in Sect. 2.2 but for all possible depth $t \in [0, 1]$ instead of only the final one:

$$\mathcal{R}^{\text{tube}}_{\text{neural ODE}}(\mathcal{X}_{in}) = \{\Phi(t, u) \in \mathbb{R}^n \mid t \in [0, 1],\, u \in \mathcal{X}_{in}\}.$$

Since in most cases this set cannot be computed exactly, we instead use off-the-shelf reachability analysis toolboxes to compute an over-approximating set $\Omega_{\text{neural ODE}}^{\text{tube}}(\mathcal{X}_{in})$ such that $\mathcal{R}_{\text{neural ODE}}^{\text{tube}}(\mathcal{X}_{in}) \subseteq \Omega_{\text{neural ODE}}^{\text{tube}}(\mathcal{X}_{in})$.

The error set can then be re-written based on the above reachable tube definition, by replacing $\Phi(t^*, u)$ (with $t^* \in [0, 1]$ and $u \in \mathcal{X}_{in}$) in (9) by $x \in \mathcal{R}_{\text{neural ODE}}^{\text{tube}}(\mathcal{X}_{in})$.

$$\mathcal{R}_\varepsilon(\mathcal{X}_{in}) = \left\{ \frac{1}{2} f'(x) f(x) \;\middle|\; x \in \mathcal{R}_{\text{neural ODE}}^{\text{tube}}(\mathcal{X}_{in}) \right\}$$
$$\subseteq \left\{ \frac{1}{2} f'(x) f(x) \;\middle|\; x \in \Omega_{\text{neural ODE}}^{\text{tube}}(\mathcal{X}_{in}) \right\}. \quad (10)$$

The next step, in line 2 of Algorithm 1, is to over-approximate this error set $\mathcal{R}_\varepsilon(\mathcal{X}_{in})$. One possible approach to achieve this is to define the static function $\varepsilon = \frac{1}{2} f'(x) f(x)$ and apply to it some set-propagation techniques (such as interval arithmetic [12], Taylor models [19], or affine arithmetic [6]) to bound the set of output errors ε corresponding to any state $x \in \Omega_{\text{neural ODE}}^{\text{tube}}(\mathcal{X}_{in})$ in the reachable tube over-approximation. An alternative approach, which provided a tighter error bounding set in the particular case of the numerical example presented in Sect. 4, is to define the discrete-time nonlinear system $x^+ = \frac{1}{2} f'(x) f(x)$, and then use existing reachability analysis toolboxes to over-approximate the reachable set of this system after one time step, which corresponds to bounding the image of the error function. Note that in this case, it is important that this final reachable set is computed as a single step, and not decomposed into a sequence of smaller intermediate steps whose iterative updates of the internal state would have no mathematical meaning for the static (stateless) error function.

As a consequence of the equalities and set inclusions in (9)–(10) and the fact that the reachability methods to be used in the first two steps of Algorithm 1 described above guarantee that the obtained sets are over-approximations of the output or reachable sets of interest, we have thus reached a solution to Problem 1.

Theorem 1. *The set $\Omega_\varepsilon(\mathcal{X}_{in})$ obtained after applying this second step described above solves Problem 1:*

$$\mathcal{R}_\varepsilon(\mathcal{X}_{in}) = \{\Phi(1, u) - (u + f(u)) \mid u \in \mathcal{X}_{in}\} \subseteq \Omega_\varepsilon(\mathcal{X}_{in}).$$

Note that the error bound in Theorem 1 is defined as a set in the state space of the neural ODE. This differs from the approach in [26], where the error bound is defined as a positive scalar.

A second and more important difference with this work is the tightness of the obtained error bounds. Indeed, if we adapt the results from [26] to the context of our framework described in Sect. 2, their error bound is expressed as:

$$\varepsilon \leq \frac{e^L - 1}{L} \left\| \frac{1}{2} f'(x) f(x) \right\|_\infty, \; \forall x \in \mathcal{R}_{\text{neural ODE}}^{\text{tube}}(\mathcal{X}_{in}),$$

where L is a Lipschitz constant of the neural ODE vector field. The term $\left\|\frac{1}{2}f'(x)f(x)\right\|_\infty$ can be obtained by first over-approximating the error set by $\Omega_\varepsilon(\mathcal{X}_{in})$ in the same way we did, but the infinity norm forces to expand this set to make it symmetrical around 0, and then keeping only the maximum value among its components (thus corresponding to a second expansion of this set into an hypercube whose width along all dimensions is the largest width of the previous set). In addition, for any system with non-zero Lipschitz constant, the factor $\frac{e^L-1}{L}$ is always greater than 1, which increases this error bound even more.

In summary, this scalar error bound is doubly more conservative than our proposed set-based error bound. The comparison of both approaches is illustrated in the numerical example of Sect. 4.

3.4 Verification Proxy

To address Problem 2, we leverage the similar behavior between the neural ODE and ResNet models to verify safety properties on one model using the reachable set of the other, combined with the error bound from Theorem 1. Specifically, we want to verify whether the reachable output set of a model is contained in the safe set $\mathcal{X}_s$, i.e., $\mathcal{R}(\mathcal{X}_{in}) \subseteq \mathcal{X}_s$.

We first focus on the case of Algorithm 1 to verify the safety property on the neural ODE, based on the reachability analysis of the ResNet. This first verification proxy relies on the set-based version of (6) using the Minkowski sum:

$$\mathcal{R}_{\text{neural ODE}}(\mathcal{X}_{in}) \subseteq \Omega_{\text{ResNet}}(\mathcal{X}_{in}) + \Omega_\varepsilon(\mathcal{X}_{in}), \tag{11}$$

stating that the reachable output set of the neural ODE is contained in the output set over-approximation of the ResNet $\Omega_{\text{ResNet}}(\mathcal{X}_{in})$, expanded by the bounding set of the error $\Omega_\varepsilon(\mathcal{X}_{in})$ obtained after applying the first two lines of Algorithm 1 as described in Sect. 3.3.

Therefore, this verification procedure is achieved as in Algorithm 1, by first using existing set-propagation or reachability analysis tools to compute an over-approximation $\Omega_{\text{ResNet}}(\mathcal{X}_{in})$ of the ResNet output set (line 3). Then in line 4, an over-approximation of the neural ODE output set can be deduced from (11) by taking the Minkowski sum of $\Omega_{\text{ResNet}}(\mathcal{X}_{in})$ and our error bound $\Omega_\varepsilon(\mathcal{X}_{in})$. If $\Omega_{\text{neural ODE}}(\mathcal{X}_{in})$ is contained in the safe set $\mathcal{X}_s$, then the neural ODE satisfies the safety property, otherwise the result is inconclusive (line 5–9).

Reversing the roles, the case of verifying the ResNet based on the reachability analysis of the neural ODE is described in Algorithm 2. This case is very similar to the previous one, so we focus here on the main differences with Algorithm 1. The first difference is that in (8), the term representing the approximation error between the models appears with a negative sign. Therefore, when converting this equation into a set inclusion similarly to (11), we need to be careful to add the negation of the error set (and not to do a set difference, which is not the correct set operation in our case). We thus introduce the negative error set

$$\Omega_{-\varepsilon}(\mathcal{X}_{in}) = \{-\varepsilon \mid \varepsilon \in \Omega_\varepsilon(\mathcal{X}_{in})\},$$

Algorithm 1. Safety Verification Framework for neural ODE based on ResNet

Input: a neural ODE, an input set $\mathcal{X}_{in}$ and a safe set $\mathcal{X}_s$.
Output: **Safe** or **Unknown**.

1: compute an over-approximation of the reachable tube of the neural ODE $\Omega_{\text{neural ODE}}^{\text{tube}}(\mathcal{X}_{in})$;
2: compute the over-approximation of the error set $\Omega_\varepsilon(\mathcal{X}_{in})$, $\forall x \in \Omega_{\text{neural ODE}}^{\text{tube}}(\mathcal{X}_{in})$;
3: compute the over-approximation of the ResNet output $\Omega_{\text{ResNet}}(\mathcal{X}_{in})$;
4: deduce an over-approximation of the neural ODE output
  $\Omega_{\text{neural ODE}}(\mathcal{X}_{in}) = \Omega_{\text{ResNet}}(\mathcal{X}_{in}) + \Omega_\varepsilon(\mathcal{X}_{in})$;
5: **if** $\Omega_{\text{neural ODE}}(\mathcal{X}_{in}) \subseteq \mathcal{X}_s$ **then**
6:   return **Safe**
7: **else**
8:   return **Unknown**
9: **end if**

in order to convert (8) into its set-based notation as follows:

$$\mathcal{R}_{\text{ResNet}}(\mathcal{X}_{in}) \subseteq \Omega_{\text{neural ODE}}(\mathcal{X}_{in}) + \Omega_{-\varepsilon}(\mathcal{X}_{in}). \tag{12}$$

The second difference is that in line 3 of Algorithm 2, we compute an over-approximation of the reachable set of the neural ODE, using any classical tools for reachability analysis of continuous-time nonlinear systems, and add it to the negative error set to obtain an over-approximation of the ResNet output set. This final set can then similarly be used to verify the satisfaction of the safety property on the ResNet model.

Algorithm 2. Safety Verification Framework for ResNet based on neural ODE

Input: a ResNet, an input set $\mathcal{X}_{in}$ and a safe set $\mathcal{X}_s$.
Output: **Safe** or **Unknown**.

1: compute an over-approximation of the reachable tube of the neural ODE $\Omega_{\text{neural ODE}}^{\text{tube}}(\mathcal{X}_{in})$;
2: compute the over-approximation of the negative error set $\Omega_{-\varepsilon}(\mathcal{X}_{in})$, $\forall x \in \Omega_{\text{neural ODE}}^{\text{tube}}(\mathcal{X}_{in})$;
3: compute the over-approximation of the neural ODE output $\Omega_{\text{neural ODE}}(\mathcal{X}_{in})$;
4: deduce an over-approximation of the ResNet output
  $\Omega_{\text{ResNet}}(\mathcal{X}_{in}) = \Omega_{\text{neural ODE}}(\mathcal{X}_{in}) + \Omega_{-\varepsilon}(\mathcal{X}_{in})$;
5: **if** $\Omega_{\text{ResNet}}(\mathcal{X}_{in}) \subseteq \mathcal{X}_s$ **then**
6:   return **Safe**
7: **else**
8:   return **Unknown**
9: **end if**

Theorem 2 (Soundness). *For the case that either Algorithm 1 or 2 returns* **Safe***, the safety property in the sense of Problem 2 holds true [15].*

The soundness of the verification framework is guaranteed because both algorithms rely on over-approximations of the true reachable sets. Specifically, (11) ensures that $\mathcal{R}_{\text{neural ODE}}(\mathcal{X}_{in}) \subseteq \Omega_{\text{neural ODE}}(\mathcal{X}_{in})$, and (12) ensures $\mathcal{R}_{\text{ResNet}}(\mathcal{X}_{in}) \subseteq \Omega_{\text{ResNet}}(\mathcal{X}_{in})$. These inclusions hold due to the conservative nature of the considered reachability analysis and error bound computations in Sect. 3.3 (Theorem 1).

4 Numerical Illustration

In this section, a commonly used neural ODE academic example [16,17] is used to demonstrate the verification proxy between the two models, which is the Fixed-Point Attractor (FPA) [22] that consists of one nonlinear neural ODE.

Experiment Setting: All the experiments[1] herein are run on MATLAB 2024b with Continuous Reachability Analyzer (CORA) version 2024.4.0 with an Intel (R) Core (TM) i5-1145G7 CPU@2.60 GHz and 32 GB of RAM.

4.1 System Description

The FPA system is a nonlinear dynamical system with dynamics that converge to a fixed point (an equilibrium state) under certain conditions [2], and the fixed-point aspect makes it a useful model for studying convergence and stability, which are important in safety-critical applications where the system must not diverge or enter unsafe states. As in the proposed benchmark in [22], we consider here the following 5-dimensional neural ODE approximating the FPA dynamics:

$$\dot{x} = f(x) = \tau x + W \tanh(x),$$

where $x \in \mathbb{R}^5$ is the state vector, $\tau = -10^{-6}$ is a time constant for the neurons, $W \in \mathbb{R}^{5 \times 5}$ is a composite weight matrix defined as $W = \begin{pmatrix} 0_{2 \times 2} & A \\ 0_{3 \times 2} & BA \end{pmatrix}$ with $A = \begin{pmatrix} -1.20327 & -0.07202 & -0.93635 \\ 1.18810 & -1.50015 & 0.93519 \end{pmatrix}$ and $B = \begin{pmatrix} 1.21464 & -0.10502 \\ 0.12023 & 0.19387 \\ -1.36695 & 0.12201 \end{pmatrix}$, and $\tanh(x)$ is the hyperbolic tangent activation function applied element-wise to the state vector x.

We choose our safety property defined by the input set $\mathcal{X}_{in} \approx [0.45, 0.55] \times [0.72, 0.88] \times [0.47, 0.58] \times [0.19, 0.24] \times [-0.64, -0.53]$ (its exact numerical values are provided in the code linked below) and the safe set $\mathcal{X}_s = [0.2, 0.6] \times [0.3, 0.85] \subset \mathbb{R}^2$, that only focuses on the projection of the state onto its first two dimensions, i.e., using an output function $h(x) = (x_1, x_2)$. In the case of the neural ODE, we thus want to verify that for all initial state $x(0) \in \mathcal{X}_{in}$, we have $h(x(1)) \in \mathcal{X}_s$.

---

[1] Code available in the following repository: https://github.com/ab-sayed/Formal-Error-Bound-for-Safety-Verification-of-neural-ODE.

4.2 Computing the Error Bound

Using CORA [1], we compute the error bound $\Omega_\varepsilon(\mathcal{X}_{in})$ from Theorem 1 as follows. First, we over-approximate the reachable tube of the neural ODE $\mathcal{R}^{tube}_{neural\ ODE}$ over the time interval $[0,1]$ as a sequence of zonotopes, where each zonotope corresponds to an intermediate time range. For each zonotope in the reachable tube, we bound the image of the error function (7) by applying a discrete-time reachability analysis method at $t = 1$. This results in a new zonotope that over-approximates the error set starting from that particular reachable tube zonotope. The total error set is thus guaranteed to be contained in the union of these error zonotopes across all time steps. To simplify its use in the safety verification experiments in Sect. 4.3, we compute the interval hull of this union, yielding a hyperrectangle that over-approximates $\Omega_\varepsilon(\mathcal{X}_{in})$ illustrated in Fig. 2 in red, and showing 20 error zonotopes in different colors, corresponding to the error bound of each intermediate time range used in the reachable tube.

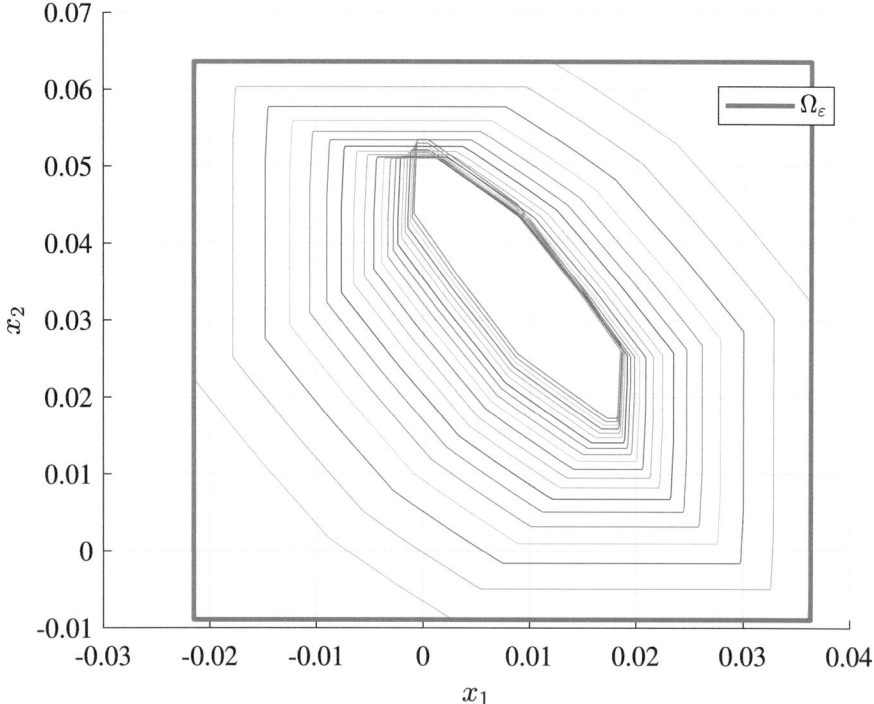

Fig. 2. Illustration of the error over-approximation

To contextualize our proposed error bound, we compare it with the error bound proposed in [26]. For that, we first compute the infinity norm of our error set $\|\Omega_\varepsilon(\mathcal{X}_{in})\|_\infty = 0.064$, which corresponds to a positive and scalar bound on the error, thus implying that its set representation in the state space (represented in yellow in Fig. 3) is necessarily symmetrical around 0 and with the width that is identical on all dimensions (since the infinity norm takes the largest width across all dimensions). The set-based error bound ($\Omega_\varepsilon(\mathcal{X}_{in})$ represented in red) obtained from our method is thus always contained in this infinity norm.

Next, we compute the Lipschitz constant for the vector field of the neural ODE $L = \|\tau + W\|_\infty = 3.62$, and then we obtain the error bound in [26] as $\frac{(e^L - 1)}{L}\|\Omega_\varepsilon(\mathcal{X}_{in})\|_\infty = 0.64$. This final error bound, represented in purple in Fig. 3, is 10 times wider (on each dimension) than the infinity norm of our error set in yellow, and about 16 millions times larger (in volume over the 5-dimensional state space) than our error set $\Omega_\varepsilon(\mathcal{X}_{in})$ in red. The improved tightness of our proposed approach is therefore very significant.

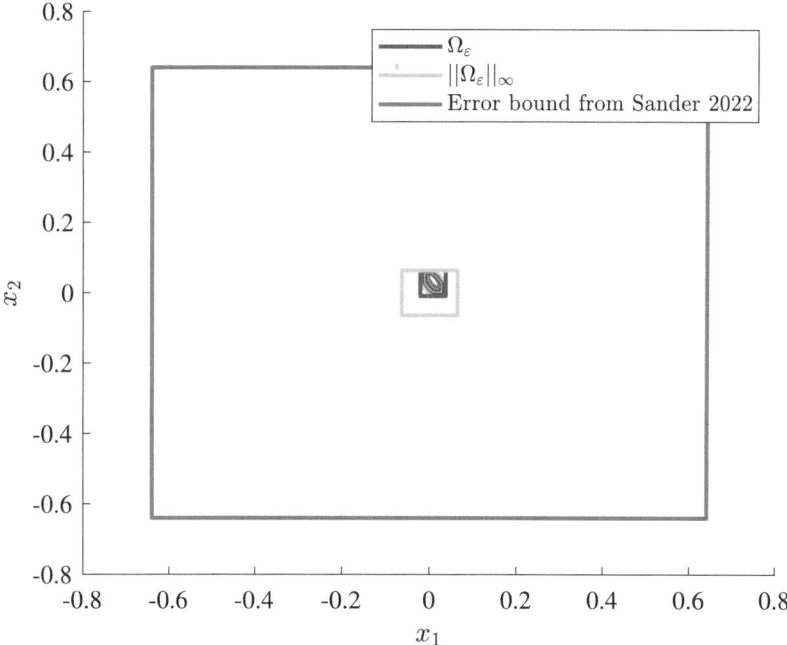

Fig. 3. Comparison of the error bounds obtained from our approach in red and the one from [26] in magenta (Color figure online)

4.3 Experiments on Safety Verification

Using the error bound computed in Sect. 4.2, we can verify safety properties for the neural ODE output set based on the ResNet output set and the error bound set (i.e., $\Omega_{\text{ResNet}}(\mathcal{X}_{in}) + \Omega_\varepsilon(\mathcal{X}_{in})$), or vice versa for the ResNet output set based on the neural ODE output set and the negative error bound set (i.e., $\Omega_{\text{neural ODE}}(\mathcal{X}_{in}) + \Omega_{-\varepsilon}(\mathcal{X}_{in})$).

In Fig. 4, we compute the over-approximation of the ResNet output set Ω_{ResNet} using simple bound propagation through the ResNet function with CORA. By adding the error bound Ω_ε, we obtain a zonotope (shown in red) that is guaranteed to contain $\mathcal{R}_{\text{neural ODE}}(\mathcal{X}_{in})$. The figure also includes black points representing neural ODE outputs for random initial conditions in $\mathcal{X}_{in}$, with their convex hull (black set) approximating the true reachable set $\mathcal{R}_{\text{neural ODE}}(\mathcal{X}_{in})$. Since the safe set $\mathcal{X}_s$ contains the over-approximation $\Omega_{\text{ResNet}}(\mathcal{X}_{in}) + \Omega_\varepsilon(\mathcal{X}_{in})$, we guarantee that the neural ODE true reachable set is safe, as:

$$\mathcal{X}_s \supseteq \Omega_{\text{ResNet}}(\mathcal{X}_{in}) + \Omega_\varepsilon(\mathcal{X}_{in}) \supseteq \mathcal{R}_{\text{neural ODE}}.$$

From Fig. 4, we can see that the ResNet and neural ODE reachable sets are very similar due to the ResNet role as a discretization of the neural ODE, but they are not identical. Indeed, some neural ODE outputs (black points) lie outside Ω_{ResNet}, highlighting the necessity of the error bound $\Omega_\varepsilon(\mathcal{X}_{in})$ to ensure that the over-approximation captures all possible neural ODE outputs.

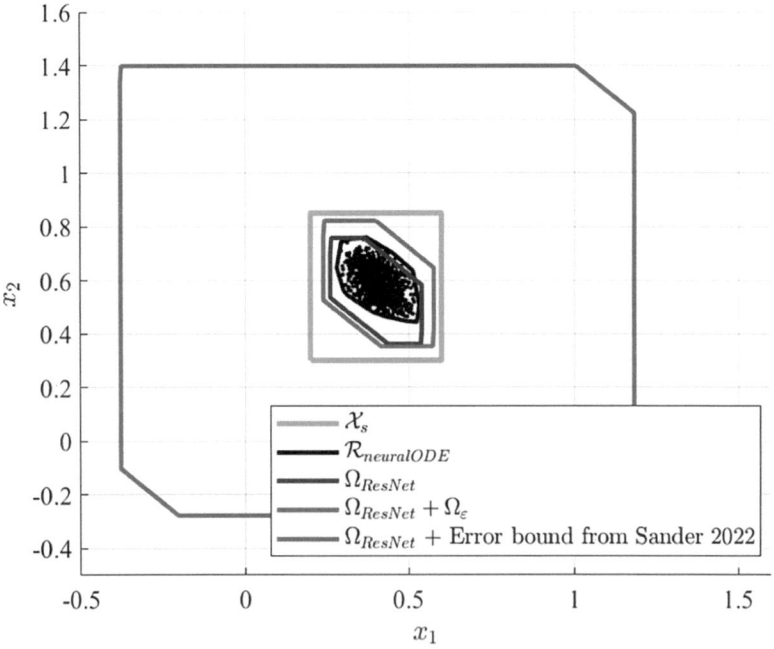

Fig. 4. Verification of neural ODE based on ResNet (Color figure online)

Conversely, in Fig. 5, we compute the over-approximation of the neural ODE reachable set $\Omega_{\text{neural ODE}}(\mathcal{X}_{in})$. By adding the negative error bound $\Omega_{-\varepsilon}$, we obtain a zonotope (shown in red) that encapsulates $\mathcal{R}_{\text{ResNet}}(\mathcal{X}_{in})$. Similarly, the figure includes blue points representing ResNet outputs for random inputs in $\mathcal{X}_{in}$, with their convex hull (blue set) approximating the true reachable set $\mathcal{R}_{\text{ResNet}}(\mathcal{X}_{in})$. Since the safe set $\mathcal{X}_s$ is a super set that contains the over-approximation $\Omega_{\text{neural ODE}}(\mathcal{X}_{in}) + \Omega_{-\varepsilon}(\mathcal{X}_{in})$, we guarantee that the ResNet true reachable set is safe, as:

$$\mathcal{X}_s \supseteq \Omega_{\text{neural ODE}}(\mathcal{X}_{in}) + \Omega_{-\varepsilon}(\mathcal{X}_{in}) \supseteq \mathcal{R}_{\text{ResNet}}.$$

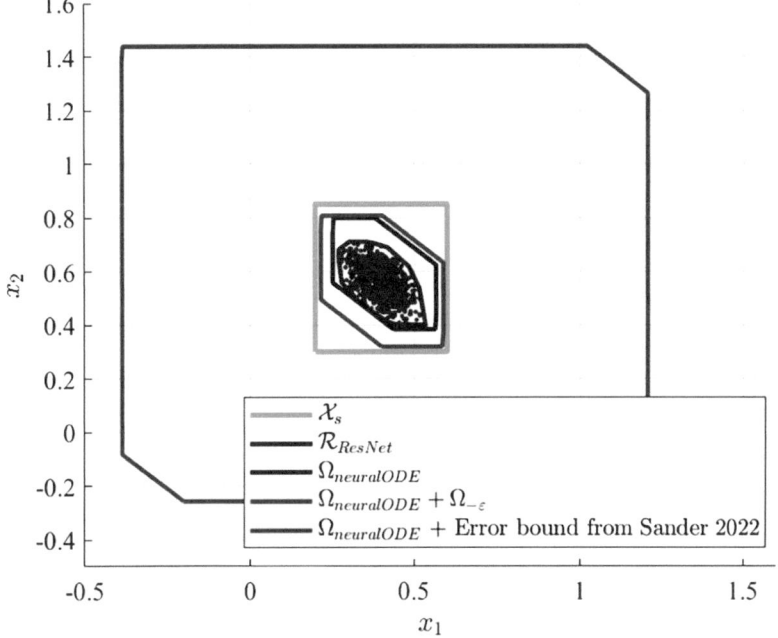

Fig. 5. Verification of ResNet based on neural ODE (Color figure online)

We can also remark that the purple obtained by adding the error bound proposed in [26] to the ResNet and neural ODE reachable sets in Figs. 4 and 5, extends significantly beyond the green safe set, preventing us from successfully guaranteeing the safety of the models.

5 Conclusion

In this paper, we propose a set-based method to bound the error between a neural ODE model and its ResNet approximation. This approach is based on reachability analysis tools applied to the Lagrange remainder in the Taylor expansion of the neural ODE trajectories, and is shown both theoretically and numerically to provide significantly tighter over-approximation of this approximation error than previous results in [26]. As the second contribution of this paper, the obtained bounding set of the approximation error between the two models is used to verify a safety property on either of the two models by applying reachability or verification tools only on the other model. This approach is fully reversible and either model can be used as the verification proxy for the other. These contributions and their improvement with respect to [26] have been illustrated on a numerical example of a fixed-point attractor system modeled as a neural ODE.

In future works, we plan to explore additional sources of complexity for these approaches, such as handling non-smooth activation functions (e.g. ReLU), and the case where the neural ODE vector field is explicitly dependent on the depth variable t, thus corresponding to ResNet with multiple residual blocks. Additionally, we aim to study the versatility of this verification proxy approach by applying it to other complex nonlinear dynamical systems or neural network architectures.

Acknowledgement. This project has received funding from the European Union's Horizon 2020 research and innovation programme under the Marie Skłodowska-Curie COFUND grant agreement No. 101034248.

References

1. Althoff, M.: An introduction to CORA 2015. In: Proceedings of the Workshop on Applied Verification for Continuous and Hybrid Systems, pp. 120–151 (2015)
2. Beer, R.D.: On the dynamics of small continuous-time recurrent neural networks. Adapt. Behav. **3**(4), 469–509 (1995)
3. Behrmann, J., Grathwohl, W., Chen, R.T., Duvenaud, D., Jacobsen, J.H.: Invertible residual networks. In: International Conference on Machine Learning, pp. 573–582. PMLR (2019)
4. Boudardara, F., Boussif, A., Meyer, P.J., Ghazel, M.: Innabstract: An inn-based abstraction method for large-scale neural network verification. IEEE Trans. Neural Netw. Learn. Syst. **35**, 18455–18469 (2023)
5. Chen, R.T., Rubanova, Y., Bettencourt, J., Duvenaud, D.K.: Neural ordinary differential equations. In: Advances in Neural Information Processing Systems, vol. 31 (2018)
6. Figueiredo, L.H., Stolfi, J.: Affine arithmetic: concepts and applications. Num. Algorithms **37**, 147–158 (2004)
7. Gruenbacher, S., Hasani, R., Lechner, M., Cyranka, J., Smolka, S.A., Grosu, R.: On the verification of neural odes with stochastic guarantees. In: Proceedings of the AAAI Conference on Artificial Intelligence, vol. 35, pp. 11525–11535 (2021)
8. Gruenbacher, S.A., et al.: GoTube: scalable statistical verification of continuous-depth models. In: Proceedings of the AAAI Conference on Artificial Intelligence, vol. 36, pp. 6755–6764 (2022)
9. Haber, E., Ruthotto, L.: Stable architectures for deep neural networks. Inverse Prob. **34**(1), 014004 (2017)

10. He, K., Zhang, X., Ren, S., Sun, J.: Deep residual learning for image recognition. In: Proceedings of the IEEE Conference on Computer Vision and Pattern Recognition, pp. 770–778 (2016)
11. Huang, X., Kwiatkowska, M., Wang, S., Wu, M.: Safety verification of deep neural networks. In: Majumdar, R., Kunčak, V. (eds.) CAV 2017. LNCS, vol. 10426, pp. 3–29. Springer, Cham (2017). https://doi.org/10.1007/978-3-319-63387-9_1
12. Jaulin, L., et al.: Interval Analysis. Springer (2001). https://doi.org/10.1007/978-1-4471-0249-6_2
13. Katz, G., Barrett, C., Dill, D.L., Julian, K., Kochenderfer, M.J.: Reluplex: an efficient SMT solver for verifying deep neural networks. In: Majumdar, R., Kunčak, V. (eds.) CAV 2017. LNCS, vol. 10426, pp. 97–117. Springer, Cham (2017). https://doi.org/10.1007/978-3-319-63387-9_5
14. Kidger, P.: On neural differential equations. Ph.D. thesis, University of Oxford (2021)
15. Liang, Z., Ren, D., Liu, W., Wang, J., Yang, W., Xue, B.: Safety verification for neural networks based on set-boundary analysis. In: International Symposium on Theoretical Aspects of Software Engineering, pp. 248–267. Springer (2023). https://doi.org/10.1007/978-3-031-35257-7_15
16. Lopez, D.M., Choi, S.W., Tran, H.D., Johnson, T.T.: NNV 2.0: the neural network verification tool. In: International Conference on Computer Aided Verification, pp. 397–412. Springer (2023). https://doi.org/10.1007/978-3-031-37703-7_19
17. Lopez, D.M., Musau, P., Hamilton, N., Johnson, T.T.: Reachability analysis of a general class of neural ordinary differential equations (2022). https://doi.org/10.1007/978-3-031-15839-1_15
18. Lu, Y., Zhong, A., Li, Q., Dong, B.: Beyond finite layer neural networks: bridging deep architectures and numerical differential equations. In: International Conference on Machine Learning, pp. 3276–3285. PMLR (2018)
19. Makino, K., Berz, M.: Taylor models and other validated functional inclusion methods. Int. J. Pure Appl. Math. **6**, 239–316 (2003)
20. Marion, P.: Generalization bounds for neural ordinary differential equations and deep residual networks. Adv. Neural. Inf. Process. Syst. **36**, 48918–48938 (2023)
21. Marion, P., Wu, Y.H., Sander, M.E., Biau, G.: Implicit regularization of deep residual networks towards neural odes (2024). https://arxiv.org/abs/2309.01213
22. Musau, P., Johnson, T.: Continuous-time recurrent neural networks (CTRNNS)(benchmark proposal). In: 5th Applied Verification for Continuous and Hybrid Systems Workshop (ARCH), Oxford, UK (2018). https://doi.org/10.29007/6czp
23. Oh, Y., Kam, S., Lee, J., Lim, D.Y., Kim, S., Bui, A.: Comprehensive review of neural differential equations for time series analysis (2025). https://arxiv.org/abs/2502.09885
24. Rackauckas, C., et al.: Universal differential equations for scientific machine learning (2021). https://arxiv.org/abs/2001.04385
25. Rudin, W.: Principles of Mathematical Analysis, 3rd edn. McGraw-Hill, New York (1976)
26. Sander, M., Ablin, P., Peyré, G.: Do residual neural networks discretize neural ordinary differential equations? Adv. Neural. Inf. Process. Syst. **35**, 36520–36532 (2022)
27. Tabuada, P.: Verification and Control of Hybrid Systems: A Symbolic Approach. Springer Science & Business Media (2009). https://doi.org/10.1007/978-1-4419-0224-5

28. Tran, H.-D., et al.: NNV: the neural network verification tool for deep neural networks and learning-enabled cyber-physical systems. In: Lahiri, S.K., Wang, C. (eds.) CAV 2020. LNCS, vol. 12224, pp. 3–17. Springer, Cham (2020). https://doi.org/10.1007/978-3-030-53288-8_1
29. Xiang, W., Shao, Z.: Approximate bisimulation relations for neural networks and application to assured neural network compression. In: 2022 American Control Conference (ACC), pp. 3248–3253. IEEE (2022)

Probabilistic Verification of Neural Networks with Sampling-Based Probability Box Propagation

Marcel Chwiałkowski[1(✉)], Eric Goubault[2], and Sylvie Putot[2]

[1] École Polytechnique, Palaiseau, France
marcel.chwialkowski@polytechnique.edu
[2] LIX, École Polytechnique, CNRS, Institut Polytechnique de Paris, 91120 Palaiseau, France
{Goubault,Putot}@lix.polytechnique.fr

Abstract. In probabilistic neural network verification, a well-chosen representation of input uncertainty ensures that theoretical analyses accurately reflect real input perturbations. A recent approach based on probability boxes (p-boxes) [9] is introduced in [10] and unifies set-based and probabilistic information on the inputs. The method allows for obtaining guaranteed probabilistic bounds for property satisfaction on feedforward ReLU networks. However, it suffers from conservatism due to employing set-based propagation methods.

In this work we investigate how to sample from p-boxes without loss of information. Based on that, we develop a sampling-based approach for propagating p-boxes through feedforward ReLU networks. We prove that with dense enough coverings of the input p-boxes, the propagated samples accurately represent the output uncertainty and provide error bounds. Additionally, we show how to create coverings for arbitrary p-boxes with various distributions. On the ACAS Xu benchmark we demonstrate that our approach is applicable in practice, both as a standalone verifier and as a way to partially assess the conservatism of the set-based approach of [10].

Keywords: Probability boxes · Neural network verification

1 Introduction

Neural networks have been proven to be powerful tools in a wide range of applications, from image recognition to autonomous systems, making their reliability and correctness critical. Neural network verification focuses on ensuring safety of trained neural networks. Specifically, verification can consist of assessing the robustness of neural networks when faced with input uncertainties or adversarial attacks. The task of verifying a neural network can be approached deterministically or probabilistically. In the classical, deterministic approach, the goal is to determine if a safety property holds for a bounded input uncertainty or provide deterministic bounds for property violation (i.e. how much of a perturbation is guaranteed to not violate the property, or conversely). Examples of such approaches include the CROWN [28], FROWN [14], and CNN-Cert [4] frameworks. Approaches such as DeepZ [21], DeepPoly [22] and Verinet [12] propagate abstractions representing input uncertainty to verify if given properties hold.

On the other hand, probabilistic verification assumes random uncertainty at input, for example generated by random noise applied to the input, and aims to provide statistical estimates on output given the input uncertainty. Much less work has been done in this domain, but examples include [24,29] using it to assess network robustness and [1,2,13,18,27] probabilistically certifying correctness under adversarial attacks. Some works, including the PROVEN [25] framework also provide guaranteed statistical estimates, that is statements of form "the probability of X occurring is guaranteed to be between a and b". Probabilistic methods for networks with ReLU activations have also been developed in [17,19] [7]. A notable family of methods that facilitate estimating statistics of outputs is covariance propagation, with examples in [16,26].

The works mentioned above operate either in a set-based or probabilistic input setting. However, as mentioned in [10], this does not accurately reflect reality, as sometimes an input can be represented with more than one probabilistic model, or a probabilistic model might have uncertain parameters. With those considerations, a recent approach introduced in [10] uses inputs described by imprecise probabilities [3,23] which unify both set-based and probabilistic inputs. This approach allows for taking into account both epistemic and aleatoric uncertainty on inputs. One realisation of imprecise probabilities is the concept of a probability box (p-box) [9] - a set of cumulative distribution functions (CDF), bounded by a lower and an upper boundary CDF. Representing input uncertainty with a p-box permits the input value to come from any of these distributions.

Propagating p-boxes has been extensively studied in the context of differential equations - for example for ODEs, as in [6] and PDEs, as in [11]. Moreover, P-boxes can be transformed into Dempster-Shafer Interval structures (DSI) [9], their discrete over-approximations, and algorithms for arithmetic operations on DSI allow for propagating DSI through neural networks, as done in [10] for feedforward ReLU networks. However, this approach suffers from conservativeness, and the resulting DSI might be much less tight than in reality. To alleviate that, [10] introduces a new abstraction, Zonotopic Dempster-Schafer structures (DSZ), which generalise DSI and produce much tighter results when propagating through neural networks. The authors of [10] use their propagation algorithms for DSI and DSZ to provide guaranteed probabilistic bounds on the outputs of the neural network satisfying a safety property. While both the probabilistic bounds and resulting DSI/DSZ are robust, their quality, i.e. how tight they are with respect to reality, is difficult to fully assess.

In this work we develop and prove the validity of a systematic approach for propagating p-boxes through neural networks. Our method is based on sampling from dense-enough coverings of input p-boxes, passing the samples through the network and constructing output p-boxes or verifying safety properties. Dependent on parameters of our methods and the Lipschitz constant of the underlying neural network, we also provide accuracy bounds for our results. Our method is applicable also without knowledge of the Lipschitz constant or when the Lipschitz constant is large, but in these cases it lacks the accuracy bounds on the results. In the case of neural networks with inputs represented by parametric p-boxes, a particular class of p-boxes where the distributions they contain are explicitly parameterised, we are able to implement and demonstrate our approach on the ACAS Xu benchmark. We compare these results to the output p-box estimates produced by the DSZ propagation algorithm from [10], although the latter is not restricted to the parametric case.

Additionally, we demonstrate ways of constructing coverings of parametric and non-parametric p-boxes and prove error bounds for our method - that is, we show that any output which our method did not account for is sufficiently close to an output that our method produced. However, we chose not to report on sampling non-parametric p-boxes as, for now, the methods with guarantees we presented are of exponential complexity in the size of the p-boxes.

1.1 Notation

Throughout the paper, we adhere to the following notations:

- $\mathbf{X}, \mathbf{Y}$, etc. denote multi-dimensional random variables, while X, Y, etc. denote one-dimensional random variables. Samples corresponding to these variables are denoted as $\mathbf{x}$ and x, respectively.
- For each random variable X, F_X denotes its cumulative distribution function (CDF), given by $F_X(x) = \mathbb{P}(X \leq x)$.

2 Problem Statement

We consider a ReLU feedforward neural network f with n independent inputs and m outputs. Values fed to f belong to probabilistic input sets:

Definition 1 (Probabilistic input set). *For two cumulative distribution functions $\underline{F}$ and $\overline{F}$, a probabilistic input set is $\mathcal{X} = \{\mathbf{X} : \underline{F}(\mathbf{x}) \leq F_X(x) \leq \overline{F}(\mathbf{x}), \forall \mathbf{x}\}$. A value belongs to a probabilistic input set if it is a sample from one of the distributions within it.*

As the inputs to f are independent, considering one n-dimensional probabilistic input set $\mathcal{X}$ is equivalent to considering n marginal input sets $\mathcal{X}_1, \ldots \mathcal{X}_n$.

Probabilistic Output Sets. A probabilistic output set is defined as $\mathcal{Y} = \{\mathbf{Y} := f(\mathbf{X}) | \mathbf{X} \in \mathcal{X}\}$, and can also be expressed in terms of some boundary CDFs $\underline{F}$ and $\overline{F}$. Marginal output sets $\mathcal{Y}_i$ for $i \in [m]$ are defined as $\mathcal{Y}_i = \{\mathbf{Y}[i] := f(\mathbf{X})[i] | \mathbf{X} \in \mathcal{X}\}$. Given $\mathcal{Y}$, it is possible to derive $\mathcal{Y}_1, \ldots \mathcal{Y}_m$. However, since the outputs of f are not guaranteed to be independent, knowing $\mathcal{Y}_1 \ldots \mathcal{Y}_m$ alone is not sufficient to characterise $\mathcal{Y}$.

We solve the following problems:

P1 Find approximate marginal output sets $\hat{\mathcal{Y}}_1, \ldots \hat{\mathcal{Y}}_m$, such that for a given $\varepsilon > 0$, and $i \in [m]$, for any $Y \in \mathcal{Y}_i$ there exists $\hat{Y} \in \hat{\mathcal{Y}}_i$ s.t. $||F_Y - F_{\hat{Y}}||_1 \leq \varepsilon$,

P2 Approximate the probability bounds of an output vector **y** satisfying a linear safety property $A\mathbf{y} \leq v$.

The work of [10] solves variants of these problems using DSZ propagation - it finds an approximate output set $\hat{\mathcal{Y}}$, guaranteed to contain $\mathcal{Y}$. Similarly, it finds guaranteed probabilistic bounds of an output vector **y** satisfying a linear safety property.

Our contributions include a sampling-based method for solving these problems, which can be used either as a standalone verifier or to assess the conservativeness of the bounds derived by [10].

3 Preliminaries

Probabilistic input sets are represented by probability boxes.

Definition 2 (P-box [9]). *Let 2 cumulative distribution functions $\underline{F}, \overline{F}$ satisfy $\underline{F}(x) \leq \overline{F}(x)$ for every $x \in \mathbb{R}$. The probability box:*

$$\mathcal{X} = [\underline{F}, \overline{F}] := \{\underline{F} \leq F \leq \overline{F}\}$$

is the set of CDFs bounded below by $\underline{F}$ and above by $\overline{F}$. A random variable X belongs to $\mathcal{X}$ (written $X \in \mathcal{X}$) if and only if $F_X \in \mathcal{X}$.

Expressing Uncertainty. A p-box encodes a measurement that exhibits both aleatoric and epistemic uncertainty. The span of the p-box reflects epistemic uncertainty, while the shape of each admissible F represents aleatoric uncertainty.

Definition 3 (Parametric p-box). *Let $\{F_\theta\}_{\theta \in \Theta}$ be a distribution family with Θ_0 being the set of admissible parameters. Then $\mathcal{X} = \{F_\theta \mid \theta \in \Theta_0\}$ is a parametric p-box; for instance $\mathcal{N}(\mu \in [0,1], \sigma = 1)$ bounds every Gaussian with mean in $[0,1]$ and unit variance.*

A parametric p-box corresponds to a measurement with a parametrised epistemic uncertainty - for example, when the mean of the data is known to belong to an interval $[a,b]$, but the actual value is unknown.

3.1 Sampling from P-Boxes

We present a method for sampling values from p-boxes that allows for constructing p-boxes from data. For a p-box $\mathcal{X}$:

1. **Distribution selection** - A distribution $X \in \mathcal{X}$ is chosen,
2. **Sampling from the distribution** - s samples are drawn from X,
3. **Propagation** - For each sample x, $f(x)$ is calculated and the empirical distribution of $f(X) \in f(\mathcal{X})$ is calculated.

Repeating the process with different distribution selections $X_1, X_2, \ldots$ yields outputs $f(X_1), f(X_2), \ldots$ which can approximate the shape of $f(\mathcal{X})$.

It is desirable to pick distributions $X_1, X_2, \ldots X_i$ that approximate $\mathcal{X}$ well in order to lose as little information conveyed by $\mathcal{X}$ as possible. This is formalised by the concept of covering:

Definition 4 (Covering). *Let $\mathcal{X}$ be a p-box and ε a positive real number. A subset $\hat{\mathcal{X}} \subseteq \mathcal{X}$ is an ε-covering of $\mathcal{X}$ if for any $X \in \mathcal{X}$ there exists $\hat{X} \in \hat{\mathcal{X}}$ such that $\|F_X - F_{\hat{X}}\|_1 \leq \varepsilon$.*

Given a covering $\hat{\mathcal{X}}$ of $\mathcal{X}$ we can rerun the sampling process, each time choosing a different distribution from $\hat{\mathcal{X}}$ to sample from distributions representing the overall shape of the input.

3.2 General Sampling-Based P-Box Propagation

Sampling from multivariate probabilistic input set is similar. We are interested specifically in finite coverings - Algorithm 1 defines a procedure that can be used to solve problems **P1** and **P2** given finite coverings of the input p-boxes $\hat{\mathcal{X}}_1, \ldots \hat{\mathcal{X}}_n$. The correctness of algorithm 1 and the ε constant of the coverings that it creates are specified in the next section.

Algorithm 1: Sampling-based p-box propagation

---
1 Input: finite coverings of the input p-boxes, $\hat{\mathcal{X}}_1, \ldots \hat{\mathcal{X}}_n$
2 Output: finite coverings of the output p-boxes $\hat{\mathcal{Y}}_1 \ldots \hat{\mathcal{Y}}_m$
3 **foreach** $\mathbf{X} := (X_1, \ldots X_n)$ s.t. $X_1 \in \hat{\mathcal{X}}_1, \ldots X_n \in \hat{\mathcal{X}}_n$ **do**
4   **for** $j \leftarrow 1$ **to** s **do**
5   Draw $\mathbf{x_{i,j}} \sim \mathbf{X}_i$
6          $\mathbf{y_{i,j}} \leftarrow f(\mathbf{x}_{i,j})$;
7      $\hat{\mathbf{Y}}_i \leftarrow$ Empirical Distribution$(\mathbf{y}_{i,1}, \ldots \mathbf{y}_{i,s})$
8   Calculate the marginals of $\hat{\mathbf{Y}}_i$, i.e. $\hat{Y}_i^1, \ldots \hat{Y}_i^m$
9   **for** $j \leftarrow 1$ **to** m **do**
10         $\hat{\mathcal{Y}}_j \leftarrow \hat{Y}_i^j$
11 **return** $\{\hat{\mathcal{Y}}_1, \ldots \hat{\mathcal{Y}}_m\}$

Complexity. Algorithm 1 propagates $\prod_{i=1}^{n} |\hat{\mathcal{X}}_i|$ distributions through the network. When propagating a single distribution, s inputs vectors are passed forward and m marginal distributions are built from the outputs. We assume that passing forward an input vector takes constant time, thus the cost associated to sample propagation is $O(s)$. Building a single marginal output distribution takes $O(s \log s)$, as it requires sorting all samples with respect to one of the coordinates. As m distributions need to be built, and each time the sorting is done over a different coordinate, building m marginal output distributions takes $O(ms \log s)$. Overall, propagating a single distributions costs $O(ms \log s)$, so the complexity of Algorithm 1 is $O(ms \log s E^n)$, where $E = \sup_{i \in [n]} |\hat{\mathcal{X}}_i|$.

4 Main Theoretical Result

We show that for Lipschitz continuous neural networks, Algorithm 1 yields sets of distributions $\hat{\mathcal{Y}}_1, \ldots \hat{\mathcal{Y}}_m$ which form coverings of the marginal output sets $\mathcal{Y}_1, \ldots \mathcal{Y}_m$ and we quantify the precision of these coverings.

Theorem 1. *Given a neural network f with n independent inputs, m outputs, an $||\cdot||_1$-norm Lipschitz constant of at most L and ε-coverings for each input, Algorithm 1 produces a $nL\varepsilon$-covering of each marginal output set.*

Below we introduce Wasserstein distance which allows for passing random variables through Lipschitz continuous functions:

Definition 5 (Wasserstein Distance). *Wasserstein-k distance for $k \in \mathbb{N}$ between two random variables $\mathbf{P}$ and $\mathbf{Q}$ is defined as:*

$$W_k(P, Q) = \inf_{\gamma \in \Pi(P,Q)} (\mathbb{E}_{(\mathbf{x},\mathbf{y}) \sim \gamma}[d(\mathbf{x}, \mathbf{y})^k])^{\frac{1}{k}}$$

where d is a distance and Π is the set of all couplings between $\mathbf{P}$ and $\mathbf{Q}$. For one-dimensional distributions P and Q it holds that:

$$W_1(P, Q) = ||F_P - F_Q||_1$$

We state properties of the Wasserstein distance relevant to our problem, with proofs given in the appendix.

Lemma 1 (Subadditivity of Wasserstein distance). *For 2 n-dimensional random vectors $\mathbf{X} := (X_1, X_2, \ldots X_n)$ and $\mathbf{Y} := (Y_1, Y_2, \ldots Y_n)$ equipped with the $||\cdot||_1$ norm it holds that:*

$$W_1(\mathbf{X}, \mathbf{Y}) \leq W_1(X_1, Y_1) + W_1\left(\begin{pmatrix} X_2 \\ \vdots \\ X_n \end{pmatrix}, \begin{pmatrix} Y_2 \\ \vdots \\ Y_n \end{pmatrix}\right)$$

Lemma 2 (Projection of Wasserstein distance). *For 2 n-dimensional random vectors $\mathbf{X} = (X_1, X_2 \ldots X_n)$ and $\mathbf{Y} = (Y_1, Y_2 \ldots Y_n)$ equipped with the $||\cdot||_1$ norm it holds that:*

$$W_1(X_1, Y_1) \leq W_1(\mathbf{X}, \mathbf{Y})$$

Lemma 3 (Passing Wasserstein-1 distance through Lipschitz functions). *For a Lipschitz function f with a $||\cdot||_1$-norm Lipschitz constant of at most L and 2 random vectors $\mathbf{X}$ and $\mathbf{Y}$ it holds that:*

$$W_1(f(\mathbf{X}), f(\mathbf{Y})) \leq L W_1(\mathbf{X}, \mathbf{Y})$$

We prove our main result, Theorem 1:

Proof. Let $\mathcal{X}_1, \mathcal{X}_2 \ldots \mathcal{X}_n$ denote the input p-boxes and $\hat{\mathcal{X}}_1, \hat{\mathcal{X}}_2 \ldots \hat{\mathcal{X}}_n$ their ε-coverings. Consider n random variables $X_1, \ldots X_n$ with their CDFs $F_1, \ldots F_n$ in the respective input p-boxes. By definition of a covering, there exist $\hat{X}_1, \hat{X}_2 \ldots \hat{X}_n$ with CDFs $\hat{F}_1 \in \hat{\mathcal{X}}_1, \hat{F}_2 \in \hat{\mathcal{X}}_2 \ldots \hat{F}_n \in \hat{\mathcal{X}}_n$, such that for each $i \in [n]$, $||F_i - \hat{F}_i||_1 \leq \varepsilon$.

We estimate the Wasserstein-1 distance between $\mathbf{X} := (X_1, X_2, \ldots X_n)$ and $\hat{\mathbf{X}} := (\hat{X}_1, \hat{X}_2, \ldots \hat{X}_n)$. Applying Lemma 1 n times with the fact that in one dimension, the Wasserstein distance is equivalent to the $||\cdot||_1$ distance between CDFs we can write:

$$W_1(\mathbf{X}, \hat{\mathbf{X}}) \leq \sum_{i=1}^{n} W_1(X_i, \hat{X}_i) \leq n\varepsilon$$

Using the fact that f is Lipschitz and Lemma 2 we have:

$$W_1(f(\mathbf{X}), f(\hat{\mathbf{X}})) \leq L W_1(\mathbf{X}, \hat{\mathbf{X}})$$

We write $(Y_1, \ldots Y_m) = \mathbf{Y} = f(\mathbf{X})$ and $(\hat{Y}_1, \ldots \hat{Y}_m) = \hat{\mathbf{Y}} = f(\hat{\mathbf{X}})$. Applying Lemma 3 for each $i \in [m]$ we obtain:

$$W_1(Y_i, \hat{Y}_i) \leq W_1(\mathbf{Y}, \hat{\mathbf{Y}})$$

The whole approximation gives us:

$$W_1(Y_i, \hat{Y}_i) \leq nL\varepsilon$$

Since Y_i and $\hat{Y}_i$ are one-dimensional, the Wasserstein-1 distance is the $||\cdot||_1$ distance between the CDFs. This shows that $\hat{\mathcal{Y}}_i$ forms a $nL\varepsilon$-covering of $\mathcal{Y}_i$. □

5 Practical Considerations

This section explains how we implement a solution utilising Algorithm 1.

5.1 Bounding the Lipschitz Constant of f

Calculating the exact Lipschitz constant of a neural network is NP-hard [20]. We use the LipSDP software introduced in [8] which estimates the upper bound of the Lipschitz constant for f. The Lipschitz constant returned by LipSDP is in $||\cdot||_2$ norm and we find the bound for the Lipschitz constant in $||\cdot||_1$ using the inequality between power means.

5.2 Inaccuracy of Empirical CDFs

We briefly describe how output CDFs are approximated with ECDFs and provide an accuracy bound when the input distributions have bounded supports.

Definition 6 (Empirical cumulative distribution function). *Let X be a random variable and let $x^{(1)}, \ldots, x^{(s)} \sim X$ be s i.i.d. samples. The empirical CDF (ECDF) of X based on these samples is:*

$$\widehat{F}_{X,s}(t) := \frac{1}{s} \sum_{k=1}^{s} \mathbf{1}\{x^{(k)} \leq t\}, \qquad t \in \mathbb{R},$$

In Algorithm 1, instead of first constructing the $\widehat{F}_{\mathbf{Y},s}$ and then considering its marginals, we construct the empirical marginal distributions $F_{Y_i,s}$ straight away from the samples.

Error Bound. The strong law of large numbers implies that as the number of samples approaches infinity, the empirical distribution of a variable almost surely approaches the true value of the distribution. Due to Glivenko-Cantelli theorem, the convergence is uniform. The Dworetzky-Kiefer-Wolfowitz inequality allows us to estimate the error between an ECDF and a CDF given the number of samples:

Theorem 2 (Dworetzky-Kiefer-Wolfowitz inequality). *For an empirical distribution function from n samples $F_{X,n}$ and a CDF F_X, it holds for any $\varepsilon > 0$ that:*

$$\mathbb{P}\left(\sup_{x \in \mathbb{R}} |F_{X,n}(x) - F_X(x)| \geq \varepsilon\right) \leq C e^{-2n\varepsilon^2}$$

where C is a constant ([15] proves that the inequality holds for $C = 2$).

Incorporating DKW into the Result of Theorem. 1 If all input p-boxes have bounded support, the following result holds:

Theorem 3. *Consider a neural network f with n independent inputs, m outputs, an $||\cdot||_1$-norm Lipschitz constant of at most L, and ε-coverings for each input. Given that the marginal output sets have bounded support, for each $i \in [m]$ denoted by $[a_i, b_i]$, then with a probability of at least $1 - 2e^{-2s\varepsilon'^2}$ for any $\varepsilon' > 0$, Algorithm 1 produces $nL\varepsilon + (b_i - a_i)\varepsilon'$ coverings of each marginal output set.*

The Case of Unbounded Support. If some of the input p-boxes have unbounded support, the above does not hold. However, DKW can be used to derive additional guarantees in $||\cdot||_\infty$.

6 Constructing Coverings of P-Boxes

To perform Algorithm 1, finite ε-coverings of each input p-box are required. We present two approaches to constructing coverings:

Step-Function Coverings. As step functions are dense in $L_1(\mathbb{R})$, it is possible to use them to construct coverings of p-boxes. To generate a covering of $\mathcal{X}$ consisting of staircase functions, we overlay a grid with rectangles of size $x \times y$ onto $\mathcal{X}$, and enumerate all staircase functions which turn only at the points of the grid and are entirely contained within $\mathcal{X}$. This approach may not produce a covering if the bounding distributions of $\mathcal{X}$ have heavy tails - however, in appendix B we show that posing a restriction on the tails is sufficient for this procedure to generate a covering with $\varepsilon := x + y$.

Coverings for Parametric P-Boxes. When a p-box is defined by a parameter range within a known distribution family, in order to construct a covering it usually suffices to consider a set of distributions from this family with varied parameters. For example, consider the parametric p-box:

$$\mathcal{X} = \left\{ N(\mu, \sigma^2) \,\middle|\, \mu \in [\mu_1, \mu_2] \right\}$$

with fixed σ. Choosing $n+1$ distributions with equidistant means $\mu_i = \mu_1 + i\Delta$ with $\Delta = (\mu_2 - \mu_1)/n$ yields a covering $\{N(\mu_i, \sigma^2)\}$ that forms a $(\Delta/2)$-covering. This strategy was used in our experiments, where it provides a tight and scalable approximation of the full p-box.

These constructions offer a trade-off between generality and efficiency: step-function coverings are applicable for arbitrary p-boxes with some restrictions on the tails but are poorly scalable due to combinatorial explosion - we were unable to generate step-function coverings with a precision high enough to be used in our experiments. Parametric coverings are easy to generate and scale well with precision, but they convey less information. In our experiments we only consider parametric p-boxes and parametric coverings due to the scalability advantage.

7 Property Verification

In this section we show how to estimate the probability of safety property satisfaction. We bound the probability of an output $\mathbf{y}$ satisfying a safety property P: $A\mathbf{y} < v$ for some matrix A and a vector v.

Guaranteed Probabilistic Bounds. Given a probabilistic output set $\mathcal{Y}$, the guaranteed probabilistic bounds for P are defined as an interval $[lb, ub]$ where:

$$lb = \inf_{\mathbf{Y} \in \mathcal{Y}} \left(\mathbb{P}(A\mathbf{y} < v | \mathbf{y} \sim \mathbf{Y}) \right)$$
$$ub = \sup_{\mathbf{Y} \in \mathcal{Y}} \left(\mathbb{P}(A\mathbf{y} < v | \mathbf{y} \sim \mathbf{Y}) \right)$$

Estimating Probabilistic Bounds. By running Algorithm 1, we obtain sets of samples from output vectors $\mathbf{Y}_1, \mathbf{Y}_2, \ldots$ For a single random vector $\mathbf{Y}$, the probability of it satisfying P is estimated by:

$$\mathbb{P}(A\mathbf{y} < v | \mathbf{y} \sim \mathbf{Y}) \sim \frac{\text{number of samples from } \mathbf{Y} \text{ that satisfy } P}{s}$$

Aggregating these estimates for the output vectors $\mathbf{Y}_1, \mathbf{Y}_2, \ldots$ we obtain approximate probability bounds for satisfying P.

We obtain only approximate probability bounds because of the following:

1. *Approximation error of empirical distributions.* Determining the probability of $\mathbf{Y}$ satisfying P is equivalent to estimating the CDF of $A\mathbf{Y}$ at v. Effectively, we calculate the ECDF of $A\mathbf{Y}$ at v, and the approximation error of the ECDF can be estimated with Multivariate DKW inequality:

Theorem 4. *For a m-dimensional empirical distribution function from s samples $F_{s,\mathbf{X}}$ and a true CDF $F_\mathbf{X}$, it holds for any $\varepsilon > 0$ that:*

$$\mathbb{P}(\sup_{\theta \in \mathbb{R}^m} |F_{s,\mathbf{X}}(\theta) - F_\mathbf{X}(\theta)| > \varepsilon) \leq m(s+1)e^{-2s\varepsilon^2}$$

2. *Not considering a covering of the whole output space in $||\cdot||_\infty$* If we had a set of vectors $\hat{\mathcal{Y}}$ which formed a covering of $\mathcal{Y}$ in $||\cdot||_\infty$, then for an output vector $\mathbf{Y}$ there would exist $\hat{\mathbf{Y}} \in \hat{\mathcal{Y}}$ such that $||F_{\hat{\mathbf{Y}}} - F_\mathbf{Y}||_\infty < \varepsilon$. Specifically, this would allow us to explicitly derive the maximal difference between $\mathbb{P}(A\mathbf{y} < v | \mathbf{y} \sim \mathbf{Y})$ and $\mathbb{P}(A\hat{\mathbf{y}} < v | \mathbf{y} \sim \hat{\mathbf{Y}})$. However, since the vectors output by Algorithm 1 are not guaranteed to form a covering of $\mathcal{Y}$ in $||\cdot||_\infty$, it is possible that there exists an output vector $\mathbf{Y}$, for which the probability of satisfying P lies outside of the property satisfaction bounds that we derived.

Due to the points above, the property satisfaction bounds that we provide in the experiments section are estimates and not guaranteed probabilistic bounds.

8 Experiments

Toy Example. We consider a neural network f:

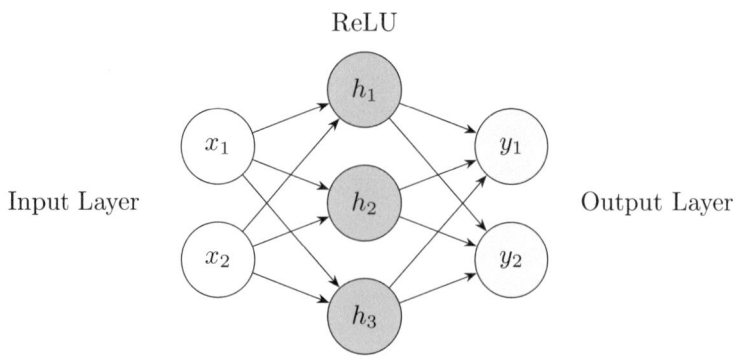

with weights given by $W_1 = \begin{bmatrix} 1.0 & -1.0 \\ 1.0 & 1.0 \\ -1.0 & 2.0 \end{bmatrix}$, $b_1 = \begin{bmatrix} 0.0 \\ 0.0 \\ 0.0 \end{bmatrix}$, $W_2 = \begin{bmatrix} 1.0 & -1.0 & 1.0 \\ 1.0 & -1.0 & 2.0 \end{bmatrix}$, $b_2 = \begin{bmatrix} 0.0 \\ 0.0 \end{bmatrix}$. Both inputs are parametric p-boxes of Gaussians with uncertain mean: $N(\mu \in [0,1], \sigma = 1)$. We generate 0.005-coverings for each input. The Lipschitz constant is bounded from above by 7.07. Running Algorithm 1 with $s = 1000$ samples we obtain 0.07-coverings of the marginal output sets. Figure shows how these coverings compare to the p-boxes obtained with the first method from [10], DSI propagation. However, the software from [10] treats all p-boxes non-parametrically, which can cause some of the discrepancy between the results.

As Gaussian distributions have unbounded supports, Theorem 3 is inapplicable here. However, DKW inequality implies that with a probability of at least 0.9, each empirical distribution is at most 0.001 away from the true distribution in terms of $||\cdot||_\infty$ (Fig. 1).

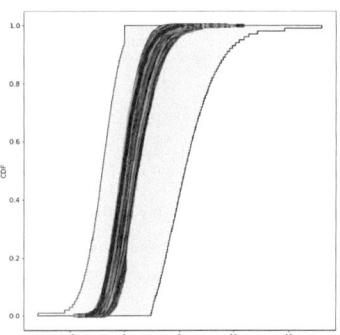 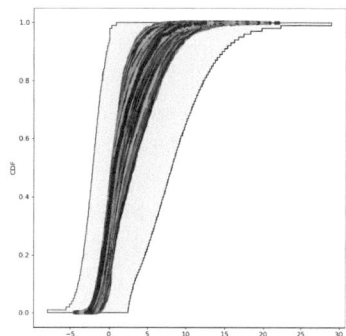

Fig. 1. Output coverings produced by Algorithm 1 (colorful), compared with output p-boxes produced by DSI propagation (grey). The left figure shows the results for the first dimension of the output, the right one those for the second dimension. (Color figure online)

8.1 ACAS Xu

We reproduce the property verification for the ACAS Xu example done in [10]. ACAS Xu is a set of 46 networks, each with 5 inputs and 5 outputs. As the complexity of Algorithm 1 is exponential with respect to the input size, $n = 5$ limits the covering precision that we can achieve in this experiment. The ACAS Xu networks' Lipschitz constant (L) estimates obtained by LipSPD are of order 10^4. This prevents us from providing an accurate theoretical guarantee on our results - the accuracy of the output coverings depend on the value of L and the accuracy of the input coverings, both of which are limited. Therefore, there can exist output distributions far away in terms of the $||\cdot||_1$ distance from any output distribution obtained by algorithm 1. However, LipSPD calculates L without taking into account input constraints, and the points which force L to be large can be very few. This lets us hypothesise that choosing a method of approximating L that incorporates the local input constraints can yield a lower value of L. Thus, we conduct the experiment regardless of the lack of theoretical guarantee on the results.

The exponential complexity of Algorithm 1 forces us to represent input uncertainty with parametric p-boxes, as the covering sizes of non-parametric p-boxes are too large.

Setting. Inputs to each ACAS Xu network are parametrised by 2 vectors, ub and lb. Initially, each scalar input is a Gaussian with mean $\mu_i = (ub[i] + lb[i])/2$ and standard deviation $\sigma_i = (ub[i] - \mu_i)/3$. Uncertainty is added by representing each input as a Gaussian parametric p-box defined by $N(\mu \in [\mu_i - 0.001 \cdot r[i], \mu_i + 0.001 \cdot r[i]], \sigma = \sigma_i)$ with $r[i] = ub[i] - lb[i]$. We generate 0.00005-coverings for each input. We remark that despite having the same precision, these coverings are of drastically different sizes - respectively, for each input, 3, 21, 21, 2, 2. This gives us an approximate cost of running Algorithm 1 with $s = 1000$ samples at $3 \times 21 \times 21 \times 2 \times 2 \times 1000 \times C = 5292000C = 5 \times 10^6 C$, where C is the cost of passing a single sample through the network. For speeding-up, Algorithm 1 can be parallelised as subsequent iterations of the main loop are independent of each other.

We verify a safety property considered by [10] - $P_2 : y_1 > y_2 \wedge y_1 > y_3 \wedge y_1 > y_4 \wedge y_1 > y_5$ on a number of networks in ACAS Xu. We also recreate this experiment with input p-boxes of the same shape with the software from [10] and compare the results in Table 1.

A single run of Algorithm 1 with 12 threads on an ACAS Xu network on an Apple M3 Pro chip terminates in under one minute. DSZ propagation terminates in around one minute as well.

Results. In each case, the probabilistic bounds obtained via B are tighter than in A. In certain cases, the difference is larger than one order of magnitude. However, this is not only due to the conservatism of A, as discussed in the next paragraph.

Differences Between the Experiments. Table 2 shows the differences between the setting of experiments A and B. The first difference can be resolved by setting a high discretization factor in A and propagating more samples in B, however we were neither able to quantify nor to alleviate the rest.

9 Future Work

We highlight below the important directions for future work:

Table 1. Probability bounds for the ACAS Xu example.

Prop	Net	DSZ propagation from [10] Experiment A $\mathbb{P}$	Empirical property verification Experiment B $\mathbb{P}$
2	1–6	[0, 0.03]	[0, 0.001]
2	2–2	[0, 0.09]	[0.022, 0.054]
2	2–9	[0, 0.09]	[0, 0.007]
2	3–1	[0.010, 0.102]	[0.029, 0.066]
2	3–6	[0.013, 0.141]	[0.018, 0.058]
2	3–7	[0, 0.176]	[0, 0.014]
2	4–1	[0, 0.071]	[0, 0.010]
2	4–7	[0.006, 0.136]	[0.028, 0.062]
2	5–3	[0, 0.051]	[0, 0.001]

Table 2. Comparison between experiments A and B.

#	A	B
1	Precision depends on the input discretization	Precision depends on the number of samples propagated
2	Considers non-parametric p-boxes	Considers parametric p-boxes (potential loss of information)
3	The probabilistic bounds can be too broad due to conservativeness	The probabilistic bounds can be too tight, as extremal distributions might not have been sampled.

1. *Lipschitz constant approximation.* As shown in the ACAS Xu example, the Lipschitz constant estimate provided by LipSDP can be large enough to prevent us from guaranteeing the correctness of the results with Theorem 1. Future work should explore different methods for estimating the Lipschitz constant that incorporate the input constraints.
2. *Relaxations to the theory.* The assumption that the inputs to f are independent rarely holds in reality and lifting it is an important next step.
3. *Parametric vs non-parametric P-boxes.* The approach in [10] could be modified to handle the restriction to parametric p-boxes, as an alternative to designing tractable non-parametric coverings.
4. $||\cdot||_\infty$ *instead of* $||\cdot||_1$. Reproducing Theorem 1 with the infinity norm would allow for integrating DKW into the main result without assumptions on the support. Moreover, in the context of property verification, obtaining a covering of the whole output space in $||\cdot||_\infty$ would allow for providing property satisfaction probabilities with guaranteed error bounds, as explained in Sect. 7.
5. *Coverings using Gaussian mixture distributions.* As shown in [5], Gaussian mixtures can approximate arbitrary probability densities - for any PDF $f \in L_2(\mathbb{R})$ and $\varepsilon > 0$, there exists a Gaussian mixture $\hat{f}$ such that:

$$||\hat{f} - f||_2 \leq \varepsilon$$

A promising direction for future extensions is extending this to obtain a result for approximating arbitrary CDFs with CDFs of Gaussian mixtures, and based on it find a method for constructing coverings with Gaussian mixtures.

6. *Reducing the complexity of Algorithm 1.* For a probability box delimited by $\underline{F}$ and $\overline{F}$, distributions close to $\underline{F}$ and $\overline{F}$ carry more information on the shape of the p-box. In our case, being able to predict which input vectors $\mathbf{X}$ after propagation produce vectors $f(\mathbf{X})$ which are close to the boundaries of the output sets would let us reduce the number of vectors that we propagate. Namely, we would only need to propagate these vectors, as the others would not provide additional information. For a random variable, checking whether after propagation it generates an extremal distribution can be heuristically approximated by its expected value - namely, distributions with lower mean tend to be closer to $\overline{F}$, and conversely. To give an example, in our setting, given that the input vectors are parametric, finding an input vector that is likely to produce an extremal distribution on the first output of f is done by solving:

$$\underset{\mathbf{X}=(X_i \sim F_{\theta_i}),\ (Y_1,...Y_m):=\mathbf{Y} \sim f(\mathbf{X})}{argmin} \mathbb{E}(Y_1)$$

for the parameters $\theta_1, \ldots \theta_n$. Given a polynomial approximation P of f this can be rewritten as:

$$\underset{\mathbf{X}=(X_i \sim F_{\theta_i}),\ (Y_1,...Y_m):=\mathbf{Y} \sim P(\mathbf{X})}{argmin} \mathbb{E}(Y_1)$$

If the distributions that we are considering are Gaussian mixtures and P is of order 1, this is reduced to a linear programming problem. However, for polynomials of higher order and for different distributions, this is a non-trivial problem.

10 Conclusions

To the best of our knowledge, this work is the first study to analyse how to sample from p-box representations and build a verification algorithm around it. Moreover, it provides methods for generating coverings of p-boxes to be used in Algorithm 1. However, due to its exponential complexity, Algorithm 1 has certain limitations - considering neural networks with non-parametric p-boxes as inputs is currently completely intractable, as is running the algorithm on neural networks with larger input dimensions. With the propositions listed in the future work section, we hope to adapt it to more general input settings, derive guaranteed bounds for property satisfaction and lower the complexity to allow treating larger neural networks.

Acknowledgments. This work was partially supported by the SAIF project, funded by the France 2030 government investment plan managed by the French National Research Agency, under the reference ANR-23-PEIA-0006, and by the 2021 project FARO, funded by Agence de l'Innovation de Défense AID through the Centre Interdisciplinaire d'Etudes pour la Défense et la Sécurité CIEDS.

A Proofs of Theorems

Proof (of lemma 1). We write:

$$W_1(\mathbf{X}, \mathbf{Y}) = \inf_{\gamma \in \Pi} \mathbb{E}\, d\left(\begin{pmatrix} x_1 \\ x_2 \\ \vdots \\ x_n \end{pmatrix}, \begin{pmatrix} y_1 \\ y_2 \\ \vdots \\ y_n \end{pmatrix}\right)$$

Consider the optimal couplings between X_1 and Y_1 and between $(X_2, \ldots X_n)$ and $(Y_2, \ldots Y_n)$: γ_1 and γ_2. Then $\gamma = \gamma_1 \gamma_2$ is a coupling between all the variables and we have:

$$\mathbb{E}_\gamma\, d\left(\begin{pmatrix} x_1 \\ x_2 \\ \vdots \\ x_n \end{pmatrix}, \begin{pmatrix} y_1 \\ y_2 \\ \vdots \\ y_n \end{pmatrix}\right)$$

$$= \mathbb{E}_\gamma \left(d(x_1, y_1) + d\left(\begin{pmatrix} x_2 \\ \vdots \\ x_n \end{pmatrix}, \begin{pmatrix} y_2 \\ \vdots \\ y_n \end{pmatrix}\right)\right)$$

$$= \mathbb{E}_{\gamma_1} d(x_1, y_1) + \mathbb{E}_{\gamma_2} d\left(\begin{pmatrix} x_2 \\ \vdots \\ x_n \end{pmatrix}, \begin{pmatrix} y_2 \\ \vdots \\ y_n \end{pmatrix}\right)$$

As γ is some coupling, not necessarily optimal, we have:

$$W_1(\mathbf{X}, \mathbf{Y}) \leq W_1(X_1, Y_1) + W_1\left(\begin{pmatrix} X_2 \\ \vdots \\ X_n \end{pmatrix}, \begin{pmatrix} X_2 \\ \vdots \\ X_n \end{pmatrix}\right)$$

□

Proof (of lemma 2). Observe that for a given coupling γ we have:

$$\mathbb{E}_\gamma \, d\left(\begin{pmatrix} x_1 \\ x_2 \\ \vdots \\ x_n \end{pmatrix}, \begin{pmatrix} y_1 \\ y_2 \\ \vdots \\ y_n \end{pmatrix}\right)$$

$$= \mathbb{E}_\gamma \left(d(x_1, y_1) + d\left(\begin{pmatrix} x_2 \\ \vdots \\ x_n \end{pmatrix}, \begin{pmatrix} y_2 \\ \vdots \\ y_n \end{pmatrix}\right) \right)$$

$$= \mathbb{E}_\gamma d(x_1, y_1) + \mathbb{E}_\gamma d\left(\begin{pmatrix} x_2 \\ \vdots \\ x_n \end{pmatrix}, \begin{pmatrix} y_2 \\ \vdots \\ y_n \end{pmatrix}\right)$$

Therefore:

$$\mathbb{E}_\gamma \, d\left(\begin{pmatrix} x_1 \\ x_2 \\ \vdots \\ x_n \end{pmatrix}, \begin{pmatrix} y_1 \\ y_2 \\ \vdots \\ y_n \end{pmatrix}\right) \geq \mathbb{E}_\gamma d(x_1, y_1)$$

Taking the infimum over all couplings between (X_1, Y_1) and $(X_2, \ldots X_n), (Y_2, \ldots Y_n)$ we get the desired result. It is important to remark that all couplings γ cover all the possible couplings between X_1 and Y_1. This is not difficult, as for any such coupling γ_1, a coupling γ_2 between $(X_2, \ldots X_n)$ and $(Y_2 \ldots Y_n)$ (independent of γ_1) can be considered and then $\gamma = \gamma_1 \gamma_2$ is a valid coupling between (X_1, Y_1) and $(X_2, \ldots X_n), (Y_2, \ldots Y_n)$. □

Proof (of lemma 3). For a coupling γ between $\mathbf{X}$ and $\mathbf{Y}$ and $\mathbf{x}, \mathbf{y} \sim \gamma$ we have:

$$||f(\mathbf{x}) - f(\mathbf{y})|| \leq L||\mathbf{x} - \mathbf{y}||$$

Therefore:

$$\mathbb{E}_{\mathbf{x},\mathbf{y}\sim\gamma}||f(\mathbf{x}) - f(\mathbf{y})|| \leq L\mathbb{E}_{\mathbf{x},\mathbf{y}\sim\gamma}||\mathbf{x} - \mathbf{y}||$$

Since this holds for any coupling, we can take the infimum and obtain:

$$W_1(f(\mathbf{X}), f(\mathbf{Y})) \leq L W_1(\mathbf{X}, \mathbf{Y})$$

□

Proof (of theorem 3). Theorem 1 yields a covering result on true CDFs - i.e. for a single output with the constrained probabilistic output set on this output having a compact support $[a, b]$, any output CDF F is at most $nL\varepsilon$ away in terms of $||\cdot||_1$ from an output CDF $\hat{F}$ belonging to the propagated input covering. When propagating empirically, instead of $\hat{F}$ we have an empirical distribution $\hat{F}_s$ estimating $\hat{F}$. By Hölder's inequality, on the interval $[a, b]$ it holds that:

$$||\hat{F}_s - \hat{F}||_1 \leq (b - a)||\hat{F}_n - \hat{F}||_\infty$$

By DKW, for any $\varepsilon' \geq 0$ it holds that:

$$\mathbb{P}\left(||\hat{F}_s - \hat{F}||_1 \geq (b-a)\varepsilon'\right) \leq 2e^{-2s\varepsilon'^2}$$

Therefore, with a probability of at least $1 - 2e^{-2s\varepsilon'^2}$, it holds that:

$$||\hat{F}_s - F||_1 \leq \varepsilon + (b-a)\varepsilon'$$

Deriving this on each output dimension gives us the desired result. □

B Precision of Covering a P-Box with Staircase Functions on a Grid

We present the method of generating a covering of a p-box with staircase functions on a grid and quantify its precision. Consider a p-box $\mathcal{X}$ bounded by $\underline{F}$ and $\overline{F}$, such that for some $x_l \in \mathbb{R}$ $\int_{-\infty}^{x_l} \overline{F}(t)dt$ is close to 0 and for some $x_r \in \mathbb{R}$, $\int_{x_r}^{\infty}(1 - \underline{F}(t))dt$ is close to 0. Let G be a grid of points in $\mathbb{R}^2$, with rectangles of size $x \times y$ for some $x, y \in \mathbb{R}$ - that is, $G = \{(a,b) | \exists n, m \in \mathbb{Z} : a = mx, b = ny, x_l \leq a \leq x_r, 0 \leq b \leq 1\}$. We show that the set $\hat{\mathcal{X}}$ of staircase functions that turn only on points belonging to G and are entirely contained within $\mathcal{X}$ is a covering of $\mathcal{X}$.

The assumption on the tails of $\underline{F}$ and $\overline{F}$ allows us to disregard everything outside of $[x_l, x_r]$ - all the functions in $\hat{\mathcal{X}}$ are identically zero before x_l and identically one after x_r. Therefore, given $\mathbf{X} \in \mathcal{X}$ and $\hat{\mathbf{X}} \in \hat{\mathcal{X}}$, the distance between $F_{\mathbf{X}}$ and $F_{\hat{\mathbf{X}}}$ on $(-\infty, x_l) \cup (x_r, \infty)$ is at most $\int_{-\infty}^{x_l} \overline{F}(t)dt + \int_{x_r}^{\infty}(1 - \underline{F}(t))dt$.

We prove an auxilliary statement:

Theorem 5. *The set of all staircase functions that turn only on points belonging to G is a ε-covering of the set of all CDFs defined on $[x_l, x_r]$, and $\varepsilon = O(x+y)$.*

Proof. Consider an arbitrary CDF F defined on $[x_l, x_r]$. For simplicity, we denote $a_0 := x_l, a_1 := x_l + x, \ldots a_m := x_l + mx$. We approximate it with a staircase function F_1 defined as:

$$F_1(t) = \begin{cases} F(a_i), & \text{if } t \in [a_i, a_{i+1}) \text{ for each } i \in 0, \ldots m-1 \\ F(a_m) & \text{if } t = a_m \end{cases}$$

Since F is an increasing functions, we can bound the $||\cdot||_1$ difference between F and F_1 on each interval $[a_i, a_{i+1}]$ - namely, for each $i \in 0, \ldots m-1$:

$$\int_{a_i}^{a_{i+1}} |F_1(t) - F(t)|dt \leq \int_{a_i}^{a_{i+1}} |F(a_i) - F(a_{i+1})|dt = x(F(a_{i+1}) - F(a_i))$$

Summing those differences up, we get:

$$\int_{a_0}^{a_m} |F_1(t) - F(t)| dt \leq x \sum_{i=0}^{m-1} F(a_{i+1}) - F(a_i) \leq x$$

Now, we approximate F_1 with a staircase function F_2 going only on the grid. Define a function round(t), that rounds a value in $[0, 1]$ to the closest mutliple of y, rounding down if it is halfway between 2 values. Then, F_2 is defined as:

$$F_2(t) = \text{round}(F_1(t))$$

By definition of the round function, we have that for any $t \in [x_l, x_r]$, $|F_2(t) - F_1(t)| \leq \frac{y}{2}$. Therefore:

$$||F_2 - F_1||_1 \leq \frac{y(x_r - x_l)}{2}$$

And:

$$||F_2 - F||_1 \leq ||F_2 - F_1||_1 + ||F_1 - F||_1 \leq x + \frac{y(x_r - x_l)}{2} = O(x + y)$$

$\square$

We generalise this result to hold with the additional restriction of staying within $\mathcal{X}$:

Theorem 6. *Given the setting and notations of theorem 5, consider $F \in \mathcal{X}$. Then, if $\hat{\mathcal{X}}$ is non-empty, there exists a grid staircase $F_3 \in \mathcal{X}$ such that $||F_3 - F_2||_1 \leq (x_r - x_l)y$ and*

Proof. Assume that $\hat{\mathcal{X}}$ is non-empty. We consider all the intervals $I_i := [a_i, a_{i+1})$ for $i \in 0, \ldots m - 1$. On each interval I_i one of three things can happen:

1. F_2 is entirely within $\mathcal{X}$,
2. certain values of F_2 are above corresponding values of $\overline{F}$, which implies that $F_2(a_i) > \overline{F}(a_i)$,
3. certain values of F_2 are below corresponding values of $\underline{F}$, which implies that $\lim_{a \to a_{i+1}} F_2(a) < \underline{F}(a_{i+1})$.

Note that if situations 2 and 3 occur at the same time, it means that $\hat{\mathcal{X}}$ is empty, as all grid points with the y-coordinate equal to $F_2(a_i)$ are outside of $\mathcal{X}$.

We consider a staircase function F_3 constructed the following way - on each interval I_i:

1. If situation 1 occurs, F_3 is identically equal to F_2 on this interval,
2. if situation 2 occurs F_3 is F_2 shifted down by y on this interval,
3. if situation 3 occurs, F_3 is F_2 shifted up by y on this interval.

It remains to show that F_3 is still increasing, and contained within $\mathcal{X}$. There are multiple ways of this happening: for example, at some interval I_i, F_3 is F_2 shifted up, and on the next interval F_3 is F_2 shifted down. However, all of those situations reduce to $\hat{\mathcal{X}}$ being empty. To show that F_3 is within $\mathcal{X}$ we remark that shifting F_2 up or down on an interval I_i, we switch from approximating F from above or from below. If we shift, that means that one of these approximations is outside of the $\mathcal{X}$ on I_i. Therefore, if the shift results in the other approximation also being outside of $\mathcal{X}$ on I_i, then $\mathcal{X}$ admits no grid staircases inside it, so $\hat{\mathcal{X}}$ is empty.

By construction of F_3, on each interval I_i the difference between F_3 and F_2 in terms of $||\cdot||_1$ is at most xy. Summing this up, we obtain the desired result:

$$||F_3 - F_2||_1 \leq (x_r - x_l)y$$

$\square$

Combining the results of Theorems 5 and 6 we obtain that for any $F \in \mathcal{X}$ there exists a grid staircase function $F_3 \in \mathcal{X}$ such that $||F - F_3||_1 = O(x + y)$.

References

1. Baluta, T., Chua, Z.L., Meel, K.S., Saxena, P.: Scalable quantitative verification for deep neural networks. In: Proceedings of the 43rd International Conference on Software Engineering, pp. 312–323. ICSE 2021, IEEE Press (2021)
2. Baluta, T., Shen, S., Shinde, S., Meel, K.S., Saxena, P.: Quantitative verification of neural networks and its security applications. In: Proceedings of the 2019 ACM SIGSAC Conference on Computer and Communications Security, pp. 1249–1264. CCS 2019, Association for Computing Machinery, New York, NY, USA (2019)
3. Beer, M., Ferson, S., Kreinovich, V.: Imprecise probabilities in engineering analyses. Mech. Syst. Signal Process. **37**(1–2), 4–29 (2013)
4. Boopathy, A., Weng, T.W., Chen, P.Y., Liu, S., Daniel, L.: CNN-CERT: an efficient framework for certifying robustness of convolutional neural networks. In: Proceedings of the Thirty-Third AAAI Conference on Artificial Intelligence and Thirty-First Innovative Applications of Artificial Intelligence Conference and Ninth AAAI Symposium on Educational Advances in Artificial Intelligence. AAAI 2019/IAAI19/EAAI 2019, AAAI Press (2019)
5. Calcaterra, C., Boldt, A.: Approximating with Gaussians (2008). https://arxiv.org/abs/0805.3795
6. Enszer, J.A., Lin, Y., Ferson, S., Corliss, G.F., Stadtherr, M.A.: Propagating uncertainties in modeling nonlinear dynamic systems. In: Proceedings of the 3rd International Workshop on Reliable Engineering, Computing, Georgia Institute of Technology, Savannah, GA,: 89. vol. 105 (2008)
7. Fazlyab, M., Morari, M., Pappas, G.J.: Probabilistic verification and reachability analysis of neural networks via semidefinite programming. In: 2019 IEEE 58th Conference on Decision and Control (CDC), pp. 2726–2731. IEEE (2019)
8. Fazlyab, M., Robey, A., Hassani, H., Morari, M., Pappas, G.J.: Efficient and Accurate Estimation of Lipschitz Constants for Deep Neural Networks. Curran Associates Inc., Red Hook, NY, USA (2019)

9. Ferson, S., Kreinovich, V., Ginzburg, L., Myers, D., Sentz, K.: Constructing probability boxes and Dempster-Shafer structures. Sandia Report (2003)
10. Goubault, E., Putot, S.: A zonotopic Dempster-Shafer approach to the quantitative verification of neural networks. In: Formal Methods: 26th International Symposium, FM 2024, Milan, Italy, 9–13 September 2024, Proceedings, Part I, pp. 324–342. Springer-Verlag, Heidelberg (2024). https://doi.org/10.1007/978-3-031-71162-6_17
11. Gray, A., Gopakumar, V., Rousseau, S., Desterke, S.: Guaranteed confidence-band enclosures for PDE surrogates. arXiv preprint arXiv:2501.18426 (2025)
12. Henriksen, P., Lomuscio, A.: Efficient neural network verification via adaptive refinement and adversarial search. In: ECAI 2020, pp. 2513–2520. IOS Press (2020)
13. Huang, C., Hu, Z., Huang, X., Pei, K.: Statistical certification of acceptable robustness for neural networks. In: Farkaš, I., Masulli, P., Otte, S., Wermter, S. (eds.) Artificial Neural Networks and Machine Learning - ICANN 2021, pp. 79–90. Springer International Publishing, Cham (2021). https://doi.org/10.1007/978-3-030-86362-3_7
14. Lyu, Z., Ko, C.Y., Kong, Z., Wong, N., Lin, D., Daniel, L.: Fastened crown: tightened neural network robustness certificates. In: Proceedings of the AAAI Conference on Artificial Intelligence, vol. 34, no. 04, pp. 5037–5044 (2020)
15. Massart, P.: The tight constant in the Dvoretzky-Kiefer-Wolfowitz inequality. Ann. Probab. **18**(3), 1269–1283 (1990)
16. Monchot, P., Coquelin, L., Petit, S.J., Marmin, S., Le Pennec, E., Fischer, N.: Input uncertainty propagation through trained neural networks. In: Krause, A., Brunskill, E., Cho, K., Engelhardt, B., Sabato, S., Scarlett, J. (eds.) Proceedings of the 40th International Conference on Machine Learning. Proceedings of Machine Learning Research, vol. 202, pp. 25140–25173. PMLR (2023)
17. Păsăreanu, C., Converse, H., Filieri, A., Gopinath, D.: On the probabilistic analysis of neural networks. In: Proceedings of the IEEE/ACM 15th International Symposium on Software Engineering for Adaptive and Self-Managing Systems, pp. 5–8 (2020)
18. Pautov, M., Tursynbek, N., Munkhoeva, M., Muravev, N., Petiushko, A., Oseledets, I.: CC-CERT: a probabilistic approach to certify general robustness of neural networks. In: Proceedings of the AAAI Conference on Artificial Intelligence, vol. 36, pp. 7975–7983 (2022)
19. Pilipovsky, J., Sivaramakrishnan, V., Oishi, M., Tsiotras, P.: Probabilistic verification of RELU neural networks via characteristic functions. In: Learning for Dynamics and Control Conference, pp. 966–979. PMLR (2023)
20. Scaman, K., Virmaux, A.: Lipschitz regularity of deep neural networks: analysis and efficient estimation. In: Proceedings of the 32nd International Conference on Neural Information Processing Systems, pp. 3839–3848. NIPS 2018, Curran Associates Inc., Red Hook, NY, USA (2018)
21. Singh, G., Gehr, T., Mirman, M., Püschel, M., Vechev, M.: Fast and effective robustness certification. In: Bengio, S., Wallach, H., Larochelle, H., Grauman, K., Cesa-Bianchi, N., Garnett, R. (eds.) Advances in Neural Information Processing Systems, vol. 31. Curran Associates, Inc. (2018)
22. Singh, G., Gehr, T., Püschel, M., Vechev, M.: An abstract domain for certifying neural networks. Proc. ACM Program. Lang. **3**(POPL), 1–30 (2019)
23. Walley, P.: Statistical Reasoning with Imprecise Probabilities. Chapman & Hall/CRC Monographs on Statistics & Applied Probability, Taylor & Francis (1991)

24. Webb, S., Rainforth, T., Teh, Y.W., Kumar, M.P.: A statistical approach to assessing neural network robustness. In: 7th International Conference on Learning Representations, ICLR 2019, New Orleans, LA, USA, 6-9 May 2019. OpenReview.net (2019)
25. Weng, L., et al.: PROVEN: Verifying robustness of neural networks with a probabilistic approach. In: Chaudhuri, K., Salakhutdinov, R. (eds.) Proceedings of the 36th International Conference on Machine Learning. Proceedings of Machine Learning Research, vol. 97, pp. 6727–6736. PMLR (2019)
26. Wright, O., Nakahira, Y., Moura, J.M.: An analytic solution to covariance propagation in neural networks. In: International Conference on Artificial Intelligence and Statistics. pp. 4087–4095. PMLR (2024)
27. Zhang, D., Ye, M., Gong, C., Zhu, Z., Liu, Q.: Black-box certification with randomized smoothing: a functional optimization based framework. In: Proceedings of the 34th International Conference on Neural Information Processing Systems. NIPS 2020, Curran Associates Inc., Red Hook, NY, USA (2020)
28. Zhang, H., Weng, T.W., Chen, P.Y., Hsieh, C.J., Daniel, L.: Efficient neural network robustness certification with general activation functions. In: Proceedings of the 32nd International Conference on Neural Information Processing Systems, pp. 4944–4953. NIPS 2018, Curran Associates Inc., Red Hook, NY, USA (2018)
29. Zhang, T., Ruan, W., Fieldsend, J.E.: PRoA: a probabilistic robustness assessment against functional perturbations. In: Amini, MR., Canu, S., Fischer, A., Guns, T., Kralj Novak, P., Tsoumakas, G. (eds.) Machine Learning and Knowledge Discovery in Databases: European Conference, ECML PKDD 2022, Grenoble, France, 19–23 September 2022, Proceedings, Part III, pp. 154–170. Springer-Verlag, Heidelberg (2023). https://doi.org/10.1007/978-3-031-26409-2_10

How to Verify Generalization Capability of a Neural Network with Formal Methods

Arthur Clavière[1](✉) [iD], Dmitrii Kirov[2] [iD], and Darren Cofer[3] [iD]

[1] Collins Aerospace, Toulouse, France
arthur.claviere@collins.com
[2] Collins Aerospace, Trento, Italy
dmitrii.kirov@collins.com
[3] Collins Aerospace, Minneapolis, USA
darren.cofer@collins.com

Abstract. Generalization of a machine learning (ML) model is its capability to maintain desired performance on input data to which it was not exposed during training. A bound on the model generalization error can provide important evidence of the absence of unintended behavior of the model, which is the key requirement for safety-critical systems and software. Such bounds are typically estimated statistically and provide a level of confidence that the bound holds. In this paper, we show how ML model generalization capability and bound can be assessed using *formal* methods providing a rigorous mathematical guarantee. We focus on applications that use neural networks to approximate a function with a low-dimensional, well-defined and bounded input space. We propose an iterative procedure that starts with partitioning the neural network input space into regions using one or multiple resolutions. Within each region, we formalize a property that the error made by the neural network on *any* data point inside the region is below a given tolerance. Proving such property provides a formal generalization guarantee for a given region. We employ an abstract interpretation solver to verify these properties over the entire input space partition. We iteratively refine the regions in which the proof could not be achieved by sampling or generating new data, forming a new local partition with higher granularity. This refinement follows a heuristic that aims to minimize the amount of new data to be produced. We demonstrate our methodology by proving generalization capability of a neural network-based avionics function.

Keywords: Neural Networks · Verification · Formal Methods

1 Introduction

Machine Learning (ML) is an enabling technology in aviation. ML models, such as neural networks (NNs), can be used to develop advanced avionics algorithms for decision making, planning, and perception. They can also efficiently approximate existing software, reducing its memory and computational costs [13]. Such

© The Author(s), under exclusive license to Springer Nature Switzerland AG 2026
M. Giacobbe and A. Lukina (Eds.): SAIV 2025, LNCS 15947, pp. 136–155, 2026.
https://doi.org/10.1007/978-3-031-99991-8_7

ML-enabled components and systems are typically safety-critical. Therefore, they must undergo rigorous design assurance and certification processes to be deployed onboard aircraft. Data-driven ML approaches are not fully amenable to existing standards for assuring safety-critical software, such as DO-178C [19], due to several gaps [20]. Aviation industry together with global certification authorities has made significant progress towards new ML-specific standard and guidance that is expected to appear in the next few years [21]. This standard will cover assurance objectives that are specific to ML.

One of the key ML assurance objectives is to provide evidence of the *generalization* capability of the ML model, i.e., its capability to maintain desired performance on input data to which it was not exposed during training. Such evidence must be provided over the entire Operational Design Domain (ODD), i.e., space of inputs where the model is designed to operate. The concept of generalization is not new in the ML community, and the widely accepted best practice for assessing it is to measure the *in-sample* error of the ML model (also called empirical risk) using a test dataset. While in-sample error can help to detect overfitting problems, it does not provide knowledge on how the model would perform on *unseen* data that may occur during operation. Such *out-of-sample* inputs may be sources of unintended behavior of the model, which is not acceptable in safety-critical aviation applications. The European Union Aviation Safety Agency (EASA) in their AI Concept Paper [3] suggests statistical learning theory methods to estimate model generalization bounds. Similar objectives appear in the upcoming ML assurance standard ARP6983 [21] jointly developed by SAE G-34 and EUROCAE WG-114 working groups. The Federal Aviation Administration (FAA) also requests to measure both the empirical error and the level of confidence that this error holds over the entire input domain [18].

While statistical methods can instrument generalization assessment, it is not yet clear whether a probabilistic measure of the bound would be acceptable, especially in high-criticality ML applications. In this paper, we consider a different perspective by looking for more rigorous, formal generalization guarantees for ML models. To provide a useful and tangible result, we focus on low-complexity NN models (tens to thousands learnable parameters) with low-dimensional (in the order of 10) well-defined and bounded input spaces. Such a class of NN applications is very well represented in the aviation domain (ACAS-XU is one example). We employ formal methods, which recently have been shown to be effective in ML assurance [10], to define and verify the NN generalization property.

Our approach is an iterative procedure that starts with partitioning the NN input space into regions using one or multiple resolutions. We call these regions "hyperrectangles". Their corners correspond to labeled data points from the existing dataset, which allows us to formalize a local property that the error made by the NN on *any* data point inside the hyperrectangle is below a given tolerance. Proving such property provides a formal generalization guarantee for a hyperrectangle, essentially representing a bound on the out-of-sample error. We employ an abstract interpretation solver to verify these properties over the entire input space partition. We iteratively refine hyperrectangles in which the proof could not be achieved by sampling or generating new data, forming a new local partition with higher granularity. This refinement follows a heuristic that aims to minimize the amount of new data to be produced.

Our contributions can be summarized as follows:

- We propose a mathematical formalization of the NN generalization property, and a method to prove this property over the entire input domain using NN verifiers with abstract interpretation. We discuss the assumptions and the limitations of the approach.
- We develop a verification procedure that iteratively refines regions where the property could not be proven valid (e.g., due to over-approximations used in the verifiers) to maximize the volume of the input space where generalization proof could be obtained.
- We demonstrate our approach by assessing generalization of a NN-based advisory system for pilots, which is a safety-critical avionics function.

Our method is currently applicable to NNs with low-dimensional input spaces (indicatively, number of inputs in the order of 10). Such NNs have a lot of applications in safety-critical aviation, as well as other domains. We assess the computational complexity of our algorithm in the paper, and discuss several performance improvements to enhance scalability.

2 Background

2.1 Neural Network Generalization Assessment

The purpose of generalization assessment is to see how well the NN performs on the data that it was not exposed to during training. Traditional practice suggests using a test (holdout) dataset to measure the generalization capability of the model. Test dataset allows to measure a so-called *empirical risk*, i.e., to understand the performance of the NN using the examples (test points) available in the dataset. Emerging aviation guidance, such as EASA AI Concept Paper [3], goes beyond this and prescribes an analytical bound on the generalization error to be estimated. The goal is to estimate a worst-case error that the NN (more generally, the ML model) could make on *any* unseen data within its ODD. It is called the *out-of-sample error* (or theoretical risk), while the empirical risk on the test dataset is called the *in-sample error*. The difference between the two is the *generalization gap* [9]. Statistical bounds are typically used to assess generalization of ML models, while this paper proposes an alternative approach using formal methods.

2.2 Neural Network Formal Verification

Formal analysis of NNs is focused mainly on robustness verification i.e., checking that a perturbation of an input yields a bounded deviation of the outputs [10]. To verify such properties, several formal verification approaches and solvers were introduced. These approaches can be roughly split into complete methods (e.g., see [11,23,25]) and incomplete methods (e.g., see [12,22,24,26]). The former provide sound and complete verification, i.e., can always prove or disprove the property, but incur higher computational complexity. The latter rely on sound over-approximations and trade completeness (i.e., can return *Unknown* answers) with higher performance. Improvements in state-of-the-art NN verifiers can be observed from the results of the annual Verification of NNs Competition (VNNComp) [5], where we also submitted several benchmark problems over the recent years [14,15].

3 Verification Method

Our proposed method applies to *regression problems* i.e., when the NN outputs values in $\mathbb{R}$. In the remainder of this section, for the sake of simplicity, we consider a NN with a single output (Remark 1 explains how the method can be generalized to multiple outputs).

We adopt the following notation:

- $I = \times_{i=1,\ldots,N}[l_i, u_i]$ is the Operational Design Domain (ODD) of the NN, captured as a Cartesian product of admissible ranges along the input dimensions, where l_i and u_i are, respectively, the lower and the upper bound of the i-th dimension (feature), and N is the dimensionality of I;
- $\mathcal{N} : I \to \mathbb{R}$ is the NN to be verified;
- $f : I \to \mathbb{R}$ is the ground truth function, i.e., the target function to be approximated with $\mathcal{N}$;
- $\mathbf{H} = (H_1, \ldots, H_Q)$ is a set of hyperrectangles that form a partition of I;
- $H_j = \times_{i=1,\ldots,N}[l_{i,j}, u_{i,j}]$ is the jth hyperrectangle in $\mathbf{H}$;
- $\mathcal{N}(H_j) = [l_{\mathcal{N},j}, u_{\mathcal{N},j}]$ is the range of outputs of $\mathcal{N}$ corresponding to input points contained in H_j;
- $f(H_j) = [l_{f,j}, u_{f,j}]$ is the range of outputs of f corresponding to input points contained in H_j;
- $\mathbf{D} = (\mathbf{X}, \mathbf{Y})$ is a dataset where $\mathbf{X} = \{x_l\}_{l=1,\ldots,L}$ is a list of inputs and $\mathbf{Y} = \{y_l\}_{l=1,\ldots,L}$ is the list of corresponding outputs (labels), i.e., $\forall l : 1 \le l \le L, y_l = f(x_l)$;
- $e(x) = |f(x) - \mathcal{N}(x)|$ is the error made by $\mathcal{N}$ on input $x \in I$;
- $\tau \in \mathbb{R}$ is the error tolerance of $\mathcal{N}$.

3.1 Prerequisites and Assumptions

Prerequisite 1. *The ODD of the NN can be represented as a hyperrectangle $I = \times_{i=1,\ldots,N}[l_i, u_i]$.*

This is a reasonable prerequisite for NNs that model processes grounded in physical principles. The lower and upper bounds (l_i, u_i) on each input dimension can be derived from sensor saturations or from the limitations due to physics (e.g., an aircraft has a limited set of operating conditions, including limited range for speed and altitude).

Prerequisite 2. *The dataset* **D** *is such that the inputs* **X** *constitute a grid covering the entire ODD. Formally*

- Each input dimension i is sampled with k_i values $S_i = \{x_{i,1}, \ldots, x_{i,k_i}\}$ where $x_{i,1} = l_i \leq x_{i,2} \leq \ldots \leq x_{i,k_i} = u_i$;
- The list of inputs **X** is the combination of all the possible sampled values along every input dimension:

$$\mathbf{X} = \{(x_{1,l} \ \ldots \ x_{N,l}) \mid \forall i = 1, \ldots, N, x_{i,l} \in S_i\} \tag{1}$$

Same as Prerequisite 1, this is reasonable when the NN is used to model a physical process. The ground truth f is often computable for every input in the grid **X**, e.g., through a physics-based simulation model. Moreover, the sampled values along input dimensions can be obtained with sensitivity analysis.

Informally, Prerequisites 1 and 2 prescribe that the input domain of $\mathcal{N}$ is well defined, and the admissible range of each feature can be explicitly defined. Additionally, we specify the following assumption:

Assumption 1. *The ground truth function f has a known variation in between the points of the dataset* **D**. *For instance, f can monotonic or K-Lipschitz between the points of* **D**, *i.e., its slope can be bounded by a constant $K \in \mathbb{R}$.*

3.2 Property Formalization

In our approach, NN generalization capability is formalized by considering the behavior of the NN on *any* possible input, i.e., any input within its the ODD. More specifically, we consider a property $\mathcal{P}$ which states that the error made by $\mathcal{N}$ on any input x shall be less than a given tolerance τ:

$$\mathcal{P} : \forall x \in I, \quad e(x) = |\mathcal{N}(x) - f(x)| \leq \tau \tag{2}$$

The property $\mathcal{P}$ states that the worst case error of $\mathcal{N}$ on any input within its ODD I shall not exceed the tolerance τ. This tolerance represents a bound on the out-of-sample error of the NN and can be allocated from NN performance requirements.

$\mathcal{P}$ is a *global* property because it is imposed for the entire ODD of the NN. To facilitate its verification, we break it down into a collection of *local* properties. This formalization relies on:

- A partition of the ODD into a set of hyperrectangles $\mathbf{H} = (H_1, \ldots, H_Q)$;
- A set of local properties $\mathcal{P}_1, \ldots, \mathcal{P}_Q$, where the property $\mathcal{P}_j$ states that the error made by $\mathcal{N}$ in the hyperrectangle H_j shall not exceed τ:

$$\mathcal{P}_j : \forall x \in H_j, \quad e(x) = |\mathcal{N}(x) - f(x)| \leq \tau \tag{3}$$

Since the set **H** constitutes a partition of the ODD, then $\mathcal{P}_1 \wedge \ldots \wedge \mathcal{P}_Q \Rightarrow \mathcal{P}$.

Remark 1. The formalization above can be extended to the case where $\mathcal{N}$ has $M > 1$ outputs. A possible formulation is to specify a dedicated error tolerance for each NN output. The formulation of $\mathcal{P}$ then becomes

$$\mathcal{P}' : \forall m = 1, \ldots, M, \ e(x)_m = |f(x)_m - \mathcal{N}(x)_m| \leq \tau_m \tag{4}$$

where $e(x)_m$ is the error made by $\mathcal{N}$ on its mth output and τ_m is the error tolerance for the mth output of $\mathcal{N}$.

3.3 Verification Algorithm

To verify the properties formalized above, we propose an algorithm that consists of four main steps, which are illustrated in Fig. 1 and described below.

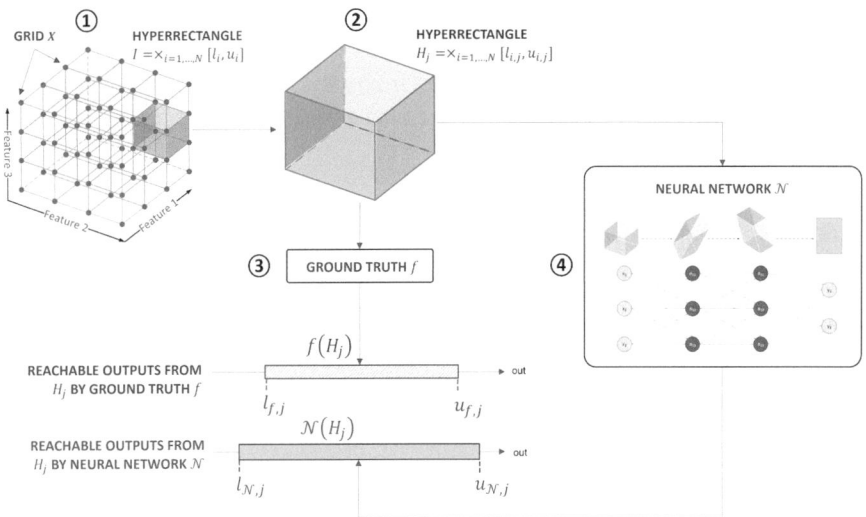

Fig. 1. Formal verification algorithm for NN generalization assessment.

Step 1 (Partitioning). The first step is the partitioning of the ODD in a set of hyperrectangles $\mathbf{H} = (H_1, \ldots, H_Q)$, the corners of which are the points $\mathbf{X} = \{x_l\}_{l=1,\ldots,L}$ of the dataset **D**. This step is made possible given that the ODD can be represented by a hyperrectangle I (see Prerequisite 1) and that the inputs **X** form a grid which covers the entire set I (see Prerequisite 2).

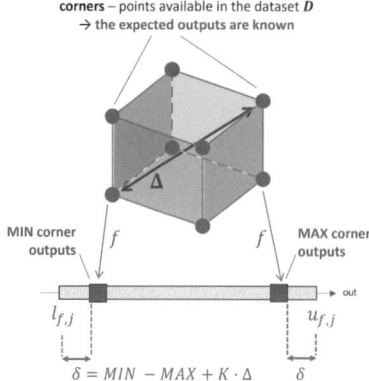

Fig. 2. Over-approximation of $f(H_j)$ when f is K-Lipschitz.

Step 2 (Hyperrectangle Retrieval). The second step consists in retrieving the bounds $(l_{i,j}, u_{i,j})$ of a hyperrectangle H_j from **H**.

Step 3 (Computing the Reachable Outputs of f). This step computes a sound approximation $f(H_j)$ of the range of the reachable outputs of f from H_j by:

1. Retrieving the expected outputs at the n_j corners of the hyperrectangle H_j, denoted by $y_{1,j}, \ldots, y_{n_j,j}$, which are by definition available in the dataset **D**;
2. Computing the range $f(H_j) = [l_{f,j}, u_{f,j}]$ by leveraging Assumption 1 i.e., the knowledge available on the variation of the ground truth f in between the corners of H_j. For instance:
   - If f is monotonic inside H_j, then exact bounds can be computed: $l_{f,j} = \text{MIN} := \min_{l=1,\ldots,n_j}(y_{l,j})$ is the minimum values among of the expected outputs at the corners and $u_{f,j} = \text{MAX} := \max_{l=1,\ldots,n_j}(y_{l,j})$ is the maximum value;
   - If f is K-Lipschitz inside H_j and K is known, then over-approximating bounds $(l_{f,j}, u_{f,j})$ can be computed (see Fig. 2):

$$\begin{cases} l_{f,j} = \text{MIN} - \delta \\ u_{f,j} = \text{MAX} + \delta \end{cases} \quad (5)$$

where $\delta = \text{MIN} - \text{MAX} + K \cdot \Delta$ and Δ is the maximum distance between two inputs in H_j i.e., $\Delta = |(l_{1,j}, \ldots, l_{N,j}) - (u_{1,j}, \ldots, u_{N,j})|$, where $l_{i,j}$ is the lower bound of H_j along the ith dimension and $u_{i,j}$ is the upper bound of H_j along the ith dimension.

Step 4 (Computing the Reachable Outputs of $\mathcal{N}$). This step computes a sound approximation $\mathcal{N}(H_j)$ of the range of the reachable outputs of $\mathcal{N}$ from H_j. It can be computed, for example, based on abstract interpretation, i.e., by relying on an abstract transformer $\mathcal{N}^{\#}$ that soundly approximates the semantics of $\mathcal{N}$:

$$\mathcal{N}(H_j) = \mathcal{N}^{\#}(H_j) \tag{6}$$

Remark 2. If $\mathcal{N}$ involves pre-processing and post-processing functions, they also need to be handled by dedicated abstract transformers. Since pre-processing and post-processing are often linear transformations that do not introduce any dependency among input variables, they can be handled efficiently with a transformer based on interval abstract domain.

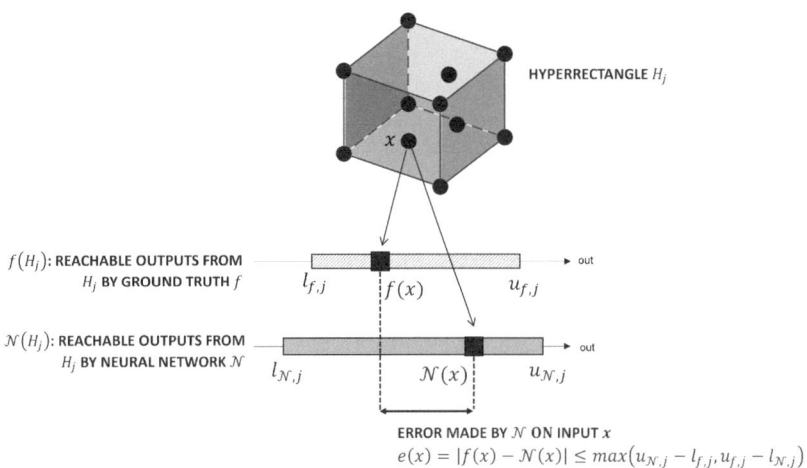

Fig. 3. Computation of an upper bound on the error made by $\mathcal{N}$ in the hyperrectangle H_j.

Once the range $\mathcal{N}(H_j)$ is computed, it is compared to the range $f(H_j)$ from Step 3 to determine an upper bound on the error made by the NN in the hyperrectangle H_j (Fig. 3) i.e., a bound $E_j \in \mathbb{R}$ such that:

$$\forall x \in H_j, e(x) = |f(x) - \mathcal{N}(x)| \leq E_j \tag{7}$$

where $e(x)$ is the error made by $\mathcal{N}$ on the input $x \in H_j$.

By definition, for all input x in H_j:

$$\begin{cases} f(x) \in f(H_j) = [l_{f,j}, u_{f,j}] \\ \mathcal{N}(x) \in \mathcal{N}(H_j) = [l_{\mathcal{N},j}, u_{\mathcal{N},j}] \end{cases} \tag{8}$$

Hence,

$$f(x) - \mathcal{N}(x) \in [l_{f,j} - u_{\mathcal{N},j}, u_{f,j} - l_{\mathcal{N},j}]$$
$$\Rightarrow |f(x) - \mathcal{N}(x)| \leq \underbrace{\max(|l_{f,j} - u_{\mathcal{N},j}|, |u_{f,j} - l_{\mathcal{N},j}|)}_{E_j} \quad (9)$$

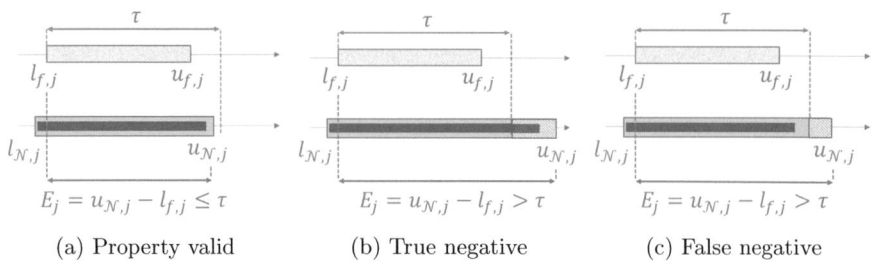

Fig. 4. Examples of outcomes of Step 4 of the algorithm. The exact set of the reachable outputs of $\mathcal{N}$ is represented in dark purple for illustrative purposes.

Finally, it can be checked if the bound on the error $E_j := \max(|l_{f,j} - u_{\mathcal{N},j}|, |u_{f,j} - l_{\mathcal{N},j}|)$ is less than the error tolerance τ. There are two possible outcomes:

- If $E_j \leq \tau$, the property $\mathcal{P}_j$ is proven *valid* i.e., the error made by $\mathcal{N}$ in H_j is effectively less than the error tolerance τ (see Fig. 4a);
- If $E_j > \tau$, no conclusion can be drawn on the validity of the property $\mathcal{P}_j$ which remains *Unknown*. Indeed, two cases are possible:
  1. *True negative*: the property $\mathcal{P}_j$ is *invalid* and there exist a counterexample i.e., an input $x^* \in H_j$ such that $e(x^*) > \tau$ (see Fig. 4b);
  2. *False negative*: the property $\mathcal{P}_j$ is *valid*, yet, due to the approximation of the reachable outputs of either f or $\mathcal{N}$, the bound E_j on the error is too conservative and does not allow to prove $\mathcal{P}_j$ valid (see Fig. 4c).

In the latter case where $E_j > \tau$, to decide whether this is a true negative or a false negative, a simple counterexample search can be performed. The error can be computed for every corner of the hyperrectangle H_j, for which the expected outputs $y_{1,j}, \ldots, y_{n_j,j}$ are available in the dataset. If there exists a corner where the error is greater than τ then this is a counterexample which disproves that the property $\mathcal{P}_j$ holds. Otherwise, a refinement of the hyperrectangle H_j can be performed, as explained in Sect. 4.

Steps 2, 3 and 4 are repeated until all the hyperrectangles composing the set **H** are analyzed. Once the analysis is complete, one can:

- Determine the ratio of the volume of the ODD where the generalization property is valid;

– Record the list $\mathbf{H}_{unknown}$ of all the hyperrectangles of $\mathbf{H}$ where the validity of the property $\mathcal{P}_j$ remains unknown.

The latter output can be used to design a monitor that during operation can detect whether the incoming input belongs to one of the unproven hyperrectangles, in which case the NN is not activated (e.g., a backup algorithm can be used instead or a warning can be shown). This can ensure a safe usage of the NN.

Remark 3. While we employ abstract interpretation to compute NN reachable outputs at Step 4, other approaches can also be used, such as SMT solvers, if the NN has piecewise linear activation functions. One can express the existence of a counterexample as the existence of an x in H_j such that the following disjunction holds:

$$(\mathcal{N}(x) - l_{f,j} \geq \tau) \vee (l_{f,j} - \mathcal{N}(x) \geq \tau) \vee (u_{f,j} - \mathcal{N}(x) \geq \tau) \vee (\mathcal{N}(x) - u_{f,j} \geq \tau)$$

The four clauses in this disjunction can be checked with SMT. If none of them is satisfiable, i.e., there exists no x such that they are satisfied, then there exists no counterexample and the property $\mathcal{P}_j$ can be concluded valid.

3.4 Implementation and Optimizations

The verification method is currently implemented in MATLAB and the abstract transformer $\mathcal{N}^\#$ of $\mathcal{N}$ relies on the MATLAB Deep Learning Toolbox Verification Library [1] which implements the DeepPoly approach [22]. This approach leverages a dedicated, polytope-based abstract domain for the analysis of NNs. It offers a good balance between accuracy (i.e., tightness of the bounds of the range $\mathcal{N}(H_j)$ of the reachable outputs of $\mathcal{N}$) and cost of the analysis (time to compute the range $\mathcal{N}(H_j)$ with $\mathcal{N}^\#$). In addition, *vectorization* and *sorting and indexing*, have been implemented to accelerate the execution of the method. These optimizations are described below.

Vectorization. Current hardware and software provide direct support for vector operations where a single instruction is applied to multiple data. This offers a faster execution time compared to applying the instruction to a single data. Therefore, Steps 2, 3 and 4 of the method are vectorized such that the corresponding operations are applied not to a single hyperrectangle but to a *batch* of hyperrectangles: Step 2 retrieves a batch $H_{j_1}, \ldots, H_{j_B}$ of B hyperrectangles. Then Steps 3 and 4 are applied to these B hyperrectangles to assess the validity of the corresponding batch of properties $\mathcal{P}_{j_1}, \ldots, \mathcal{P}_{j_B}$.

Sorting and Indexing. When the dataset $\mathbf{D}$ is large, searching $\mathbf{D}$ for the expected outputs at the corners of a specific hyperrectangle (as needed in Step 3) is a costly operation, which may take significant time compared to the computation of the reachable outputs of the NN with abstract interpretation. To mitigate this, the dataset $\mathbf{D}$ can be sorted and the set $\mathbf{H}$ can be indexed. In our implementation, the dataset is sorted based on the values of the inputs: $\mathbf{X}$ is sorted in ascending order of the value of the first input dimension, then where the value of the first input dimension is identical, $\mathbf{X}$ is sorted in ascending order of the value of the second input dimension, and this is repeated until last input dimension. The list $\mathbf{Y}$ is then sorted such that its lth element is the expected output for the lth input in the sorted list $\mathbf{X}$. The indexing of the set of hyperrectangles is done by considering that $\mathbf{H}$ is ordered in ascending order of the lower bound of the first input dimension, then where the lower bound of the first input dimension is identical, $\mathbf{H}$ is ordered in ascending order of the lower bound of the second input dimension, and this is repeated until last input dimension:

$$\begin{aligned} H_1 &= [x_{1,1}, x_{1,2}] \times \ldots \times [x_{N,1}, x_{N,2}] \\ H_2 &= [x_{1,1}, x_{1,2}] \times \ldots \times [x_{N,2}, x_{N,3}] \\ H_3 &= [x_{1,1}, x_{1,2}] \times \ldots \times [x_{N,3}, x_{N,4}] \\ &\vdots \\ H_Q &= [x_{1,k_1-1}, x_{1,k_1}] \times \ldots \times [x_{N,k_N-1}, x_{N,k_N}] \end{aligned} \quad (10)$$

where, as indicated in Prerequisite 2, the values $x_{i,1}, \ldots, x_{i,k_i}$ are the sampled values along the ith input dimension, defining the inputs in $\mathbf{X}$ and thus the corners of the hyperrectangles. The hyperrectangle H_j of index j is the jth hyperrectangle in this ordered set. Considering this indexing of $\mathbf{H}$ and the sorting of the dataset $\mathbf{D}$:

- At Step 1, the set $\mathbf{H}$ needs not to be stored: it can be represented simply with the list $(Q_i)_{i=1,\ldots,N}$ where Q_i is the number of hyperrectangles along the ith input dimension i.e., $Q_i = k_i - 1$, and the total number of hyperrectangles $Q = \prod_{i=1,\ldots,N} Q_i$. The set $\mathbf{H}$ can be explored by iterating over the index j between 1 and Q;
- At Step 2, the bounds of the hyperrectangle H_j of index j can be determined based on the sampled values along each inputs dimension and an iterative euclidean division of the index j by the values Q_i;
- At Step 3, similarly as the retrieving of the bounds of H_j, the expected outputs $y_{1,j}, \ldots, y_{n_j,j}$ at the corners of H_j can be retrieved by determining their indices in the sorted list $\mathbf{Y}$ with iterative euclidean divisions, alleviating the cost of searching $\mathbf{Y}$ for the combination of the N input values defining each corner of H_j.

3.5 Complexity

The computational complexity of the verification method was computed, based on the following considerations:

- The number of hyperretangles to be analyzed is in $O(L)$ where L is the size of the dataset $\mathbf{D}$. Indeed, $L = \prod_{i=1,\ldots,N} k_i$ where k_i is the number of sampled values along the ith input dimension and the number of hyperrectangles is $Q = \prod_{i=1,\ldots,N} k_i - 1$;

- With sorting the data and indexing the hyperrectangle, the retrieval of the N bounds of a hyperrectangle H_j from $\mathbf{H}$ is in $O(N)$ where N is the number of input dimensions. Moreover, the retrieval of the expected outputs at the corners of a hyperrectangle is in $O(2^N)$ i.e., the number of corners of the hyperrectangle;
- The complexity of the computation of the reachable outputs of $\mathcal{N}$ from a hyperrectangle H_j with the DeepPoly approach is in $O(n_{layers}^2 \cdot n_{neurons}^3)$ where n_{layers} is the number of layers of $\mathcal{N}$ and $n_{neurons}$ is the maximum number of neurons in one layer [22].

Consequently, as the verification consists in retrieving the bounds and expected outputs at the corners of the Q hyperrectangles, and apply the DeepPoly approach on each of them, the total complexity is in $O(L \cdot 2^N \cdot n_{layers}^2 \cdot n_{neurons}^3)$. The applicability of the method is thus limited by three factors being: (1) the size of the dataset, (2) the number of input dimension and (2) the size of the NN. In practice, the method is applicable for low dimensional input spaces (N in the order of 10) and low-complexity NNs (number of learnable parameters in the order of $100 - 1000$).

4 Verification Workflow

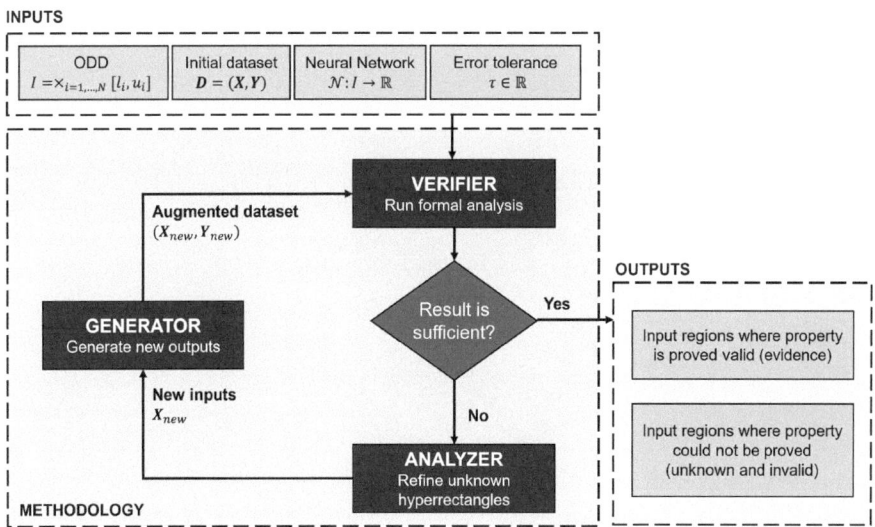

Fig. 5. Iterative workflow with verification-driven refinement.

The possibility of proving the property (3) depends on the size of the hyperrectangle. Larger intervals lead to coarser approximations during verification and increase the risk of not being able to prove the property, i.e., to get an *Unknown* answer from the solver. A possible mitigation is to create a dataset with very high resolution, so that the hyperrectangles are "small enough". This may not be practical, for example, if running simulations to create data points are expensive or data generation is owned by a third party. Therefore, it is highly desirable to minimize the number of data points required to obtain the proof.

To this end, we propose a verification workflow that iteratively verifies the property and refines *only* those regions where the property could not be proven, which we call *verification-driven* data generation. This is implemented by a dedicated verification workflow, illustrated in Fig. 5, which is composed of three main blocks: a *Verifier*, an *Analyzer* and a *Generator*. These three blocks are executed sequentially, as follows:

1. The Verifier implements the verification method described in Sect. 3, partitioning the ODD into a set $\mathbf{H}$ of hyperrectangles and checking the local property $\mathcal{P}_j$ in every of these hyperrectangles. It outputs the list $\mathbf{H}_{unknown}$ of the hyperrectangles where the validity of the property $\mathcal{P}_j$ remains unknown;
2. The Analyzer performs a *refinement* that splits the hyperrectangles pertaining to $\mathbf{H}_{unknown}$ into smaller hyperrectangles (see Fig. 6). It outputs a list of new inputs $\mathbf{X}_{new}$, which are the corners of the smaller hyperrectangles, for which the expected outputs need to be computed to apply the verification method;
3. The Generator computes the outputs $\mathbf{Y}_{new} = f(\mathbf{X}_{new})$ for the corners of refined hyperrectangles, i.e., it is a labeling procedure.

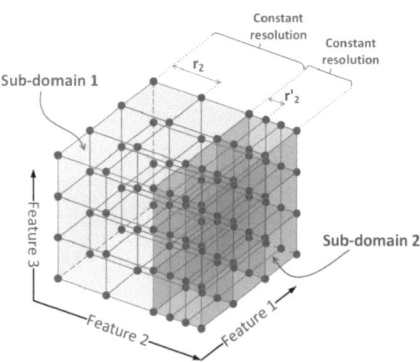

Fig. 6. The Analyzer splits the hyperrectangles where the property is unknown, with a hyperrectangles of size r'_2 smaller than the original size r_2.

These three steps are repeated iteratively, until a termination criteria is reached. Such a criteria can be either:

1. The maximum resolution of inputs is reached;

2. Making further refinements is too costly;
3. The results are acceptable e.g., the volume of the regions where the property could not be proven is sufficiently small with respect to NN or system requirements.

An important hyperparameter of this workflow is the refinement performed by the Analyzer i.e., how every hyperrectangle dimension is split at each iteration. To determine this refinement, a hyperparameter tuning process is performed before running the verification workflow. This hyperparameter tuning relies on a heuristic that aims to find the refinement which maximizes the number of properties $\mathcal{P}_j$ proven valid after a given number of iterations, while minimizing the number of new data to be generated through the iterations. This heuristic consists in (1) defining a set of candidate refinements and (2) estimating the efficiency of these candidate refinements. For (1), a grid search approach can be followed e.g., consider the refinements which bisect all possible combinations of hyperrectangle dimensions. Expert knowledge about the ground truth or sensitivity analysis may also be used to identify the hyperrectangle dimensions to be split preferentially, and define a set of candidate refinements which split only these specific hyperrectangle dimensions. For (2), every candidate refinement is evaluated by running a modified version of the verification workflow, where the Generator is replaced with *linear interpolation*. The use of linear interpolation in this context allows estimating the efficiency of the candidate refinement i.e., the number of new data generated and the number of properties proven valid after a given number of iterations. Moreover, it avoids the cost of computing the ground truth function f for generating the new data.

5 Evaluation

5.1 Pilot Advisory System Case Study

The verification workflow presented in Sect. 4 is evaluated against an advisory system used onboard aircraft to provide the pilot with the optimal altitude. This advisory system takes as inputs a candidate optimal altitude as well as several variables describing the current state of the aircraft (weight, speed) and the weather conditions (wind, temperature). It outputs the cost of flying at the candidate altitude given the current state of the aircraft and the weather conditions.

This advisory system is implemented as a NN with ReLU activation functions and two hidden layers of 13 neurons each. This NN aims to approximate a traditional implementation of the advisory system while offering reduced execution time and memory footprint. Regarding generalization capabilities, it is expected that, for any input in the ODD, the relative error made by the NN is less than 5% compared to the traditional implementation. Formally, if $\mathcal{N}$ denotes the NN implementing the advisory system, f the traditional implementation and I the ODD, the desired property is:

$$\mathcal{P}_{5\%} : \forall x \in I, \ e(x) = |f(x) - \mathcal{N}(x)| \leq 5\% \cdot |f(x)| \qquad (11)$$

where the tolerance on the error made by $\mathcal{N}$ on input x i.e., the quantity $5\% \cdot |f(x)|$, depends on the value of the input x. As one can note, this is slightly different from the property $\mathcal{P}$ addressed by our verification method, where the tolerance on the error is a fixed value $\tau \in \mathbb{R}$ (see Eq. 2). This difference was handled by reformulating each local property $\mathcal{P}_j$ as:

$$\mathcal{P}_{j,5\%} : \forall x \in H_j,\ e(x) = |f(x) - \mathcal{N}(x)| \leq \tau_{j,5\%} \tag{12}$$

where τ_j is such that:

$$\forall x \in H_j,\ \tau_{j,5\%} \leq 0.05 \cdot |f(x)| \tag{13}$$

To satisfy this condition, $\tau_{j,5\%}$ was taken equal to 5% of the minimum of $|f(x)|$ in H_j i.e. $\tau_{j,5\%} := l_{f,j}$ where $l_{f,j}$ is the lower bound on the reachable outputs of f from H_j. Indeed, $\min_{x \in H_j}|f(x)| = \min_{x \in H_j} f(x) = l_{f,j}$ since $f(x)$ is a cost, assumed to take positive values only.

5.2 Experiments

The verification of the advisory system was performed with a dataset $\mathbf{D} = (\mathbf{X}, \mathbf{Y})$ containing 4 million points. As required by Prerequisite 2, this dataset $\mathbf{D}$ constitutes a grid which covers the entire ODD of the advisory system. In addition, the variation of the traditional implementation f is known (monotonic) in between the points of this dataset $\mathbf{D}$, satisfying Assumption 1.

Table 1. Results of the generalization assessment of the advisory system with 3 iterations of the verification workflow, run on Windows machine and NVIDIA RTX A6000 GPU with 48GB memory.

	Iteration 1	Iteration 2	Iteration 3
Number of Data	4M	66M	171M
Number of Hyperrectangles	2M	48M	164M
Ratio of volume proven valid	0%	59%	91%
Ratio of volume proven invalid	4%	2%	2%
Ratio of volume unknown	96%	39%	7%
Time elapsed[a]	3 minute	15 minutes	35 minutes

[a] This time includes only the time to run the Verifier and the Analyzer, excluding the time to run the Generator which computes the new outputs by executing the traditional implementation f.

The generalization assessment of the advisory system was performed with the following choice of hyperparameters:

- A number of 3 iterations of the verification workflow i.e., three executions of the Verifier, Analyzer and Generator;

- A batch size B of 1 million hyperrectangles for the vectorization of the operations involved in the Verifier and the Analyzer;
- A refinement (i.e., how the Analyzer refines the unknown hyperrectangles at each iteration) determined with the heuristic described in Sect. 4: several candidate refinements were defined, based on expert knowledge and sensitivity analysis, and tested by running 3 iterations of the workflow and using *linear interpolation* to generate the new data instead of the ground truth.

The results of the generalization assessment are given in Table 1, which shows, for each iteration of the workflow:

- Amount of data generated since first iteration. At iteration 1, this number is the size of dataset **D** while at iteration 2, it is the size of **D** plus the number of data generated to refine the unknown hyperrectangles $\mathbf{H}_{unknown}$ in iteration 1;
- Number of hyperrectangles analyzed since first iteration;
- Ratio of the volume of the Operational Design Domain I where the desired property $\mathcal{P}_{j,5\%}$ is proven valid i.e., the ratio between (i) the sum of the volumes of the hyperrectangles H_j where $\mathcal{P}_{j,5\%}$ is proven valid and (ii) the total volume of the ODD;
- Ratio of the volume of the ODD I where the desired property $\mathcal{P}_{j,5\%}$ is proven invalid (through counterexamples found at one corner of the invalid hyperrectangles);
- Ratio of the volume of the ODD I where the validity of the desired property $\mathcal{P}_{j,5\%}$ remains unknown;
- Time elapsed since the first iteration (excluding the time to run the Generator which computes new outputs with f).

It can be seen that after 3 iterations of the workflow, the desired property can be proven valid in 91% of the total volume of the ODD, requiring a total of 171 million data points to be generated and 35 minutes of verification time. The iterative refinements of the unknown hyperrectangles provide a significant increase of the volume where the property is proven valid, from 0% at iteration 1, due to the large size of the hyperrectangles defined by the initial dataset **D**, to 59% at iteration 2 and 91% at iteration 3. In the remaining 9% of volume at iteration 3, 7% remains unknown and 2% is proven invalid. This ratio where the property is proven invalid decreases along the iterations. This is due to the fact that invalid hyperrectangles are also refined along iterations: only some of the refined hyperrectangles have invalid corners while the other refined hyperrectangles are not invalid, hence the decreasing ratio of invalid areas.

Comparison with Statistical Methods. As mentioned in the related work, several statistical methods can also be applied to assess the property $\mathcal{P}_{j,5\%}$ which we verified formally with our workflow. These statistical methods were also applied to the advisory system [6]. To reach the desired confidence level, statistical methods required to generate 10^9 data, which is one order of magnitude above the amount of data generated in our verification, representing additional computational cost. Moreover, one advantage of the formal verification compared to statistical methods is the possibility to identify the hyperrectangles where the property cannot be proven valid. This information can be leveraged for instance to design a real-time monitoring mechanism, such as a safety net [7], which switches to the traditional implementation f when the input lies in one of these areas.

Evaluation of Optimizations. The acceleration of the verification time due to optimizations discussed in Sect. 3.4 was also measured. It was observed that the vectorization of the operations with batches of 1 million hyperrectangles, parallelized on a 48GB memory GPU, provides an acceleration by a factor in the order of 10^4. Regarding the sorting and indexing of data and hyperrectangles, it was observed that it provides an acceleration by a factor in the order of 10^2 to 10^3, depending on the size of the dataset and the number of hyperrectangles.

6 Related Work

Model generalization is an important topic in theoretical machine learning, specifically in the field of statistical learning theory. The study of quantitative generalization bounds has a rich history that started with seminal works, such as VC-dimension and Rademacher complexity, and produced various forms of bounds since then [9]. Many bounds are based on the Probably Approximately Correct (PAC) Bayesian theory (e.g., see [8,17]). Such bounds are often vacuous and thus impractical for deep learning applications [16], but can be computed sufficiently tight for low-complexity NNs, which are the focus of this work. Still, to achieve high confidence levels (e.g., 99.9% and beyond) that is required for assuring a safety-critical NN, very large sample may be needed, whereas producing additional data points may incur high costs due to various reasons (expensive to generate, data owned by a third party, etc.). In contrast to statistical methods, our generalization assessment approach is based on formal methods and provides mathematical guarantees on the validity of the generalization property (basically, a 100% confidence). We have also shown that this approach requires significantly less data points for the analysis.

The use of formal methods for learning assurance of safety-critical ML applications in aviation is discussed in [10] and [2]. The report provides seminal ideas for generalization assessment guarantees, but no practical solution, which is instead materialized in this paper. Additionally, a similar approach for dividing the NN input space into sub-regions (called "boxes") has been presented in [7]. However, their work focuses on verification of the ACAS-XU system, which is based on classification NNs. Our current result has been produced for regression NNs, however, the generalization property can be reformulated for classification networks as well, so that the method would apply to ACAS-XU and similar problems. This merely depends on how the tolerance is defined in the property.

In [4], formal methods are used for NN generalization assessment: several NNs are trained independently and formal methods are used to identify the NNs which are in agreement across all inputs in a specific domain. This approach evaluates generalization by comparing several independently trained NNs, implying that the NNs which are in agreement have learned decision rules that generalize well to all inputs. However, our work focuses on verifying a NN against the ground truth and providing a proof that the error made by the NN, compared to the ground truth, is below a given tolerance.

Finally, it is worth noting that generalization capability is one of the key ML assurance objectives in the emerging aviation guidance, including [3,18,21]. These documents may use different terminology (for example, the FAA does not explicitly speak about generalization, but rather refers to measuring expected empirical error and level of confidence that it corresponds to the true error), but the expected evidence is the same. Our approach can complement the anticipated means of compliance for generalization objectives with formal methods-based approaches that have a clear benefit of providing formal guarantees rather than statistical. Even though analyzing deep learning models remains a challenge for formal methods due to scalability barriers, this approach can extensively support low-complexity NNs that find many applications in safety-critical aviation systems.

7 Conclusion

We presented a mathematical formalization of the generalization property for NNs, and a method to prove this property with formal analysis. We also proposed a workflow that limits the amount of data required for obtaining the proof by combining the verification method with an iterative refinement of the regions where the property could not be proven valid. We demonstrated the applicability of the approach on a realistic case study of a safety-critical pilot advisory system that uses a low-complexity regression NN. Our results provided *formal* generalization guarantees for the significant portion of the NN input space and used orders of magnitude fewer data points compared to an existing statistical method that was employed to verify this NN. Future work will focus on enhancing the choice of the workflow hyperparameters, such as the choice of the optimal refinement strategy. We further plan to extend the workflow to support NN improvements (e.g., fine tuning). Finally, we also plan to assess the scalability of the approach on higher complexity NNs to identify further optimizations.

References

1. Deep learning toolbox verification library. https://fr.mathworks.com/products/deep-learning-verification-library.html. Accessed 29 Apr 2025

2. Machine Learning in Certified Systems. Tech. rep., DEEL Certification Working group (2020)
3. EASA Artificial Intelligence Concept Paper Issue 2: Guidance for Level 1&2 machine learning applications. Tech. rep., EASA (March 2024)
4. Amir, G., Maayan, O., Zelazny, T., Katz, G., Schapira, M.: Verifying generalization in deep learning. In: Computer Aided Verification, pp. 438–455. Springer (2023). https://doi.org/10.1007/978-3-031-37703-7_21
5. Brix, C., Bak, S., Johnson, T.T., Wu, H.: The fifth international verification of neural networks competition (VNN-COMP 2024): summary and results. arXiv preprint arXiv:2412.19985 (2024)
6. Collins Aerospace: Certification aspects of Collins Aerospace recommended cruise level neural network development. Tech. rep. (2023)
7. Damour, M., et al.: Towards certification of a reduced footprint ACAS-XU system: a hybrid ML-based solution. In: Proceedings of SAFECOMP, pp. 34–48. Springer (2021). https://doi.org/10.1007/978-3-030-83903-1_3
8. Dziugaite, G.K., Roy, D.M.: Computing nonvacuous generalization bounds for deep (stochastic) neural networks with many more parameters than training data. arXiv:1703.11008 (2017)
9. EASA AI Task Force and Daedalean, AG: Concepts of design assurance for neural networks (CoDANN). Tech. rep. (2020)
10. EASA and Collins Aerospace: Formal methods use for learning assurance (ForMuLA). Tech. rep. (2023)
11. Ehlers, R.: Formal verification of piece-wise linear feed-forward neural networks. In: Automated Technology for Verification and Analysis (2017)
12. Gehr, T., Mirman, M., Drachsler-Cohen, D., Tsankov, P., Chaudhuri, S., Vechev, M.: AI^2: Safety and robustness certification of neural networks with abstract interpretation. In: 2018 IEEE Symposium on Security and Privacy (SP), pp. 3–18 (2018). https://doi.org/10.1109/SP.2018.00058
13. Julian, K.D., Kochenderfer, M.J., Owen, M.P.: Deep neural network compression for aircraft collision avoidance systems. J. Guid. Control. Dyn. **42**(3), 598–608 (2019). https://doi.org/10.2514/1.G003724
14. Kirov, D., Rollini, S.F.: Benchmark: remaining useful life predictor for aircraft equipment. In: Proceedings of AISOLA, pp. 299–304. Springer (2023). https://doi.org/10.1007/978-3-031-46002-9_18
15. Kirov, D., Rollini, S.F., Chandrahas, R., Chandupatla, S.R., Sawant, R.: Benchmark: object detection for maritime search and rescue. In: Proceedings of AISOLA, pp. 305–310. Springer (2023). https://doi.org/10.1007/978-3-031-46002-9_19
16. MLEAP Consortium: EASA Research – Machine Learning Application Approval (MLEAP) final report. HORIZON Europe research and innovation programme report, EASA (2024)
17. Pérez-Ortiz, M., Rivasplata, O., Shawe-Taylor, J., Szepesvári, C.: Tighter risk certificates for neural networks. J. Mach. Learn. Res. **22**(227), 1–40 (2021)
18. Pham, T.: Technical concept paper 1: verification of an artificial neural net model developed through machine learning. Tech. rep, FAA (2024)
19. RTCA/DO-178C: Software Considerations in Airborne Systems and Equipment Certification (2011)
20. SAE G-34 Artificial Intelligence in Aviation: Artificial intelligence in aeronautical systems: statement of concerns (2021)
21. SAE G34 / EUROCAE WG-114: ARP6983 / ED-324: Process Standard for Development and Certification/Approval of Aeronautical Safety-Related Products Implementing AI (DRAFT 6b) (2024)

22. Singh, G., Gehr, T., Püschel, M., Vechev, M.: An abstract domain for certifying neural networks. Proc. ACM Program. Lang. **3**(POPL) (2019). https://doi.org/10.1145/3290354
23. Tjeng, V., Xiao, K.Y., Tedrake, R.: Evaluating robustness of neural networks with mixed integer programming. In: International Conference on Learning Representations (2019)
24. Wang, S., Pei, K., Whitehouse, J., Yang, J., Jana, S.S.: Formal security analysis of neural networks using symbolic intervals. In: USENIX Security Symposium. USENIX Association (2018)
25. Wu, H., et al.: Parallelization techniques for verifying neural networks. In: 2020 Formal Methods in Computer Aided Design (FMCAD), pp. 128–137. IEEE (2020). https://doi.org/10.34727/2020/isbn.978-3-85448-042-6_20
26. Zhang, H., Weng, T.W., Chen, P.Y., Hsieh, C.J., Daniel, L.: Efficient neural network robustness certification with general activation functions. In: NIPS'18, Proceedings of the 32nd International Conference on Neural Information Processing Systems, pp. 4944–4953. Curran Associates Inc. (2018)

Certified Error Analysis of Homomorphically Encrypted Neural Networks

Philipp Kern[1], Edoardo Manino[2(✉)], and Carsten Sinz[1,3]

[1] Karlsruhe Institute of Technology, 76131 Karlsruhe, Germany
{philipp.kern,carsten.sinz}@kit.edu
[2] The University of Manchester, Manchester M13 9PL, UK
edoardo.manino@manchester.ac.uk
[3] Karlsruhe University of Applied Sciences, 76133 Karlsruhe, Germany
carsten.sinz@h-ka.de

Abstract. Fully-Homomorphic Encryption (FHE) has been touted as the ultimate solution for preserving user data privacy in Machine Learning as a Service (MLaaS) applications. Under this scheme, the server never sees the user data in clear, but executes the ML model on encrypted data instead. Unfortunately, efficient FHE schemes only support addition and multiplication operations, which cannot exactly represent common activation functions in neural networks. Substituting activation functions with polynomial approximations may cause significant output deviations. In this paper, we propose ZONOPOLY, an efficient algorithm to compute guaranteed bounds on the maximum output deviation of FHE neural networks. We implement our algorithm in the VERYDIFF framework by extending its zonotope-based reachability analysis primitives to support high-degree polynomials. Experimental results show that ZONOPOLY produces approximately 3× tighter bounds than existing methods in most cases.

Keywords: Fully-homomorphic encryption · Privacy-preserving machine learning · Neural network verification · Equivalence checking

1 Introduction

The past decade has seen an increasing use of cloud computing services to run large machine learning models, a product often referred to as Machine Learning as a Service (MLaaS) [37]. On the one hand, MLaaS has the advantage of lifting the high computational requirements of machine learning away from edge devices and providing on-demand infrastructure for large-scale use cases. On the other hand, MLaaS introduces privacy risks, as the user data is transferred to a third-party server for processing.

While there are many ways to mitigate the privacy risk in MLaaS, including anonymising the data prior to transmission, the most principled solution is Fully-Homomorphic Encryption (FHE). This family of cryptographic primitives allows

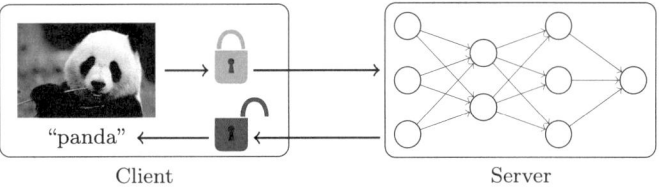

Fig. 1. In FHE-enabled MLaaS, the server operates on encrypted data.

a third party – the server – to execute a computer program on encrypted data, without ever accessing the plaintext. After that, the still-encrypted output can be sent back to the user, who decrypts it and recovers the plaintext output (see Fig. 1). With such FHE scheme, a MLaaS provider could offer fully-confidential execution of arbitrary ML models.

In this light, the introduction of modern FHE schemes has rapidly sparked interest in the feasibility of running large ML models and neural networks with it [22]. In addition to the considerable computational overhead [12], a key challenge with FHE is that it imposes strict limitations on the operations that can be performed on encrypted data [35]. For the most ML-friendly FHE schemes like CKKS [11], these restrictions can go as far as allowing only the execution of additions and multiplications, but not the non-linear activation functions of neural networks like ReLU. Consequently, activation functions must be replaced with approximating high-degree polynomials, often also requiring a retraining of the network.

After a number of early attempts at training and fine-tuning neural networks with quadratic and low-degree polynomial activations, the field has realised that they degrade the accuracy of the model too much. As a result, the state of the art solution is replacing each activation function in a neural network with a high-degree polynomial approximation. Since higher-degree polynomials increase FHE's computational cost, an acceptable compromise between accuracy and execution time needs to be found via repeated experimentation.

Attempts at computing verified error bounds between the original and modified network exist [28], but have not yet become mainstream.

In this paper, we present ZONOPOLY, an efficient algorithm to compute verified error bounds between a neural network and its polynomial counterpart. With it, we demonstrate that it is possible to derive tighter bounds on the error of FHE polynomial approximations of neural networks, improving upon existing approaches. We believe that our algorithm represents an important step towards integrating neural network verification methods into the design of FHE-enabled neural networks for ML-as-a-Service (MLaaS) applications.

More in detail, we make the following contributions to the state of the art:

– We propose ZONOPOLY, a zonotope-based method capable of both synthesizing neural networks with polynomial activation functions and computing verified bounds on the output difference between the original and polynomial approximated networks.

- We implement our ZONOPOLY algorithm in the VERYDIFF framework, thus extending its reachability analysis engine to support polynomial transformations.
- We compare ZONOPOLY with LIGAR [28], the only existing formal method baseline in this domain, and show that we can derive 3.37× tighter bounds on average.

2 Background

For the sake of simplicity, we will assume that our ML model is a feedforward neural network $\mathcal{N} : \mathbb{R}^m \to \mathbb{R}^n$ with L fully-connected layers h_l, such that $\mathcal{N} = h_L \circ h_{L-1} \circ \cdots \circ h_1$. Each layer h_l has the following form:

$$h_l(\boldsymbol{x}_l) = \sigma\big(W_l\boldsymbol{x}_l + \boldsymbol{b}_l\big) \ , \tag{1}$$

where W_l is a matrix, $\boldsymbol{b}_l$ a column vector, and $\sigma(x) = \max(x, 0)$ the element-wise ReLU activation function. Our algorithm is – in principle – extensible to more sophisticated neural architectures, but we leave that effort to future work (see Sect. 5).

2.1 Fully-Homomorphic Encryption (FHE) Schemes

We define a homomorphic encryption scheme as follows.

Definition 1 (Homomorphic Encryption). *Let $\mathcal{E} = (\mathsf{Gen}, \mathsf{Enc}, \mathsf{Dec})$ be an encryption scheme, m_1, m_2 two plaintext messages, and g a function. Further assume that $m_3 = g(m_1, m_2)$ is the result of applying function g to the plaintext messages m_1, m_2, and $c_3 \equiv g(c_1, c_2)$ is the result of applying function g on the corresponding cyphertexts $c_1 \equiv \mathsf{Enc}(m_1)$ and $c_2 \equiv \mathsf{Enc}(m_2)$. Then $\mathcal{E}$ is homomorphic with respect to function g if we have $\mathsf{Dec}(c_3) = m_3$.*

Early attempts at creating a homomorphic scheme are limited to one operation g alone [3]. For example, the scheme in [32] supports only homomorphic addition $g(m_1, m_2) = m_1 + m_2$, whereas RSA encryption [38] supports only multiplication $g(m_1, m_2) = m_1 m_2$. The first scheme that supports both addition and multiplication, while also allowing the computation of programs of arbitrary depth, is by Gentry [20]. After that, the field has focused on leveraging more efficient computational problems, i.e. Learning With Errors (LWE) [7] and Ring Learning With Error (RLWE) [8], to reduce the computational overhead of FHE.

Introduction of *approximate* FHE schemes like CKKS [11] has enabled practical execution of machine learning algorithms. Instead of representing individual binary values, the CKKS scheme and its variants are able to manipulate vectors of real numbers $m = (x_1, x_2, \ldots, x_n)$, which makes them more efficient for machine learning purposes [35]. The downside is that the results are not *exact* [15]: for each homomorphic operation g, we have $\mathsf{Dec}(g(c_1, c_2)) = g(m_1, m_2) + \eta$, where the error term η depends on the user's encryption key and the value of the plaintext messages m_1, m_2. For the purpose of MLaaS, the error η can be arbitrarily reduced by changing the parameters of the FHE scheme, at the cost of increasing the computational overhead [1,6]. As such, we assume the intrinsic encryption error η is negligible and focus on the error introduced by approximating activation functions by polynomials (see Sect. 2.2) in the remainder of the paper.

2.2 Design of FHE Neural Networks

One of the main challenges in the execution of FHE neural networks is dealing with activation functions, as they cannot be represented as a computational circuit of additions and multiplications [35]. Instead, early attempts try to replace all activations with approximating low-degree polynomials, such as quadratic activations [10,22,29]. Unfortunately, any polynomial activation of degree $d \geq 2$ has unbounded derivatives, which cause gradient instability during training and fine-tuning. Furthermore, reusing the original weights is not viable as the approximation error at each activation accumulates, yielding low overall predictive accuracy [19].

A more recent approach consists of keeping the trained model unmodified and building close approximations $p_d(x) \approx \sigma(x)$ of the activation functions with high-degree polynomials ($d \approx 100$ or more) [26,27]. In order to improve numerical stability, some authors prefer to build approximations in Chebyshev basis [39] or employ custom hierarchical factorisations [25]. Still, these approximations minimize the error for a specific input range $x \in [l, u]$, while becoming increasingly worse outside of it (see Fig. 2). To our knowledge, the existing literature does not explore the problem of correctly estimating the ranges $[l, u]$. Instead, most works seem to rely on symmetric ranges $[-c, +c]$ and either fix their width a priori (e.g. $c = 3$) [10,30] or use some unspecified empirical approach to estimate its value (up to $c = 50$ for a CIFAR-10 model) [27,39].

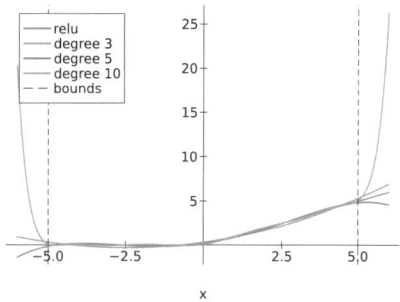

Fig. 2. Polynomial approximations quickly deviate to $\pm \infty$ outside of the approximation interval.

Certified Design. The only existing attempt at designing a FHE neural network with formal guarantees is the LiGAR algorithm [28]. Its authors propose to abstract the polynomial approximation error by injecting an additional symbolic input after every activation function. Then, they compute a certified bound on the activation ranges $[l, u]$, and estimate the numerical stability of the network by computing its Lipschitz constant (for a definition see, e.g., [28]). With it, they can optimize the polynomial degree of each activation to achieve a desired output error bound.

Still, LiGAR employs relatively inefficient neural network verification techniques, including parallel linear bounds for reachability analysis [45] and Lipschitz bounds for equivalence checking [40]. Furthermore, it simplifies the optimisation problem by replacing the objective function with an asymptotic approximation of its value [44]. Together, these factors cause LiGAR to yield very conservative estimates, as we show in Sect. 4.3.

2.3 Equivalence Checking of ReLU Neural Networks

In this paper, we cast the problem of analysing the difference between polynomial FHE networks and original ReLU networks as an *equivalence checking* problem. Specifically, we are interested in the following definition of equivalence:

Definition 2 (ε-Equivalence). *The neural networks $\mathcal{N}_1$ and $\mathcal{N}_2$ are equivalent in the domain $\mathcal{D}$ according to norm $\|\cdot\|_p$, if for any input $x \in \mathcal{D}$ we have $\|\mathcal{N}_1(x) - \mathcal{N}_2(x)\|_p \leq \varepsilon$.*

In general, checking the equivalence of two ReLU networks $\mathcal{N}_1$ and $\mathcal{N}_2$ is a coNP-complete problem [42]. As such, exact verification techniques, such as mixed integer programming [23] and SMT solving [17], struggle to scale to reasonably-sized networks. Popular alternatives use incomplete verification techniques that over-approximate the set of outputs that are reachable from the input domain $\mathcal{D}$ [33,34,43], as detailed in Sect. 2.4.

2.4 Zonotope-Based Reachability Analysis

In this paper, we use *zonotopes* [21,41,43] to represent reachable sets:

Definition 3 (Zonotope). *A zonotope $\mathcal{Z} = (c, G)$ with n generators and dimension m is an affine transformation of the hypercube $[-1, 1]^n$ described by*

$$\mathcal{Z} = \{x \in \mathbb{R}^m \mid G\epsilon + c = x, \epsilon \in [-1,1]^n\} \, , \tag{2}$$

where $G \in \mathbb{R}^{m \times n}$ and $c \in \mathbb{R}^m$ are the generator matrix and center of the zonotope, respectively. The columns of G are called generators of the zonotope.

Affine Layers. A zonotope $\mathcal{Z} = (c, G)$ can be propagated through an affine transformation $x \mapsto Ax + b$ without introducing any over-approximation. The resulting zonotope $\hat{\mathcal{Z}}$ can be computed as

$$\hat{\mathcal{Z}} = A\mathcal{Z} + b = (Ac + b, AG) \, . \tag{3}$$

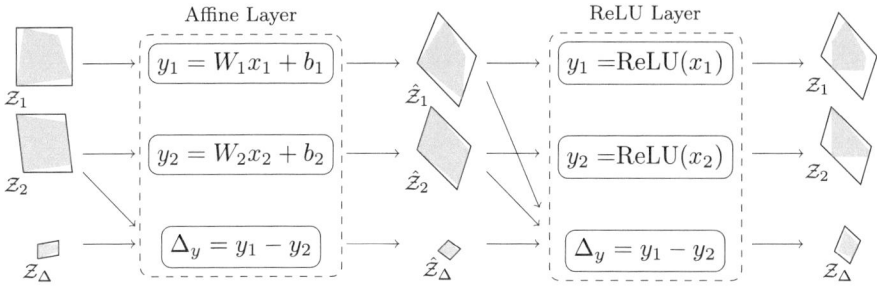

Fig. 3. Zonotope propagation (black) over-approximates the reachable sets (gray) at every layer. Differential verification keeps track of the explicit difference $\mathcal{Z}_\Delta$. (Color figure online)

ReLU Layers. A zonotope $\mathcal{Z} = (\mathbf{c}, G)$ cannot be propagated through a non-linear function like ReLU without over-approximation [41]. More specifically, assume that $\sigma : \mathbb{R} \to \mathbb{R}$ is a non-linear activation function. Also, assume that σ is bounded in the interval domains $I_i = [l_i, u_i]$, $1 \leq i \leq m$, such that $\forall x_i \in I_i : |\alpha_i x_i + \beta_i - \sigma(x_i)| \leq \gamma_i$ for some $\alpha_i, \beta_i \in \mathbb{R}$ and error bounds $\gamma_i \in \mathbb{R}$. The resulting over-approximated zonotope $\hat{\mathcal{Z}}$ becomes:

$$\hat{\mathcal{Z}} = \boldsymbol{\alpha} \odot \mathcal{Z} + \boldsymbol{\beta} + \boldsymbol{\gamma} \odot \boldsymbol{\epsilon}, \quad \boldsymbol{\epsilon} \in [-1,1]^m \qquad (4)$$

$$= \left(\boldsymbol{\alpha} \odot \mathbf{c} + \boldsymbol{\beta}, [\boldsymbol{\alpha} \odot G \;\; \text{diag}(\boldsymbol{\gamma})]\right), \qquad (5)$$

where $\odot$ represents element-wise multiplication and $\text{diag}(\cdot)$ turns a vector into a diagonal matrix. The fresh variables $\boldsymbol{\epsilon}$ in Eq. (4) allow each dimension to independently vary within its error bounds [14]. To capture this concept in the zonotope formalism, the error bounds $\boldsymbol{\gamma}$ are appended as a diagonal matrix to the end of the scaled original generator matrix G.

2.5 Differential Verification

Computing the output sets of $\mathcal{N}_1$ and $\mathcal{N}_2$ may not be enough to prove their equivalence, since the over-approximation grows due to the contribution of γ at every ReLU layer (see Eq. (4)). Instead, both the pioneering work of Paulsen [33,34] and the VERYDIFF tool [43] show that we should keep track of a third reachability set over the difference function between $\mathcal{N}_1$ and $\mathcal{N}_2$ (see Fig. 3). When $\mathcal{N}_1$ and $\mathcal{N}_2$ have similar architecture and weights, this *differential verification* approach allows us to greatly reduce the over-approximation.

Affine Layers. Given affine transformations $y_i = W_i x_i + b_i$ for $i \in \{1, 2\}$ and $\Delta_x = x_1 - x_2$, the difference function $\Delta_y = y_1 - y_2$ can be written as

$$\Delta_y = y_1 - y_2 \tag{6}$$
$$= W_1 x_1 + b_1 - (W_2 x_2 + b_2) \tag{7}$$
$$= W_1 ((x_1 - x_2) + x_2) + b_1 - (W_2 x_2 + b_2) \tag{8}$$
$$= W_1 (\Delta_x + x_2) + b_1 - (W_2 x_2 + b_2) \tag{9}$$
$$= (W_1 - W_2) x_2 + W_1 \Delta_x + (b_1 - b_2) \tag{10}$$

which depends only on x_2 and $\Delta_x = x_1 - x_2$ as inputs.

Proposition 1 (Affine Differential Zonotope [43]). *Given zonotopes $\mathcal{Z}_1$ with $x_1 \in \mathcal{Z}_1$ (written in the following as $\mathcal{Z}_1 \ni x_1$), $\mathcal{Z}_\Delta \ni x_1 - x_2$, $\mathcal{Z}_2 \ni x_2$ and affine transformations $y_i = W_i x_i + b_i$ for $i \in \{1, 2\}$, the zonotopes*

$$\hat{\mathcal{Z}}_1 = W_1 \mathcal{Z}_1 + b_1 \tag{11}$$
$$\hat{\mathcal{Z}}_\Delta = (W_1 - W_2) \mathcal{Z}_2 + W_1 \mathcal{Z}_\Delta + (b_1 - b_2) \tag{12}$$
$$\hat{\mathcal{Z}}_2 = W_2 \mathcal{Z}_2 + b_2 \tag{13}$$

over-approximate $y_1, y_1 - y_2$ and y_2.

ReLU Layers. Similarly to the propagation through the affine layer, the ReLU-difference function $\Delta_y^R = \mathrm{ReLU}(x_1) - \mathrm{ReLU}(x_2)$ can again be expressed as

$$\Delta_y^R = \mathrm{ReLU}(x_1) - \mathrm{ReLU}(x_2) \tag{14}$$
$$= \mathrm{ReLU}((x_1 - x_2) + x_2) - \mathrm{ReLU}(x_2) \tag{15}$$
$$= \mathrm{ReLU}(\Delta_x + x_2) - \mathrm{ReLU}(x_2) \tag{16}$$
$$= \mathrm{ReLU}(x_1) - \mathrm{ReLU}(x_1 - (x_1 - x_2)) \tag{17}$$
$$= \mathrm{ReLU}(x_1) - \mathrm{ReLU}(x_1 - \Delta_x) \tag{18}$$

which depends on either x_1 and Δ_x (Eq. (18)) or x_2 and Δ_x (Eq. (16)).

Proposition 2 (ReLU Differential Zonotope [43]). *Given zonotopes $\mathcal{Z}_1 \ni x_1, \mathcal{Z}_\Delta \ni x_1 - x_2, \mathcal{Z}_2 \ni x_2$ and $y_1 = \mathrm{ReLU}(x_1), y_2 = \mathrm{ReLU}(x_2)$, the zonotopes*

$$\hat{\mathcal{Z}}_1 = \lambda_1 \odot \mathcal{Z}_1 + \xi_1 + \xi_1 \epsilon_1 \tag{19}$$
$$\hat{\mathcal{Z}}_\Delta = a_1 \odot \mathcal{Z}_1 + a_2 \odot \mathcal{Z}_2 + a_\Delta \odot \mathcal{Z}_\Delta + b + c\epsilon_\Delta \tag{20}$$
$$\hat{\mathcal{Z}}_2 = \lambda_2 \odot \mathcal{Z}_2 + \xi_2 + \xi_2 \epsilon_2 \tag{21}$$

over-approximate $y_1, y_1 - y_2$ and y_2. Where $\epsilon_1, \epsilon_2, \epsilon_\Delta$ are new independent generators,

$$\lambda_i = \frac{u_i}{u_i - l_i}, \quad \xi_i = \frac{-l_i \lambda_i}{2} \tag{22}$$

for $l_i \leq \mathcal{Z}_i \leq u_i$ element-wise and the values of a_1, a_2, a_Δ, b, c are set according to Table 1.

Table 1. Case distinction for differential ReLU propagation. Different ReLU phases are denoted by $-$ (negative), $+$ (positive) and $\sim$ (unstable). The values for λ_i, ξ_i are defined in (22). $\alpha_i = \frac{-l_i}{u_i - l_i}, \mu_i = \frac{1}{2}\lambda_i u_i$ and $\lambda_\Delta = \text{clamp}\left(\frac{u_\Delta}{u_\Delta - l_\Delta}, 0, 1\right)$, $\mu_\Delta = \frac{1}{2}\max(-l_\Delta, u_\Delta)$, $\nu_\Delta = \lambda_\Delta \max(0, -l_\Delta)$

ReLU		Factor				
σ_1	σ_2	a_1	a_2	a_Δ	b	c
$-$	$-$	0	0	0	0	0
$-$	$+$	0	-1	0	0	0
$+$	$-$	1	0	0	0	0
$+$	$+$	0	0	1	0	0
$\sim$	$-$	λ_1	0	0	ξ_1	0
$-$	$\sim$	0	$-\lambda_2$	0	$-\xi_2$	0
$\sim$	$+$	$-\alpha_1$	0	1	μ_1	μ_1
$+$	$\sim$	0	α_2	1	$-\mu_2$	μ_2
$\sim$	$\sim$	0	0	λ_Δ	$\nu_\Delta - \mu_\Delta$	μ_Δ

3 Methodology

In this section, we present ZONOPOLY, an algorithm to synthesise polynomial approximation networks with certified error bound. In contrast to previous work [28], ZONOPOLY constructs concrete polynomials instead of abstracting them away. As such, ZONOPOLY produces tighter error estimates than [28] at the expense of increased computational cost (see Sect. 4.3). At the same time, manipulating high degree polynomials can lead to numerical instability: we show how to mitigate such risk in Sect. 3.3.

At high level, the process of running ZONOPOLY can be divided in two stages. First, we construct a polynomial network using verified bounds, as described in Sect. 3.1. We output not only the polynomial degrees (as in [28]), but the concrete coefficients of the polynomial activation functions as well as the bounds used for approximation. Second, we compute a certified bound on the output difference between the original network $\mathcal{N}_1$ and the corresponding polynomial network $\mathcal{N}_2$. To do so, we augment the zonotope-based differential verification approach of VERYDIFF with a novel relaxation for $p(x) - \text{ReLU}(x - \Delta)$, as described in Sect. 3.2.

3.1 Verified Construction of Polynomial Networks

In order to synthesize networks with polynomial activation functions, we need estimates over the pre-activation ranges $[l, u]$ of each neuron (see Sect. 2.2). Then, we can compute the polynomial approximation $p(x) \approx \text{ReLU}(x)$ that minimises the absolute error over $[l, u]$, by using the Remez algorithm [36]. Since the approximation error quickly diverges to $\pm \infty$ outside of $[l, u]$ (see Fig. 2), we need verified

Algorithm 1. Construction of network with polynomial approximations as activation functions using verified bounds

---
1: **function** CONSTRUCT_NETWORK($\langle W_l, b_l \rangle_{l=1}^{L}, l_0, u_0, d$)
Require: $\langle W_l, b_l \rangle_{l=1}^{L}$ neural network parameters, l_0, u_0 concrete bounds on the network inputs, d degree of the polynomial approximations
Ensure: Pre-activation bounds $\langle l_l \rangle_{l=1}^{L-1}$, $\langle u_l \rangle_{l=1}^{L-1}$, list of vectors of polynomials $\langle p_l \rangle_{l=1}^{L-1}$
2:     $\mathcal{Z} \leftarrow$ zonotope(l_0, u_0)
3:     **for** $l \leftarrow 1, \ldots, L-1$ **do**
4:         $\mathcal{Z} \leftarrow W_l \mathcal{Z} + b_l$
5:         $l_l, u_l \leftarrow$ bounds($\mathcal{Z}$)
6:         $p_l, \_ =$ remez(ReLU, l_l, u_l, d)   ▷ element-wise for each neuron
7:         $\mathcal{Z} \leftarrow p(\mathcal{Z})$ ▷ Proposition 3
8:     **end for**
9: **end function**

---

bounds over the ranges $[l, u]$ that contain all possible values attainable by concrete execution of the network.

Furthermore, the bounds $[l, u]$ on the ranges of neurons at layer $l \in [2, L]$ depend on the error introduced by all approximations $p(x)$ at previous layers $j \in [1, l-1]$. Therefore, it is not sufficient to compute the bounds by running reachability analysis on the original network with ReLU activations. Instead, we have to track the approximation error we introduce at each layer l and propagate it correctly to the next layers. We formally describe the resulting procedure in Algorithm 1.

There, we use the zonotope propagation rules for affine layers presented in Eq. (3) (Line 4). The resulting zonotope gives us an easy way to compute bounds on the pre-activation ranges (Line 5). With them, we can compute polynomial approximations of the activation functions (Line 6). Finally, we need to propagate the zonotope through the polynomial activations (Line 7). For this purpose, we propose a way to over-approximate each univariate polynomial activation $p(x)$ with linear parallel bounds (see Fig. 4). More formally:

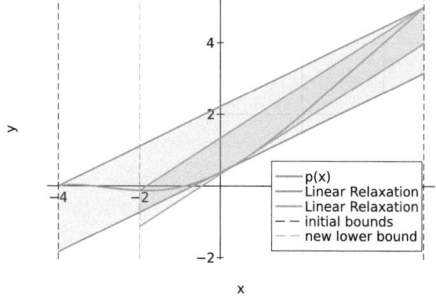

Fig. 4. Two zonotope relaxations of a polynomial activation $p(x)$. Note how the zonotope relaxation for a smaller input domain (orange) might not be fully contained in the one for a larger input domain (green). (Color figure online)

Proposition 3 (Linear Relaxation of Polynomials). *Given $y = p(x)$ for a vector of univariate polynomials $p(x) = (p_1(x_1), \ldots, p_n(x_n))$ and a zonotope $\mathcal{Z} \ni x$, we obtain a linear relaxation (a polynomial of degree 1) using*

$$\hat{p}, \gamma = \mathrm{remez}(p, l, u, 1) \,, \tag{23}$$

where $\hat{p}(x) = \boldsymbol{\alpha} \odot x + \beta$ and $l \leq x \leq u$ are obtained from $\mathcal{Z}$ and $\boldsymbol{\alpha} \odot x + \beta - \gamma \leq p(x) \leq \boldsymbol{\alpha} \odot x + \beta + \gamma$ for all $x \in [l, u]$. The new zonotope $\hat{\mathcal{Z}} \ni y$ is then given by

$$\hat{\mathcal{Z}} = \boldsymbol{\alpha} \odot \mathcal{Z} + \beta + \gamma \odot \epsilon, \tag{24}$$

where $\epsilon \in [-1, 1]^n$ are new error symbols.

3.2 Differential Verification of Polynomial and ReLU Networks

In Sect. 2.5, we reviewed how existing work models the difference between two ReLU activation functions. Here, we instead consider the difference $\Delta_y = p(x_1) - \text{ReLU}(x_2)$ between a polynomial and a ReLU activation. We can still take inspiration from Eqs. (14)–(18) and write the following:

$$\Delta_y = p(x_1) - \text{ReLU}(x_2) \tag{25}$$
$$= p(\Delta_x + x_2) - \text{ReLU}(x_2) \tag{26}$$
$$= p(x_1) - \text{ReLU}(x_1 - \Delta_x), \tag{27}$$

While Eq. (26) requires reasoning over a multivariate polynomial of possibly high degree, Eq. (27) is much easier to handle. Indeed, we can analyse the two linear segments of $\text{ReLU}(x_1 - \Delta_x)$ separately, thus splitting Eq. (27) into two cases:

$$p(x_1) - \text{ReLU}(x_1 - \Delta_x) = \begin{cases} p(x_1) & x_1 \leq \Delta_x \\ (p(x_1) - x_1) + \Delta_x & x_1 > \Delta_x \end{cases} \tag{28}$$

The advantage of Eq. (28) is that we only need to reason about the *univariate* polynomials $p(x_1)$ and $p(x_1) - x_1$, while treating the addition of Δ_x independently. Furthermore, we are left with only three possible activation patterns, rather than the nine required when comparing two ReLU networks (see Table 1). More specifically, let the pre-activation ranges be $x_1 \in [l_1, u_1], x_2 \in [l_2, u_2]$ and $\Delta_x \in [l_\Delta, u_\Delta]$. Then, we can distinguish between always inactive, always active, and unstable ReLU as follows.

Inactive ReLU. If $u_2 \leq 0$, then $\text{ReLU}(x_2)$ is always inactive. In this case, the difference function simplifies to $p(x_1) - \text{ReLU}(x_2) = p(x_1)$. As such, the difference zonotope is identical to the zonotope of the polynomial network, which we compute according to Proposition 3.

Active ReLU. If $l_2 \geq 0$, then $\text{ReLU}(x_2)$ is always active. In this case, the difference function simplifies to $p(x_1) - \text{ReLU}(x_2) = (p(x_1) - x_1) + \Delta_x$. Thus, we can first compute a linear over-approximation of the univariate polynomial $p(x_1) - x_1$ and then add the linear term Δ_x. In particular, let:

$$\hat{p}, \gamma = \text{remez}(p(x_1) - x_1, l_1, u_1, 1), \tag{29}$$

where $\hat{p}(x_1) = \alpha x_1 + \beta$ and $\alpha x_1 + \beta - \gamma \leq p(x_1) - x_1 \leq \alpha x_1 + \beta + \gamma$ for $x_1 \in [l_1, u_1]$. Then, the final linear relaxation is:

$$\alpha x_1 + \Delta_x + \beta - \gamma \leq (p(x_1) - x_1) + \Delta_x \leq \alpha x_1 + \Delta_x + \beta + \gamma. \tag{30}$$

Unstable ReLU. If $l_2 < 0 < u_2$, then we do not know whether ReLU(x_2) is active or inactive. In this case, we need to find a linear relaxation $a_1 x_1 + a_\Delta \Delta_x + b \pm c$ that satisfies:

$$a_1 x_1 + a_\Delta \Delta_x + b - c \leq p(x_1) - \text{ReLU}(x_1 - \Delta_x) \leq a_1 x_1 + a_\Delta \Delta_x + b + c \tag{31}$$

In ZONOPOLY, we construct a valid over-approximation by guessing the values of a_1, a_Δ and optimising for the values of b, c. Specifically, we take the values of a_1, a_Δ from Table 1, which are the slopes VERYDIFF uses for comparing ReLU activations [43]. Since we have $p(x) \approx \text{ReLU}(x)$ for all neurons, the values of a_1, a_Δ are not far from optimal.

Relaxation Error. Given the values of a_1, a_Δ, the relaxation error is:

$$g(x_1, \Delta_x) = (p(x_1) - \text{ReLU}(x_1 - \Delta_x)) - (a_1 x_1 + a_\Delta \Delta_x) \tag{32}$$

and we can set:

$$b = \frac{\max g + \min g}{2}, \quad c = \frac{\max g - \min g}{2} \tag{33}$$

For simplicity, we only describe how to compute the maximum relaxation error. The minimum can be computed in a similar fashion.

Error Maximisation. Since Eq. 32 contains a ReLU activation, we split the domain of the maximisation problem into two regions: $x_1 \leq \Delta_x$ (inactive) and $x_1 \geq \Delta_x$ (active). More formally, we have $\max g(x_1, \Delta_x) = \max\{\mu_\leq, \mu_\geq\}$, where:

$$\mu_\leq = \max\ p(x_1) - a_1 x_1 - a_\Delta \Delta_x, \qquad \text{s.t. } x_1 \leq \Delta_x \tag{34}$$
$$\mu_\geq = \max\ p(x_1) - (1+a_1)x_1 - (a_\Delta - 1)\Delta_x, \qquad \text{s.t. } x_1 \geq \Delta_x \tag{35}$$

with $x_1 \in [l_1, u_1]$ and $\Delta_x \in [l_\Delta, u_\Delta]$. Note that both objective functions can be expressed as $p(x_1) + \alpha x_1 + \beta \Delta_x$ for suitable choices of α and β. Thus, solving the above optimization problems requires finding the maximum of a polynomial on a compact bounded set (Fig. 5).

Critical Points. Since $g(x_1, \Delta_x) = p(x_1) + \alpha x_1 + \beta \Delta_x$ is a linear function in Δ_x, the maximum is always located at one of the three boundaries $\Delta_x = l_\Delta$, $\Delta_x = u_\Delta$, or $\Delta_x = x_1$. For the first two boundaries, define the critical points of the univariate polynomial $g(x_1, 0)$ as follows:

$$\mathcal{C}_{\Delta_x = 0} = \left\{ x : \frac{d}{dx}\left(p(x) + \alpha x\right) = 0 \right\} \cup \{l_1, u_1\} \tag{36}$$

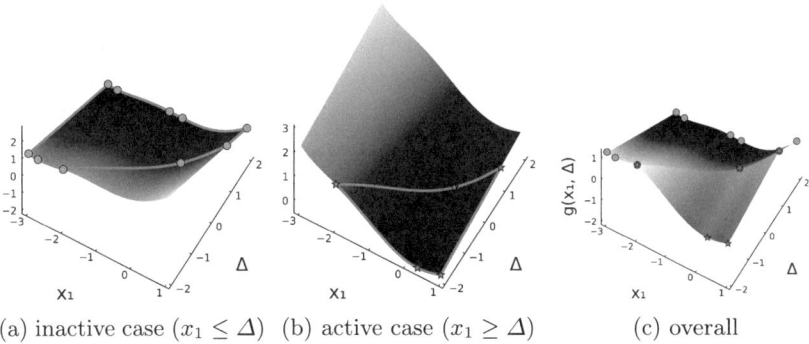

(a) inactive case ($x_1 \leq \Delta$) (b) active case ($x_1 \geq \Delta$) (c) overall

Fig. 5. Critical points for $g(x_1, \Delta_x) = (p(x_1) - \text{ReLU}(x_1 - \Delta_x)) - (-1/7 x_1 + 8/10 \Delta_x)$. The two subproblems are shown on the left with the boundary of their domain shown as green lines. The overall relaxation error function with its critical points computed via the subproblems is shown on the right.

For the latter boundary $\Delta_x = x_1$, define the critical points of another univariate polynomial $g(x_1, x_1)$ as:

$$\mathcal{C}_{\Delta_x = x_1} = \left\{ x : \frac{d}{dx}\left(p(x) + \alpha x + \beta x\right) = 0 \right\} \cup \left\{ l_1, u_1, l_\Delta, u_\Delta \right\} \qquad (37)$$

Then, we can build our final set of critical points, which is guaranteed to contain the solution to the optimisation problems in Eqs. 34 and 35:

$$\hat{\mathcal{C}} = \left\{ (x_1, \Delta_x) : x_1 \in \mathcal{C}_{\Delta_x=0}, \Delta_x \in \{l_\Delta, u_\Delta\} \right\} \cup \left\{ (x_1, x_1) : x_1 \in \mathcal{C}_{\Delta_x = x_1} \right\} \qquad (38)$$

Since $\hat{\mathcal{C}}$ is finite, ZONOPOLY simply searches over its feasible subset.

3.3 Numerical Stability

Polynomial Basis. The methods we introduce in Sects. 3.1 and 3.2 require the manipulation of polynomials of arbitrary degree and rely on common primitives such as evaluation, interpolation, and root finding. It is well known that their implementation in monomial basis can lead to numerical instability [44]. We show an example of this in Fig. 6.

To avoid these numerical difficulties, we follow the recommendations of [44] and represent all polynomials in Chebyshev basis with inputs normalized to $[-1, 1]$. Each polynomial is stored as a triple $(\mathbf{c}, l, u)$ of its Chebyshev coefficients $\mathbf{c}$ and original input range $x \in [l, u]$. With it, we can implement the following:

Evaluation and Interpolation. For the former, we use Clenshaw recurrence [13]. For the latter, we implement the version of the Remez algorithm described in [31], which was originally developed for the CHEBFUN system [16].

Root Finding. Given the Chebyshev coefficients, finding the roots of the polynomial reduces to finding the eigenvalues of the corresponding colleague matrix [44]. The correctness of the critical points in Eqs. 36 and 37 depends on the soundness of the underlying eigenvalue solver. In our Julia implementation, we use the built-in `eigvals` command [5].

Zonotope Monotonicity. Zonotope relaxations of activation functions are not monotonic in the size of the input domain (see Fig. 4). As a consequence, running differential verification for a smaller input domain $\mathcal{D}' \subseteq \mathcal{D}$ may lead to non-overlapping input range bounds $[l', u'] \not\subseteq [l, u]$ for some neurons in the network. If the new bounds $[l', u']$ exceed the domain where the polynomial activation is well behaved (see Fig. 2), numerical issues arise. We mitigate this risk by storing the *verified* bounds $[l, u]$ that we compute via Algorithm 1, and tightening any range estimate $[l', u']$ that exceeds them during differential verification.

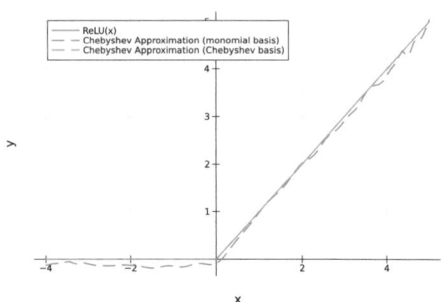

Fig. 6. Chebyshev approximation of degree 100 of ReLU(x) for $x \in [-4, 5]$. Determining monomial coefficients by solving a linear system and standard evaluation in monomial form vs. Chebyshev coefficients and evaluation using Clenshaw recurrence.

4 Experiments

We integrated the ZONOPOLY algorithms for synthesis and differential verification of polynomially approximated networks in the VERYDIFF [43] tool implemented in Julia [5]. The code of our implementation[1] and experiments[2] is available on GitHub. All experiments were run on a 4-core Intel Xeon E5-2670 CPU and 128 GB of RAM using single-threaded execution.

In our evaluation, we examine the accuracy of the polynomial networks constructed by ZONOPOLY and compare the tightness of their differential bounds with the state-of-the-art tool LIGAR [28]. To ensure a fair comparison, we modify the latter to construct neural networks with uniform (rather than heterogeneous) polynomial degree. Furthermore, we introduce a LIGAR+CHEBY variant that outputs concrete polynomials in Chebyshev basis, rather than just asymptotic bounds over minimax polynomials.

4.1 Benchmarks

We evaluate our approach on neural networks trained for privacy critical applications like credit scoring and human activity recognition as well as standard image classification:

---
[1] https://github.com/samysweb/VeryDiff/tree/PolynomialEquivalence.
[2] https://github.com/phK3/VeryDiffPolyExperiments.

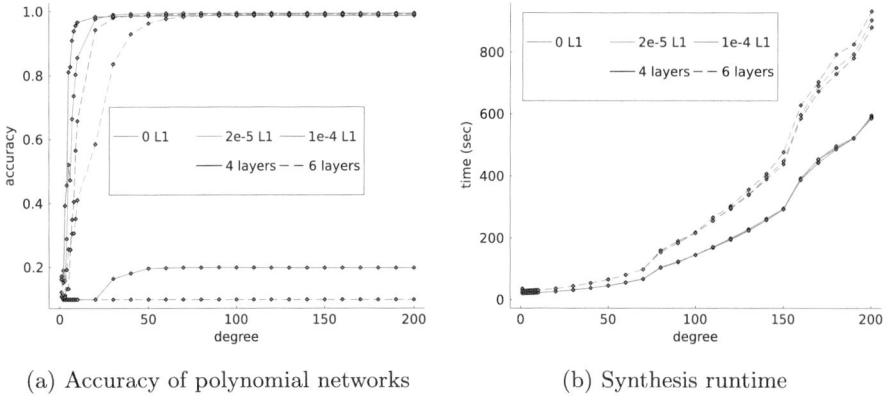

(a) Accuracy of polynomial networks (b) Synthesis runtime

Fig. 7. Accuracy of polynomial networks generated by ZONOPOLY for different polynomial degrees and base ReLU networks and runtime of ZONOPOLY for synthesis.

MNIST. [24] The machine learning task in MNIST is to correctly classify the handwritten digit shown on 28×28 pixel grayscale images. Each pixel can attain the values from $[0, 1]$ leading to an input set of $[0, 1]^{784}$. We use two base networks of size 4×256 (4 hidden layers of 256 neurons each) and 6×256 taken from the annual competition VNN-COMP[3]. For each of the networks, we train two networks of the same architecture, but with additional L_1-regularization with weights 2×10^{-5} and 10^{-4}.

HAR. [2] Given 561 statistical aggregates computed from smartphone gyroscopic data, the goal is to correctly predict human activity out of 6 candidates (standing, sitting, lying, walking, walking downstairs and walking upstairs). Each input dimension was normalized to $[-1, 1]$. We evaluate on the 1×500 network already used in the evaluations of RELUDIFF [33] and NEURODIFF [34]. We also train two networks ourselves with the same structure and L_1-penalties with weights 2×10^{-5} and 10^{-4}.

HELOC. The *home equity line of credit* dataset was part of the FICO explainable machine learning challenge [18]. Given 23 features, the goal is to classify whether or not a person is credit-worthy. We normalized all features to $[0, 1]$ and trained two neural networks – one with standard training and one with L_1-penalty of 2×10^{-5}. Despite their small size (only two hidden layers of 64 and 32 neurons respectively) the networks achieve comparable accuracy to the models submitted to the FICO challenge [4].

4.2 Synthesis of Polynomially Approximated Neural Networks

Predictive Accuracy. To examine the quality of polynomial networks generated by ZONOPOLY, we constructed an initial zonotope containing the *whole*

---

[3] https://github.com/stanleybak/vnncomp2021.

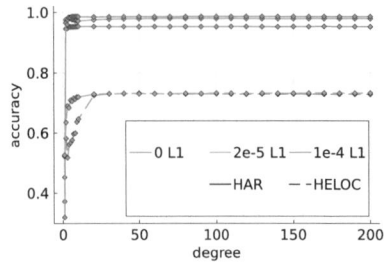
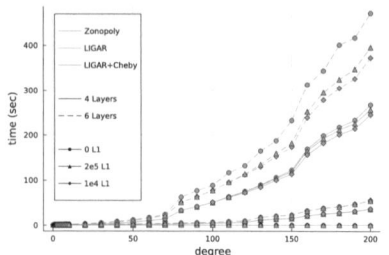

Fig. 8. Accuracy of polynomial networks generated by ZONOPOLY for different base ReLU networks and polynomial degrees for HAR and HELOC.

Fig. 9. Runtime for computation of verified bounds on polynomially approximated MNIST networks.

input set (e.g. $[0, 1]^{784}$ for the MNIST networks) and propagated that zonotope through the network to generate verified bounds and polynomial approximations according to Algorithm 1 for polynomial degrees of $1, 2, \ldots, 10, 20, 30, \ldots, 200$. Subsequently, we *statistically* evaluated the accuracy of the generated networks, as well as the maximum difference $\max_i \|\hat{\mathcal{N}}(x_i) - \mathcal{N}(x_i)\|_\infty$ between the polynomially approximated and the original network over the associated dataset. Results for *verified* bounds on the difference are reported in Sect. 4.3.

At least in the MNIST case, the most important factor for achieving good accuracy and low statistical difference from the original network is whether standard training or training with L_1 penalty was used. As shown in Fig. 7a, ZONOPOLY was able to generate polynomial networks that match the accuracy of the ReLU networks trained with some form of L_1 penalty for polynomials of degree 80 in the worst case. For the two networks that only used standard training, however, the accuracy of the generated polynomial networks never rises or gets stuck on a plateau even for high degrees – despite small improvements in the sampled maximum error shown in the left of Fig. 10. Shallower networks also achieved better accuracy for smaller polynomial degrees than deeper networks.

For the one-layer HAR networks and small HELOC networks, ZONOPOLY is also able to generate polynomial networks of matching accuracy for the ReLU networks obtained via standard training. However, the networks trained with L_1 penalty achieve better accuracy (Fig. 8) and lower sampled error for smaller polynomial degrees (deferred to Appendix A.2).

Overall, the quality of the synthesized polynomial networks seems to be good whenever small bounds can be obtained via zonotope propagation. This in turn allows the polynomial approximation to be fitted to a small approximation interval and thus less error is incurred. Training using L_1 regularization was already shown to improve verification performance [46] by encouraging a smaller range of attainable values at the neurons.

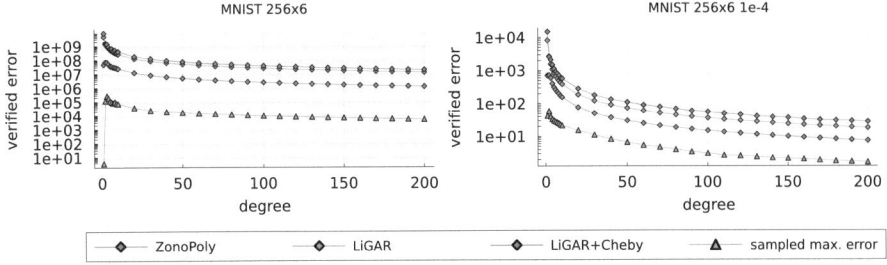

Fig. 10. Verified error bounds for polynomially approximated networks of different degree for different ReLU base networks for MNIST

Synthesis Time. The synthesis time for a polynomially approximated network is primarily influenced by the number of neurons in the network and the degree of the polynomial approximation. This trend is illustrated in the MNIST case (Fig. 7b), where the runtime increases with the polynomial degree. Networks with the same number of layers—corresponding to the same number of neurons in this case—exhibit overlapping runtime curves. Runtime curves for the other datasets are qualitatively similar and are deferred to Appendix A.1.

The dominant factor contributing to ZONOPOLY's synthesis time is the computation of the approximation error between the current polynomial $p(x)$ and the ReLU function ReLU(x) over the interval $x \in [l, u]$ during each step of the Remez algorithm. This error must be evaluated for each neuron and becomes increasingly costly for higher-degree polynomials.

4.3 Verified Error Bounds

Bound Tightness. We now compare the verified bounds on the error $\|\hat{\mathcal{N}}(x) - \mathcal{N}(x)\|_\infty$ between the polynomially approximated and the original ReLU networks computed by ZONOPOLY to the verified bounds produced by LIGAR and LIGAR+CHEBY. For ZONOPOLY, we use the networks generated in the previous section and let both LIGAR versions compute their own polynomial networks. Here, we only log verification time, not generation time.

For each benchmark, we computed verified error bounds over the *whole* input set (e.g. $[0,1]^{784}$ for the MNIST networks). Even for this large input set, ZONOPOLY was able to produce useful bounds especially for the HELOC and HAR benchmarks and (to a lesser extent) also for the MNIST networks that were trained using L_1 regularization.

The change of the verified error for all tools as well as the sampled error over the MNIST training dataset is illustrated in Fig. 10 on the left for the 256×6 MNIST network trained using standard training and the network with the same architecture trained with an L_1 penalty of 10^{-4} on the right. Graphs for other benchmarks follow a similar pattern and are deferred to Appendix A.2.

ZONOPOLY was able to compute tighter bounds than LIGAR and LIGAR+CHEBY on all benchmarks. For higher polynomial degrees, the relative improvement of the bounds seems to converge to a constant factor for each base network

Table 2. Verified bounds for the error $|\hat{\mathcal{N}}(x) - \mathcal{N}(x)|$ between polynomial networks and different ReLU base networks

base network		Error at degree 200			relative improvement	
Structure	L_1 weight	LiGAR	LiGAR+Cheby	ZonoPoly	$\frac{\text{LiGAR}}{\text{ZonoPoly}}$	$\frac{\text{LiGAR+Cheby}}{\text{ZonoPoly}}$
MNIST						
256×4	0	14240.51	21342.21	3472.10	4.10	6.15
256×4	2×10^{-5}	29.00	41.14	10.39	2.79	3.96
256×4	10^{-4}	5.55	8.06	2.15	2.58	3.74
256×6	0	1.25×10^7	1.87×10^7	1.21×10^6	10.35	15.49
256×6	2×10^{-5}	131.68	187.80	42.16	3.12	4.45
256×6	10^{-4}	17.94	27.54	7.42	2.42	3.71
HELOC						
$64 - 32$	0	0.54	0.80	0.31	1.73	2.57
$64 - 32$	2×10^{-5}	0.19	0.29	0.11	1.73	2.69
HAR						
500×1	0	0.66	0.82	0.27	2.43	3.02
500×1	2×10^{-5}	0.65	0.73	0.21	3.03	3.43
500×1	10^{-4}	0.63	0.72	0.23	2.79	3.18

(parallel lines in the logarithmic plot in Fig. 10), which is shown alongside the absolute verified error for degree 200 in Table 2. The relative improvement for smaller degrees is slightly larger.

Verification Time. However, the improvements in the verified bounds do not come for free. While LiGAR works on an efficient abstraction of the polynomial activations, ZonoPoly has to consider their actual coefficients and compute roots and linear approximations to these possibly high degree polynomials. Therefore – as illustrated in Fig. 9 for MNIST – verification time grows much quicker with the degree of the polynomials compared to LiGAR whose runtime is constant in that regard.

It is also expected that ZonoPoly is slower than LiGAR+Cheby since this augmentation of LiGAR only has to fit the Chebyshev approximation and compute its error once for each neuron whereas ZonoPoly has to compute the error between the linear relaxation and the polynomial for every iteration of the Remez algorithm. The number of Remez iterations required can also be dependent on the width of the approximation interval of a polynomial. This may also explain, why differential verification for the MNIST network trained with standard training takes more time than verification of the L_1 trained networks of the same structure.

4.4 Verified Error for Samples

Neural network verifiers are commonly evaluated in the context of adversarial robustness for small ϵ-balls around points in a training dataset. We also perform

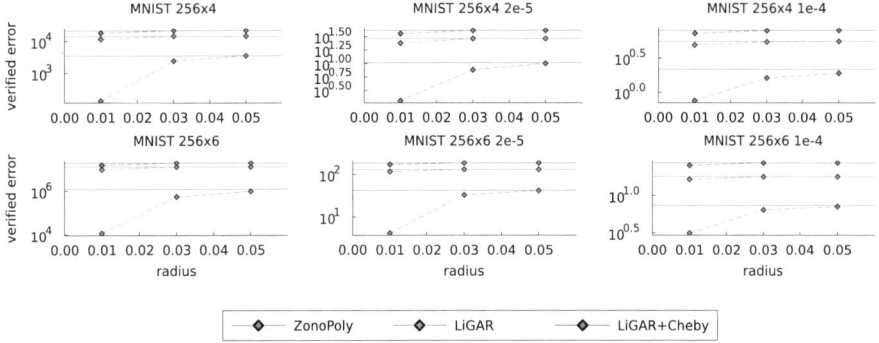

Fig. 11. Verified error bounds for ϵ-balls of different radii around the first 10 samples of the MNIST training dataset. The solid lines represent the globally-valid bounds (for the total input set of $[0,1]^{784}$) for each tool.

a small comparison of the difference bounds computed by ZONOPOLY against LIGAR and LIGAR+CHEBY for ϵ-balls of different radii around samples of MNIST images. Due to ZONOPOLY's runtime, we only evaluated on the first 10 samples of the MNIST training dataset. While equivalence is only checked for the ϵ-balls around the samples, we consider polynomial networks that were generated using verified bounds for the whole MNIST input set.

Figure 11, shows the bounds computed by each tool for the whole MNIST input set as solid horizontal lines, while the dashed lines represent the maximum verified difference among the ϵ-balls around the 10 center images. The bounds computed by ZONOPOLY for the whole MNIST input set are already tighter than the verified bounds for LIGAR and LIGAR+CHEBY for radius 0.01. With smaller radii, ZONOPOLY also improves its bounds more than both other tools.

5 Conclusions

In this paper, we tackle the problem of designing polynomial activations for FHE neural networks. Our ZONOPOLY algorithm employs a zonotope-based differential verification approach to propagate the approximation error through the network. As a result, ZONOPOLY can construct a stable polynomial network with verified neuron ranges and output error. Our evaluation shows that ZONOPOLY produces tighter bounds than existing certified techniques such as LIGAR.

Acknowledgment. The authors thank Samuel Teuber for technical support with VERYDIFF. Edoardo Manino is partially funded by the EPSRC grant EP/T026995/1 entitled "EnnCore: End-to-End Conceptual Guarding of Neural Architectures" under *Security for all in an AI enabled society*. Philipp Kern's work was supported by funding from the pilot program Core-Informatics of the Helmholtz Association (HGF).

Disclosure of Interests. The authors have no competing interests to declare that are relevant to the content of this article.

A Further Results

We omitted detailed figures for some benchmarks from the evaluation section, since the results are qualitatively similar to results of other benchmarks.

For completeness, we print the omitted figures for the accuracy of generated polynomial networks in Sect. A.1 and for the verified difference between generated and original networks in Sect. A.2.

A.1 Synthesis of Polynomially Approximated Networks

(Figs. 12 and 13)

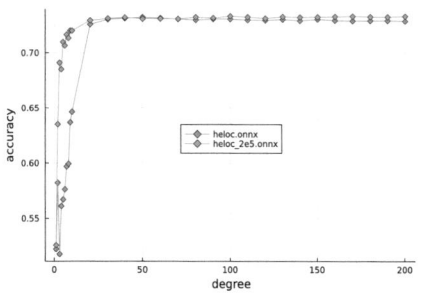 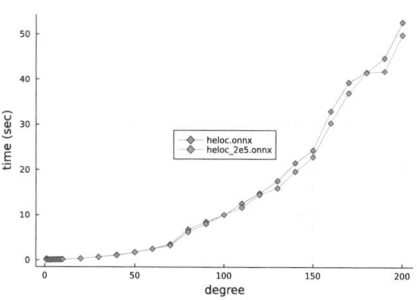

(a) Accuracy for polynomially approximated HELOC networks for polynomials of different degrees and different base ReLU networks.

(b) Runtime of ZONOPOLY to synthesize polynomially approximated networks for different degrees and base ReLU networks

Fig. 12. Accuracy of runtime of ZONOPOLY for different synthesized polynomially approximated networks for HELOC.

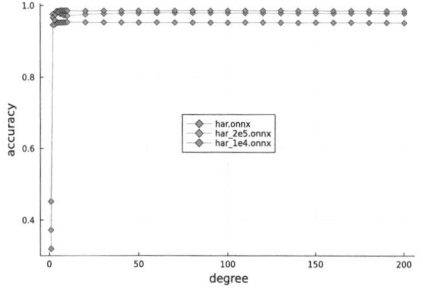 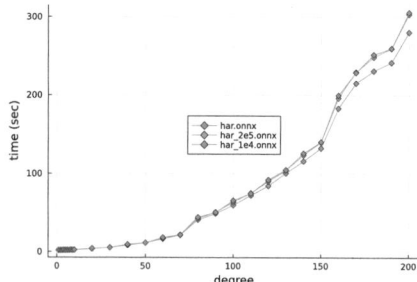

(a) Accuracy for polynomially approximated HAR networks for polynomials of different degrees and different base ReLU networks.

(b) Runtime of ZONOPOLY to synthesize polynomially approximated networks for different degrees and base ReLU networks

Fig. 13. Accuracy of runtime of ZONOPOLY for different synthesized polynomially approximated networks for HAR.

A.2 Verified Error Bounds

(Figs. 14, 15 and 16)

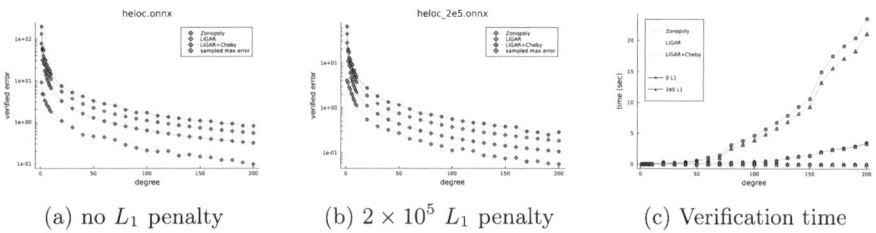

(a) no L_1 penalty (b) 2×10^5 L_1 penalty (c) Verification time

Fig. 14. Verified error bounds for networks trained on the HELOC dataset and runtime for their computation.

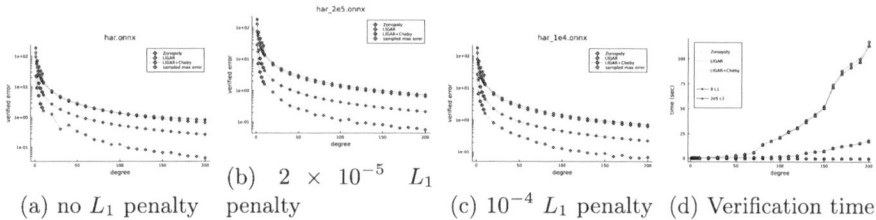

(a) no L_1 penalty (b) 2×10^{-5} L_1 penalty (c) 10^{-4} L_1 penalty (d) Verification time

Fig. 15. Verified error bounds for networks trained on the HAR dataset and runtime for their computation.

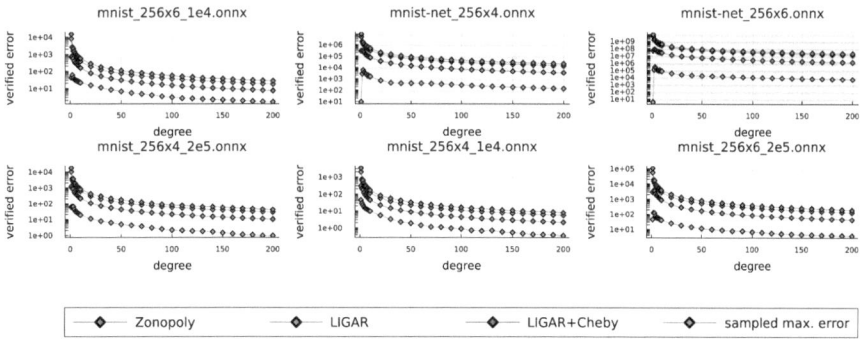

Fig. 16. Verified error bounds for polynomially approximated networks of different degree for different ReLU base networks for MNIST

A somewhat surprising effect which can be seen in Fig. 16 is that for the MNIST networks, the output error of the degree-1 (linear) approximations is often smaller than for quadratic polynomials. This is because the zonotopes we use during synthesis of the polynomial networks, can exactly represent linear transformations, resulting in tight bounds for neuron inputs. In contrast, higher-degree approximations introduce overapproximation error, which causes wider input intervals and poorer polynomial fits. While this difference is minor in most networks, it is significant for the MNIST networks from VNN-COMP [9], where the true output ranges are very narrow. As less overapproximation is introduced for linear approximations, they lead to smaller output ranges and thus to smaller absolute output errors. While the output ranges are small for the linear networks, the outputs themselves are not necessarily useful. As shown in Fig. 7a, the classification accuracy is still not high.

References

1. Albrecht, M., et al.: Homomorphic encryption standard. Cryptology ePrint Archive, Paper 2019/939 (2019). https://eprint.iacr.org/2019/939
2. Anguita, D., Ghio, A., Oneto, L., Parra, X., Reyes-Ortiz, J.L.: A public domain dataset for human activity recognition using smartphones. In: 21st European Symposium on Artificial Neural Networks, ESANN 2013, Bruges, Belgium, April 24–26, 2013 (2013). https://www.esann.org/sites/default/files/proceedings/legacy/es2013-84.pdf
3. Armknecht, F., et al.: A guide to fully homomorphic encryption. Cryptology ePrint Archive, Paper 2015/1192 (2015). https://eprint.iacr.org/2015/1192
4. Arya, V., et al.: AI explainability 360: impact and design. In: Thirty-Sixth AAAI Conference on Artificial Intelligence, AAAI 2022, Thirty-Fourth Conference on Innovative Applications of Artificial Intelligence, IAAI 2022, The Twelveth Symposium on Educational Advances in Artificial Intelligence, EAAI 2022 Virtual Event, February 22–March 1, 2022, pp. 12651–12657. AAAI Press (2022). https://doi.org/10.1609/AAAI.V36I11.21540
5. Bezanson, J., Edelman, A., Karpinski, S., Shah, V.B.: Julia: a fresh approach to numerical computing. SIAM Rev. **59**(1), 65–98 (2017). https://doi.org/10.1137/141000671
6. Bossuat, J.P., et al.: Security guidelines for implementing homomorphic encryption. Cryptology ePrint Archive, Paper 2024/463 (2024). https://eprint.iacr.org/2024/463
7. Brakerski, Z., Vaikuntanathan, V.: Efficient fully homomorphic encryption from (standard) LWE. In: Ostrovsky, R. (ed.) IEEE 52nd Annual Symposium on Foundations of Computer Science, FOCS 2011, Palm Springs, CA, USA, October 22–25, 2011, pp. 97–106. IEEE Computer Society (2011). https://doi.org/10.1109/FOCS.2011.12
8. Brakerski, Z., Vaikuntanathan, V.: Fully homomorphic encryption from ring-lwe and security for key dependent messages. In: Rogaway, P. (ed.) Advances in Cryptology - CRYPTO 2011 - 31st Annual Cryptology Conference, Santa Barbara, CA, USA, August 14–18, 2011. Proceedings. Lecture Notes in Computer Science, vol. 6841, pp. 505–524. Springer (2011). https://doi.org/10.1007/978-3-642-22792-9_29
9. Brix, C., Müller, M.N., Bak, S., Johnson, T.T., Liu, C.: First three years of the international verification of neural networks competition (VNN-COMP). Int. J. Softw. Tools Technol. Transf. **25**(3), 329–339 (2023)

10. Chabanne, H., de Wargny, A., Milgram, J., Morel, C., Prouff, E.: Privacy-preserving classification on deep neural network. Cryptology ePrint Archive, Paper 2017/035 (2017). https://eprint.iacr.org/2017/035
11. Cheon, J.H., Kim, A., Kim, M., Song, Y.: Homomorphic encryption for arithmetic of approximate numbers. In: Takagi, T., Peyrin, T. (eds.) Advances in Cryptology - ASIACRYPT 2017, pp. 409–437. Springer International Publishing, Cham (2017)
12. Chillotti, I., Joye, M., Paillier, P.: Programmable bootstrapping enables efficient homomorphic inference of deep neural networks. In: Dolev, S., Margalit, O., Pinkas, B., Schwarzmann, A. (eds.) Cyber Security Cryptography and Machine Learning, pp. 1–19. Springer International Publishing, Cham (2021)
13. Clenshaw, C.W.: A note on the summation of chebyshev series. Math. Comput. **9**, 118–120 (1955). https://doi.org/10.1090/S0025-5718-1955-0071856-0
14. Comba, J.L.D., Stolfi, J.: Affine arithmetic and its applications to computer graphics. In: SIBGRAPI 1993, Recife, PE (Brazil) (1993)
15. Costache, A., Curtis, B.R., Hales, E., Murphy, S., Ogilvie, T., Player, R.: On the precision loss in approximate homomorphic encryption. In: Carlet, C., Mandal, K., Rijmen, V. (eds.) Selected Areas in Cryptography - SAC 2023, pp. 325–345. Springer Nature Switzerland, Cham (2024)
16. Driscoll, T.A., Hale, N., Trefethen, L.N.: Chebfun Guide. Pafnuty Publications (2014). http://www.chebfun.org/docs/guide/
17. Eleftheriadis, C., Kekatos, N., Katsaros, P., Tripakis, S.: On neural network equivalence checking using SMT solvers. In: Bogomolov, S., Parker, D. (eds.) Formal Modeling and Analysis of Timed Systems - 20th International Conference, FORMATS 2022, Warsaw, Poland, September 13–15, 2022, Proceedings. LNCS, vol. 13465, pp. 237–257. Springer (2022). https://doi.org/10.1007/978-3-031-15839-1_14
18. FICO: Fico explainable machine learning challenge (2018). https://community.fico.com/s/explainable-machinelearning-challenge
19. Garimella, K., Jha, N.K., Reagen, B.: Sisyphus: a cautionary tale of using low-degree polynomial activations in privacy-preserving deep learning. arXiv:2107.12342 (2021)
20. Gentry, C.: Fully homomorphic encryption using ideal lattices. In: Mitzenmacher, M. (ed.) Proceedings of the 41st Annual ACM Symposium on Theory of Computing, STOC 2009, Bethesda, MD, USA, May 31–June 2, 2009, pp. 169–178. ACM (2009). https://doi.org/10.1145/1536414.1536440
21. Ghorbal, K., Goubault, E., Putot, S.: The zonotope abstract domain taylor1+. In: Bouajjani, A., Maler, O. (eds.) Computer Aided Verification, 21st International Conference, CAV 2009, Grenoble, France, June 26–July 2, 2009. Proceedings. Lecture Notes in Computer Science, vol. 5643, pp. 627–633. Springer (2009). https://doi.org/10.1007/978-3-642-02658-4_47
22. Gilad-Bachrach, R., Dowlin, N., Laine, K., Lauter, K., Naehrig, M., Wernsing, J.: Cryptonets: applying neural networks to encrypted data with high throughput and accuracy. In: Balcan, M.F., Weinberger, K.Q. (eds.) Proceedings of The 33rd International Conference on Machine Learning. Proceedings of Machine Learning Research, vol. 48, pp. 201–210. PMLR, New York, New York, USA (2016). https://proceedings.mlr.press/v48/gilad-bachrach16.html
23. Kleine Büning, M., Kern, P., Sinz, C.: Verifying equivalence properties of neural networks with ReLU activation functions. In: Simonis, H. (ed.) Principles and Practice of Constraint Programming - 26th International Conference, CP 2020, Louvain-la-Neuve, Belgium, September 7–11, 2020, Proceedings. LNCS, vol. 12333, pp. 868–884. Springer (2020). https://doi.org/10.1007/978-3-030-58475-7_50

24. Lecun, Y., Bottou, L., Bengio, Y., Haffner, P.: Gradient-based learning applied to document recognition. Proc. IEEE **86**(11), 2278–2324 (1998). https://doi.org/10.1109/5.726791
25. Lee, E., Lee, J.W., No, J.S., Kim, Y.S.: Minimax approximation of sign function by composite polynomial for homomorphic comparison. IEEE Trans. Dependable Secure Comput. **19**(6), 3711–3727 (2022). https://doi.org/10.1109/TDSC.2021.3105111
26. Lee, J.W., et al.: Privacy-preserving machine learning with fully homomorphic encryption for deep neural network. IEEE Access **10**, 30039–30054 (2022). https://doi.org/10.1109/ACCESS.2022.3159694
27. Lee, J., Lee, E., Lee, J.W., Kim, Y., Kim, Y.S., No, J.S.: Precise approximation of convolutional neural networks for homomorphically encrypted data. IEEE Access **11**, 62062–62076 (2023). https://doi.org/10.1109/ACCESS.2023.3287564
28. Manino, E., Magri, B., Mustafa, M., Cordeiro, L.: Certified private inference on neural networks via Lipschitz-guided abstraction refinement. In: Narodytska, N., Amir, G., Katz, G., Isac, O. (eds.) Proceedings of the 6th Workshop on Formal Methods for ML-Enabled Autonomous Systems. Kalpa Publications in Computing, vol. 16, pp. 35–46. EasyChair (2023). https://doi.org/10.29007/59w3
29. Mishra, P., Lehmkuhl, R., Srinivasan, A., Zheng, W., Popa, R.A.: Delphi: a cryptographic inference service for neural networks. In: 29th USENIX Security Symposium (USENIX Security 20), pp. 2505–2522. USENIX Association (2020). https://www.usenix.org/conference/usenixsecurity20/presentation/mishra
30. Obla, S., Gong, X., Aloufi, A., Hu, P., Takabi, D.: Effective activation functions for homomorphic evaluation of deep neural networks. IEEE Access **8**, 153098–153112 (2020). https://doi.org/10.1109/ACCESS.2020.3017436
31. Pachón, R., Trefethen, L.N.: Barycentric-remez algorithms for best polynomial approximation in the chebfun system. BIT Numer. Math. **49**, 721–741 (2009). https://doi.org/10.1007/s10543-009-0240-1
32. Paillier, P.: Public-key cryptosystems based on composite degree residuosity classes. In: Stern, J. (ed.) Advances in Cryptology – EUROCRYPT '99, pp. 223–238. Springer, Berlin Heidelberg (1999)
33. Paulsen, B., Wang, J., Wang, C.: ReluDiff: differential verification of deep neural networks. In: Rothermel, G., Bae, D. (eds.) ICSE 2020: 42nd International Conference on Software Engineering, Seoul, South Korea, 27 June–19 July, 2020, pp. 714–726. ACM (2020). https://doi.org/10.1145/3377811.3380337
34. Paulsen, B., Wang, J., Wang, J., Wang, C.: NeuroDiff: scalable differential verification of neural networks using fine-grained approximation. In: 35th IEEE/ACM International Conference on Automated Software Engineering, ASE 2020, Melbourne, Australia, September 21–25, 2020, pp. 784–796. IEEE (2020). https://doi.org/10.1145/3324884.3416560
35. Pulido-Gaytan, B., et al.: Privacy-preserving neural networks with homomorphic encryption: challenges and opportunities. Peer-to-Peer Networking Appl. **14**(3), 1666–1691 (2021)
36. Remes, E.: Sur un procédé convergent d'approximations successives pour déterminer les polynômes d'approximation. CR Acad. Sci. Paris **198**, 2063–2065 (1934)
37. Ribeiro, M., Grolinger, K., Capretz, M.A.: Mlaas: machine learning as a service. In: 2015 IEEE 14th International Conference on Machine Learning and Applications (ICMLA), pp. 896–902 (2015). https://doi.org/10.1109/ICMLA.2015.152
38. Rivest, R.L., Shamir, A., Adleman, L.M.: A method for obtaining digital signatures and public-key cryptosystems. Commun. ACM **21**(2), 120–126 (1978). https://doi.org/10.1145/359340.359342

39. Rovida, L., Leporati, A.: Encrypted image classification with low memory footprint using fully homomorphic encryption. Int. J. Neural Syst. **34**(5), 2450025 (2024). https://doi.org/10.1142/S0129065724500254
40. Shi, Z., Wang, Y., Zhang, H., Kolter, J.Z., Hsieh, C.J.: Efficiently computing local lipschitz constants of neural networks via bound propagation. In: Koyejo, S., Mohamed, S., Agarwal, A., Belgrave, D., Cho, K., Oh, A. (eds.) Advances in Neural Information Processing Systems, vol. 35, pp. 2350–2364. Curran Associates, Inc. (2022). https://proceedings.neurips.cc/paper_files/paper/2022/file/0ff54b4ec4f70b3ae12c8621ca8a49f4-Paper-Conference.pdf
41. Singh, G., Gehr, T., Mirman, M., Püschel, M., Vechev, M.T.: Fast and effective robustness certification. In: Bengio, S., Wallach, H.M., Larochelle, H., Grauman, K., Cesa-Bianchi, N., Garnett, R. (eds.) Advances in Neural Information Processing Systems 31: Annual Conference on Neural Information Processing Systems 2018, NeurIPS 2018, December 3–8, 2018, Montréal, Canada, pp. 10825–10836 (2018). https://proceedings.neurips.cc/paper/2018/hash/f2f446980d8e971ef3da97af089481c3-Abstract.html
42. Teuber, S., Büning, M.K., Kern, P., Sinz, C.: Geometric path enumeration for equivalence verification of neural networks. In: 33rd IEEE International Conference on Tools with Artificial Intelligence, ICTAI 2021, Washington, DC, USA, November 1–3, 2021, pp. 200–208. IEEE (2021). https://doi.org/10.1109/ICTAI52525.2021.00035
43. Teuber, S., Kern, P., Janzen, M., Beckert, B.: Revisiting differential verification: equivalence verification with confidence. CoRR arXiv:2410.20207 (2024)
44. Trefethen, L.N.: Approximation Theory and Approximation Practice, Extended Edition. SIAM (2019)
45. Weng, L., et al.: Towards fast computation of certified robustness for ReLU networks. In: Dy, J., Krause, A. (eds.) Proceedings of the 35th International Conference on Machine Learning. Proceedings of Machine Learning Research, vol. 80, pp. 5276–5285. PMLR (2018). https://proceedings.mlr.press/v80/weng18a.html
46. Xiao, K.Y., Tjeng, V., Shafiullah, N.M.M., Madry, A.: Training for faster adversarial robustness verification via inducing ReLu stability. In: 7th International Conference on Learning Representations, ICLR 2019, New Orleans, LA, USA, May 6–9, 2019. OpenReview.net (2019). https://openreview.net/forum?id=BJfIVjAcKm

Neural Network Verification for Gliding Drone Control: A Case Study

Colin Kessler[1,2](✉), Ekaterina Komendantskaya[1], Marco Casadio[1], Ignazio Maria Viola[2], Thomas Flinkow[3], Albaraa Ammar Othman[1], Alistair Malhotra[1], and Robbie McPherson[1]

[1] Heriot-Watt University and Edinburgh Centre for Robotics, Edinburgh, UK
ck2049@hw.ac.uk
[2] School of Engineering, University of Edinburgh, Edinburgh, UK
[3] Maynooth University, Maynooth, Ireland

Abstract. As machine learning is increasingly deployed in autonomous systems, verification of neural network controllers is becoming an active research domain. Existing tools and annual verification competitions suggest that soon this technology will become effective for real-world applications. Our application comes from the emerging field of microflyers that are passively transported by the wind, which may have various uses in weather or pollution monitoring. Specifically, we investigate centimetre-scale bio-inspired gliding drones that resemble *Alsomitra macrocarpa* diaspores. In this paper, we propose a new case study on verifying *Alsomitra*-inspired drones with neural network controllers, with the aim of adhering closely to a target trajectory. We show that our system differs substantially from existing VNN and ARCH competition benchmarks, and show that a combination of tools holds promise for verifying such systems in the future, if certain shortcomings can be overcome. We propose a novel method for robust training of regression networks, and investigate formalisations of this case study in Vehicle and CORA. Our verification results suggest that the investigated training methods do improve performance and robustness of neural network controllers in this application, but are limited in scope and usefulness. This is due to systematic limitations of both Vehicle and CORA, and the complexity of our system reducing the scale of reachability, which we investigate in detail. If these limitations can be overcome, it will enable engineers to develop safe and robust technologies that improve people's lives and reduce our impact on the environment.

Keywords: Neural Network Control · Bioinspired Robots · Verification of Cyber-Physical Systems · Machine Learning

1 Introduction

A recent research trend in drone design concerns the development of gliding microdrones, which could serve a function as airborne sensors and remain aloft for extended periods of time [15,17,20,34]. Current research focuses on the aerodynamics of seeds that have exceptional wind dispersal mechanisms: for example, *Taraxacum* (dandelion) [9] and *Alsomitra* (Javan cucumber). This case study focuses specifically on *Alsomitra*-inspired drones (Figs. 1 and 4) as the aerodynamics underlying the flight of this diaspore is unique in the plant kingdom, enhancing the dispersal mechanism provided by the wind by an efficient gliding flight. This allows one of the heaviest seeds (314 mg) [4] to reach a similar descent velocity as some of the lightest seeds such as the dandelion (0.6 mg) [9]. Because of this unique feature, several authors have considered this diaspore as a bioinspiration for microdrones [25,34]. Such drones could function as distributed sensors in the atmosphere, for weather monitoring or detecting pollutants [15,17,20,25,34]. This could be particularly useful for environmental monitoring and meteorology, with research and regulations moving towards incorporating drone observations to improve weather predictions [11,35]. It has been demonstrated that such systems are capable of sustained flight with active control and internal electronics [17], although more work on effective actuation and control methods is needed in the future.

Neural networks (NNs) have been widely investigated for drone control, for both quadcopters [3,24] and fixed-wing designs [30,32]. The control of small passive gliders is a relatively unexplored field, with the most relevant works involving larger aircraft [1,32] or without continuous control [17]. For our application, we consider NN control since it has been shown to achieve accurate and robust control for systems with uncertain dynamics [16], it is particularly applicable to controlling swarms [29], and improvements to low-order aerodynamic modelling [23] facilitates easier simulations of such drones. This approach could facilitate particularly lightweight and low-cost drones; such as with analogue network circuits printed on flexible substrates acting as the body of the gliding drone [27,31]. One could alternatively consider uncontrolled flying sensors [15,20,34] or traditional approaches such as state-space or model predictive control. However, one should consider that such systems will need to be verifiably safe with regard to people, other air users, and the environment [35]. These drones could collide with each other, veer into unsafe airspace, fall into an endangered ecosystem, or otherwise cause harm. The utility of uncontrolled flyers would be hampered by such issues, unless they can be made biodegradable. Traditional control methods may be applied, but NN methods have advantages in that they can be made data-driven and adaptive, and printed NN circuits could lead to lighter designs than digital microcontrollers.

1.1 Contributions

Our first aim is the introduction of a novel case study (outlined in Sect. 4) in the verification of *Alsomitra*-inspired drone controllers (our modelling methods are explained in Sect. 3), that differs significantly from existing benchmarks. Unlike VNN-COMP benchmarks such as ACAS Xu, our study involves regression control and continuous dynamic equations. Compared to ARCH-COMP benchmarks

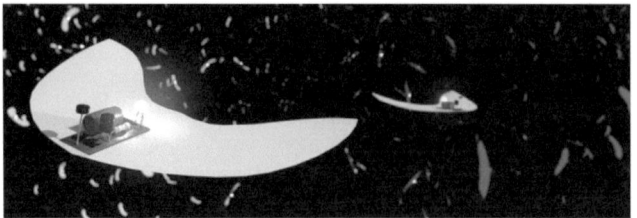

Fig. 1. An artist's impression of a swarm of gliding drones inspired by *Alsomitra* seeds [7].

such as QUAD, our system involves differential equations that are far more complex in terms of the number of non-linear terms. Moreover, unlike the majority of ARCH-COMP cases, this problem does not have as natural a notion of the start, goal, safe, and unsafe states; and thus requires an out-of-the-box approach to property specification.

We propose our ideal formalisation of the problem in Sect. 4.1, and distil the formalisation down to properties that can be handled with available tools (Marabou [19] implemented with Vehicle [10], and CORA [2]) in Sects. 6 and 7. The choice is motivated by the fact that each can be seen as a representative of a set of tools that come from the research communities of VNN-COMP [5] and ARCH-COMP [14], respectively. We present a new implementation of adversarial training for Lipschitz robustness applied to regression training for our controllers in Sect. 5, and present the results of verifying those properties with our robust networks in Sects. 6.3 and 7.2.

Our second aim is to present the lessons learnt from investigating this case study, to help inform the development of relevant tools for similar real-life cyber-physical projects in the future (Sect. 8). The main lesson learnt is that no single existing tool ticks all the desirable boxes. Moreover, each individual tool we chose would benefit from further development in several aspects that are crucial for real-life models. Concretely:

- On the Vehicle side, the verification properties that arise in the presented study are more complex than the usual VNN-COMP benchmarks in at least three ways.
  - Firstly, the constraints on the input vector are more complex: instead of constraining individual vector elements by constants (as e.g. in $a \leq x_i \leq b$), as is the case in the majority of benchmarks including ACAS XU [18], the constraints establish relation between different vector elements, as e.g. in $x_i \leq cx_j$. This changes mathematical interpretation of the verification problem: it no longer boils down to defining a hyper-rectangle (or other constant shape) on the input space and propagating it through the network layers, but gives a more general case of linear programming that works on arbitrary input space constraints. Not every VNN-COMP [5] verifier will be able to deal with such verification properties: Marabou is

one of the most general tools in this family of tools and this case study suggests this generality may play a bigger role in the future.
- Secondly, for verification of Lipschitz robustness, we implemented *relational properties*, i.e. properties that compare different outputs of a neural network. These properties are not natively supported by Marabou or Vehicle yet, and required some additional plumbing. On-going implementation of support for relational verification in Marabou will be useful for cases such as this.
- Finally, some novelty of our verification approach is derived from the fact that, unlike most benchmarks in VNN-COMP, our models are regression models, rather than verification models. Some of the methods for training and verification are specialised to classification tasks only, and we predict that this has to change with occurrence of new engineering-inspired benchmarks.

– On the CORA side, the system outlined in this study required several workarounds in order to compute reachability:
  - The complexity of our system of equations [23] far exceeds that of all ARCH-COMP [14] benchmarks, in the number of non-linear terms. This would cause the Jacobian and Hessian matrices to far exceed the maximum number of terms supported by MATLAB, and fail to run. The equations were simplified (Sect. 3.2) by constraining the pitch angle and using an angle-of-attack definition, solving the complexity issue, but (for any reasonably large initial set) the reachable set still tended to expand exponentially after relatively few timesteps. This was solved by dividing the initial set into smaller subsets, computing reachable sets for each, and combining the results.
  - CORA expects a NN controller that takes the system variables as inputs, with relatively few layer types supported [2]. Certain parameters occupy wider ranges than others (for example, $\theta \in [-0.93, -0.07]$, $x \in [0.48, 41.7]$) but unlike Vehicle, input normalisation (keeping all inputs between 0 and 1) is not supported. This is problematic since we intend to observe the effect of adversarial training, for which the input ranges should to be normalised, such that Projected Gradient Descent (PGD) attacks occur in ϵ ranges that are not imbalanced between input dimensions. A workaround was found by training an adversarial network on normalised data, then implementing normalisation layers to the start and end of the network.

In summary, our study aims to provide insights into the challenges and successes in applying neural network verification to *Alsomitra*-inspired drones for environmental monitoring, with a focus on safety and robustness evaluation of controllers. Although this study considers only one type of gliding drones, most of the paper's conclusions will be common between their different modifications, such as e.g. dandelion-inspired drones, and the lessons learnt can be broadly applied to other continuous control tasks. All relevant files are publicly available here.

2 Background

2.1 Neural Network Control

For our control method, we will use the common closed-loop negative feedback method, an overview of which can be seen in Fig. 2. In simple terms, the controller in a drone is given information about its current state (such as position, relative to some desired state) as input, and outputs a command to an actuator which affects how the drone flies. The controller can be considered as an equation linking the system states to an actuation force that changes the states over time according to the system dynamics, where the controller design affects how the drone behaves. If a traditional control theory approach is difficult (such as if the dynamics are highly complex) or a data-driven approach is desirable (if collecting data is easier than modelling the system, or if adaption based on new data is required), an engineer might consider implementing a NN controller.

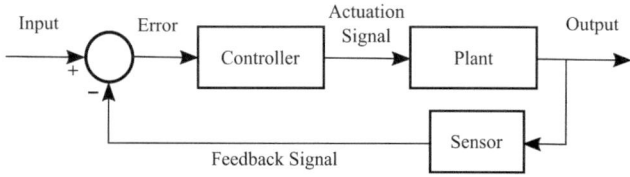

Fig. 2. Overview of a negative feedback control system. For each control iteration, an error signal is calculated by subtracting the current system state (feedback) from the desired system state (input). A controller computes an actuation based on this error, which is applied to a simulated or real system (plant), resulting in some new output state.

2.2 Verification Tools

The case study will rely on the following three groups of neural network verification (NNV) tools. The first group concerns verification of infinite time-horizon properties of controllers in isolation from verification of the overall system dynamics. The most famous benchmark in the domain is ACASXu, and the representative verifier is Marabou [19]; other tools, such as ERAN [26], Pyrat [22] or $\alpha\beta$-CROWN [36] could be interchangeably used for the verification tasks in which Marabou is deployed in this paper; we refer the reader to VNN-Comp [5] for an in depth discussion of existing tools in this category. In addition, we use Vehicle [10], a higher-level interface on top of Marabou, and take advantage of its facility in bridging the *embedding gap* [8] between the physical domains and vector representation of data.

The second group of methods considers the neural controller together with the overall system dynamics to ensure that the entire system avoids unsafe states,

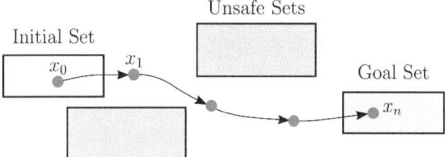

Fig. 3. General form of reachability specifications - dots represent the system at successive control time steps, and arrows represent the continuous trajectory of the system. Any trajectory starting in the initial set should never intersect an unsafe set, and always finish in the goal set.

see Fig. 3. This class of problems is also known under the umbrella term reachability verification and representative examples include e.g. POLAR-Express [33], and CORA [2], see [24] for an exhaustive overview of the mainstream tools in this category. Representative benchmarks include simple dynamic problems such as the inverted pendulum, and more complex problems such as the quadcopter, space docking, and 2-wheeled obstacle avoidance. Each benchmark has a predetermined set of dynamic equations and a NN controller, with a mix of supervised learning (through behaviour-cloning) and reinforcement learning. The limitations of these benchmarks are in the complexity of the networks (large networks require reduction methods), complexity of the equations (systems are either linear, or relatively simple non-linear differential equations), and verification of complex properties (no tools can successfully verify the Spacecraft Docking benchmark as of the most recent results [14]).

Finally, an important group of methods for practical NNV cases comes from machine learning domain, under the umbrella term of *property-driven training (PDT)*. These methods allow to optimise a given neural network for satisfying a desired verification property, with a view of improving the verification success [6, 12, 13]. Although methods in this group vary, they usually deploy a form of training with PGD [21]. PGD methods involve finding the worst-case perturbed example in a region around a data point, which can then be implemented as a loss function during training:

$$\min_{\theta} E_{(x,y)\sim\mathcal{D}} \left[\max_{\delta \in \Delta} \mathcal{L}(f_\theta(x+\delta), y) \right]$$

where θ represents the parameters of the NN; $(x,y) \sim \mathcal{D}$ are input-label pairs sampled from the data distribution $\mathcal{D}$; E is the expected value, averaging the loss over all samples in the data distribution $\mathcal{D}$; $\delta \in \Delta$ is the adversarial perturbation constrained within a feasible set Δ (e.g., $\|\delta\|_p \leq \epsilon$) and $\mathcal{L}$ is the loss function (e.g., RMSE, MAE) measuring the discrepancy between the predicted output $f_\theta(x+\delta)$ and the true label y.

The inner maximisation, which identifies the *worst-case* adversarial perturbation $\delta \in \Delta$, is performed using PGD that iteratively adjusts δ by ascending the gradient of the loss function with respect to the input, followed by projection back onto the feasible set Δ (e.g., ensuring $\|\delta\|_p \leq \epsilon$).

The outer minimisation, aimed at optimising the neural network parameters θ to minimise the adversarial loss, is achieved using gradient descent.

3 Modelling Methodology

3.1 Alsomitra Macrocarpa

A dynamics model (Fig. 4) was derived from [23] resulting in a system of equations for falling plates with displaced centre of mass (CoM), as defined in Sect. 3.2. Based on experimental measurements, our model accurately describes the falling trajectories of *Alsomitra* seeds by inferring aerodynamic forces from the angle of attack [23]. The flight characteristics are highly dependent on the CoM displacement (e_x, Fig. 4), providing us with a convenient actuation method for an *Alsomitra*-inspired drone.

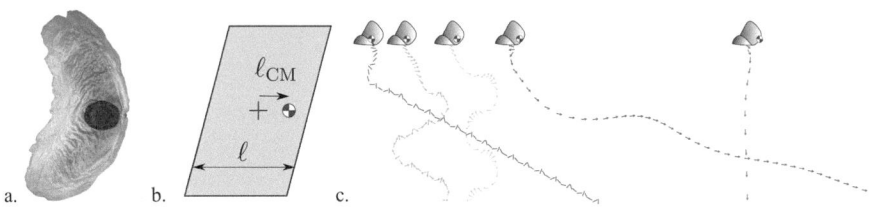

Fig. 4. (a) An *Alsomitra* seed [7]. (b) A two-dimensional approximation of an *Alsomitra* seed, with centre of mass (CoM) displaced by ℓ_{CM} (nondimensional form $e_x = \ell_{\text{CM}}/\ell$). (c) Effect of various e_x on gliding trajectories; according to a quasi-steady aerodynamic model ([23], Sect. 3.2). As the CoM is displaced the trajectory behaviour is affected significantly.

3.2 Equations

The following equations describe falling plates with a displaced centre of mass [23], with six system variables ($x_{1...6}$, Eqs. 11 ... 16), involving mechanical and aerodynamic constants chosen to match that of *Alsomitra* seeds [7].

The main assumptions of the model are that the aerodynamic behaviour of the plate is quasi-steady and independent of previous motion. The three most important aerodynamic force coefficients (lift 3, drag 4, and the location of the center of pressure 5) are defined as functions of the instantaneous angle of attack 1. This approximation has been found to capture the interesting aspects of *Alsomitra* flight (especially the effects of the CoM position on flight modes), without requiring expensive numerical simulations of the flow field around the seed. A more detailed overview can be seen in Appendix A.1

$$\tan \alpha = (x_2 - x_3 y_1 \ell)/x_1 \approx x_2/x_1 \tag{1}$$

Table 1. *Alsomitra* model constants defined according to [7,23]

Constant(s)	Definition(s)	Value(s)
ℓ, m, I	Plate length [m], mass [kg], inertia [kgm^2]	0.07, 3.175e-04, 0.0796
ρ_f, g	Fluid Density [kg/m^3], gravity [m/s^2]	1.225, 9.81
α_0, δ	Critical α at stall, transition smoothness [°]	14, 6
C_L^1, C_L^2	Lift coefficient components	5.1822, 0.80751
$C_D^0, C_D^1, C_D^{\pi/2}$	Drag Coefficient components	0.10598, 4.9368, 1.4996
$C_{CP}^0, C_{CP}^1, C_{CP}^2$	CoP components	0.2386, 2.8529, 0.3689
C_R	Rotational lift	1.73

$$f = (1 - \tanh((\alpha - \alpha_0)/\delta))/2 \tag{2}$$

$$-C_L = f(|\alpha|)C_L^1 \sin(|\alpha|) + (1 - f(|\alpha|))C_L^2 \sin(2|\alpha|) \tag{3}$$

$$C_D = f(|\alpha|)(C_D^0 + C_D^1 \sin^2(|\alpha|)) + (1 - f(|\alpha|))C_D^{\pi/2} \sin^2(|\alpha|) \tag{4}$$

$$\ell_{CP}/\ell = f(|\alpha|)(C_{CP}^0 - C_{CP}^1 \alpha^2) + C_{CP}^2[1 - f(|\alpha|)](1 - |\alpha|/(\pi/2)) \tag{5}$$

$$L_T = \frac{1}{2}\rho_f \ell C_L \sqrt{x_1^2 + (x_2 - x_3 y_1 \ell)^2} \, (x_2 - x_3 y_1 \ell, x_1) \tag{6}$$

$$L_R = -\frac{1}{2}\rho_f \ell^2 C_R x_3 (x_2 - x_3 y_1 \ell, x_1) \tag{7}$$

$$D = -\frac{1}{2}\rho_f \ell C_D \sqrt{x_1^2 + (x_2 - x_3 y_1 \ell)^2} \, (x_1, x_2 - x_3 y_1 \ell) \tag{8}$$

$$\tau_T = -\frac{1}{2}\rho_f \ell \sqrt{x_1^2 + (x_2 - x_3 y_1 \ell)^2} \, [C_L x_1 + C_D (x_2 - x_3 y_1 \ell)](\ell_{CP} - \ell_{CM}) \tag{9}$$

$$\tau_R = -\frac{1}{128}\rho_f \ell^4 C_D^{\pi/2} x_3 |x_3| \left[(2y_1 + 1)^4 \pm (2y_1 + 1)^4\right] \tag{10}$$

$$m\dot{x}_1 = (m + \pi\rho_f \ell^2/4)\, x_3 x_2 - (\pi\rho_f \ell^2/4) x_3^2 \ell_{CM} + L_T^{x'} + L_R^{x'} + D^{x'} - m'g \sin x_4 \tag{11}$$

$$(m + \pi\rho_f \ell^2/4)\,\dot{x}_2 = -m x_3 x_1 + (\pi\rho_f \ell^2/4)\dot{x}_3 \ell_{CM} + L_T^{y'} + L_R^{y'} + D^{y'} - m'g \cos x_4 \tag{12}$$

$$I\ddot{x}_3 = \tau_T + \tau_R \tag{13}$$

$$\dot{x}_4 = x_3 \tag{14}$$

$$\dot{x}_5 = x_1 \cos x_4 - x_2 \sin x_4 \tag{15}$$

$$\dot{x}_6 = x_1 \sin x_4 + x_2 \cos x_4 \tag{16}$$

4 Verification Task

Our *Alsomitra* model from Sect. 3.2 is used as the basis of a feedback control system with a NN controller, as described in Sect. 2.1. In our case, the plant is the aerodynamic model, and the desired input is a linear reference trajectory in x_5 and x_6 (translational x and y):

$$x_6 = -x_5 \tag{17}$$

The feedback signal consists of the six system states, and the CoM displacement is actuated by a controller aiming to follow the target trajectory (Fig. 5).

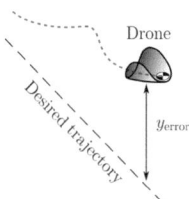

Fig. 5. As a control problem, we consider an *Alsomitra*-inspired microdrone and attempt to follow a linear trajectory in two dimensions.

As per the ARCH-COMP airplane and pendulum benchmarks [14], the neural network controller is trained using behaviour cloning. All simulations ran for a total of 20 s, with a model timestep of 0.01 s and a control timestep of 0.5 s. A PID controller actuates y_1 (e_x) based on an error in x_6, and the gains are tuned manually until the control system performs well for a range of starting x_6 positions. For each controller actuation (24 per simulation, for nine simulations), the system states, x_6 error, and PID actuation are recorded for use as training data. This data is imported to Python for standard regression learning, and networks are exported in .onnx format for evaluation (Fig. 6) and verification. All networks have 6 inputs, 3 hidden layers with 6, 4, and 1 nodes respectively with ReLU activation functions, and 1 output.

4.1 Formalisation

The core of this case study lies in examining the challenges in adopting the existing NNV methods in this new domain. Our ideal formalisation of the problem is as follows. We consider a hybrid program where the six system states $x_1, ..., x_6$ change over continuous time t according the dynamics model shown in Sect. 3.2, and a NN controller acts to change the system state discretely every 0.5 s. For any starting state $x_1, ..., x_6(0)$, after some time t^* the trajectory of the drone will always be within some small distance y^* of the target trajectory (ideally, $x_6 = -x_5$). This boils down to the following ideal verification property:

$$\forall t \geq t^*, \forall x_1, ..., x_6(0) \in \mathbb{R} : |x_6(t) + x_5(t)| \leq y^* \tag{18}$$

There are several features that distinguishes this system from standard NNV benchmarks, and we aim to explain the technical implications of these challenges for existing verification technologies, and propose ways in which these challenges can be overcome:

1. The system dynamics are continuous, therefore unlike standard control verification benchmarks (such as ACAS Xu [5]), control is modelled as a regression task as oppose to classification.
2. Unlike the ARCH-COMP benchmarks [24] that have a pre-defined notion of safe and unsafe state, these gliding drones do not have a notion of safety in the sense of a pre-defined coordinate region. A safe state is instead defined in a relational way, as adhesion to certain safe trajectory.
3. Unlike many ARCH-COMP benchmarks, our verification task requires modelling with an infinite-time horizon. Each drone could stay airborne for an arbitrary duration of time, depending on the surrounding airflow.
4. As defined by our model, the dynamics of gliding drones are more complex than what is currently handled by the ARCH-COMP benchmarks and tools, and in particular it is more complex than the dynamics handled by tools that can verify infinite-time horizon systems, such as KeyMaeraX [28].

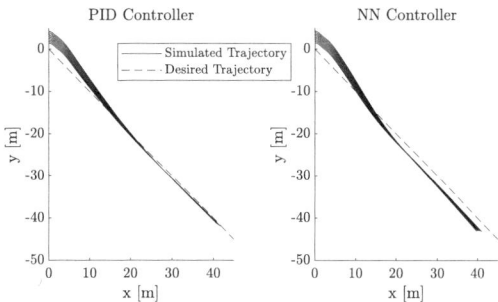

Fig. 6. PID and basic NN controller performance on an *Alsomitra*-inspired drone. The naive network is trained on regression data obtained from simulations with the PID controller, and the resulting performance is similar but not perfect.

The available verification tools (Sect. 2.2) do not allow us to formalise this idealised goal directly, since CORA does not support infinite time, and Marabou does not support differential equations (and in that sense, it does not directly support analysis of the system evolution). As a result, we simplified this general task as two simpler tasks (in the first case sacrificing the analysis of the overall system dynamics, and in the second case the infinite-time horizon and relational definition of the target state):

1. The NN will never command the drone to deviate significantly from the target trajectory. This task was implemented in Marabou, using the Vehicle specification language since it facilitates complex property definition.
2. Given an interval of initial positions in space and a finite-time horizon, the NN-controlled drone will always reach a goal region, defined as a region around the target trajectory within this finite time frame. This task was verified in CORA.

We note that task 1 resembles a robustness property in some ways [6], except for now we deal with a regression NN and robustness relative to a line rather than a given data point.

5 Robustness Training for Regression

Since robustness is critically important for drone safety, it seems reasonable to attempt a form of adversarial training based on PGD methods for our controller. The guiding hypothesis was that a general improvement in NN robustness should lead to improved verification performance. Since our neural network is a regression model, the classification-based training methods surveyed in Sect. 2.2 could not easily be used without modification. We therefore had to modify the PGD algorithm to use an RMSE loss function instead of cross-entropy, and modify other aspects of the adversarial training algorithm that relied on the presence of discrete classes.

We focused on two notion of robustness, *standard* and *Lipschitz* robustness [6]. Given $x^* \in \mathcal{D}$ and constants $\epsilon, \delta, L \in R$,

$$\forall x \in R^n : \|x - x^*\| \leq \epsilon \implies \|f(x) - f(x^*)\| \leq \delta \tag{19}$$

$$\forall x \in R^n : \|x - x^*\| \leq \epsilon \implies \|f(x) - f(x^*)\| \leq L \|x - x^*\| \tag{20}$$

Since the latter has been proven to be strictly stronger than the former in [6], we implemented a form of PGD training with a Lipschitz loss function. During each training epoch, the algorithm finds the worst-case adversarial example $(x^*, f(x^*))$ in an ϵ-ball around each training point $(x, f(x))$. To optimise the regression model for Lipschitz robustness, we dynamically compute the highest value of L from the training and adversarial points (according to Eq. 20), which is summed to the training RMSE loss, penalising the network for large gradients about each data point. This is expected to result in a network with a smoother and therefore more robust output, at the expense of some accuracy.

6 Vehicle Implementation

Task 1 was broken down into five simpler specifications to be implemented in Vehicle (a detailed introduction to which can be found in [10]), to ensure the NNs control the drone as desired in various ways. Global properties relating to the controller's output relative to the target trajectory are introduced in Sect. 6.1, and a local robustness property is introduced in Sect. 6.2. Global properties are verified for all inputs bounded by the training data (representing the entire parameter space over which our controller is trained), and the local property is evaluated about ϵ-balls from the training data.

6.1 Global Property Specifications

Our first goal is to ensure the controller never causes the drone to deviate from the target trajectory. To establish a performance criteria, properties 1–4 include y^* (a threshold distance from the target trajectory, Eqs. 17, 18), such that a critical y^* can be found per network per property where verification succeeds. For example, for properties 1 and 2, a lower critical y^* would indicate a controller that better adheres to the target trajectory:

1. *If the drone is above the line by some threshold y^*, the NN output will always make the drone pitch down* (Listing 1)

$$x_6 \geq -x_5 + y^* \Rightarrow f(x) \geq 0.187 \tag{21}$$

2. *If the drone is below the line by some threshold y^*, the NN output will always make the drone pitch up*

$$x_6 \leq -x_5 - y^* \Rightarrow f(x) \leq 0.187 \tag{22}$$

Our third property is reversed, where a larger y^* would indicate better adherence to a larger region around the target trajectory:

3. *If the drone is close to the line by some threshold y^*, and at an intermediate pitch angle, the NN output will always be intermediate* (Listing 2)

$$-x_5 - y^* \leq x_6 \leq -x_5 + y^* \wedge -0.786 \leq x_4 \leq -0.747 \Rightarrow 0.184 \leq f(x) \leq 0.19 \tag{23}$$

Our fourth property is more complex, and represents a desireable behaviour not present in the data:

4. *If the drone is above and close to the line, pitching down quickly and moving fast, the NN output will always make the drone pitch up*

$$-x_5 \leq x_6 \leq -x_5 + y^* \wedge x_3 \leq -0.12 \wedge x_2 \leq -0.3 \Rightarrow f(x) \leq 0.187 \tag{24}$$

```
droneFarAboveLine : UnnormalisedInputVector -> Bool
droneFarAboveLine x =
        x ! d_y >= - x ! d_x + ystar

@property
property1 : Bool
property1 = forall x . validInput x and droneFarAboveLine x =>
  alsomitra x ! e_x >= 0.187
```

Listing 1: Property 1 implemented in Vehicle.

```
intermediatePitch : UnnormalisedInputVector -> Bool
intermediatePitch x =
        -0.786 <= x ! d_theta <= -0.747

closeToLine : UnnormalisedInputVector -> Bool
closeToLine x =
        x ! d_y >= -x ! d_x - ystar and
        x ! d_y <= - x ! d_x + ystar

@property
property3 : Bool
property3 = forall x . validInput x and intermediatePitch x
and closeToLine x => 0.184 <= alsomitra x ! e_x <= 0.19
```

Listing 2: Property 3 implemented in Vehicle.

In our Vehicle code, *alsomitra* represent the NN, *validInput* represents the input space bounded by the training data, and the parameter *ystar* is defined during runtime.

6.2 Local Robustness Specification

Our fifth property is an evaluation of robustness around ϵ-balls with respect to the training dataset, as defined in Sect. 5. A detailed introduction to ϵ-ball robustness for image classification implemented in Vehicle can be found in [10]. Similarly to properties 1–4, we are interested in finding at what threshold L value (L^*) does each network pass verification. Similarly to properties 1–4, we expect the verification results for this property to depend on the strictness of L, which we consider as the parameter L^*. However, due to Marabou limitations, this was evaluated with respect to the training dataset, where for each network Property 5 was evaluated for each training point, given fixed $L*$ and ϵ values. Additionally, the distance between points was computed with L^∞ and the input distance could not be included in the formula, leading use to use a different robustness definition:

5. *For any given input point x, the network output $f(x^*)$ of any perturbed point x^* within an ϵ-ball around x, will have a distance less than or equal to $L^*\epsilon$ to $f(x)$ (Listing 3)*

$$\forall x \in R^n : \|x - x^*\| \leq \epsilon \implies \|f(x) - f(x^*)\| \leq L^*\epsilon \qquad (25)$$

This definition is less strict than our definition of Lipschitz robustness (Eq. 20), since it is effectively equivalent to standard robustness (Eq. 19) where $L^*\epsilon = \delta$. This means that any counterexample to Property 5 will also violate Lipschitz robustness where $L = L^*$, but not the other way around. Since we train for the stronger definition (Sect. 5), we expect to see improved robustness with regard to this weaker definition.

In our Vehicle code, parameters *epsilon* and *Lipschitz* are defined during runtime, and n is inferred from the training data (provided in idx format [10]).

```
myList : List Rat
myList = [0, 1, 2, 3, 4, 5]

boundedByEpsilon : InputVector -> Bool
boundedByEpsilon x = forall i in myList . -epsilon <= x ! i - x ! i + 6 <= epsilon

validPerturbation : InputVector -> Bool
validPerturbation x = forall i in myList . x ! i == 0.0

standardRobustness : InputVector -> OutputVector -> Bool
standardRobustness input output = forall pertubation .
        let perturbedInput = input - pertubation in validPerturbation pertubation and
        validInput perturbedInput and boundedByEpsilon perturbedInput =>
        (output ! e_x - alsomitra perturbedInput ! e_x2) <= Lipschitz * epsilon and
        alsomitra perturbedInput ! e_x2 - output ! e_x <= Lipschitz * epsilon

@property
property4 : Vector Bool n
property4 = foreach i . standardRobustness (trainingInputs ! i) (trainingOutputs ! i)
```

Listing 3: Property 5 implemented in Vehicle. In this case, the states are defined in normalised terms to avoid scaling issues. Instead of calling the network twice to evaluate $f(x)$ and $f(x^*)$, the NN is doubled in onnx format so that two sets of inputs and outputs can be evaluated at once.

6.3 Verification Results

These results provide interesting insights from an engineering perspective. From Table 2 there is a clear improvement in performance for Property 1 when implementing adversarial training, suggesting that our approach has been successful. However, Properties 1 and 2 only succeed with very large values of y^* - our

Table 2. Critical y^* values for properties 1–4 (Sect. 6.1), for naive and adversarially trained NNs (Sect. 5). For properties 1, 2, and 4, a lower y^* indicates a controller that better adheres to the target trajectory, and the inverse for Property 3.

Property	Naive	Adversarial
1 (21)	46	30
2 (22)	42	42
3 (22)	Failed	Failed
4 (23)	0	0

Table 3. Verification success rates (%) of Property 5 (Sect. 6.2) for naive and adversarial NNs (Sect. 5), per L^* values and ϵ, with respect to the training dataset. A higher success rate means that the NN is robust with respect to more of the training data points. As ϵ increases we are increasing the radius for perturbation around each training point, and a decreasing L^* results in a stricter maximum gradient threshold. Empty cells represent properties that timed out before verifying 100 data points.

Naive		$L^*\epsilon$			
		10^{-3}	10^{-2}	10^{-1}	10^0
ϵ	10^{-5}				100
	10^{-4}			96.1	100
	10^{-3}		17.0	98.5	100
	10^{-2}	-	-	-	100

Adversarial		$L^*\epsilon$			
		10^{-3}	10^{-2}	10^{-1}	10^0
ϵ	10^{-5}				100
	10^{-4}			99.7	100
	10^{-3}		23.9	99.7	100
	10^{-2}	0	13.6	92.5	100

controllers only adhere to a region around the target trajectory so wide as to be useless in real applications. Properties 3 and 4 failed and succeeded, for all y^* values, for all the tested networks, suggesting that they are particularly difficult and easy to verify respectively. Table 3 shows a marginal improvement in robustness performance for our adversarial network, suggesting that our approach has been moderately successful.

7 CORA Implementation

7.1 Reachability Specification

Since our case study is based on the QUAD benchmark from the ARCH competition [24], our reachability specification is defined similarly. The initial set is:
$$x_1 = 1, x_2 = 0, x_3 = 0, x_4 = 0, x_5 = 0, x_6 \in [1.43, 4.29] \tag{26}$$

The reachability goal is for the drone to always be within a distance $y^* = 2$ of the target trajectory after 20 s. To compute reachability, CORA uses set representations (such as zonotopes [2]) and set operations to over-approximate the continuous time reachable set in discrete time steps. Additional considerations include the initial set representation, time step size, controller type, and reachability algorithm - in our case we use a zonotope, 0.01 s, a NN controller, and conservative linearization.

7.2 Reachability Results

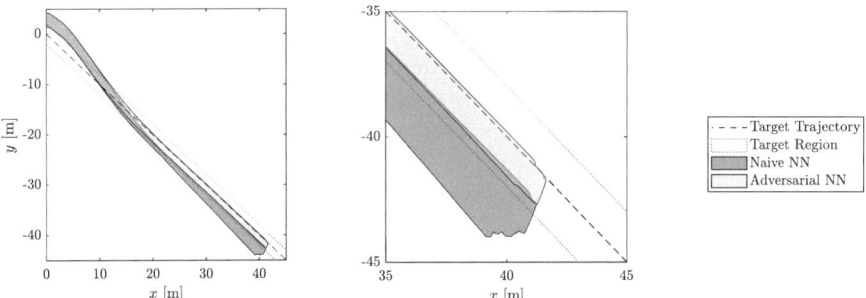

Fig. 7. Reachable regions in x_5 and x_6 for naive and adversarial NNs implemented as controllers, from the initial set defined in Eq. 26. The naive NN fails to reach a region bounded by $y^* = 2$ after 20 s, and the adversarial NN succeeds.

This result shows significant improvement from the adversarial network compared to the naive (these networks are identical to those from Tables 2 and 3), with the adversarial network adhering much closer to the target trajectory. This would suggest that our adversarial training has been successful, but we note that whilst these networks are identical in terms of structure, training data, and training epochs, the discrepancy in this plot could be partly due to differences in regression performance.

8 Discussion

8.1 Limitations and Lessons Learned

Use cases such as ours requires multiple tools to verify, each with benefits and drawbacks. Although standard methods apply, modifications are needed for proper implementation, such as with robustness training (Sect. 5). Vehicle does not have integration with Python, and our dynamics model and CORA are in Matlab, requiring the use of three programming languages for our case study. Marabou does not support multiple network calls, so a workaround involving doubling of the NN (in .onnx format) was required to evaluate robustness in Vehicle (Listing. 3). Additionally, for our local robustness property, certain Marabou queries timed out after a few data points (Table 3). Correct handling of normalisation was found to be very important since the implemented robustness training and verification methods require normalisation, yet CORA does not support normalisation. To evaluate reachability in CORA with normalised networks required another workaround, incorporating the normalisation arithmetic as extra layers in the network. Furthermore, CORA could not evaluate reachability for the full system of equations described in Sect. 3.2, due to their complexity and the size of the starting set.

Implementing CORA for our application was difficult due to set explosions, where the complexity of the reachability computation would cause an exponential expansion in the set, causing a crash. To reduce the complexity of the equations, we modified the angle of attack definition (1). To solve the initial set size issue, the initial set was divided in x_6, and the resulting subsets combined to a final reachable set. The reachability timesteps still needed to be small (0.01 s) to avoid set explosions; resulting in long computation times for full reachable sets (over 8 h in some cases). All reachable sets only involve a starting interval in x_6 (starting values are constants in every other dimension), since increasing the starting interval size in multiple dimensions would cause set explosions. These limitations in CORA were found to stem from the complexity of the partial derivative matrices (Jacobian and Hessian), especially due to a large number of nonlinear terms. CORA could be improved significantly by faster approximations of these derivatives, such as with finite differences instead of symbolic methods, but performing such calculations over sets was found to be non-trivial. ReLU activation functions were also found to reduce computation times compared to sigmoid.

Another consideration for future work is the trade-off between robustness and regression performance for such a controller. For our verification implementations we assume that each NN is capable of controlling the drone relatively well, but that may not always have been the case. A better comparison could be made using NNs with equivalent regression performance on a test set of data, using a coefficient such as R^2.

8.2 Conclusion

In this paper, we introduce a novel case study in the verification of gliding drones (Sect. 4), and evaluate the utility and challenges involved in the tools used. We developed a two-dimensional model for *Alsomitra*-inspired drones in Sect. 3, presented an ideal verification formalisation in Sect. 4.1, reduced the formalisation into properties manageable by current tools (Vehicle and CORA, Sects. 6 and 7), and presented verification results in Sects. 6.3 and 7.2. We noted challenges that this class of problems presents, among which are its more complex dynamics, under-defined notion of safe and unsafe states, preference for infinite-time horizon guarantees, and its different learning-as-regression regimes. We have shown that in principle, a combination of existing verification tools (Sect. 2.2) and novel training methods (Sects. 5 could be effectively adopted in order to enable future inclusion of this class of benchmarks into NNV portfolios. We note, however, that verification tasks like this motivate strongly development of tools that cross the boundaries of ARCH-COMP and VNN-COMP on the one hand, and incorporate these tools more smoothly with machine learning toolboxes on the other hand; cohering perhaps with the general agenda of building more complex programming language interfaces for such more complex verification tasks [8]. Technical problems such as insufficient support for normalisation (as reported here) can make a difference between verification success and failure, yet they are often over-looked in papers and tools that are dedicated to implementing NNV algorithms. Whilst we can define and verify for the behaviours that we want to a certain extent, the state of tools makes it difficult to say exactly how well

NNs will fulfil their role - even for our relatively simple (two-dimensional, non-turbulent) drone system. For example, Table 2 suggests that our NNs are only guaranteed to adhere to a very large region around the line, and Fig. 7 shows reachable regions but for which the initial set is relatively small (zero-width in 5 dimensions). All of these issues will likely be found on any comparable regression task with complex dynamic equations. If these limitations can be overcome, it will help enable engineers to develop safe and robust control and modelling methods for technologies that improve people's lives and reduce our impact on the environment.

A Appendix

A.1 Equations

Table 4. 2D quasi-steady equations for falling plates with a displaced centre of mass [23], with six system variables $(x, y, \theta, v_{x'}, v_{y'}, \omega)$. When integrated over time, the force coefficients are derived from the angle of attack (5–7), the forces are calculated (8–12), followed by the equations of motion (13–18). For simplicity the plate is assumed to be infinitesimally thin, and to always have an angle of attack within the region $\alpha \in [-\pi/2, 0]$.

Constant(s)	Definition(s)	Value(s)
ℓ, m	Plate length [m] and mass [kg]	0.07, 3.175e-04
ρ_f	Fluid Density [kg/m^3]	1.225
α_0, δ	Critical α at stall, stall transition smoothness [°]	14, 6
$C_L^1, C_L^2, C_D^0, C_D^1, C_D^{\pi/2}, C_{CP}^0, C_{CP}^1, C_{CP}^2, C_R$	System-specific aerodynamic coefficients	0.23857, 2.8529, 0.36893, 5.1822, 0.80751, 0.10598, 4.9368, 1.4996, 1.73
a, b	Elliptical semi axes [m]	0.03375, 5e-04

No.	Variable	PDE expression
1	CoM displacement, ℓ_{CM}/ℓ or e_x	Defined by controller, in the range $[0.181, 0.193]$
2	Moment of Inertia, I [kgm^2]	$I = (m(a^2 + b^2)/(\rho_f \ell^4)) + 1/32 + (\ell_{CM}/\ell)^2$
3	Angle of attack, α (p15)	$\tan \alpha = (v_{y'} - \omega \ell_{CM})/v_{x'} \approx v_{y'}/v_{x'}$
4	Selection function, $f(\alpha)$ (5.2)	$f = (1 - \tanh((\alpha - \alpha_0)/\delta))/2$
5	Lift coefficient, $C_L(\alpha)$ (5.1, 5.3)	$-C_L = f(|\alpha|)C_L^1 \sin(|\alpha|) + (1 - f(|\alpha|))C_L^2 \sin(2|\alpha|)$
6	Drag coefficient, $C_D(\alpha)$ (5.4, 5.5)	$C_D = f(|\alpha|)(C_D^0 + C_D^1 \sin^2(|\alpha|)) + (1 - f(|\alpha|))C_D^{\pi/2} \sin^2(|\alpha|)$
7	Center of pressure, $\ell_{CP}(\alpha)$ (5.6, 5.7)	$\ell_{CP}/\ell = f(|\alpha|)(C_{CP}^0 - C_{CP}^1 \alpha^2) + C_{CP}^2[1 - f(|\alpha|)](1 - |\alpha|/(\pi/2))$
8	Translational lift force, L_T (4.10)	$L_T = \frac{1}{2}\rho_f \ell C_L \sqrt{v_{x'}^2 + (v_{y'} - \omega \ell_{CM})^2}\,(v_{y'} - \omega \ell_{CM}, v_{x'})$
9	Rotational lift force, L_R (4.11)	$L_R = -\frac{1}{2}\rho_f \ell^2 C_R \omega\,(v_{y'} - \omega \ell_{CM}, v_{x'})$
10	Drag force, D (4.13)	$D = -\frac{1}{2}\rho_f \ell C_D \sqrt{v_{x'}^2 + (v_{y'} - \omega \ell_{CM})^2}\,(v_{x'}, v_{y'} - \omega \ell_{CM})$
11	Torque from transl. forces, τ_T (4.14)	$\tau_T = -\frac{1}{2}\rho_f \ell \sqrt{v_{x'}^2 + (v_{y'} - \omega \ell_{CM})^2}\,[C_L v_{x'} + C_D(v_{y'} - \omega \ell_{CM})](\ell_{CP} - \ell_{CM})$
12	Aerodynamic rot. resistance, τ_R (4.15)	$\tau_R = -\frac{1}{128}\rho_f \ell^4 C_D^{\pi/2} \omega |\omega|\left[\left(\frac{2\ell_{CM}}{\ell} + 1\right)^4 \pm \left(\frac{2\ell_{CM}}{\ell} - 1\right)^4\right]$
13	Fixed frame x velocity, $\dot{x}$ (4.4)	$\dot{x} = v_{x'} \cos \theta - v_{y'} \sin \theta$
14	Fixed frame y velocity, $\dot{y}$ (4.5)	$\dot{y} = v_{x'} \sin \theta + v_{y'} \cos \theta$
15	Angular velocity, $\dot{\theta}$ (4.6)	$\dot{\theta} = \omega$
16	Platewise x' acceleration, $\dot{v}_{x'}$ (4.7)	$m\dot{v}_{x'} = (m + \pi \rho_f \ell^2/4)\omega v_{y'} - (\pi \rho_f \ell^2/4)\omega^2 \ell_{CM} + L_T^{x'} + L_R^{x'} + D^{x'} - m'g \sin \theta$
17	Platewise y' acceleration, $\dot{v}_{y'}$ (4.8)	$(m + \pi \rho_f \ell^2/4)\dot{v}_{y'} = -m\omega v_{x'} + (\pi \rho_f \ell^2/4)\dot{\omega}\ell_{CM} + L_T^{y'} + L_R^{y'} + D_{y'} - m'g \cos \theta$
18	Angular acceleration, $\dot{\omega}$ (4.9)	$I\dot{\omega} = \tau_T + \tau_R$

References

1. Abouheaf, M., Mailhot, N., Gueaieb, W.: An online reinforcement learning wing-tracking mechanism for flexible wing aircraft. In: 2019 IEEE International Symposium on Robotic and Sensors Environments (ROSE), pp. 1–7 (2019). https://doi.org/10.1109/ROSE.2019.8790425
2. Althoff, M., Kochdumper, N., Ladner, T., Wetzlinger, M.: Manual v2025 (2024). https://tumcps.github.io/CORA/data/archive/manual/Cora2025Manual.pdf
3. Amer, K., Samy, M., Shaker, M., ElHelw, M.: Deep convolutional neural network based autonomous drone navigation. In: Proceedings of the Thirteenth International Conference on Machine Vision, vol. 11605, p. 1160503 (2021). https://doi.org/10.1117/12.2587105
4. Azuma, A., Okuno, Y.: Flight of a samara, alsomitra macrocarpa. J. Theor. Biol. **129**(3), 263–274 (1987). https://doi.org/10.1016/S0022-5193(87)80001-2
5. Brix, C., Bak, S., Johnson, T.T., Wu, H.: The 5th international verification of neural networks competition (vnn-comp 2024): summary and results (2024). https://www.arxiv.org/pdf/2412.19985
6. Casadio, M., et al.: Neural network robustness as a verification property: a principled case study. Comput. Aided Verif. 219–231 (2022)
7. Certini, D.: The flight of Alsomitra macrocarpa. Phd thesis, University of Edinburgh (2023)
8. Cordeiro, L.C., et al.: Neural network verification is a programming language challenge (2025). https://arxiv.org/abs/2501.05867
9. Cummins, C., et al.: A separated vortex ring underlies the flight of the dandelion. Nature **562**, 414–418 (2018). https://doi.org/10.1038/s41586-018-0604-2
10. Daggitt, M., et al.: A vehicle tutorial (2024). https://vehicle-lang.github.io/tutorial/
11. ERC: A dandelion-inspired drone for swarm sensing. https://cordis.europa.eu/project/id/101001499
12. Fischer, M., Balunović, M., Drachsler-Cohen, D., Gehr, T., Zhang, C., Vechev, M.: DL2: training and querying neural networks with logic. In: International Conference on Machine Learning (2019)
13. Flinkow, T., Pearlmutter, B.A., Monahan, R.: Comparing differentiable logics for learning with logical constraints. Sci. Comput. Program. **244**, 103280 (2025). https://doi.org/10.1016/j.scico.2025.103280
14. Frehse, G., Althoff, M.: Arch-comp24: volume information proceedings of the 11th international workshop on applied verification for continuous and hybrid systems. EPiC Ser. Comput. **103** (2024). https://easychair.org/publications/volume/ARCH-COMP24
15. Iyer, V., Gaensbauer, H., Daniel, T.L., Gollakota, S.: Wind dispersal of battery-free wireless devices. Nature **603**, 427–433 (2022)
16. Li, J., Yang, Q., Fan, B., Sun, Y.: Robust state/output-feedback control of coaxial-rotor MAVs based on adaptive NN approach (2019). https://ieeexplore.ieee.org/document/8715436
17. Johnson, K., et al.: Solar-powered shape-changing origami microfliers. Sci. Robot. **8**(82) (2023). https://www.science.org/doi/abs/10.1126/scirobotics.adg4276
18. Katz, G., Barrett, C., Dill, D., Julian, K., Kochenderfer, M.: Reluplex: an efficient SMT solver for verifying deep neural networks (2017). https://arxiv.org/abs/1702.01135

19. Katz, G., et al.: The marabou framework for verification and analysis of deep neural networks, pp. 443–452 (2019)
20. Kim, B.H., et al.: Three-dimensional electronic microfliers inspired by wind-dispersed seeds. Nature (2021). https://doi.org/10.1038/s41586-021-03847-y
21. Kolter, Z., Madry, A.: Adversarial robustness—theory and practice. NeurIPS 2018 tutorial (2018). https://adversarial-ml-tutorial.org/
22. Lemesle, A., Lehmann, J., Le Gall, T.: Neural network verification with pyrat (2024). https://arxiv.org/abs/2410.23903
23. Li, H., Goodwill, T., Jane Wang, Z., Ristroph, L.: Centre of mass location, flight modes, stability and dynamic modelling of gliders. J. Fluid Mech. **937**, A6 (2022). https://doi.org/10.1017/jfm.2022.89
24. Lopez, D.M., et al.: Arch-comp24 category report: artificial intelligence and neural network control systems (AINNCS) for continuous and hybrid systems plants. EPiC Ser. Comput. **103**, 64–121 (2024). https://easychair.org/publications/paper/WsgX
25. Lumini, M.: Pherodrone1.0: an innovative inflatable UAV's concept, inspired by zanonia macrocarpa's samara flying-wing and to insect's sensillae, designed for the biological control of harmful insects in pa (precision agriculture). Bionics and Sustainable Design (2022)
26. Müller, M.N., et al.: Eran (2025). https://github.com/eth-sri/eran
27. Oshima, K., Kuribara, K., Sato, T.: Flex-snn: spiking neural network on flexible substrate. IEEE Sens. Lett. **7**(5), 1–4 (2023)
28. Platzer, A.: Logical Foundations of Cyber-Physical Systems. Springer, Cham (2018). https://doi.org/10.1007/978-3-319-63588-0
29. Qamar, S., Khan, S.H., Arshad, M.A., Qamar, M., Gwak, J., Khan, A.: Autonomous drone swarm navigation and multitarget tracking with island policy-based optimization framework. IEEE Access **10**, 91073–91091 (2022). https://doi.org/10.1109/ACCESS.2022.3202208
30. Richter, D.J., Calix, R.A., Kim, K.: A review of reinforcement learning for fixed-wing aircraft control tasks. IEEE Access **12**, 103026–103048 (2024). https://doi.org/10.1109/ACCESS.2024.3433540
31. Singaraju, S.A., Weller, D.D., Gspann, T.S., Aghassi-Hagmann, J., Tahoori, M.B.: Artificial neurons on flexible substrates: a fully printed approach for neuromorphic sensing. Sensors **22** (2022)
32. Wada, D., Araujo-Estrada, S.A., Windsor, S.: Unmanned aerial vehicle pitch control using deep reinforcement learning with discrete actions in wind tunnel test. Aerospace **8**, 18 (2021). https://doi.org/10.3390/aerospace8010018
33. Wang, Y., et al.: Polar-express: efficient and precise formal reachability analysis of neural-network controlled systems. IEEE Trans. Comput. Aided Des. Integr. Circuits Syst. **43**(3), 994–1007 (2024). https://doi.org/10.1109/TCAD.2023.3331215
34. Wiesemüller, F., et al.: Transient bio-inspired gliders with embodied humidity responsive actuators for environmental sensing. Front. Robot. AI (2023)
35. WMO: Global Demonstration Campaign for Evaluating the Use of Uncrewed Aircraft Systems in Operational Meteorology: White Paper. Technical report (2023)
36. Zhang, H., Weng, T.W., Chen, P.Y., Hsieh, C.J., Daniel, L.: Efficient neural network robustness certification with general activation functions. In: Advances in Neural Information Processing Systems, vol. 31, pp. 4939–4948 (2018). https://arxiv.org/pdf/1811.00866.pdf

Extended Abstracts

Abstraction-Based Proof Production in Formal Verification of Neural Networks (Extended Abstract)

Yizhak Yisrael Elboher[1(✉)], Omri Isac[1], Guy Katz[1], Tobias Ladner[2], and Haoze Wu[3]

[1] The Hebrew University of Jerusalem, Jerusalem, Israel
`yizhak.elboher@mail.huji.ac.il`
[2] Technical University of Munich, Munich, Germany
[3] Amherst College, Amherst, USA

Abstract. Modern verification tools for deep neural networks (DNNs) increasingly rely on abstraction to scale to realistic architectures. In parallel, proof production is becoming a critical requirement for increasing the reliability of DNN verification results. However, current proof-producing verifiers do not support abstraction-based reasoning, creating a gap between scalability and provable guarantees. We address this gap by introducing a novel framework for proof-producing abstraction-based DNN verification. Our approach modularly separates the verification task into two components: (i) proving the correctness of an abstract network, and (ii) proving the soundness of the abstraction with respect to the original DNN. The former can be handled by existing proof-producing verifiers, whereas we propose the first method for generating formal proofs for the latter. This preliminary work aims to enable scalable and trustworthy verification by supporting common abstraction techniques within a formal proof framework.

Keywords: Neural Networks · Formal Verification · Proof Production · Abstraction

1 Introduction

Deep Neural Networks (DNNs) [18,32] have demonstrated exceptional performance in various domains, including vision [29], language [48], audio [47] and video [2] analysis, achieving state-of-the-art accuracy in complex tasks [41,42]. However, despite their success, DNNs function as black-box models, making their decision-making processes difficult to interpret and trust [33,43].

DNN verification [13,26,34] provides formal methods and tools (*verifiers*), to ensure or refute that DNNs comply with required specifications, offering formal guarantees of correctness. However, although verification algorithms are theoretically sound, their implementation occasionally introduce bugs and vulnerabilities [16,25,50], compromising their soundness and undermining the confidence in the verifier.

A notable approach to tackle these issues is by producing *formal proofs*, i.e., mathematical objects that can be checked by an independent program and witness the verifier's correctness. Proof production was explored in SMT and SAT solvers [6,20], and recently also in DNN verification [23,45]. Although proofs enhance the reliability of the verification process, their generation limits the scalability of the verifier in two ways: (a) the generated proofs tend to be large, which substantially increases the verifier's memory consumption; and (b) some verifier optimizations are not supported by the proof mechanism, and are disabled whenever proof generation is used—slowing down the verifier. Scalability is a key challenge for DNN verification, which is an NP-complete problem [44] in simple cases, and modern solvers might solve verification queries in worst-case exponential time with respect to DNN size (number of neurons) [7]. A common attempt to overcome this obstacle is to apply *abstraction*. This well-established technique in formal verification [9,10,12] is used to manage the complexity of analyzing large systems by creating a simpler, abstract model that retains the essential properties of the original system. In the context of DNNs, abstraction has gained attention as a method to enhance the scalability and efficiency of verification [3,14,31]. Specifically, DNN abstraction involves the construction of a reduced or approximate representation of the network such that the verification of the abstract network provides meaningful guarantees for the original network. Using abstraction, verification tools can handle larger networks and more complex properties, making it a promising approach for scalable and efficient formal analysis of DNNs.

This work-in-progress addresses two key challenges in DNN verification: enabling proof production for abstraction-based solvers and generating more compact proofs. While abstraction improves scalability by simplifying the network, existing proof-producing tools do not support it. To bridge this gap, we propose the notion of an *abstract proof*—a modular proof consisting of (i) a proof that the required specification holds in the abstract network, and (ii) a proof that the abstraction over-approximates the original network, which means that if the property holds for the abstract network, it is guaranteed to hold for the original network as well.

Therefore, our approach extends proof support to scalable abstraction-based solvers, while at the same time reducing proof size; since the abstract networks are typically smaller than the original DNNs (i.e., contain fewer neurons) and their verification time is faster, it is expected that size of the proof will be considerably reduced as well. Figure 1 illustrates the improved proof workflow and expected efficiency gains compared to the standard approach.

We regard this work as an attempt to lay a solid foundation, to be followed in the future by an implementation and evaluation.

Inspired by CEGAR [9], our main contributions are:

1. We introduce the concept of an abstract proof for DNN verification.
2. We design an abstraction-refinement mechanism for proof production.
3. We formalize a verifiable proof of the abstraction process itself, using the Marabou DNN verifier [49] and the CORA abstraction engine [1].

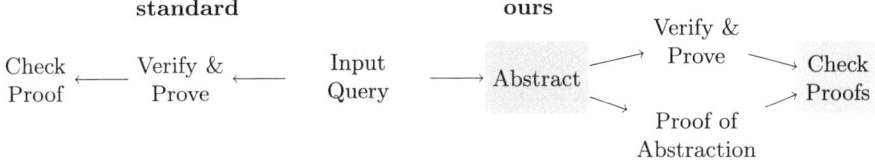

Fig. 1. Proof production flowchart: standard (left) versus ours (right). Bold colors represent cheaper operations.

The paper is organized as follows: Section 2 provides background on DNNs, DNN verification and abstraction, and proof production. Section 3 introduces our modular framework for constructing abstract proofs, describes the challenge of aligning proofs between the original and abstract networks, and presents a general abstraction-refinement algorithm for efficient proof production. Section 4 explains the abstraction process in CORA, and adapts it to our formulation. Section 5 details our implementation using Marabou (for proof production) and CORA (for abstraction), including how to verify abstract networks and generate corresponding proofs. Section 6 reviews relevant literature, and Sect. 7 summarizes our contributions and outlines future work.

2 Preliminaries

2.1 Deep Neural Networks (DNNs)

A *Deep Neural Network (DNN)* is a parameterized function $f\colon \mathbb{R}^{n_0} \to \mathbb{R}^{n_L}$, composed of multiple layers of interconnected neurons. Each layer performs an affine transformation followed by a nonlinear activation function. Formally, given an input $\mathbf{x} \in \mathbb{R}^{n_0}$, the output $\mathbf{y} = f(\mathbf{x})$ is computed as follows:

$$\mathbf{h}_0 = \mathbf{x}, \qquad \mathbf{h}_k = \phi_k(\mathbf{W}_k \mathbf{h}_{k-1} + \mathbf{b}_k), \qquad \mathbf{y} = \mathbf{h}_L, \qquad k \in [L]. \quad (1)$$

where $\mathbf{W}_k \in \mathbb{R}^{n_k \times n_{k-1}}$ is the weight matrix, $\mathbf{b}_k \in \mathbb{R}^{n_k}$ is the bias vector, and ϕ_k is the nonlinear activation function (e.g., ReLU [38] or sigmoid) for the k-th layer. An illustration of a neural network f appears in Fig. 2.

2.2 DNN Verification

A *verification query* is a triplet $\langle f, \mathcal{P}, \mathcal{Q} \rangle$ where $f\colon \mathbb{R}^{n_0} \to \mathbb{R}^{n_L}$ is a DNN, $\mathcal{P} \subset \mathbb{R}^{n_0}$ is an input property and $\mathcal{Q} \subset \mathbb{R}^{n_L}$ is an output property. *DNN Verification* aims to solve verification queries by deciding whether there exists an input satisfying $\mathcal{P}$ for which its output of f satisfies $\mathcal{Q}$:

$$\exists \mathbf{x}.\ \mathbf{x} \in \mathcal{P} \land f(\mathbf{x}) \in \mathcal{Q}. \quad (2)$$

Typically, $\mathcal{Q}$ is a set that characterizes an undesired behavior, such as vulnerability of f to adversarial perturbations or danger conditions. If an input $\mathbf{x} \in \mathcal{P}$ is

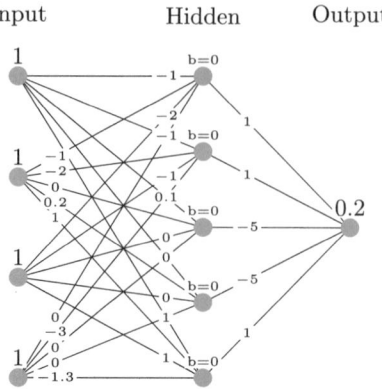

Fig. 2. A neural network f for which f(1, 1, 1, 1) = 0.2. All biases are 0.

found whose output $f(\mathbf{x}) \in \mathcal{Q}$, we say the query is SAT, and $\mathbf{x}$ serves as a counterexample to the desired property. Otherwise, if no such input exists, we say the query is UNSAT, and thus the desired property is valid. To ease notation, we also denote the latter case as $\text{unsat}(\langle f, \mathcal{P}, \mathcal{Q} \rangle)$. This can be captured as follows:

$$\text{unsat}(\langle f, \mathcal{P}, \mathcal{Q} \rangle) \equiv \forall \mathbf{x}.\ \mathbf{x} \in \mathcal{P} \implies f(\mathbf{x}) \notin \mathcal{Q}. \qquad (3)$$

For simplicity, we assume for this work that $\mathcal{P}$ is a hyperrectangle, although our approach can be generalized to any closed set $\mathcal{P}$, e.g., by over-approximating $\mathcal{P}$ with a bounding box thereof. An example of a verification query is $\langle f_1, \mathcal{P}_1, \mathcal{Q}_1 \rangle$ where f_1 is the network in Fig. 2, $\mathcal{P}_1 = \{(1 \pm \epsilon, 1 \pm \epsilon, 1 \pm \epsilon, 1) \mid \epsilon \in [0, 0.1]\}$ and $\mathcal{Q}_1 = \mathbb{R}_{\leq 0}$.

2.3 DNN Abstraction for Formal Verification

To accelerate DNN verification, it is often beneficial to reduce the size of the network through abstraction. However, since the verification target is the original DNN, one must ensure that any conclusions drawn from the abstract (simplified) model also apply to the original. The over-approximation requirement is represented as follows, where $f, \hat{f}$ are the original and abstract networks, respectively:

$$\text{unsat}(\langle \hat{f}, \mathcal{P}, \mathcal{Q} \rangle) \implies \text{unsat}(\langle f, \mathcal{P}, \mathcal{Q} \rangle).$$

If the abstraction is too coarse and yields a SAT result with a spurious example, i.e. one that is not a counter example in the original model, the abstract model is iteratively *refined*—made into a more precise, albeit a larger, over-approximation—until the verification query can be resolved correctly.

Our framework is designed to be compatible with a wide range of abstraction methods. In this work, we focus on CORA [1], a MATLAB toolbox used for formal verification of neural networks via reachability analysis. With its recent abstraction-refinement extension [31], CORA improves performance by replacing the original network with a smaller abstract model that is iteratively refined as needed. We leverage CORA as a backend for abstraction in our framework. Other approaches to network abstraction are discussed in Sect. 6. In some abstraction methods, including the one used in CORA, the abstract network does not follow a standard neural network structure. Section 3.1 discusses this gap in more detail.

2.4 Proof Production for DNN Verification

As a satisfiability problem, proving that a DNN verification query is SAT is straightforward, using a satisfying assignment that could be checked by evaluation over the network. Proving UNSAT, however, is more complicated due to the NP-hardness of DNN verification [27,44]. Thus, bookkeeping the whole proof may require large memory consumption, even for small DNNs.

In this work, we focus on the proof producing version of Marabou [23,49], a state-of-the-art DNN verifier, which encodes verification queries as satisfiability problems, utilizing satisfiability modulo theories (SMT) solving and linear programming (LP) to analyze properties of interest. It handles nonlinear activation functions, such as ReLU, through case-splitting and relaxation techniques. Marabou's proof of UNSAT is represented by a *proof-tree*. By construction, the proof's size heavily depends on the number of splits performed by Marabou, which could be exponential in the number of neurons.

3 Method

We intend to accelerate verification by applying abstraction to reduce the DNN size and prove the property over the abstract DNN. However, a proof over the abstract network alone is insufficient—it does not guarantee that the property holds for the original network. To overcome this, we introduce a general framework for constructing end-to-end proofs that remain sound while leveraging abstraction.

3.1 Proving Abstraction-Based DNN Verification

The verification of DNNs using abstraction consists of two main components: constructing the abstraction and verifying the abstract network. To match this structure, our proof method for UNSAT cases follows the same modular approach. This modularity ensures that our method remains agnostic to the underlying DNN verifier and abstraction technique, making it broadly applicable. Specifically, it enables combining any DNN verification tool capable of producing proofs with any abstraction method that comes with a corresponding proof rule.

Our method constructs a proof that consists of two independent parts. First, given a candidate DNN f, an abstract netrowk $\widehat{f}$ and properties $\mathcal{P}, \mathcal{Q}$, we establish that if $\langle \hat{f}, \mathcal{P}, \mathcal{Q} \rangle$ is UNSAT, then so is $\langle f, \mathcal{P}, \mathcal{Q} \rangle$. This forms the *proof of over-approximation*, i.e., proof of abstraction correctness, which ensures that verification results transfer from the abstract network to the original one. The second part is the verification proof for the abstract network, i.e., the proof that $\langle \hat{f}, \mathcal{P}, \mathcal{Q} \rangle$ is indeed UNSAT. These two proofs, when combined, yield the *abstract proof* following the proof rule in Fig. 3. Even though this rule is a private case of implication elimination (modus ponens), we define it to clearly indicate our modular approach.

$$\text{abs} - \text{proof}: \frac{\text{unsat}(\langle \hat{f}, \mathcal{P}, \mathcal{Q} \rangle) \implies \text{unsat}(\langle f, \mathcal{P}, \mathcal{Q} \rangle) \quad \text{unsat}(\langle \hat{f}, \mathcal{P}, \mathcal{Q} \rangle)}{\text{unsat}(\langle f, \mathcal{P}, \mathcal{Q} \rangle)}$$

Fig. 3. Proof rule for proving DNN verification with abstraction.

As a proof system for verifying DNNs (i.e., the top right part of the rule) has been introduced in prior work [23], we focus on constructing the proof of over-approximation (i.e., the top left part). We exemplify this in Sect. 5.2. Also note that in the cases where $\hat{f}$ is not precisely a DNN, we should also formalize $\langle \hat{f}, \mathcal{P}, \mathcal{Q} \rangle$ and its unsatisfiability, as part of the abstraction's definition. Furthermore, we are required to show how $\langle \hat{f}, \mathcal{P}, \mathcal{Q} \rangle$ can be reduced to a DNN verification query. We do so for CORA in Sect. 4 and in Sect. 5.1, respectively.

3.2 Main Algorithm

We propose Algorithm 1 to improve proof production via abstraction-refinement. The algorithm begins (line 1) by generating an abstract version of the original network, then iteratively verifies the correctness of the desired property on the abstract network.

Unless the condition in line 6 is met, only verification is performed; proof production is attempted only after an UNSAT result has been established. This avoids redundant proof attempts and improves performance in each iteration. An additional advantage is modularity: any verifier can be used to check the property, not just those with proof production capabilities or specific configurations that support it.

The procedures `prove-over-approximation` and `verify-with-proofs` represent the generation of a proof for the over-approximation and for the abstract query, respectively, and are described in more detail in Sect. 5. The pair $\langle p_a, p_q \rangle$ denotes the concatenation of the two components into a full proof.

Algorithm 1. Proof Production with Abstraction

Input: f, $\mathcal{P}$, $\mathcal{Q}$. **Output:** proof that $\texttt{unsat}(\langle f, \mathcal{P}, \mathcal{Q} \rangle)$, or counterexample.

1: $\widehat{f} = \texttt{abstract}(f, \mathcal{P})$
2: **while** true **do**
3:    result, example $= \texttt{verify}(\widehat{f}, \mathcal{P}, \mathcal{Q})$
4:    **if** result $==$ SAT and example is not spurious **then**
5:       **return** result, example
6:    **else if** result $==$ UNSAT **then**
7:       $p_a = \texttt{prove-over-approximation}(\widehat{f}, f, \mathcal{P}, \mathcal{Q})$
8:       $p_q = \texttt{verify-with-proofs}(\widehat{f}, \mathcal{P}, \mathcal{Q})$
9:       **if** p_a and p_q were successfully generated **then**
10:         **return** UNSAT, $\langle p_a, p_q \rangle$
11:       **end if**
12:    **end if**
13:    $\widehat{f} = \texttt{refine}(\widehat{f}, f)$
14: **end while**

4 Abstraction in CORA

We provide an overview on how abstraction in CORA works and how it can be integrated into the verification process. We refer the reader to [1,31] for additional details.

Given a neural network f as in (1) and an input set $\mathcal{P}$, the exact output set $\mathcal{Y}^* = f(\mathcal{P})$ is computed by

$$\mathcal{H}_0^* = \mathcal{P}, \qquad \mathcal{H}_k^* = \phi_k(\mathbf{W}_k \mathcal{H}_{k-1}^* + \mathbf{b}_k), \qquad \mathcal{Y}^* = \mathcal{H}_L^*, \qquad k \in [L]. \qquad (4)$$

These exact sets are generally expensive to compute [26]. Thus, we over approximate the output of each layer $\mathcal{H}_k \supseteq \mathcal{H}_k^*$. In this work, we only consider the set $\mathcal{H}_k$ to be represented as hyperrectangles, although more sophisticated set representations exist [4,17,28,30,37].

Since DNNs usually contain a large number of neurons per layer, their verification can be computationally expensive as well. Thus, [31] suggests a construction of an abstract network that soundly merges neurons with similar bounds to reduce the network size, which in turn decreases the verification time by decreasing the computation time. The bounds are determined by a one-step look-ahead algorithm using interval bound propagation (IBP) [19]. In particular, we compute the output interval bounds of layer k as follows [31, Alg. 2]:

$$\mathcal{I}_k = \phi_k(\mathbf{W}_k \cdot \texttt{bounds}(\mathcal{H}_{k-1})) + \mathbf{b}_k) \supseteq \mathcal{H}_k, \qquad (5)$$

where $\texttt{bounds}(\cdot)$ computes the interval bounds of the given set $\mathcal{H}_{k-1}$. In order to preserve soundness, multiple neurons with similar bounds are merged and the resulting error is bounded by adapting the bias term in the next layer, converting them from scalars into intervals. These bias intervals bound the deviation between the abstract network and the original network of each layer in the network and, thus, also the output of both networks.

More formally, given a neural network, [31, Prop. 4] defines a way to merge the neurons in the k-th layer, constructing the weights and biases such that the output of the $k+1$-th layer of the original neural network is contained in the output of the $k+1$-th layer of the abstract network. Notice that the terminology in [31] splits each layer into two layers, namely the linear layer and the nonlinear layer, and indexes them separately. Here, we similarly treat each layer as having two parts, but do not handle these as different layers.

Proposition 1 (Neuron Merging [31, Prop. 4]). *Given a nonlinear hidden layer $k \in [L-1]$ of a network f with n_k neurons, output interval bounds $\mathcal{I}_k \supseteq \mathcal{H}_k^*$, a merge bucket $\mathcal{B} \subset [n_k]$ containing the indices of the merged neurons, and $\bar{\mathcal{B}} = [n_k] \setminus \mathcal{B}$, we can construct an abstract network $\widehat{f}$, where we remove the merged neurons by adjusting the layers k and $k+1$ as follows:*

$$\widehat{\mathbf{W}}_k = \mathbf{W}_{k(\bar{\mathcal{B}},\cdot)}, \qquad \widehat{\mathbf{b}}_k = \mathbf{b}_{k(\bar{\mathcal{B}})}, \qquad \widehat{\mathcal{I}}_k = \widehat{\mathcal{I}}_{k(\bar{\mathcal{B}})},$$
$$\widehat{\mathbf{W}}_{k+1} = \mathbf{W}_{k+1(\cdot,\bar{\mathcal{B}})}, \qquad \widehat{\mathbf{b}}_{k+1} = \mathbf{b}_{k+1}, \qquad \widehat{\mathcal{I}}_{k+1} = \mathbf{W}_{k+1(\cdot,\mathcal{B})} \mathcal{I}_{k(\mathcal{B})}.$$

where for $\mathcal{S} \in \{\mathcal{B}, \bar{\mathcal{B}}\}$, $\square_{(\mathcal{S},\cdot)}$ and $\square_{(\cdot,\mathcal{S})}$ represent the rows and columns with the indices in $\mathcal{S}$ in lexicographic order, respectively. The interval bounds $\widehat{\mathcal{I}}_k$ require us to extend the formulation for a neural network f as in (1) to an abstract network $\widehat{f}$. Figure 4 illustrates this extension for the neural network $\mathbf{f}$.

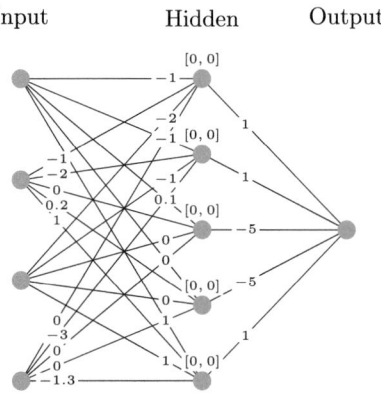

Fig. 4. $\widehat{\mathbf{f}}_0$, the extension of $\mathbf{f}$ with the new formulation for abstract networks, where the biases of $\mathbf{f}$ (zeros) are converted to intervals (singletones).

Given an input $\mathbf{x} \in \mathcal{P}$, the output $\widehat{\mathcal{Y}} = \widehat{f}(\mathbf{x})$ is computed by

$$\widehat{\mathcal{H}}_0 = \{\mathbf{x}\}, \qquad \widehat{\mathcal{H}}_k = \phi_k(\widehat{\mathbf{W}}_k \widehat{\mathcal{H}}_{k-1} \oplus \widehat{\mathbf{b}}_k \oplus \widehat{\mathcal{I}}_k), \qquad \widehat{\mathcal{Y}} = \widehat{\mathcal{H}}_L, \qquad k \in [L], \qquad (6)$$

where all $\widehat{\mathcal{I}}_k$ are initialized with $\{\mathbf{0}\}$, or equivalently $[\mathbf{0},\mathbf{0}]$, and $\oplus$ denotes the Minkowski sum of two sets, i.e., given $\mathcal{S}_1, \mathcal{S}_2 \subset \mathbb{R}^n$, $\mathcal{S}_1 \oplus \mathcal{S}_2 = \{s_1 + s_2 \mid s_1 \in \mathcal{S}_1, s_2 \in \mathcal{S}_1\}$. If either summand of the Minkowski sum is given as a vector, it is implicitly converted to a singleton. The interval biases $\widehat{\mathbf{b}}_k \oplus \widehat{\mathcal{I}}_k$ capture the error between the abstract network and the original network. Thus, initially it holds that:

$$\forall \mathbf{x} \in \mathcal{P} \colon f(\mathbf{x}) \in \widehat{f}(\mathbf{x}) = \{f(\mathbf{x})\}. \tag{7}$$

As an abstract network outputs a set instead of a single vector, we also have to generalize (3) to abstract networks:

$$\mathtt{unsat}(\langle \widehat{f}, \mathcal{P}, \mathcal{Q} \rangle) \equiv \forall \mathbf{x}.\ \mathbf{x} \in \mathcal{P} \implies \widehat{f}(\mathbf{x}) \cap \mathcal{Q} = \emptyset. \tag{8}$$

This formulation enables us the following corollary:

Corollary 1. *Given an input set $\mathcal{P}$, an abstract neural network $\widehat{f}$ where Proposition 1 is applied to all layers $k' \leq k \in [L]$, we can merge the neurons in layer k using Proposition 1 such that for the obtained abstract network $\widehat{f}'$, it holds that:*

$$\forall \mathbf{x} \in \mathcal{P} \colon \widehat{f}(\mathbf{x}) \subseteq \widehat{f}'(\mathbf{x}).$$

In particular, it holds that:

$$\mathtt{unsat}(\langle \widehat{f}', \mathcal{P}, \mathcal{Q} \rangle) \implies \mathtt{unsat}(\langle \widehat{f}, \mathcal{P}, \mathcal{Q} \rangle).$$

Proof. Let $\widehat{\mathcal{H}}_k$ and $\widehat{\mathcal{H}}'_k$ denote the output of the k-th layer of $\widehat{f}$ and $\widehat{f}'$, respectively. Note that Proposition 1 only alters layer k and $k+1$, thus, all other layers are identical between $\widehat{f}$ and $\widehat{f}'$ (6). In particular, we know that $\widehat{\mathcal{H}}_{k-1} = \widehat{\mathcal{H}}'_{k-1}$

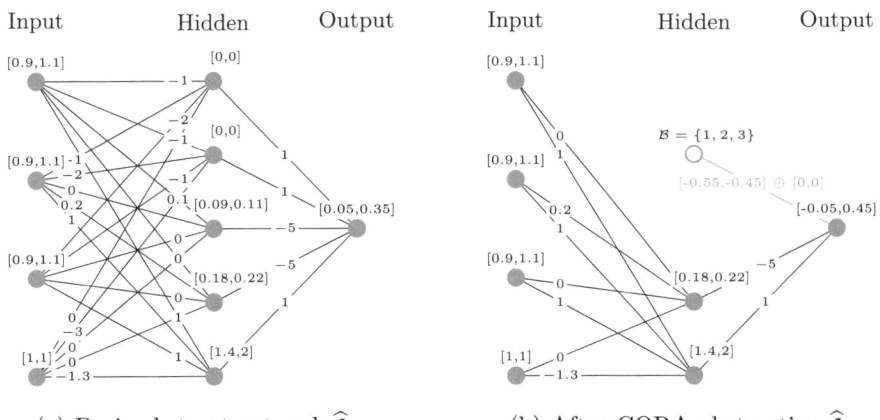

(a) Basic abstract network $\widehat{\mathbf{f}}_1$ (b) After CORA-abstraction $\widehat{\mathbf{f}}$

Fig. 5. Example of abstraction, given the input property $\mathcal{P}_1$. The basic abstract network $\widehat{\mathbf{f}}_1$ (left) is reduced to another abstract network $\widehat{\mathbf{f}}$ (right).

holds. We now show that $\widehat{\mathcal{H}}_{k+1} \subseteq \widehat{\mathcal{H}}'_{k+1}$ holds by contradiction. Let us assume that there exist a $\bar{\mathbf{h}}_{k-1} \in \widehat{\mathcal{H}}_{k-1}$ for which the respective $\bar{\mathbf{h}}_{k+1} \in \widehat{\mathcal{H}}_{k+1}$ but $\bar{\mathbf{h}}_{k+1} \notin \widehat{\mathcal{H}}'_{k+1}$. However, this cannot be true as the values of the merged neurons are captured by $\widehat{\mathcal{I}}_{k+1}$, which is computed over-approximative using IBP ((5), Proposition 1), and all remaining neurons are kept equal (Proposition 1). Thus, $\widehat{\mathcal{H}}_{k+1} \subseteq \widehat{\mathcal{H}}'_{k+1}$ holds, which directly shows that $\widehat{f}(\mathbf{x}) \subseteq \widehat{f}'(\mathbf{x})$ as all subsequent layers are again identical. The implication directly follows due to the subset relation and (8).

Example: An example of abstraction for f is shown in Fig. 5. Given the input set $\mathcal{P}_1$, the output bounds of the abstract network $\widehat{f}_1$ contain the output bounds of the basic abstract network $\widehat{f}_0$. The first three hidden neurons have similar bounds, making them a merge bucket $\mathcal{B} = \{1, 2, 3\}$, and are thus merged into an abstract neuron (in white). The set of bounds of the bucket ([0,0], [0,0] and [0.09,0.11]) is embedded into the bias ([0,0]) of the neuron in the output layer using IBP $(1 \cdot [0,0] + 1 \cdot [0,0] - 5 \cdot [0.09, 0.11] = [-0.55, -0.45])$ and Minkowski sum $(\oplus)$, resulting with output bounds of $[-0.05, 0.45] = -5 \cdot [0.18, 0.22] + 1 \cdot [1.4, 2] + [-0.55, -0.45]$. This results in the final abstract network $\widehat{f}$.

5 Proving CORA Abstraction and Marabou Verification

In this work, we focus on the proof-producing version of Marabou [23,49], a state-of-the-art verification tool with the ability to produce proofs of its UNSAT results. The abstraction process used in this work was suggested in [31] and is implemented to improve set-based DNN verification and is part of CORA [1]. In this section, we explain how to implement verify-with-proofs and prove-over-approximation in Algorithm 1 with these tools.

We start with explaining (in Sect. 5.1) the details about the verification process in Marabou, and then show how to implement verify-with-proofs and apply Marabou on an abstract network obtained by the abstraction process in CORA. In Sect. 5.2, we show how to implement prove-over-approximation and produce a proof that the abstraction process is correct. By doing so, we accomplish both necessary results as outlined in Sect. 3.1.

5.1 Proving Correctness of Abstract Network Queries in Marabou

The abstract networks obtained by the abstraction process in CORA generalize DNNs. As a result, the verification process should be adapted from solving $\langle f, \mathcal{P}, \mathcal{Q} \rangle$ and proving (3) to solving $\langle \widehat{f}, \mathcal{P}, \mathcal{Q} \rangle$ and proving (8). In the following, we show how the latter can be represented as a query that the Marabou verifier supports. This allows implementing verify-with-proofs, since the proofs generated by Marabou during the verification of $\langle \widehat{f}, \mathcal{P}, \mathcal{Q} \rangle$ can be used as proofs for (8). Recall that Marabou handles verification queries by trying to find satisfying assignments to the linear constraints in f with LP methods [8,21] and check the solution against the other, non-linear, constraints.

There are two differences to consider when using Marabou to solve queries over abstract networks. First, the output of an abstract network is a set of vectors and not a single vector. This does not require any change in the verification query, as Marabou is capable of handling constraints that define continuous sets in both input and output. Second, the abstract network $\widehat{f}$ structure expresses biases as intervals or singletons, instead of scalars. To address this, we propose two options for encoding the verification query in a form supported by Marabou:

1. The architecture of the original network f is encoded in Marabou using equations. Since the backend LP solver used in Marabou supports linear inequalities, linear constraints in an abstract network are represented directly as inequalities, where the lower and upper bounds reflect the abstracted bias interval. More formally, suppose the bias term $\widehat{b}_{ki}$ in the abstract network $\widehat{f}$ lies in the interval $[\widehat{b}^l_{ki}, \widehat{b}^u_{ki}]$. We can then express the linear constraint as the following pair of inequalities:

$$n_{ki} \geq \sum_j \mathbf{W}^{k-1}_{ji} x^{k-1}_j + \widehat{b}^l_{ki}, \quad \text{and} \quad n_{ki} \leq \sum_j \mathbf{W}^{k-1}_{ji} x^{k-1}_j + \widehat{b}^u_{ki}.$$

As an example, consider the output neuron in the network f_1, which is originally encoded by the equation:

$$n_{\text{out}} = \sum_{i=1}^{5} \mathbf{W}^1_{i1} n_{1i} + 0.0,$$

where n_{1i} denotes the i-th neuron in the hidden layer, and the final term is the bias. After converting f_1 into its abstract counterpart $\widehat{f}_1$, the output neuron is instead represented using the pair of inequalities:

$$n_{\text{out}} \geq \sum_{i=1}^{5} \mathbf{W}^1_{i1} n_{1i} + 0.0, \quad \text{and} \quad n_{\text{out}} \leq \sum_{i=1}^{5} \mathbf{W}^1_{i1} n_{1i} + 0.0.$$

since its bias lies in the interval $[0, 0]$. After applying further abstraction to obtain $\widehat{f}'_1$, these inequalities are updated to reflect the new bounds:

$$n_{\text{out}} \geq \sum_{i=1}^{5} \mathbf{W}^1_{i1} n_{1i} - 0.05, \quad \text{and} \quad n_{\text{out}} \leq \sum_{i=1}^{5} \mathbf{W}^1_{i1} n_{1i} + 0.45.$$

2. The Marabou solver supports skip connections, as these can be represented as additional linear constraints, which are seamlessly handled by the underlying LP solver. Consequently, for each bias term $\mathbf{b}_{ki}$ in an abstract network $\widehat{f}$, we can introduce a fresh input variable p_{ki} that is connected via a skip connection of weight 1 directly to the neuron n_{ki}. The set $\mathcal{P}$ is then extended with a constraint that enforces the interval bounds associated with p_{ki}.

For example, in the network $\widehat{f}'_1$, the bias of the output neuron is encoded through an additional input variable p_{out}, and $\mathcal{P}_1$ is updated to include the constraint $-0.05 \leq p_{\text{out}} \leq 0.45$.

Both methods allow us to verify $\langle \widehat{f}, \mathcal{P}, \mathcal{Q} \rangle$ directly with Marabou; the first introduces additional inequalities, whereas the second requires a larger number of variables.

5.2 Proving Correctness of the CORA Abstraction

After explaining the implementation of verify-with-proofs in the previous section, we are left with showing how prove-over-approximation for the CORA abstraction can be implemented. In this section, we describe this formalization.

A scheme of proof rules for a DNN with L layers is depicted in Fig. 6. As abstract DNNs are generalizations of DNNs, we first reason about any DNN and its trivial abstraction. For that, we use the proof rule triv − abs, based on (7). Recall that the correctness of the CORA abstraction is established based on Proposition 1 and Corollary 1, applied sequentially to all layers of the network. This yields the main part of the proof, depicted in the base − abs and the l_k − abs rules. base − abs established the correctness of CORA for the first layer based on any hyperrectangle $\mathcal{I}_1$ bounding the input property $\mathcal{P}$. Then, using l_k − abs repeatedly on each layer of the abstract network. Then, we can conclude the correctness of CORA using the CORA − L rule for a DNN with L layers. Then, these rules can be integrated into the proof construction scheme described in Sect. 3.1. To ease notation, we assume that all networks' internal variables are well defined as in (1) and (6). To ease notation further, we define the following:

$$f(\mathbf{x}) = \phi_L(\mathbf{W}_L \cdots \phi_1(\mathbf{W}_1 \mathbf{x} + \mathbf{b}_1) \cdots + \mathbf{b}_L),$$
$$\widehat{f}_0(\mathbf{x}) = \phi_L(\mathbf{W}_L \cdots \phi_1(\mathbf{W}_1 \mathbf{x} + \mathbf{b}_1 \oplus \{\mathbf{0}\}) \cdots + \mathbf{b}_L \oplus \{\mathbf{0}\}),$$
$$\widehat{f}_k(\mathbf{x}) = \phi_L(\mathbf{W}_L \cdots \phi_k(\widehat{\mathbf{W}}_K \cdots \phi_1(\widehat{\mathbf{W}}_1 \mathbf{x} + \widehat{\mathbf{b}}_1 \oplus \widehat{\mathcal{I}}_1) \cdots \widehat{\mathbf{b}}_k \oplus \widehat{\mathcal{I}}_k) \cdots + \mathbf{b}_L \oplus \{\mathbf{0}\}),$$
$$\widehat{f}(\mathbf{x}) = \widehat{f}_L(\mathbf{x}) = \phi_L(\widehat{\mathbf{W}}_L \cdots \phi_1(\widehat{\mathbf{W}}_1 \mathbf{x} + \widehat{\mathbf{b}}_1 \oplus \widehat{\mathcal{I}}_1) \cdots + \widehat{\mathbf{b}}_L \oplus \widehat{\mathcal{I}}_L)$$

and use the left hand side as an abbreviation of the right hand side.

Proof checking. In order to check a proof witness for CORA abstraction, the checker needs to receive the original DNN verification query $\langle f, \mathcal{P}, \mathcal{Q} \rangle$, as well as the candidate abstract network $\widehat{f}$. Then, any intermediate abstract network $\widehat{f}_k$ can be constructed during the checking process based on $\widehat{f}$ and f. Note that in contrary to CORA, the proof checker is not required to construct abstract networks. In addition, it could be implemented with formal guarantees of correctness (e.g., by using arbitrarily-precise arithmetic for its computation), prioritizing reliability over scalability.

Example: an example for a proof, proving the abstraction presented in Fig. 5, appears in Fig. 7. The proof uses the concrete DNN f and the abstract networks $\widehat{f}_0, \widehat{f}_1, \widehat{f}$. For simplicity, we omit the direct definitions of all matrices. However, we can see that the underlying weight matrices of $\widehat{f}$ can be obtained by removing

$$\text{triv} - \text{abs}: \frac{f \quad \widehat{f}_0 \quad \mathbf{x} \in \mathbb{R}^{n_0}}{f(\mathbf{x}) \in \widehat{f}_0(\mathbf{x})} \qquad \text{base} - \text{abs}: \frac{\widehat{f}_0 \quad \widehat{f}_1 \quad \mathbf{x} \in \mathcal{P} \subseteq \widehat{\mathcal{I}}_1}{\forall x \in \mathcal{P}. \ \widehat{f}_0(\mathbf{x}) \subseteq \widehat{f}_1(\mathbf{x})}$$

$$\mathsf{l}_k - \text{abs}: \frac{\begin{array}{c} k \in \{2, \cdots, L-1\} \quad \mathcal{B} \subset [n_k] \quad \widehat{f}_k \quad \widehat{f}_{k+1} \\ \widehat{\mathbf{W}}_k = \mathbf{W}_{k(\bar{\mathcal{B}}, \cdot)} \quad \widehat{\mathbf{b}}_k = \mathbf{b}_{k(\bar{\mathcal{B}})} \quad \widehat{\mathbf{W}}_{k+1} = \mathbf{W}_{k+1(\cdot, \bar{\mathcal{B}})} \quad \widehat{\mathbf{b}}_{k+1} = \mathbf{b}_{k+1} \\ \widehat{\mathcal{I}}_k = \widehat{\mathcal{I}}_{k(\bar{\mathcal{B}})} \quad \widehat{\mathcal{I}}_{k+1} = \mathbf{W}_{k+1(\cdot, \mathcal{B})} \mathcal{I}_{k(\mathcal{B})} \end{array}}{\forall x \in \mathcal{P}. \ \widehat{f}_k(\mathbf{x}) \subseteq \widehat{f}_{k+1}(\mathbf{x})}$$

$$\text{CORA} - \mathsf{L}: \frac{f(\mathbf{x}) \in \widehat{f}_0(\mathbf{x}) \quad \forall x \in \mathcal{P}. \ \widehat{f}_0(\mathbf{x}) \subseteq \widehat{f}_1(\mathbf{x}) \quad \cdots \quad \forall x \in \mathcal{P}. \ \widehat{f}_{L-1}(\mathbf{x}) \subseteq \widehat{f}(\mathbf{x}) \quad \mathcal{Q} \subset \mathbb{R}^{n_L}}{\text{unsat}(\langle \widehat{f}, \mathcal{P}, \mathcal{Q} \rangle) \implies \text{unsat}(\langle f, \mathcal{P}, \mathcal{Q} \rangle)}$$

Fig. 6. A scheme of proof rules for CORA abstraction of a DNN with L layers.

rows from the weight matrices of f. Furthermore, $\widehat{\mathcal{I}}_2 = [-0.55, -0.45]$ is indeed obtained (in Fig. 5) by multiplying the input bounds and their weights, for the indices corresponding to the bucket, i.e., we indeed have that $\widehat{\mathcal{I}}_2 = \mathbf{W}_{2(\cdot, \mathcal{B})} \widehat{\mathcal{I}}_{1(\mathcal{B})}$.

$$\frac{\dfrac{\mathsf{f} \quad \widehat{\mathsf{f}}_0 \quad \mathbf{x} \in \mathbb{R}^4}{\mathsf{f}(\mathbf{x}) \in \widehat{\mathsf{f}}_0(\mathbf{x})} \quad \dfrac{\widehat{\mathsf{f}}_0 \quad \widehat{\mathsf{f}}_1 \quad \mathbf{x} \in \mathcal{P}_1 := \widehat{\mathcal{I}}_1}{\forall x \in \mathcal{P}. \ \widehat{\mathsf{f}}_0(\mathbf{x}) \subseteq \widehat{\mathsf{f}}_1(\mathbf{x})} \quad \dfrac{\begin{array}{c} \mathcal{B} = \{1,2,3\} \quad \widehat{\mathsf{f}}_1 \quad \widehat{\mathsf{f}} \\ \widehat{\mathbf{W}}_1 = \mathbf{W}_{1(\bar{\mathcal{B}}, \cdot)} \quad \widehat{\mathbf{b}}_1 = \mathbf{b}_{1(\bar{\mathcal{B}})} \\ \widehat{\mathbf{W}}_2 = \mathbf{W}_{2(\cdot, \bar{\mathcal{B}})} \quad \widehat{\mathbf{b}}_2 = \mathbf{b}_2 \quad \mathcal{Q}_1 \subset \mathbb{R} \\ \widehat{\mathcal{I}}_1 = \widehat{\mathcal{I}}_{1(\bar{\mathcal{B}})} \quad \widehat{\mathcal{I}}_2 = \mathbf{W}_{2(\cdot, \mathcal{B})} \mathcal{I}_{1(\mathcal{B})} \end{array}}{\forall x \in \mathcal{P}. \ \widehat{\mathsf{f}}_1(\mathbf{x}) \subseteq \widehat{\mathsf{f}}(\mathbf{x})}}{\text{unsat}(\langle \widehat{\mathsf{f}}, \mathcal{P}_1, \mathcal{Q}_1 \rangle) \implies \text{unsat}(\langle \mathsf{f}, \mathcal{P}_1, \mathcal{Q}_1 \rangle)}$$

Fig. 7. An example of a proof of an abstraction, for the DNN f and the abstract network $\widehat{\mathsf{f}}$.

6 Related Work

This work builds on two main pillars in DNN verification: proof production and abstraction.

Proof production is a well-established area in formal verification, particularly within SAT and SMT solvers [5,22,39] among many others, where the generation of proofs or certificates serves to improve trust in automated verification results. These proofs can be independently checked, enhancing the reliability of verification pipelines. Despite its importance in traditional verification, proof production remains largely unexplored in the context of DNN verification, and most existing tools do not provide formal proofs as part of their output.

Abstraction [9,10,12] is a classical technique in formal verification, widely used to tackle scalability and complexity challenges. In the domain of DNN verification, abstraction has been actively studied through two main lenses. The first is *abstract interpretation*, which over-approximates neural network behavior using abstract domains [17,46]. The second is *abstraction refinement*, where the verifier incrementally refines the abstraction based on counterexamples or property violations, improving precision over time [3,11,14,15,31,35,40]. These techniques have proven effective in improving both scalability and verification success rates.

However, the intersection of abstraction and proof production has received very limited attention, in both directions: how proofs can influence abstraction, and how abstraction can contribute to proof construction. An early example of the former, in the SAT domain, is the work of [22], where proofs are used to guide and refine the abstraction process.

As for the latter, our work is, to the best of our knowledge, among the first to investigate how abstraction mechanisms can be directly integrated into the production of formal proofs in the context of DNN verification. In a recent work [45], a Domain Specific Language (DSL), designed for defining and certifying the soundness of abstract interpretation DNN verifiers, is introduced and evaluated over several DNN verifiers. This work is focused on proving DNN verifiers that employ linear over-approximations of activation functions, while our method focuses on separate proofs for neuron-merging abstraction process, and for the verification process. An interesting future work would be to formalize our scheme using the DSL of [45].

7 Conclusion and Future Work

This work-in-progress aims to bridge abstraction and proof production in DNN verification. On one hand, incorporating abstraction enhances the efficiency and compactness of proof production in the formal verification of neural networks. On the other hand, proofs can be generated for verification tools that apply abstraction to improve performance of reliable verifiers. To achieve this, we allow the abstraction process itself to be certified. By introducing a modular proof rule that separates the verification proof from the abstraction proof, we establish a foundation for generating complete proofs while using abstraction to aid in their construction. This modular approach allows integration with existing proof-producing verifiers for the verification component, while enabling the development of novel proof mechanisms specific to abstraction. We presented a general algorithm for abstraction-refinement-based proof production in DNN verification and demonstrated how it can be instantiated using current tools for both proof generation and abstraction.

The next steps of our work include the implementation and evaluation of our method with respect to proof size, verification time, and proof-checking time; over real-world benchmarks. Looking forward, we identify two promising directions for future work. First, integrating residual reasoning [15] could improve the effectiveness of abstraction refinement procedures. Second, leveraging abstract proofs within CDCL-based frameworks [24,36] offers a compelling avenue for bridging abstraction and clause learning-based proof systems.

Acknowledgements. The research presented in this paper was partially funded by the project FAI under project number 286525601 funded by the German Research Foundation (Deutsche Forschungsgemeinschaft, DFG).

This work was partially funded by the European Union (ERC, VeriDeL, 101112713). Views and opinions expressed are however those of the author(s) only and do not necessarily reflect those of the European Union or the European Research Council Executive Agency. Neither the European Union nor the granting authority can be held responsible for them.

This work was performed in part using high-performance computing equipment obtained under NSF Grant #2117377.

Disclosure of Interests. The authors have no competing interests to declare that are relevant to the content of this article.

References

1. Althoff, M.: An introduction to CORA 2015. In: Proceedings of 1st and 2nd International Workshop on Applied Verification for Continuous and Hybrid Systems (ARCH), pp. 120–151 (2015)
2. Arnab, A., Dehghani, M., Heigold, G., Sun, C., Lučić, M., Schmid, C.: ViViT: a video vision transformer. In: Proceedings of International Conference on Computer Vision (ICCV), pp. 6816–6826 (2021)
3. Ashok, P., Hashemi, V., Křetínský, J., Mohr, S.: DeepAbstract: neural network abstraction for accelerating verification. In: Proceedings of 18th International Symposium on Automated Technology for Verification and Analysis (ATVA), pp. 92–107 (2020)
4. Bak, S.: nnenum: verification of ReLU neural networks with optimized abstraction refinement. In: Proceedings of 13th NASA Formal Methods Symposium (NFM), pp. 19–36 (2021)
5. Barbosa, H., et al.: Flexible proof production in an industrial-strength SMT solver. In: Proceedings of 11th International Joint Conference on Automated Reasoning (IJCAR), pp. 15–35 (2022)
6. Barrett, C., de Moura, L., Fontaine, P.: Proofs in satisfiability modulo theories. In: All about Proofs, Proofs for All, pp. 23–44. College Publications (2015)
7. Brix, C., Müller, M., Bak, S., Johnson, T., Liu, C.: First three years of the international verification of neural networks competition (VNN-COMP). In: International Journal on Software Tools for Technology Transfer (STTT), pp. 1–11 (2023)
8. Chvátal, V.: Linear Programming. Macmillan (1983)
9. Clarke, E., Grumberg, O., Jha, S., Lu, Y., Veith, H.: Counterexample-guided abstraction refinement. In: Proceedings of 12th International Conference on Computer Aided Verification (CAV), pp. 154–169 (2000)
10. Clarke, E., Grumberg, O., Long, D.: Model checking and abstraction. ACM Trans. Programm. Lang. Syst. (TOPLAS) 1512–1542 (1994)
11. Cohen, E., Elboher, Y.Y., Barrett, C., Katz, G.: Tighter abstract queries in neural network verification. In: Proceedings of of 24th International Conference on Logic for Programming, Artificial Intelligence and Reasoning (LPAR), pp. 124–143 (2023)

12. Cousot, P., Cousot, R.: Abstract interpretation: a unified lattice model for static analysis of programs by construction or approximation of fixpoints. In: Proceedings of 4th ACM SIGACT-SIGPLAN Symposium on Principles of Programming Languages (POPL), pp. 238–252 (1977)
13. Ehlers, R.: Formal verification of piece-wise linear feed-forward neural networks. In: D'Souza, D., Narayan Kumar, K. (eds.) ATVA 2017. LNCS, vol. 10482, pp. 269–286. Springer, Cham (2017). https://doi.org/10.1007/978-3-319-68167-2_19
14. Elboher, Y.Y., Gottschlich, J., Katz, G.: An abstraction-based framework for neural network verification. In: Lahiri, S.K., Wang, C. (eds.) CAV 2020. LNCS, vol. 12224, pp. 43–65. Springer, Cham (2020). https://doi.org/10.1007/978-3-030-53288-8_3
15. Elboher, Y.Y., Cohen, E., Katz, G.: Neural network verification using residual reasoning. In: Proceedings of 20th International Conference on Software Engineering and Formal Methods (SEFM), pp. 173–189 (2022)
16. Elsaleh, R., Katz, G.: DelBugV: delta-debugging neural network verifiers. In: Proceedings of 23rd International Conference Formal Methods in Computer-Aided Design (FMCAD), pp. 34–43 (2023)
17. Gehr, T., Mirman, M., Drachsler-Cohen, D., Tsankov, E., Chaudhuri, S., Vechev, M.: AI2: safety and robustness certification of neural networks with abstract interpretation. In: Proceedings of 39th IEEE Symposium on Security and Privacy (S&P), pp. 3–18 (2018)
18. Goodfellow, I., Bengio, Y., Courville, A.: Deep Learning. MIT Press Cambridge (2016)
19. Gowal, S., et al.: On the Effectiveness of Interval Bound Propagation for Training Verifiably Robust Models (2019). Technical Report. https://arxiv.org/abs/1810.12715
20. Griggio, A., Roveri, M., Tonetta, S.: Certifying Proofs for SAT-Based Model Checking. Formal Methods in System Design (FMSD), pp. 178–210 (2021)
21. Gurobi Optimization, LLC: Gurobi Optimizer Reference Manual (2024). https://www.gurobi.com
22. Henzinger, T., Jhala, R., Majumdar, R., McMillan, K.: Abstractions from proofs. In: Proceedings of 31st ACM SIGACT-SIGPLAN Symposium on Principles of Programming Languages (POPL), p. 232–244 (2004)
23. Isac, O., Barrett, C., Zhang, M., Katz, G.: Neural network verification with proof production. In: Proceedings of 22nd International Conference on Formal Methods in Computer-Aided Design (FMCAD), pp. 38–48 (2022)
24. Isac, O., Refaeli, I., Wu, H., Barrett, C., Katz, G.: Proof-Driven Clause Learning in Neural Network Verification (2025). Technical Report. http://arxiv.org/abs/2503.12083
25. Jia, K., Rinard, M.: Exploiting verified neural networks via floating point numerical error. In: Drăgoi, C., Mukherjee, S., Namjoshi, K. (eds.) SAS 2021. LNCS, vol. 12913, pp. 191–205. Springer, Cham (2021). https://doi.org/10.1007/978-3-030-88806-0_9
26. Katz, G., Barrett, C., Dill, D.L., Julian, K., Kochenderfer, M.J.: Reluplex: an efficient SMT solver for verifying deep neural networks. In: Majumdar, R., Kunčak, V. (eds.) CAV 2017. LNCS, vol. 10426, pp. 97–117. Springer, Cham (2017). https://doi.org/10.1007/978-3-319-63387-9_5
27. Katz, G., Barrett, C., Dill, D., Julian, K., Kochenderfer, M.: Reluplex: a Calculus for Reasoning about Deep Neural Networks. Formal Methods in System Design (FMSD) (2021)

28. Kochdumper, N., Schilling, C., Althoff, M., Bak, S.: Open- and closed-loop neural network verification using polynomial zonotopes. In: Proceedings of 15th NASA Formal Methods Symposium (NFM), pp. 16–36 (2023)
29. Krizhevsky, A., Sutskever, I., Hinton, G.: ImageNet classification with deep convolutional neural networks. In: Proceedings of Advances in Neural Information Processing Systems (NeuRIPS) (2012)
30. Ladner, T., Althoff, M.: Automatic abstraction refinement in neural network verification using sensitivity analysis. In: Proceedings of 26th ACM International Conference on Hybrid Systems: Computation and Control (HSCC), pp. 1–13 (2023)
31. Ladner, T., Althoff, M.: Fully Automatic Neural Network Reduction for Formal Verification (2023). Technical Report. http://arxiv.org/abs/2305.01932
32. LeCun, Y., Bengio, Y., Hinton, G.: Deep learning. Nature 436–444 (2015)
33. Lipton, Z.: The mythos of model interpretability: In machine learning, the concept of interpretability is both important and slippery. Queue 31–57 (2018)
34. Liu, C., Arnon, T., Lazarus, C., Strong, C., Barrett, C., Kochenderfer, M.: Algorithms for verifying deep neural networks. Found. Trends Optimiz. 244–404 (2021)
35. Liu, J., Xing, Y., Shi, X., Song, F., Xu, Z., Ming, Z.: Abstraction and refinement: towards scalable and exact verification of neural networks. ACM Trans. Softw. Eng. Methodol. (TOSEM) 1–35 (2024)
36. Liu, Z., Yang, P., Zhang, L., Huang, X.: DeepCDCL: a CDCL-based neural network verification framework. In: Proceedings of 18th International Symposium on Theoretical Aspects of Software Engineering (TASE), pp. 343–355 (2024)
37. Lopez, D., Choi, S., Tran, H.D., Johnson, T.: NNV 2.0: the neural network nerification tool. In: Proceedings of 35th International Conference on Computer Aided Verification (CAV), pp. 397–412 (2023)
38. Nair, V., Hinton, G.: Rectified linear units improve restricted Boltzmann machines. In: Proceedings of 27th International Conference on Machine Learning (ICML), pp. 807–814 (2010)
39. Niemetz, A., Preiner, M., Reynolds, A., Zohar, Y., Barrett, C., Tinelli, C.: Towards bit-width-independent proofs in SMT solvers. In: Fontaine, P. (ed.) CADE 2019. LNCS (LNAI), vol. 11716, pp. 366–384. Springer, Cham (2019). https://doi.org/10.1007/978-3-030-29436-6_22
40. Ostrovsky, M., Barrett, C., Katz, G.: An abstraction-refinement approach to verifying convolutional neural networks. In: Proceedings of 20th International Symposium on Automated Technology for Verification and Analysis (ATVA), pp. 391–396 (2022)
41. Radford, A., et al.: Learning transferable visual models from natural language supervision. In: Proceedings of 38th International Conference on Machine Learning (ICML) (2021)
42. Radford, A., Kim, J.W., Xu, T., Brockman, G., McLeavey, C., Sutskever, I.: Robust speech recognition via large-scale weak supervision. In: Proceedings of 40th International Conference on Machine Learning (ICML) (2023)
43. Rudin, C.: Stop explaining black box machine learning models for high stakes decisions and use interpretable models instead. Nat. Mach. Intell. 206–215 (2019)
44. Sälzer, M., Lange, M.: Reachability is NP-complete even for the simplest neural networks. In: Proceedings of 15th International Conference on Reachability Problems (RP), pp. 149–164 (2021)
45. Singh, A., Sarita, Y., Mendis, C., Singh, G.: Automated verification of soundness of DNN certifiers. In: Proceedings of ACM on Programming Languages (PACMPL) (2025)

46. Singh, G., Gehr, T., Püschel, M., Vechev, M.: An abstract domain for certifying neural networks. In: Proceedings of 46th ACM SIGACT-SIGPLAN Symposium on Principles of Programming Languages (POPL), pp. 1–30 (2019)
47. van den Oord, A., et al.: WaveNet: a generative model for raw audio. In: Proceedings of 9th ISCA Workshop on Speech Synthesis Workshop (SSW), p. 125 (2016)
48. Vaswani, A., et al.: Attention is all you need. In: Proceedings of 31st Conference on Advances in Neural Information Processing Systems (NeuRIPS) (2017)
49. Wu, H., et al.: Marabou 2.0: a versatile formal analyzer of neural networks. In: Proceedings of 36th International Conference on Computer Aided Verification (CAV) (2024)
50. Zombori, D., Bánhelyi, B., Csendes, T., Megyeri, I., Jelasity, M.: Fooling a complete neural network verifier. In: Proceedings of 9th International Conference on Learning Representations (ICLR) (2021)

On the Complexity of Formal Reasoning in State Space Models (Extended Abstract)

Eric Alsmann[✉] and Martin Lange

University of Kassel, Kassel, Germany
{eric.alsmann,martin.lange}@uni-kassel.de

Abstract. We study the computational complexity of the satisfiability problem for state space models (SSMSAT), a recurrent architecture that has recently emerged as a promising alternative to the widely used transformer architecture in language modelling. We show that SSMSAT is undecidable in the general case. However, under certain practically motivated restrictions, the problem becomes decidable, and we establish complexity bounds for these cases. When the context length is bounded, SSMSAT is NP-complete. When the model is quantised, i.e. restricted to fixed-width arithmetic, satisfiability remains decidable. Nevertheless, the problem remains computationally hard: depending on the encoding, we identify instances where SSMSAT, when restricted to fixed-width arithmetic, is PSPACE-complete or lies between PSPACE and EXPSPACE, depending on the encoding of the bit-width. Given these results, we discuss possible implications for the verification of state-space models used in language modelling.

Keywords: state space models · formal reasoning · complexity

1 Introduction

State Space Models (SSM) have recently emerged as an promising alternative to transformer-based architectures for sequence modeling tasks. By relying on linear recurrences and pointwise transformations, SSM are able to capture long-range dependencies while maintaining computational simplicity. This structural difference compared to transformers raises new questions about the formal properties of SSM. While the empirical performance of SSM has been studied extensively, their formal verification remains largely unexplored. In particular, understanding the complexity of basic reasoning tasks, such as satisfiability and reachability, is essential for assessing the reliability and robustness of models deployed in safety-critical applications.

In this paper, we initiate a systematic investigation of the satisfiability problem for SSM. The satisfiability problem asks whether there exists an input sequence that causes the model to reach an accepting configuration. We first show that, in full generality, the problem is undecidable by a reduction from the halting problem for Minsky machines. Motivated by practical settings, we then consider two natural restrictions that make the problem decidable. First, we study SSM under bounded context length, a common assumption in deployed language models. We show that in this case, the satisfiability problem is NP-complete. Second, we investigate SSM operating over fixed-width arithmetic, reflecting the use of quantised computation in practical implementations. We prove that the satisfiability problem is PSPACE-complete when the bit-width is constant or encoded in unary and in EXPSPACE when the bit-width is encoded in binary.

These results establish a first complexity landscape for formal reasoning in SSM. They provide a foundation for future work on verification techniques and a better theoretical understanding of the strengths and limitations of SSM.

Recent work has explored the expressive power of SSM. Sarrof et al. [11] showed that general SSM can express all star-free regular languages and that a restricted class of SSM exactly characterises the star-free languages. Furthermore, Merrill et al. [7] proved that quantised SSM can recognise only languages contained in the class TC^0. Related complexity questions have also been investigated for transformer architectures: Sälzer et al. [10] studied the satisfiability problem for transformer encoders, establishing computational hardness results similar to ours.

2 State Space Models

We consider State Space Models (SSM) in the sense of [4], adopting the formalisation introduced in [11] for a structured analysis. An SSM layer takes an input sequence $\boldsymbol{x}_1 \cdots \boldsymbol{x}_n$ and maintains a hidden state $\boldsymbol{h}_t$ that evolves via an input-dependent linear recurrence and produces outputs through a pointwise transformation ϕ.

$$\boldsymbol{h}_t = A(\boldsymbol{x}_t) \cdot \boldsymbol{h}_{t-1} + B(\boldsymbol{x}_t)$$
$$\boldsymbol{y}_t = \phi(\boldsymbol{x}_t, \boldsymbol{h}_t)$$

A full SSM working over some finite alphabet Σ comprises a sequence of such layers, followed by an output projection and preceded by an embedding function which maps the input word to the initial sequence of vectors. Given an input sequence, the model applies each layer successively, using the output of one layer as the input to the next. The final output is obtained by applying the output function element-wise to the top layer's result.

SSM architectures used in practice mainly differ on the allowed functions for A, B and ϕ. While some architectures are time-invariant [6,9,12], meaning that A is not input-dependent, others allow A to be an arbitrary smooth function [1,3,13]. However, almost all architectures assume $A(\boldsymbol{x}_t)$ to be a diagonal matrix. The pointwise transformation ϕ is usually a non-linear function using some kind of linear projection together with non-linear activations like GeLU or Sigmoid. Established upper bounds will hold for any reasonable choice of functions, subsuming all variants of SSM used in practice. The only assumption we make is that all functions can be computed in polynomial-time. This ensures that for a given input word, the output of the SSM can be also computed in polynomial time, depending on the input length. For the lower bounds we use a fairly weak choice of functions by assuming A, B to be input-dependent linear maps and all pointwise applied functions to be simple Feedforward Neural Networks (FNN). In this work we only consider SSM for sequence classification. In this case the output vector of the last input symbol is used to determine whether the input sequence is accepted or not. The leads to the satisfiability problem for SSM ssmSAT which is defined as follows:

> ssmSAT
> **Input:** SSM $\mathcal{S}$ over alphabet Σ.
> **Question:** Is there a word $w \in \Sigma^*$, such that $\mathcal{S}(w) = 1$?

In order to obtain upper complexity bounds for this problem, we need to measure the representation size of an SSM. We measure this representation size in the usual way, meaning given an SSM over an alphabet Σ, with vector dimension d and number of layers L the size is $|\mathcal{S}| = |\Sigma| + L + d$. We now assume the syntactic representation of $\mathcal{S}$ to be polynomial in $|\mathcal{S}|$. For a given word, the output of an SSM is computed layer-wise and each layer only requires a linear amount of calculations. This leads to the polynomial-evaluation property for SSM.

Theorem 1. *Given an SSM $\mathcal{S}$ over an alphabet Σ and a word $w \in \Sigma^*$, the output $\mathcal{S}(w)$ can be computed in time polynomial in $|\mathcal{S}| + |w|$.*

3 Satisfiability for General SSM is Undecidable

We show the undecidability of ssmSAT by reducing from the halting problem of Minsky Machines, a classical undecidable problem [8]. The key idea is to simulate the computation of a Minsky Machine within the framework of an SSM, thereby encoding the question of whether a Minsky Machine halts as a satisfiability question for an SSM. A Minsky Machine operates on two counters and transitions between states based on increment, decrement, and conditional zero-check instructions. To simulate such computations using an SSM, the approach separates control-flow information (machine states and transition rules) from the counter values. The control flow is encoded directly into the input sequence, while the counter values are computed internally by the SSM through its linear recurrence mechanism.

We construct a SSM with three layers. The first layer reconstructs the previous machine state at each step, allowing access to state transitions. The second layer uses the linear recurrence and the pointwise applied neural network to simulate counter updates and perform consistency checks: it verifies that the encoded transition is valid, and in the case of conditional transitions, correctly handles zero-checks. A final layer ensures that the entire sequence corresponds to a valid run by aggregating error flags. The construction guarantees that the

SSM accepts a sequence if and only if it encodes a valid halting run of the given Minsky Machine.

Theorem 2. SSMSAT *is undecidable.*

4 Bounded Context Length

After establishing the undecidability of the general model, we now consider two natural restrictions that render the problem decidable and for which we establish complexity bounds. The first restriction, commonly encountered in practical language models, is a bound on the context length. When the context length is fixed and not part of the input, the satisfiability problem becomes trivial, as only a constant number of input sequences need to be checked. Therefore, we focus on the following problem, denoted SSMSAT$^\leq$:

> **SSMSAT$^\leq$**
> **Input:** SSM S over alphabet Σ and number n (in unary).
> **Question:** Is there a word $w \in \Sigma^*$ with $|w| \leq n$, such that $S(w) = 1$?

Membership in NP follows from a standard guess-and-verify approach. We non-deterministically select a word w with $|w| \leq n$ and verify whether S accepts it. Due to the assumed polynomial-evaluation property of SSM, this verification can be performed in polynomial time. To establish NP-hardness, we provide a reduction from the well-known NP-complete problem Zero-One Linear Programming [5]. In this problem, given a matrix $A \in \mathbb{R}^{d \times d}$ and a vector $\mathbf{b} \in \mathbb{R}^d$, the task is to determine whether there exists a vector $\mathbf{x} \in \{0,1\}^d$ such that $A\mathbf{x} = \mathbf{b}$. Our reduction constructs a single-layer SSM that accepts an input of maximum length d encoding $\mathbf{x}$ as a sequence of unit vectors. The linear recurrence is used to compute $A\mathbf{x}$. The output of the SSM is determined by a neural network that verifies equality with $\mathbf{b}$.

Theorem 3. SSMSAT$^\leq$ *is NP-complete.*

5 Fixed-Width Arithmetic

This section establishes the precise complexity of the satisfiability problem for SSM operating over fixed-point arithmetic. Our notion of fixed-width arithmetics are representations of numbers using a fixed amount of bits, like floating- or fixed-point arithmetic. Our results are independent of the specific choice of an implementation. We assume that all values represented in a fixed-width arithmetic use b bits for representing numbers. We say that an SSM works over fixed-with arithmetics, if all computations and values occuring in the computation of the SSM are carried out using only b bits. Therefore, for given $b \in \mathbb{N}$ we define the problem:

b-ssmSAT^{fix}
Input: SSM $\mathcal{S}$ over alphabet Σ
Question: Is there a word $w \in \Sigma^*$ such that $\mathcal{S}(w) = 1$
when $\mathcal{S}$ works over fixed-width arithmetic with b bits?

The upper bound is obtained by exploiting the finiteness of the reachable configuration space under fixed-point arithmetic. Specifically, any SSM with L layers, d-dimensional hidden states, and bit-width b can produce at most $2^{L \cdot d \cdot b}$ distinct internal states. A simple pigeonhole argument shows that if the SSM accepts any input at all, it must also accept an input of length exponential in the model size. Additionally, the next hidden state of an SSM only depends on the previous hidden state and the next vector of the input sequence. This enables a nondeterministic algorithm that guesses such an input symbol-by-symbol while tracking the internal state with polynomial space, leading to a PSPACE membership result.

The lower bound is shown via a reduction from the satisfiability problem for Linear Temporal Logic on finite traces (LTL$_f$) [2], which is known to be PSPACE-hard. The reduction constructs, for any given LTL$_f$ formula φ, a corresponding SSM $\mathcal{S}_\varphi$ that accepts exactly the models of φ. The construction encodes subformulas of φ layer-wise in the SSM, carefully respecting their structural dependencies. Atomic propositions, boolean operations and temporal operators are translated into fixed-point computations using the SSM's linear recurrence and pointwise output function ϕ. The encoding only requires fixed-point precision of 6 bits, ensuring that the hardness result holds already for modest bit-widths.

Together, these results yield the following tight characterisation:

Theorem 4. *b-ssmSAT^{fix} is PSPACE-complete when $b \geq 6$.*

When the bit-width is part of the input and encoded in unary, the PSPACE-membership still holds, because the space requirements of $L \cdot d \cdot b$ is still polynomial in the size of the input. However, when the bit-width is encoded in binary the first natural upper bound is EXPSPACE, because now an internal state has size $L \cdot d \cdot 2^b$. The question whether the problem also becomes EXPSPACE-complete is an open problem for future research.

6 Outlook

The satisfiability problem studied in this paper provides a natural foundation for the study on formal verification of State Space Models. Although abstract, it captures the core challenge underlying many verification tasks, such as proving or refuting safety properties. Its general formulation, detached from specific property types, ensures that undecidability and complexity results immediately extend to broader reasoning problems. Thus, satisfiability serves as a baseline for understanding the fundamental limits of verifying SSM and motivates future research into efficient and sound verification techniques.

References

1. De, S., et al.: Griffin: mixing gated linear recurrences with doucetlocal attention for efficient language models (2024). https://doi.org/10.48550/arXiv.2402.19427
2. De Giacomo, G., Vardi, M.Y.: Linear temporal logic and linear dynamic logic on finite traces. In: Proceedings of the Twenty-Third International Joint Conference on Artificial Intelligence, pp. 854–860. IJCAI '13, AAAI Press, Beijing, China (2013)
3. Gu, A., Dao, T.: Mamba: linear-time sequence modeling with selective state spaces. In: First Conference on Language Modeling (2024)
4. Gu, A., Goel, K., Re, C.: Efficiently modeling long sequences with structured state spaces. In: International Conference on Learning Representations (2022)
5. Karp, R.M.: Reducibility among Combinatorial Problems. In: Miller, R.E., Thatcher, J.W., Bohlinger, J.D. (eds.) Complexity of Computer Computations: Proceedings of a Symposium on the Complexity of Computer Computations, Held March 20–22, 1972, at the IBM Thomas J. Watson Research Center, Yorktown Heights, New York, and Sponsored by the Office of Naval Research, Mathematics Program, IBM World Trade Corporation, and the IBM Research Mathematical Sciences Department, pp. 85–103. Springer US, Boston, MA (1972). https://doi.org/10.1007/978-1-4684-2001-2_9
6. Mehta, H., Gupta, A., Cutkosky, A., Neyshabur, B.: Long range language modeling via gated state spaces. In: The Eleventh International Conference on Learning Representations (2023)
7. Merrill, W., Petty, J., Sabharwal, A.: The illusion of state in state-space models. In: Proceedings of the 41st International Conference on Machine Learning. ICML'24, vol. 235, pp. 35492–35506. JMLR.org, Vienna, Austria (2024)
8. Minsky, M.L.: Computation: Finite and Infinite Machines. Prentice-Hall Inc, USA (1967)
9. Orvieto, A., et al.: Resurrecting recurrent neural networks for long sequences. In: Proceedings of the 40th International Conference on Machine Learning. ICML'23, JMLR.org, Honolulu, Hawaii, USA (2023)
10. Sälzer, M., Alsmann, E., Lange, M.: Transformer encoder satisfiability: complexity and impact on formal reasoning. In: The Thirteenth International Conference on Learning Representations (2024)
11. Sarrof, Y., Veitsman, Y., Hahn, M.: The expressive capacity of state space models: a formal language perspective. In: The Thirty-eighth Annual Conference on Neural Information Processing Systems (2024)
12. Sun, Y., et al.: Retentive network: a successor to transformer for large language models (2023). https://doi.org/10.48550/arXiv.2307.08621
13. Yang, S., Wang, B., Shen, Y., Panda, R., Kim, Y.: Gated linear attention transformers with hardware-efficient training. In: Proceedings of the 41st International Conference on Machine Learning. ICML'24, JMLR.org, Vienna, Austria (2024)

Quantifiers for Differentiable Logics in Rocq (Extended Abstract)

Jairo Miguel Marulanda-Giraldo[1]([✉]), Ekaterina Komendantskaya[1,2], Alessandro Bruni[3], Reynald Affeldt[4], Matteo Capucci[5], and Enrico Marchioni[1]

[1] University of Southampton, Southampton, UK
jmmg1c24@soton.ac.uk
[2] Heriot-Watt University, Edinburgh, UK
[3] IT-University of Copenhagen, Copenhagen, Denmark
[4] National Institute of Advanced Industrial Science and Technology (AIST), Tokyo, Japan
[5] Ravenna, Italy

Abstract. The interpretation of logical expressions into loss functions has given rise to so-called differentiable logics. They function as a bridge between formal logic and machine learning, offering a novel approach for property-driven training. The added expressiveness of these logics comes at the price of a more intricate semantics for first-order quantifiers. To ease their integration into machine-learning backends, we explore how to formalize semantics for first-order differentiable logics using the Mathematical Components library in the Rocq proof assistant. We seek to give rigorous semantics for quantifiers, verify their properties with respect to other logical connectives, as well as prove the soundness and completeness of the resulting logics.

Keywords: Neural Network Verification · Formal Specifications · Loss Functions · Differentiable Logics · Interactive Theorem Proving

1 Introduction

Quantitative logics, i.e. logics that have semantics over the real numbers instead of over $\{0, 1\}$ have been studied for decades, and date back to the ideas of Kleene, Gödel, and Łukasiewicz at the start of the 20th century [10,22]. Fuzzy logics [22], and the logics of the Lawvere quantale [5,15,22] are important examples of quantitative logics. To illustrate, let us have a toy syntax with atomic propositions and conjunction, such as

$$\Phi \ni \phi := A \mid \phi \wedge \phi \qquad (1)$$

where A is interpreted in a domain $D \subseteq [-\infty, \infty]$. D varies among logics and restricts the interpretation of connectives. For example, the Gödel logic has a

---

Komendantskaya and Capucci are funded by the Advanced Research + Invention Agency (ARIA).
M. Capucci—Independent Researcher.

standard semantics over $[0,1]$ where the conjunction is interpreted as the minimum function.

Recently, there was a surge of interest in quantitative logics, stimulated by the growing interest in *AI safety* [13,14]. Differentiable Logics (DLs) form a family of methods that applies key insights from quantitative logics to this domain for property-driven learning [25]. Generally, it is considered desirable to be able to use machine learning algorithms in a way that imposes certain logical specifications during training [20,27]. Differentiable logics have been shown to effectively translate arbitrary logical specifications into real-valued and differentiable functions that, in turn, can be used as *loss functions* in standard gradient-descent algorithms [8]. Such loss functions help improve the adherence of the resulting neural networks to specifications [16]. At the same time, DLs have proven to be useful in compiling specifications for the back-ends of neural network verifiers [12], a process necessary to provide programming language support to property-driven training [11]. This calls for stronger guarantees about the correctness of such compilers, and rigorous semantics for DLs, as well as their soundness, completeness, and compositionality [1,8,25].

Nevertheless, there is one fundamental problem that differentiable logics face. Many specifications of interest for machine learning involve quantifiers, yet the majority of quantitative logics is propositional [5,22,25]. A canonical specification of this kind is *robustness* [9], i.e. small perturbations to the inputs of a neural network should result in small changes to its output, formally:

Definition 1 (ϵ-δ-**Robustness**). *Let $\epsilon, \delta \in \mathbb{R}^+$, $||\cdot||$ be a norm, and $f : \mathbb{R}^n \to \mathbb{R}^m$ be a measurable function. One says f is ϵ-δ-robust around $\bar{x} \in \mathbb{R}^n$ if*

$$\forall x \in \mathbb{R}^n, ||x - \bar{x}|| \leq \epsilon \Rightarrow ||f(x) - f(\bar{x})|| \leq \delta \tag{2}$$

Expanding some sound and complete propositional quantitative logics to first-order logic often comes at the expense of either completeness or continuity. For example, the first-order extension of Gödel logic is the only one, among the most prominent fuzzy logics [22,25], that is sound and complete w.r.t. models with values in $[0,1]$ and with universal and existential quantifiers interpreted as infima and suprema [3]. However, connectives of this logic are continuous and therefore not suitable for gradient-descent algorithms.

Recently, a promising solution was proposed by Capucci: interpreting quantifiers as *p-means* [7], a generalization of p-norms over a probability space [6]. This new semantics gives hope that the open problem of finding a suitable approach to quantification in DLs will find its resolution, and we can soon find a logic that is sound and complete relative to this new quantitative semantics.

With rigorous semantics for quantifiers, first-order DLs could be integrated into verifier back-ends. We must hence provide guarantees of the resulting logics, as well as of quantifiers with respect the other logical connectives. Rigorous computer formalizations of propositional semantics for DLs have been used to this end [1]. Extending these formalizations to first-order logics is a non trivial challenge that is yet to be overcome. Furthermore, the new semantics proposed by Capucci presents a particular challenge for formal verification, since, unlike the previous formalizations of DLs [1], it now also involves results from real analysis and probability. Most notably, it involves formalisations of measure spaces, probability spaces, and Lebsegue integrals, as well as the use of results such as Jensen's and Hölder's inequalities [19].

Rocq's Mathematical Components library (*MathComp*) [26], is a particularly good fit for this task, due to its extensive mathematical libraries. Many of the aforementioned standard results from measure theory are formalized in the library modules on algebra and analysis. However, some, such as the encoding of extended real numbers, still require further development.

In this extended abstract, we first quickly review the approach to quantification proposed by Capucci, explain its relation to the available mathematical libraries in Rocq, and report on our current work on formalizing the novel semantics. With this formalization, we contribute towards developing the semantics for quantifiers in DLs. Tangentially, we extend *MathComp* as necessary. In the long term, this formalization is expected to become part of a larger collaborative project [2], that develops a novel first-order quantitative logic and provides its full formalization in Rocq, including, when and if that will be proven, the formalisation of the soundness and completeness results for the logic. Our work seeks to aid in the development of programming language support for property-driven development of neural networks, as well as influence machine learning research in general [2,12].

2 Preliminaries

We introduce preliminaries from the extended arithmetic of the reals. They are an abridged version of [7], specifically we do not address the 'non-linear' fragment therein. We also diverge from *ibid.* in notation, preferring standard linear logic notation.

Our base setting are the positive extended reals $[0,\infty]$, considered as suplattice with the usual order $\leq$. The topology on $\mathbb{R}^+$ is extended to $[0,\infty]$ by adding to the opens all the intervals $(a,\infty]$. As a measure space, $[0,\infty]$ is considered equipped with completion of its Borel σ-field (i.e. the Lebesgue σ-field); and then further equipped with the obvious extension of the Lebesgue measure given by setting $\lambda((a,\infty]) = \infty$ for $a < \infty$ and $\lambda(\{\infty\}) = 0$.

Definition 2 (Multiplication). *On $[0,\infty]$, **conjunctive multiplication** and **disjunctive multiplication** are, respectively, the following operations:*

$a \otimes b$	0	$a \in (0,\infty)$	∞		$a \mathbin{⅋} b$	0	$a \in (0,\infty)$	∞
0	0	0	0		0	0	0	∞
$b \in (0,\infty)$	0	ab	∞		$b \in (0,\infty)$	0	ab	∞
∞	0	∞	∞		∞	∞	∞	∞

(3)

Notice $\otimes$ and $⅋$ differ only when a is 0 and b is ∞, or *vice versa*. Often we write ab instead of $a \otimes b$.

Definition 3 (Duality Operator). *Let $a \in [0, \infty]$. Then the **dual** of a is*

$$a^{\perp} = \begin{cases} 1/a & a \in (0, \infty) \\ \infty & a = 0 \\ 0 & a = \infty \end{cases}$$

Note $a \, \mathcal{\gamma} \, b = (a^{\perp} \otimes b^{\perp})^{\perp}$. Moreover we define $a \multimap b = a^{\perp} \, \mathcal{\gamma} \, b$, which extends the definition of b/a.

2.1 *p*-Means

The following definitions relate specifically to the new quantifier semantics. They are what are classically known as generalized weighted means [23], though geometric mean, much like multiplication above, bifurcates into a conjunctive and a disjunctive version.

Throughout the following, fix a probability space $(S, \Sigma_S, \mathbb{P})$.

Definition 4 (*p*-Means). *Let $f : S \to [0, \infty]$ be a measurable function. For $p \in (0, \infty)$, the **(generalized weighted) *p*-mean** of f is*

$$\langle f \rangle_{S,p} := \left(\int_S f(s)^p \, d\mathbb{P}(s) \right)^{1/p} \tag{4}$$

where we extended the functions $(-)^p$ as follows

$$\infty^p = \begin{cases} 1 & p = 0 \\ \infty & p > 0 \end{cases} \qquad 0^p = 0. \tag{5}$$

*Dually, the **(generalized weighted) harmonic *p*-mean** of f is*

$$\langle f \rangle_{S,-p} := \left(\langle f^{\perp} \rangle_{S,p} \right)^{\perp}. \tag{6}$$

When S can be inferred from the context, we write $\langle f \rangle_p$.

The definition of *p*-means can be extended to $p = 0$ and $p = \infty$ by taking limits [7]. First we have

Lemma 1. *As $p \to +\infty$,*

$$\langle f \rangle_{+p} \to \operatorname{ess\,sup}(f) =: \langle f \rangle_{+\infty}, \qquad \langle f \rangle_{-p} \to \operatorname{ess\,inf}(f) =: \langle f \rangle_{-\infty}. \tag{7}$$

These quantities are so defined:

Definition 5 (Essential Extrema). *Let (S, Σ_S, μ) be a measure space and $f : S \to [0, \infty]$ a measurable function.*

1. Let $U = \{a \in [0, \infty] : \mu(\{x \in X : a < f(x)\}) = 0\}$ and $\inf(U)$ be the infimum of U. The **essential supremum** of f is

$$\operatorname{ess\,sup}(f) = \inf U \tag{8}$$

recalling that $\inf \varnothing = \infty$.

2. The **essential infimum** of f is

$$\text{ess inf}(f) = -\text{ess sup}(-f) \qquad (9)$$

On the other end of the spectrum, we have:

Lemma 2. *As $p \longrightarrow 0$, both $\langle f \rangle_{+p}$ and $\langle f \rangle_{-p}$ converge to a limit, thus defining **disjunctive** and **conjunctive** geometric means:*

$$\langle f \rangle_{+p} \longrightarrow: \langle f \rangle_{+0}, \qquad \langle f \rangle_{-p} \longrightarrow: \langle f \rangle_{-0}. \qquad (10)$$

For bounded functions, these quantities coincide with the classical (weighted) geometric mean:

Definition 6 (Geometric Mean). *Let $f: S \to [0, \infty)$ be a measurable function and (S, Σ_S, μ) a measure space. The **geometric mean** of f is*

$$GM[f] = \exp\left(\frac{1}{\mu(S)} \int_S \ln f(s) \, \mathrm{d}\mu(s)\right) \qquad (11)$$

For unbounded functions, conjunctive and disjunctive geometric means may differ in the same way as $\otimes$ and $⅋$, namely in the way they handle 0 and ∞. See [7] for clarifications.

3 Proposed Language and its Semantics

We introduce the main ideas for first-order quantitative logic following Capucci [7], where the case is made that the positive reals support a family of substructural logics where the multiplicative connectives are interpreted as actual multiplication, and the additives as the p-norm and converge to the *actual* additives as $p \to \infty$. We stress that only a language (i.e. a syntax for formulae), and not a logic (i.e. an entailment relation), are defined therein. Here we propose a simplified version of that language which features only multiplicative connectives (in the style of classical multiplicative linear logic [17]).

For simplicity, we use the same symbols of Sect. 2 for our *language*.

A *first-order theory* over this language is given by a fixed set of sorts $\mathcal{S}$ and a family of atomic predicates for each context, denoted as $\{\mathcal{A}(\boldsymbol{X})\}_{\boldsymbol{X} \in \text{List}\mathcal{S}}$. Recall a context is a finite (and possibly empty) list of typed variables $\boldsymbol{X} = (x_1 : X_1, \ldots, x_n : X_n)$, where $X_i \in \mathcal{S}$. Then, for each context, and simultaneously over all contexts, we inductively define the set of formulae of the theory $\Phi(\boldsymbol{X})$ by closing the atomic predicates under duality, multiplicative conjunction, and universal and existential quantification over *fresh* variables:

$$\Phi(\boldsymbol{X}) \ni \phi(\boldsymbol{x}) := A(\boldsymbol{x}) \in \mathcal{A}(\boldsymbol{X}) \\
\mid \phi(\boldsymbol{x})^\perp \\
\mid \phi(\boldsymbol{x}) \otimes \phi(\boldsymbol{x}) \qquad (12)\\
\mid \forall^p(y \in Y).\psi(y, \boldsymbol{x}) \\
\mid \exists^p(y \in Y).\psi(y, \boldsymbol{x})$$

where $p \in [0, \infty]$ and $\psi \in \Phi(Y, \boldsymbol{X})$, where Y is another sort. Let $\Phi = \bigcup_{\boldsymbol{X}} \Phi(\boldsymbol{X})$ be the set of formulae over arbitrary contexts. We encode multiplicative disjunction and linear implication respectively as

$$\phi_1 \mathbin{\text{⅋}} \phi_2 := (\phi_1^\perp \otimes \phi_2^\perp)^\perp \qquad \phi_1 \multimap \phi_2 := \phi_1^\perp \mathbin{\text{⅋}} \phi_2$$

An interpretation of such a theory is given by (1) a choice of probability space $[\![X]\!]$ for each sort $X \in \mathcal{S}$, where, for a context $\boldsymbol{X}$ as above, we let $[\![\boldsymbol{X}]\!] = [\![X_1]\!] \times \cdots \times [\![X_n]\!]$ (as well as $[\![()]\!] = 1$); and (2) a given measurable function $[\![A]\!] : [\![\boldsymbol{X}]\!] \to [0, \infty]$ for each atomic predicate $A \in \mathcal{A}(\boldsymbol{X})$. Then the translation function (corresponding to *multiplicative semantics* in [7]) $[\![\cdot]\!] : \Phi \to [0, \infty]$ is defined inductively on the structure of formulae as follows:

$$\begin{aligned}
[\![\phi(\boldsymbol{x})^\perp]\!] &:= [\![\phi(\boldsymbol{x})]\!]^\perp \\
[\![\phi_1(\boldsymbol{x}) \otimes \phi_2(\boldsymbol{x})]\!] &:= [\![\phi_1(\boldsymbol{x})]\!][\![\phi_2(\boldsymbol{x})]\!] \\
[\![\forall^p (y \in Y).\psi(y, \boldsymbol{x})]\!] &:= \langle [\![\psi(\cdot, \boldsymbol{x})]\!] \rangle_{[\![Y]\!], -p} \\
[\![\exists^p (y \in Y).\psi(y, \boldsymbol{x})]\!] &:= \langle [\![\psi(\cdot, \boldsymbol{x})]\!] \rangle_{[\![Y]\!], p}
\end{aligned} \qquad (13)$$

Hence the semantics is defined w.r.t. the quantale $[0, \infty]_\otimes$ we described above (Definition 2, [7]), which we note is isomorphic to the *Lawvere quantale* introduced in [21] and central in [4,5].

As an example of the usefulness of this semantics, we can use it to construct the *softmax operator* [24], using the same logical formulae used for *argmax*, as shown in [7]. Indeed, suppose $f : S \to [0, \infty)$ is a measurable function we want to express the softmax of. The first-order theory of softmax has one sort X and a single atomic predicate $\phi(x) \in \mathcal{A}(X)$. We target f by interpreting X as S and set $[\![\phi(\bar{x})]\!] = f(\bar{s})$. Then the softmax of f is obtained as follows:

$$\begin{aligned}
(\text{softmax } f)(\bar{s}) &= [\![(\exists^1 (x \in X).\phi(x)) \multimap \phi(\bar{x})]\!] \\
&= [\![(\exists^1 (x \in X).\phi(x))]\!]^\perp \mathbin{\text{⅋}} [\![\phi(\bar{x})]\!] \\
&= (\langle [\![\phi(x)]\!] \rangle_{S,1})^\perp \mathbin{\text{⅋}} [\![\phi(\bar{x})]\!] \\
&= \left(\int_S [\![\phi]\!](s) \mathrm{d}\mathbb{P}(s) \right)^\perp \mathbin{\text{⅋}} [\![\phi(\bar{x})]\!] \\
&= \left(\int_S f(s) \mathrm{d}\mathbb{P}(s) \right)^\perp \mathbin{\text{⅋}} f(\bar{s}) \\
&= \frac{f(\bar{s})}{\int_S f(s) \mathrm{d}\mathbb{P}(s)}
\end{aligned} \qquad (14)$$

Note that often $f = \exp(-\beta u)$ for some scoring function $u : S \to [-\infty, \infty]$ and inverse temperature $\beta \in (0, \infty]$—this is the form most common in machine learning [18]. Similarly, $\bar{s} \in \arg\max f \iff [\![(\exists^\infty (x \in X).\phi(x)) \multimap \phi(\bar{x})]\!] \geq 1$.

For a second example, we show how the robustness property of Definition 1 can be encoded in such a language. Since this is usually a 'hard' predicate, we have many choices on how to approach it as a soft predicate, here we give a very crude such encoding, parametrised by the given constants $\epsilon, \delta \in \mathbb{R}$, the function $f \colon \mathbb{R}^m \to \mathbb{R}^n$, the point $\bar{x} \in \mathbb{R}^n$, as well as by a 'softness degree' $p \in [0, \infty]$. Thus we look at a first-order theory with one sort X and predicates $E, D \in \mathcal{A}(X)$, and we interpret it by setting

$$\llbracket X \rrbracket = \mathbb{R}^m, \quad \llbracket E \rrbracket = \mathbf{1}_{\{x \in \mathbb{R}^n \,|\, \|x - \bar{x}\| \le \epsilon\}}, \quad \llbracket D \rrbracket = \mathbf{1}_{\{x \in \mathbb{R}^n \,|\, \|f(x) - f(\bar{x})\| \le \delta\}}. \tag{15}$$

where $\mathbf{1}_A$ denotes the indicator function of a measurable set A. Then (2) is

$$\llbracket \forall^p (x \in X).(E(x) \multimap D(x)) \rrbracket = \left(\int_{\mathbb{R}^m} \left(\frac{\llbracket E \rrbracket(s)}{\llbracket D \rrbracket(s)} \right)^p \mathrm{d}\mathbb{P}(s) \right)^{-1/p} \tag{16}$$

4 Properties of Quantifiers

In the machine learning community there is a general consensus on the desirable properties of loss functions—convexity or continuity are widely considered desirable [20]. From a programming language perspective, there is no consensus as to how to define soundness for quantitative logics. In the future, we intend to follow the general approach applied by Slusarz et al. Moreover, Varnai and Dimarogonas suggest characterizing quantitative logics in terms of their *geometric properties*, valuable for optimization tasks [27]. As for quantifiers, we wish that our formulation possesses good numerical properties, as well as behave similarly to quantifiers in classical logic. Currently we are working to formalize and prove the following properties in Rocq, which were presented by Capucci [7].

Through the following, Let $\boldsymbol{X}$ be a context, Y a sort, and $\phi(\boldsymbol{x}) \in \Phi(\boldsymbol{X})$, $\psi_i(y, \boldsymbol{x}) \in \Phi(Y, \boldsymbol{X})$.

Lemma 3 (Duality).

1. $\llbracket \forall^p (y \in Y).\psi(y, \boldsymbol{x}) \rrbracket = \llbracket \exists^p (y \in Y).\psi(y, \boldsymbol{x})^\perp \rrbracket^\perp$
2. $\llbracket \exists^p (y \in Y).\psi(y, \boldsymbol{x}) \rrbracket = \llbracket \forall^p (y \in Y).\psi(y, \boldsymbol{x})^\perp \rrbracket^\perp$

Lemma 4 (Distributivity over Implication).

1. $\llbracket \phi(\boldsymbol{x}) \multimap \forall^p (y \in Y).\psi(y, \boldsymbol{x}) \rrbracket = \llbracket \forall^p (y \in Y).(\phi(\boldsymbol{x}) \multimap \psi(y, \boldsymbol{x})) \rrbracket$
2. $\llbracket \forall^p (y \in Y).(\psi(y, \boldsymbol{x}) \multimap \phi(\boldsymbol{x})) \rrbracket = \llbracket (\exists^p (y \in Y).\psi(y, \boldsymbol{x})) \multimap \phi(\boldsymbol{x}) \rrbracket$.

These lemmas will be potentially useful to prove the *residuation property*, an important feature of many quantitative logics [17].

Lemma 5 (Abductive). *Let $\llbracket Z \rrbracket \subseteq \llbracket Y \rrbracket$ then*

1. $\llbracket \exists^p (z \in Z).\psi(z, \boldsymbol{x}) \rrbracket \le \llbracket \exists^p (y \in Y).\psi(y, \boldsymbol{x}) \rrbracket$
2. $\llbracket \forall^p (y \in Y).\psi(y, \boldsymbol{x}) \rrbracket \le \llbracket \forall^p (z \in Z).\psi(z, \boldsymbol{x}) \rrbracket$.

Intuitively, confidence depends on the amount of evidence.
The following are often desirable properties of loss functions.

Lemma 6 (Monotonic). *If $[\![\psi_1]\!] \leq [\![\psi_2]\!]$ then*

1. $[\![\exists^p(y \in Y).\psi_1(y, \boldsymbol{x})]\!] \leq [\![\exists^p(y \in Y).\psi_2(y, \boldsymbol{x})]\!]$
2. $[\![\forall^p(y \in Y).\psi_1(y, \boldsymbol{x})]\!] \leq [\![\forall^p(y \in Y).\psi_2(y, \boldsymbol{x})]\!]$.

Lemma 7 (p-Monotonic and Bounded). *If $0 \leq q \leq p$ then*

1. $[\![\exists^q(y \in Y).\psi(y, \boldsymbol{x})]\!] \leq [\![\exists^p(y \in Y).\psi(y, \boldsymbol{x})]\!] \leq [\![\exists^\infty(y \in Y).\psi(y, \boldsymbol{x})]\!]$
2. $[\![\forall^\infty(y \in Y).\psi(y, \boldsymbol{x})]\!] \leq [\![\forall^p(y \in Y).\psi(y, \boldsymbol{x})]\!] \leq [\![\forall^q(y \in Y).\psi(y, \boldsymbol{x})]\!]$.

Hence we can approximate the quantifier semantics of Gödel logic while maintaining differentiability.

5 Work in Progress on the Rocq Formalization

In "Taming Differentiable Logics with Coq Formalisation" a formalization for several quantitative logics was developed [1]. We seek to expand this formalization so that it is suitable for reasoning about first-order DLs, with p-means as the semantics for quantifiers. So far we have formalized the semantics presented in Sect. 3, and some basic properties of the p-means. To illustrate, we present the encodings needed for Lemma 3. Note the following implementations have been simplified for clarity.

To encode the p-mean, we make use of the Lnorm, *MathComp*'s encoding of the p-norm [6], and add an encoding for the geometric mean.

```
Definition Lnorm P p f :=
  match p with
  | p%:E => (\int[mu]_x `|f x| `^ p) `^ p^-1
  | +oo => ess_sup P (abse \o f)
  | -oo => ess_inf P (abse \o f)
end.

Definition geo_mean P f :=
    expeR \int[P]_x (lne (f x)).

Definition pmean P p f :=
    if p == 0 then geo_mean P f else Lnorm P p f.
```

Where `ess_sup`, `ess_inf`, `geo_mean`, and `pmean` correspond respectively to the essential supremum, essential infimum, geometric mean and p-mean. For the dual, we use *MathComp*'s power function.

```
Definition dual a := if a == 0 then +oo else x `^ -1.
```

We can represent quantifiers in terms of the previous encodings, and add notations for clarity.

```
Notation "x ^'"          := (cdual x).
Notation "'forall_ p f " := (pmean P p f).
Notation "'exists_ p f " := (('forall_p (fun y => (f y)^'))^').
```

Lastly, Lemma 3 is encoded as `Lemma Duality`, using the facts that the dual is idempotent and the harmonic p-mean non-negatove, encoded as `Lemma idem_dual` and `Lemma forall_gt0`, respectively.

```
Lemma Duality p x :
    (0 < p) ->
    'forall_p (psi x) = ('exists_p (fun y => (psi x y)^'))^'.
Proof.
  by move=> ?; rewrite  (*this is true since*)
    idem_dual //=  (*the dual is idempotent and*)
    ?forall_gt0 //; (*the harmonic p-mean is non-negative and*)
  under eq_fun do rewrite (*in the body of the harmonic p-mean*)
    idem_dual //. (*the dual is idempotent.*)
Qed.
```

To formalize the rest of Sect. 4 in Rocq, as well as the lemmas in Sect. 2.1, we are currently working on extending the analysis module of *MathComp*. In particular, Hölder's inequalities must be generalized to functions that go to the extended reals. In this process, we noticed the original encoding of the power function over extended real numbers incorrectly assumed its exponent is a real number greater than or equal to zero. The implementation has now been generalized for negative exponents.

6 Conclusions and Future Work

In this extended abstract we described our work in progress. We presented the main ideas behind a first-order quantitative logic to be applied in AI verification. We presented a promising translation for quantifiers and introduced some desirable properties for this translation, following closely [7]. We argued for the usefulness of a computer formalization to provide compilation guarantees. Lastly, we presented some preliminary progress in formalization of these results in Rocq.

In the future we hope to:

1. Develop a Hilbert and Sequent Calculus for the language.
2. Prove soundness and completeness for the resulting logic.
3. Formalize the properties mentioned in Sect. 4 and the resulting proofs of soundness and completeness.
4. Test the performance of the logic for property-driven training.
5. Integrate our results into verification back-ends such as that of Vehicle [12].

Acknowledgements. J. Marulanda-Giraldo and E. Komendantskaya acknowledge the partial support of the EPSRC grant AISEC: AI Secure and Explainable by Construction (EP/T026960/1). M. Capucci and E. Komendantskaya were supported by ARIA: Mathematics for Safe AI grant. J. Marulanda-Giraldo received PhD Scholarship from the University of Southampton.

Disclosure of Interests. The authors have no competing interests to declare that are relevant to the content of this article.

References

1. Affeldt, R., Bruni, A., Komendatskaya, E., Ślusarz, N., Stark, K.: Taming differentiable logics with coq formalisation. In: Bertot, Y., Kutsia, T., Norrish, M. (eds.) 15th International Conference on Interactive Theorem Proving (ITP 2024). Leibniz International Proceedings in Informatics (LIPIcs), pp. 4:1–4:19. Schloss Dagstuhl – Leibniz-Zentrum für Informatik, Dagstuhl, Germany (2024). https://doi.org/10.4230/LIPIcs.ITP.2024.4. https://drops.dagstuhl.de/entities/document/10.4230/LIPIcs.ITP.2024.4
2. Atkey, R., Capucci, M., Komendatskaya, E., Mardare, R.: Quantitative Predicate Logic as a Foundation for Verified ML. ARIA grant (2024)
3. Baaz, M., Preining, N., Zach, R.: First-order Gödel logics. Ann. Pure Appl. Logic **147**(1), 23–47 (2007). https://doi.org/10.1016/j.apal.2007.03.001. https://www.sciencedirect.com/science/article/pii/S0168720700019X
4. Bacci, G., Mardare, R., Panangaden, P., Plotkin, G.: Polynomial Lawvere Logic (2024). arXiv:2402.03543. https://arxiv.org/abs/2402.03543. https://doi.org/10.48550/arXiv.2402.03543. Accessed 11 Jan 2024
5. Bacci, G., Mardare, R., Panangaden, P., Plotkin, G.: Propositional logics for the Lawvere quantale. Electronic Notes in Theoretical Informatics and Computer Science 3 (2023)
6. Bourgain, J.: New classes of LP-spaces. Springer (2006)
7. Capucci, M.: On Quantifiers for Quantitative Reasoning. arXiv preprint arXiv:2406.04936 (2024)
8. Casadio, M., et al.: Neural network robustness as a verification property: a principled case study. In: International Conference on Computer Aided Verification, pp. 219–231 (2022)
9. Casadio, M., et al.: Neural Network Robustness as a Verification Property: A Principled Case Study (2022). arXiv:2104.01396. https://arxiv.org/abs/2104.01396
10. Cintula, P., Hajek, P., Noguera, C., et al.: Handbook of Mathematical Fuzzy Logic Volume 1. College Publications (2011)
11. Daggitt, M., et al.: The vehicle tutorial: neural network verification with vehicle. In: Sarodysky, N., Amir, G., Katz, G., Isaac, O. (eds.) Proceedings of the 6th Workshop on Formal Methods for ML-Enabled Autonomous Systems. Kalpa Publications in Computing, pp. 1–5. EasyChair (2023). https://doi.org/10.29007/5s2x. https://easychair.org/publications/paper/Rkrv
12. Daggitt, M.L., Kokke, W., Atkey, R., Slusarz, N., Arnaboldi, L., Komendatskaya, E.: Vehicle: Bridging the Embedding Gap in the Verification of Neuro-Symbolic Programs. arXiv preprint arXiv:2401.06379 (2024)
13. Dalrymple, D.: Safeguard AI: constructing guaranteed safety (2024). https://www.aria.org.uk/media/3nhjno4/aria-safeguarded-ai-programme-thesis-v1.pdf. Programme Thesis
14. Dalrymple, D., et al.: Towards Guaranteed Safe-AI: A Framework for Ensuring Robust and Reliable AI Systems (2024). arXiv:2405.06624. https://arxiv.org/abs/2405.06624
15. Fischer, M., Balunovic, M., Drachsler-Cohen, D., Gehr, T., Zhang, C., Vechev, M.: DL2: training and querying neural networks with logic. In: International Conference on Machine Learning, pp. 1931–1941 (2019)

16. Flinkow, T., Pearlmutter, B.A., Monahan, R.: Comparing Differentiable Logics for Learning with Logical Constraints. arXiv preprint arXiv:2407.03847 (2024)
17. Galatos, N., Jipsen, P., Kowalski, T., Ono, H.: Residuated lattices: an algebraic glimpse at substructural algebras. Elsevier (2007)
18. Goodfellow, I., Bengio, Y., Courville, A.: Deep Learning. MIT Press (2016)
19. Kazarinof, N.D.: Analytic inequalities. Courier Corporation (2014)
20. Klebanov, L.B., Rachev, S.T., Fabozzi, F.J.: Robust and Non-robust Models in Statistics. Nova Science Publishers, Hauppauge (2009)
21. Lawvere, F.W.: Metric spaces, generalized logics, and closed categories. Rendiconti del seminario matematico e fisico di Milano **13**, 135–166 (1973)
22. Metcalfe, G., Olivetti, N., Gabbay, D.M.: Proof Theory for Fuzzy Logics. Springer (2008)
23. Mitrinovic, D.S., Vasic, P.M.: Analytic Inequalities. Springer (1970)
24. Ren, J., Wang, H.: Chapter 3- Calculus and optimization. In: Mathematical Methods in Data Science. Ed. by J. Ren and H. Wang, pp. 51–89. Elsevier (2023). https://doi.org/10.1016/B978-0-44-318679-0.00009-0. https://www.sciencedirect.com/science/article/pii/B9780443186790000090
25. Slusarz, N., Komendatskaya, E., Daggitt, M.L., Stewart, R.J., Stark, K.: Logic of differentiable logics: towards a uniform semantics of DL. In: Piskac, R., Voronkov, A. (eds.) LPAR 2023: Proceedings of 24th International Conference on Logic for Programming, Artificial Intelligence and Reasoning, Manizales, Colombia, 4–9 June 2023. EPiC Series in Computing, pp. 473–493. EasyChair (2023). https://doi.org/10.29007/C1NT
26. Team, M.C.: Mathematical components library (2007). https://github.com/math-comp/math-comp
27. Varnai, P., Dimarogonas, D.V.: On robustness metrics for learning STL tasks. In: 2020 American Control Conference (ACC), pp. 5394–5399 (2020)

CTRAIN - A Training Library for Certifiably Robust Neural Networks (Extended Abstract)

Konstantin Kaulen[1(✉)] and Holger H. Hoos[1,2]

[1] Chair for AI Methodology, RWTH Aachen University, Aachen, Germany
{kaulen,hh}@aim.rwth-aachen.de
[2] LIACS, Leiden University, Leiden, The Netherlands

Abstract. Despite their widespread success, neural networks are susceptible to *adversarial examples*, severely limiting their responsible deployment in safety-critical scenarios. To address this, *neural network verification* techniques have been proposed that rigorously prove the robustness of a given network against specific threats. However, the scalability of these methods remains a major challenge, with networks trained for empirical robustness still proving difficult to verify. Thus, *certified training* has been proposed to produce networks more amenable to formal robustness verification. However, there is currently no comprehensive framework allowing easy access to these training methods. To address this, we introduce `CTRAIN`, a new Python library built upon the `auto_LiRPA` package, which reimplements state-of-the-art certified training methods in a unified, modular and comprehensive manner, while offering user-friendly interfaces, enhancing accessibility for both researchers and practitioners. Additionally, `CTRAIN` integrates `SMAC3` for hyperparameter optimisation and $\alpha\beta$-CROWN for complete verification, empowering users to exploit these systems to achieve state-of-the-art certified robustness. We provide code, documentation, examples and usage instructions at https://github.com/ada-research/CTRAIN.

1 Introduction

In recent years, neural networks have shown remarkable performance across various application domains, ranging from computer vision [8] to protein structure prediction [13]. At the same time, it became evident that neural networks are typically not robust, as adversarially crafted, yet imperceptible, changes in the input can lead to to incorrect predictions [35]. This circumstance severely limits the responsible deployment of machine learning models in safety-critical use cases. To mitigate this issue, *neural network verification* techniques have been proposed, which provide provable robustness guarantees using rigorous mathematical frameworks [14,36]. Generally, these can be divided into two families; cheap incomplete methods attempt to solve the robustness verification problem by bounding the outputs of a network, but may not be able to prove a property due to overly loose bounds. Complete methods will, in principle, always return a result but have to solve an expensive $\mathcal{NP}$-complete problem [19,32]. Despite several algorithmic advancements, *e.g.*, the inclusion of sophisticated network over-approximations [5,29,34,38,43] or search techniques [3], the scalability of complete verification remains a major challenge.

Concurrently, specialised training methods were developed that aim to produce robust neural networks. While state-of-the-art empirical robustness can be achieved using *adversarial training* (see, *e.g.*, [22,41]), the resulting networks remain hard to verify. Thus, there has been a surge of training methods that yield robust neural networks amenable to formal verification, therefore mitigating the challenge of limited scalability, giving rise to the concept of *certified training* [11,26]. These methods employ an over-approximation of the worst case adversarial loss using cheap incomplete robustness verification methods as the training objective to be minimised. Several certified loss functions leveraging this concept have been proposed, gradually advancing the state-of-the-art regarding the number of input samples for which the resulting networks are provably robust [6,11,24,28,33]. However, the community to date lacks a comprehensive library that makes these techniques accessible to potentially inexperienced end users.

Therefore, we propose CTRAIN, an extensive Python library for certified training. We provide, for the first time, implementations of all current state-of-the-art methods, based on the popular neural network bounding library auto-LiRPA [39], and make these accessible via a Python package. Further, CTRAIN provides user-friendly interfaces to certifiably train neural networks based on the PyTorch framework [30]. Therefore, CTRAIN easily integrates into existing PyTorch training pipelines, neural network architecture specifications and datasets. Furthermore, we natively support sophisticated hyperparameter optimisation for certified training via the state-of-the-art optimiser SMAC3 [21]. Last but not least, CTRAIN includes several possibilities for robustness evaluation using adversarial attacks, incomplete verification and the state-of-the-art complete neural network verification system $\alpha\beta$-CROWN [38,40,44].

2 Related Work

In the following, we provide an overview of work related to CTRAIN, focusing on tools that provide functionalities for training robust neural networks. To date, several easy-to-use and performant libraries have been proposed that implement adversarial training methods. Among these, the Adversarial Robustness Toolbox (ART) [37] and DeepRobust [20] constitute the most extensive and popular libraries, having accumulated over five thousand[1] and one thousand[2] stars on GitHub, respectively. These stars allow users to indicate interest in a repository and to bookmark it. Both implement multiple adversarial training methods, *e.g.*, training for robustness on examples created through the *Projected Gradient*

---

[1] https://github.com/Trusted-AI/adversarial-robustness-toolbox
[2] https://github.com/DSE-MSU/DeepRobust

Descent (PGD) method [22], a strong iterative adversarial attack. However, these libraries lack proper support for methods that focus on producing easily verifiable networks. Specifically, ART only supports early advancements from the field that do not constitute the state of the art anymore [11,26], while DeepRobust implements no certified trainings method at all.

Recently, CTBench, a novel and unified library for certified training, has been proposed [23]. CTBench implements several state-of-the-art protocols, including SABR [28] and MTL-IBP [6], and the authors reported very strong results using their implementation. Nonetheless, CTBench cannot be easily integrated into existing code, since it relies on independent training scripts, and a Python package providing convenient options for running the CTBench training code does not exist. In addition, CTBench employs the verification system MN-BaB [10] to evaluate the certifiable robustness of trained neural networks, which has been shown to be consistently outperformed by $\alpha\beta$-CROWN [38,40,44] in recent studies and competitions [15,27]. While we acknowledge the importance of CTBench, we believe that researchers as well as end users will profit from easy-to-use alternative implementations based on the popular auto_LiRPA library. In addition, we believe that the use of $\alpha\beta$-CROWN will lead to more precise assessments of certified training methods.

3 Overview of CTRAIN

In the following, we describe the key components and features of the CTRAIN library, including supported certified training methods, affordances for evaluating the empirical and certified robustness of neural networks, and native support for hyperparameter optimisation of certified training methods.

3.1 Certified Training with CTRAIN

Selected Certified Training Methods. CTRAIN implements several state-of-the-art algorithms for certified training. In selecting these, we focused on methods that provide *deterministic* robustness guarantees against all possible perturbations included in the l_∞ norm balls with radius ϵ around input images. These perturbations constitute the properties typically examined in the neural network verification literature (see, *e.g.*, [2,15]). Furthermore, we excluded methods that rely on non-standard neural network components not natively supported by the PyTorch library [30].

The best-peforming losses for deterministic certified training are based on Interval Bound Propagation (IBP) [11], the conceptually simplest incomplete verification method. IBP employs interval arithmetic to bound the outputs of a neural network which, in turn, can be used to calculate a sound upper bound of the worst-case loss on adversarial examples. The closely related *CROWN-IBP* [42] relies on the tighter bounding method CROWN [44] in combination with IBP to improve on standard IBP-based certified training. Shi et al. [33]

propose further improvements to IBP through an initialisation procedure and loss regularisers that are specifically crafted to stabilise certified training.

Recently, significant advancements have been made by combining PGD-based adversarial training with IBP-based certified training. Those methods rely on unsound approximations of the worst-case adversarial loss, but yield strongly improved performance. *SABR* [28] uses PGD to identify adversarial examples in the l_∞ norm ball around the training instance, which are in turn used as the centre of a smaller norm ball. This smaller input region is then employed in standard IBP bounding to obtain the overall training loss. *TAPS* [24] combines adversarial and certified training by first propagating an input region through the feature extractor of a network using IBP, and by then adversarially training the classifier using latent adversarial examples that lie in the output region of the feature extractor. *STAPS* [24] works similarly to TAPS, but uses SABR instead of IBP to obtain intermediate bounds. Finally, *MTL-IBP* [6] is a representative member of the family of *expressive losses*, *i.e.*, losses that combine adversarial and certified losses through convex combinations. The MTL-IBP loss consists of the weighted sum of the certified loss obtained using IBP and the PGD-based adversarial loss.

In CTRAIN, we have included all previously mentioned certified training methods, *i.e.*, IBP, CROWN-IBP, SABR, TAPS, STAPS and MTL-IBP, ensuring comprehensive coverage of established approaches. This selection provides users with a diverse and relevant set of techniques, since methods combining adversarial and certified losses have shown the strongest results in recent literature and thus constitute the state-of-the-art (see, *e.g.*, [6,23,25]). While standard IBP and CROWN-IBP training was surpassed performance-wise, they remain the most computationally efficient and, thus, represent viable alternatives when potent hardware is not available.

Key Features of CTRAIN. In CTRAIN we provide, for the first time, an unified implementation of the state-of-the-art in certified training based on the auto_LiRPA [39] library. This package serves as the backbone of the state-of-the-art verification tool $\alpha\beta$-CROWN [38,40], is actively maintained, implements a variety of incomplete verification techniques and is popular among the neural network verification community, testified by over 250 GitHub stars[3]. Furthermore, it provides extensive support for many popular network architectures, ranging from convolutional networks to transformers.

In CTRAIN, we implemented the previously mentioned certified training methods closely following the original literature and codebases, but reimplemented all relevant parts of certified training in a modular and highly configurable fashion. Furthermore, we unified varying implementations of network bounding, loss calculation and adversarial attacks into one comprehensive code base. Therefore, CTRAIN enhances comparability between methods by standardising their shared components, such as IBP bounding or regularisation. Additionally, all components of CTRAIN are implemented using PyTorch [30]; thus, the package integrates

---

[3] https://github.com/Verified-Intelligence/auto_LiRPA.

well into common machine learning pipelines and PyTorch components such as optimisers, regularisers, and data augmentations can be seamlessly incorporated.

3.2 Evaluation

To assess whether the network actually adheres to desired robustness properties, users require easy and extensive possibilities to evaluate neural networks regarding their certified and empirical robustness, which CTRAIN provides. Notably, CTRAIN can also be used to evaluate models that were trained outside of its training workflow and, thus, also represents a valuable tool for users that do only desire to use the evaluation capabilities of CTRAIN.

Empirical Robustness. To evaluate the robustness of a given network against adversarial attacks, we implemented the *PGD* attack [22], which to date is the *de-facto* standard method to assess empirical robustness. For example, state-of-the-art verification tools such as $\alpha\beta$-CROWN [38] or MN-BaB [10] use this attack to identify counter-examples.

Incomplete Verification. To give provable guarantees of the robustness of neural networks, CTRAIN implements several incomplete verification methods using auto_LiRPA. More specifically, the incomplete bounding methods *IBP* [11], *CROWN-IBP* [42] and *CROWN* [43] are included. These methods differ in the tightness of the network bounds they compute, but also in their computational complexity. *IBP* is the cheapest and loosest incomplete method, *CROWN-IBP* gives tighter bounds at the cost of increased computational costs, and *CROWN* is the tightest and most expensive method. Users can decide whether all inputs that should be investigated are verified using one method, or whether verfication is performed in an *adaptive* fashion. In the latter case, the supported methods are progressively applied to input samples in increasing order of their computational costs. Therefore, easy verification problems are solved with cheap methods, while computationally expensive methods are only applied to problems where their tightness is required to obtain a solution (see, *e.g.*, [6,23]).

Complete Verification. Finally, CTRAIN also provides an interface to the state-of-the-art complete verification system $\alpha\beta$-CROWN. Complete verification provides the most accurate assessment of the certified robustness of a given network at the cost of significantly increased computational requirements. Especially, networks trained using recent methods based on surrogate losses, require complete verification to obtain precise robustness measurements [6,28].

To save computational resources, CTRAIN first attempts to obtain a solution to the verification query by applying its included incomplete verification techniques and by running the *PGD* adversarial attack, before invoking $\alpha\beta$-CROWN [6,23].

3.3 Hyperparameter Optimisation

All certified training methods are parametrised by a extensive and diverse set of hyperparameters, such as the number of ϵ-annealing epochs or the settings of the PGD attack. Furthermore, the values chosen for those parameters influence the training outcome strongly, ranging from training collapse to state-of-the-art results. Recent works tackle the hyperparameter optimisation problem by employing manual [6] or grid search [23] over an expert-designed configuration space. In any case, these approaches to hyperparameter tuning for certified training currently require extensive domain knowledge to identify suitable parameter choices. To mitigate this prerequisite and to therefore make hyperparameter tuning more accessible to potentially inexperienced practitioners, CTRAIN implements preconfigured hyperparameter optimisation as one of its core components.

We employ the state-of-the-art hyperparameter optimisation system SMAC3 [21] for the tuning task, since it has demonstrated remarkable performance across various recent benchmarks [9,31]. For each of the implemented certified training methods, we provide a configuration space, out of which SMAC3 attempts to find the best-performing configuration. Thus, when using CTRAIN, users do not require domain knowledge to achieve state-of-the-art results on novel datasets for which no well-performing configurations are known.

By default, CTRAIN aims to optimise the sum of natural, certified and adversarial accuracy, since all of these metrics represent desirable properties of a certifiably trained neural network, *i.e.* strong performance on natural and adversarial inputs and easy verifiability. Nevertheless, the accuracy values that should be included in the optimisation objective can be weighted according to user preferences. To keep the evaluation overhead manageable, these values are by default computed on the first 1000 samples of the validation dataset, using *CROWN*.

The CTRAIN hyperparameter optimisation procedure begins by exploring the search space through a random search for the number of iterations determined by the number of hyperparameters in the configuration space. Compared to the default of SMAC3, we limit this number, to avoid overspending on random configurations, since training and evaluation is costly. In addition, CTRAIN allows users to specify a pre-defined configuration, which is assumed to performing well. This modification to the SMAC3 optimisation procedure facilitates the exploitation of expert user knowledge. Subsequently, CTRAIN continues with the optimisation procedure until the budget is exhausted.

4 Implementation

In the following, we explain the architectural details and implementation of the CTRAIN library, highlighting its modular and well-structured design as well as its easy usability.

First and foremost, we designed CTRAIN as a Python library that can easily be installed and set up using package management tools such as pip. Furthermore, we made sure that CTRAIN seamlessly integrates into common machine learning workflows without the need to run separate scripts or to set up different environments. We implemented CTRAIN in Python 3, currently using torch in version 2.2.2 and auto_LiRPA in version 0.50 as its core libraries. Our implementation can be accessed at https://github.com/ada-research/CTRAIN.

CTRAIN.model_wrappers. As a result of our considerations for the design of CTRAIN, we provide a package implementing *model wrappers* that can be easily included into existing code. These wrappers encapsulate predefined or pretrained neural networks and expose core functionalities in an accessible manner.

We show an example of the usage of the model wrappers provided by CTRAIN in Code Example 4.1. For each of the supported training methods, there is one separate wrapper. These objects take the neural network, which must inherit from the PyTorch nn.Module class, the perturbation magnitude ϵ that defines the training and verification objectives, and the method-specific training hyperparameters as arguments. Since using a higher ϵ during training compared to evaluation might be beneficial (see, *e.g.*, [6,42]), users can define a multiplier to scale the training ϵ. Training is invoked via the train_model function, while an evaluation of natural, robust and certified performance can be carried out using the evaluate or evaluate_complete functions, respectively. The hyperparameter optimisation procedure is implemented in the hpo function, for which an optimisation budget should be provided that specifies for how long the optimisation procedure runs. Furthermore, the user may pass a default configuration to be investigated during the optimisation process.

The model_wrappers package is easily extensible, since all wrappers inherit from the common base class CTRAINWrapper, which implements method-independent functionalities such as evaluation, checkpoint saving and hyperparameter optimisation. In addition, it was of paramount importance for CTRAIN to be compatible with common PyTorch operations. Therefore, the base class inherits from the nn.Module class and, thus, all wrappers can be used in existing training and evaluation workflows.

```
from CTRAIN.model_definitions import CNN7_Shi
from CTRAIN.data_loaders import load_cifar10
from CTRAIN.model_wrappers import ShiIBPModelWrapper

train_loader, test_loader = load_cifar10(val_split=False)
in_shape = [3, 32, 32]

model = CNN7_Shi(in_shape=in_shape)
wrapped_model = ShiIBPModelWrapper(model=model,
    input_shape=in_shape, eps=2/255, num_epochs=160)

wrapped_model.train_model(train_loader)
std_acc, cert_acc, adv_acc =
    wrapped_model.evaluate(test_loader)
```

Code Example 4.1. CTRAIN is easy to use for certifiably training and evaluating neural networks: In twelve lines of code, users can load a dataset, define the standard CNN7 network architecture proposed by Shi et al. [33], certifiably train the network using IBP and evaluate it, using adversarial attacks and incomplete verification.

CTRAIN.bound. The bound module implements all bounding operations required during training and incomplete verification, based on the auto_LiRPA package. More specifically, it implements the sound bounding operations IBP, CROWN-IBP and CROWN as well as the unsound SABR and TAPS bounds.

CTRAIN.data. Although CTRAIN is fully compatible with standard PyTorch data loaders, we provide functions that load the common vision datasets MNIST [18], CIFAR-10 [16] and TinyImageNet [17].

CTRAIN.eval. The eval package provides all functions required to evaluate standard, robust and certified accuracy of neural networks, including functions to carry out incomplete and complete verification as well as adversarial attacks. Generally, all evaluation methods require the user to pass the network that should be evaluated, the perturbation magnitude ϵ and a data loader, which holds the inputs for which the robustness should be assessed. Since the evaluation procedure may be costly, especially when employing complete verification, users may also provide a number of samples for which the evaluation is carried out in the given order of the evaluation set. To utilise complete verification, users must pass, in addition to the arguments generally required for evaluation, the allowed maximum running time per verification query and the number of CPU cores $\alpha\beta$-CROWN may utilise. In addition, a dictionary including configuration values for $\alpha\beta$-CROWN that adhere to its documentation may be provided.

CTRAIN.complete_verification. Since $\alpha\beta$-CROWN is not intended to be executed directly from external libraries or codebases, CTRAIN implements several steps to ensure seamless integration in its abCROWN subpackage. First, CTRAIN exports the network in ONNX format [1] and saves the resulting file to a temporary folder. Then, it formulates the verification property in the standardised VNN-LIB format [7] and also saves the resulting file. Thereafter, CTRAIN generates a configuration file for $\alpha\beta$-CROWN that specifies the cutoff time and further parameters set by the user as well as the verification property, defined through the previously generated ONNX and VNN-LIB files. Finally, CTRAIN invokes $\alpha\beta$-CROWN by calling the function that serves as the entry point of the verification system, passing along the configuration file.

CTRAIN.attacks. CTRAIN currently only implements the PGD adversarial attack, which is used in several training losses as well as in the empirical robustness evaluation. We have made the parameters of the attack, *i.e.*, the number of restarts, the number of steps and the step size, configurable. Furthermore, users can define *decay milestones* at which the step size is reduced by a specified factor. When PGD attacks are involved in training, we set the network to *evaluation* mode when carrying out the attacks, while the loss computation based on the obtained adversarial examples is done in *training* mode. Therefore, the statistics of batch normalisation layers [12] are not influenced by the forward and backward passes performed during attacks and employ the mean and variance computed over both unperturbed and perturbed inputs at evaluation time.

CTRAIN.model_definitions. While CTRAIN is, in principle, compatible with a broad range of neural network definitions, models proposed by Shi et al. [33] emerged as the *de-facto* standard architectures for evaluating certified training methods on (see, *e.g.*, [6, 23, 28]). We provide model definitions of these networks in the `model_definitions` package.

`CTRAIN.train.certified`. This package implements all components of certified training in a functional manner. In the subpackage `losses`, we provide functions for calculating the various supported certified losses. The `initialisation` and `regularisation` packages provide implementations of the procedures proposed by Shi et al. [33] as well as an implementation of l_1 regularisation. Finally, we have implemented each supported certified training method as one separate function that is utilised in the respective model wrappers.

`CTRAIN.util`. Finally, we have implemented utility functions, such as seeding the library or exporting networks to `ONNX`, in the `util` package.

5 Conclusions and Future Work

In this work, we presented `CTRAIN`, a new Python library for certified training. `CTRAIN` implements several state-of-the-art certified training protocols and makes them accessible via model wrappers that integrate well into existing machine learning workflows based on PyTorch. Furthermore, `CTRAIN` provides a broad range of evaluation functions that can assess the robustness of a given network using adversarial attacks as well as incomplete and complete verification. Notably, using `CTRAIN`, it becomes possible to invoke the state-of-the-art complete verification system $\alpha\beta$-CROWN using only one function call. Last but not least, `CTRAIN` has native support for sophisticated hyperparameter optimisation using `SMAC3`.

In future work, we aim to maintain and further extend the functionalities of `CTRAIN`. The modular design of the library allows for easy addition of adversarial attack mechanisms, such as *AutoAttack* [4], or of complete verification systems, *e.g.*, *Oval* [5]. Furthermore, we intend to implement further enhancements to certified training, such as ReLU transformer shrinking [28]. In addition, we will perform an extensive empirical evaluation of `CTRAIN`, comparing its performance to reference implementations from the literature and examining potential improvements achieved through the use of `SMAC3` and $\alpha\beta$-CROWN. Finally, we plan to continuously update `CTRAIN` with new certified training and verification methods, maintaining `CTRAIN` as a state-of-the-art resource for certified training and its evaluation, valuable to both end-users and researchers.

Acknowledgments. The authors would like to express their sincere gratitude to Hadar Shavit for providing valuable feedback, insightful inspiration, and expert knowledge on hyperparameter optimisation. Holger H. Hoos gratefully acknowledges support through an Alexander-von-Humboldt Professorship in Artificial Intelligence. Furthermore, the authors thank the reviewers for their valuable comments.

Disclosure of Interests. The authors have no competing interests to declare that are relevant to the content of this article.

References

1. Bai, J., Lu, F., Zhang, K., et al.: ONNX: Open Neural Network Exchange (2025). https://github.com/onnx/onnx
2. Brix, C., Müller, M.N., Bak, S., Johnson, T.T., Liu, C.: First three years of the international verification of neural networks competition (VNN-COMP). Int. J. Softw. Tools Technol. Transfer **25**(3), 329–339 (2023)
3. Bunel, R., Lu, J., Turkaslan, I., Torr, P.H., Kohli, P., Kumar, M.P.: Branch and bound for piecewise linear neural network verification. J. Mach. Learn. Res. **21**(42), 1–39 (2020)
4. Croce, F., Hein, M.: Reliable evaluation of adversarial robustness with an ensemble of diverse parameter-free attacks. In: Proceedings of the 37th International Conference on Machine Learning, (ICML 2020), vol. 119, pp. 2206–2216 (2020)
5. Palma, A., Behl, H.S., Bunel, R., Torr, P.H.S., Kumar, M.P.: Scaling the convex barrier with sparse dual algorithms. J. Mach. Learn. Res. **25**(61), 1–51 (2024)
6. De Palma, A., Bunel, R., Dvijotham, K.D., Kumar, M.P., Stanforth, R., Lomuscio, A.: Expressive Losses for Verified Robustness via Convex Combinations. In: Proceedings of the 12th International Conference on Learning Representations (ICLR 2024). pp. 1–28 (2024)
7. Demarchi, S., et al.: Supporting standardization of neural networks verification with VNNLIB and CoCoNet. In: Proceedings of the 6th Workshop on Formal Methods for ML-Enabled Autonomous Systems (FoMLAS 2023), pp. 47–58 (2023)
8. Dosovitskiy, A., et al.: An image is worth 16×16 words: transformers for image recognition at scale. In: Proceedings of the 9th International Conference on Learning Representations (ICLR 2021), pp. 1–22 (2021)
9. Eggensperger, K., et al.: HPOBench: A collection of reproducible multi-fidelity benchmark problems for HPO. In: Proceedings of the 35th Conference on Neural Information Processing Systems (NeurIPS 2021) Track on Datasets and Benchmarks, pp. 1–36 (2021)
10. Ferrari, C., Mueller, M.N., Jovanović, N., Vechev, M.: Complete verification via multi-neuron relaxation guided branch-and-bound. In: Proceedings of the 10th International Conference on Learning Representations (ICLR 2022), pp. 1–15 (2022)
11. Gowal, S., et al.: Scalable verified training for provably robust image classification. In: Proceedings of the IEEE/CVF International Conference on Computer Vision, pp. 4842–4851 (2019)
12. Ioffe, S., Szegedy, C.: Batch normalization: accelerating deep network training by reducing internal covariate shift. In: Proceedings of the 32nd International Conference on Machine Learning (ICML 2015), vol. 37, pp. 448–456 (2015)
13. Jumper, J.: Highly accurate protein structure prediction with AlphaFold. Nature **596**(7873), 583–589 (2021)
14. Katz, G., Barrett, C., Dill, D.L., Julian, K., Kochenderfer, M.J.: Reluplex: An Efficient SMT Solver for Verifying Deep Neural Networks. In: Majumdar, R., Kunčak, V. (eds.) CAV 2017. LNCS, vol. 10426, pp. 97–117. Springer, Cham (2017). https://doi.org/10.1007/978-3-319-63387-9_5
15. König, M., Bosman, A.W., Hoos, H.H., Rijn, J.N.: Critically assessing the state of the art in neural network verification. J. Mach. Learn. Res. **25**(12), 1–53 (2024)
16. Krizhevsky, A., Hinton, G., et al.: Learning Multiple Layers of Features from Tiny Images (2009)
17. Le, Y., Yang, X.S.: Tiny ImageNet Visual Recognition Challenge (2015)

18. LeCun, Y.: The MNIST Database of Handwritten Digits (1998)
19. Li, L., Xie, T., Li, B.: Sok: Certified robustness for deep neural networks. In: Proceedings of the 44th IEEE Symposium on Security and Privacy (S and P 2023), pp. 1289–1310. IEEE (2023)
20. Li, Y., Jin, W., Xu, H., Tang, J.: DeepRobust: a platform for adversarial attacks and defenses. In: Proceedings of the 35th AAAI Conference on Artificial Intelligence (AAAI-21), pp. 16078–16080 (2021)
21. Lindauer, M.: SMAC3: a versatile Bayesian optimization package for hyperparameter optimization. J. Mach. Learn. Res. **23**(54), 1–9 (2022)
22. Madry, A., Makelov, A., Schmidt, L., Tsipras, D., Vladu, A.: Towards deep learning models resistant to adversarial attacks. In: Proceedings of 6th International Conference on Learning Representations (ICLR 2018), pp. 1–23 (2018)
23. Mao, Y., Balauca, S., Vechev, M.: CTBENCH: A Library and Benchmark for Certified Training. arXiv preprint arXiv:2406.04848 (2024)
24. Mao, Y., Müller, M.N., Fischer, M., Vechev, M.T.: Connecting certified and adversarial training. In: Advances in Neural Information Processing Systems 37 (NeurIPS 2023), pp. 1–19 (2023)
25. Mao, Y., Müller, M.N., Fischer, M., Vechev, M.T.: Understanding certified training with interval bound propagation. In: Proceedings of the 12th International Conference on Learning Representations (ICLR 2024), pp. 1–23 (2024)
26. Mirman, M., Gehr, T., Vechev, M.: Differentiable abstract interpretation for provably robust neural networks. In: Proceedings of the 35th International Conference on Machine Learning (ICML 2018), pp. 3578–3586. PMLR (2018)
27. Müller, M.N., Brix, C., Bak, S., Liu, C., Johnson, T.T.: The Third International Verification of Neural Networks Competition (VNN-COMP 2022): Summary and Results. arXiv preprint arXiv:2212.10376 (2022)
28. Müller, M.N., Eckert, F., Fischer, M., Vechev, M.T.: Certified training: small boxes are all you need. In: Proceedings of the 11th International Conference on Learning Representations (ICLR 2023), pp. 1–21 (2023)
29. Müller, M.N., Makarchuk, G., Singh, G., Püschel, M., Vechev, M.: PRIMA: general and precise neural network certification via scalable convex hull approximations. In: Proceedings of the 6th ACM on Programming Languages (POPL), pp. 1–33 (2022)
30. Paszke, A., et al.: PyTorch: an imperative style, high-performance deep learning library. In: Advances in Neural Information Processing Systems 33 (NeurIPS 2019), pp. 1–12 (2019)
31. Pfisterer, F., Schneider, L., Moosbauer, J., Binder, M., Bischl, B.: YAHPO Gym - an efficient multi-objective multi-fidelity benchmark for hyperparameter optimization. In: Proceedings of the First International Conference on Automated Machine Learning (AutoML-Conf 2022), vol. 188, pp. 3/1–39. PMLR (2022)
32. Sälzer, M., Lange, M.: Reachability is NP-Complete Even for the Simplest Neural Networks. In: Bell, P.C., Totzke, P., Potapov, I. (eds.) RP 2021. LNCS, vol. 13035, pp. 149–164. Springer, Cham (2021). https://doi.org/10.1007/978-3-030-89716-1_10
33. Shi, Z., Wang, Y., Zhang, H., Yi, J., Hsieh, C.: Fast certified robust training with short warmup. In: Advances in Neural Information Processing Systems 34 (NeurIPS 2021), pp. 18335–18349 (2021)
34. Singh, G., Gehr, T., Püschel, M., Vechev, M.: An abstract domain for certifying neural networks. In: Proceedings of the 3rd ACM on Programming Languages (POPL 2019), pp. 1–30 (2019)

35. Szegedy, C., et al.: Intriguing properties of neural networks. In: Proceedings of the 2nd International Conference on Learning Representations (ICLR 2014), pp. 1–10 (2014)
36. Tjeng, V., Xiao, K.Y., Tedrake, R.: Evaluating robustness of neural networks with mixed integer programming. In: Proceedings of the 7th International Conference on Learning Representations (ICLR 2019), pp. 1–21 (2019)
37. Trusted-AI: adversarial robustness toolbox (2025). https://github.com/Trusted-AI/adversarial-robustness-toolbox
38. Wang, S., et al.: Beta-CROWN: efficient bound propagation with per-neuron split constraints for neural network robustness verification. In: Advances in Neural Information Processing Systems 34 (NeurIPS 2021), pp. 29909–29921 (2021)
39. Xu, K., et al.: Automatic perturbation analysis for scalable certified robustness and beyond. In: Advances in Neural Information Processing Systems 33 (NeurIPS 2020), pp. 1–13 (2020)
40. Xu, K., et al.: Fast and complete: enabling complete neural network verification with rapid and massively parallel incomplete verifiers. In: Proceedings of the 9th International Conference on Learning Representations (ICLR 2021), pp. 1–15 (2021)
41. Zhang, H., et al.: Theoretically principled trade-off between robustness and accuracy. In: Proceedings of the 36th International Conference on Machine Learning (ICML 2019), vol. 97, pp. 7472–7482. PMLR (2019)
42. Zhang, H., et al.: Towards stable and efficient training of verifiably robust neural networks. In: Proceedings of the 8th International Conference on Learning Representations (ICLR 2020), pp. 1–15 (2019)
43. Zhang, H., et al.: General cutting planes for bound-propagation-based neural network verification. Advances in Neural Information Processing Systems 35 (NeurIPS 2022), pp. 1656–1670 (2022)
44. Zhang, H., Weng, T.W., Chen, P.Y., Hsieh, C.J., Daniel, L.: Efficient neural network robustness certification with general activation functions. In: Advances in Neural Information Processing Systems 31 (NeurIPS 2018), pp. 4944—-4953 (2018)

Competition Contributions

NeuralSAT: Scaling Constraint Solving for DNN Verification (Competition Contribution)

Hai Duong$^{(\boxtimes)}$ and ThanhVu Nguyen

George Mason University, Fairfax, USA
hduong22@gmu.edu

Abstract. We present NeuralSAT, a DNN verification tool based on the DPLL(T) framework in SAT solving with conflict clause learning. NeuralSAT participated in VNN-COMP'23 and VNN-COMP'24, with recent improvements such as parallel DPLL(T) and neuron stabilization optimizations. The theoretical foundations and algorithmic details of NeuralSAT are described in prior work, and this paper focuses on the engineering aspects of NeuralSAT, including its design, configuration, and performance in the context of the VNN-COMP evaluation framework. NeuralSAT is available at: https://github.com/dynaroars/neuralsat.

Keywords: DNN Verification · Satisfiability Solving · VNN-COMP

1 Introduction

Deep learning systems are increasingly being deployed in safety-critical domains such as autonomous driving and healthcare. However, like traditional software systems, neural networks have "bugs" and vulnerable to attacks—raising concerns on their deployment in the real-world. Deep neural network (DNN) verification has emerged as a promising research direction to address this gap, resulting in a wide variety of algorithmic techniques and supporting tools.

To foster research progress and enable fair comparison between DNN verification tools, the International Verification of Neural Networks Competition (VNN-COMP) was established in 2020 and has been held annually as a co-located event CAV. VNN-COMP [2] provides a standardized evaluation framework, including common formats for neural networks and specifications, a uniform benchmarking infrastructure on AWS cloud instances, and automated pipelines for tool installation and evaluation. Since its inception, the competition has attracted many state-of-the-art in the field.

In 2023, we introduced NeuralSAT, a DNN verification tool based on the DPLL(Davis-Putnam-Logemann-Loveland) with theory T framework [3,9], and submitted it to VNN-COMP'23. The following year, NeuralSAT was updated with features such as parallel DPLL(T) and neuron stabilization optimization [6], and participated again in VNN-COMP'24. The NeuralSAT's algorithm, along with optimizations and an in-depth evaluation, is presented in [5,6]. This contribution paper focuses on NeuralSAT's implementation and settings in the context of VNN-COMP.

2 Overview of NeuralSAT

Figure 1 summarizes the DPLL(T) framework [3,9] that NeuralSAT implements. It consists of standard DPLL components (non-shaded) and a theory solver (shaded) dedicated for DNN reasoning.

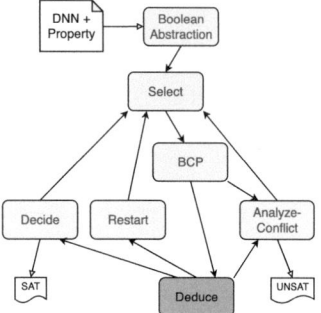

Fig. 1. NeuralSAT.

DPLL search. NeuralSAT treats DNN verification as a search for an activation pattern, represented as an assignment σ which maps truth values to the variables representing the activation status of neurons (BooleanAbstraction). Initially σ is empty, and NeuralSAT uses decision heuristics to select unassigned variables (Select) and assigns truth values to them (Decide). After each assignment, NeuralSAT infers additional assignments caused by the current assignment through Boolean constraint propagation(BCP). Next, it invokes the T-solver (Deduce) to check the feasibility of the current assignment in σ. If it is feasible, NeuralSAT continues to search for new assignments. Otherwise, NeuralSAT detects a conflict, and it learns clauses to remember and backtracks to a previous assignment (Analyze-Conflict). This process repeats until NeuralSAT can no longer backtrack, at which point it returns unsat, i.e., the DNN has the property. Otherwise, it finds a complete assignment for all Boolean variables (i.e., a satisfying activation pattern), and returns sat. The user can query for a counterexample input in the case of sat.

If the search falls into a local optima, NeuralSAT will restart by clearing all assignments that have been made. NeuralSAT retains learned conflict clauses learned, to avoid reaching the same state in the subsequent search.

Note that NeuralSAT leverages multiprocessing to parallelize its DPLL search. When assigning values to variables, NeuralSAT considers both options for each variable, and then splits the search space into two disjoint subspaces and processes them in parallel. When a conflict is detected in one subspace, NeuralSAT prunes that subspace and continues the search in the remaining subspaces. This parallelism not only speeds up the process but also facilitates information exchange such as learned clauses among search subspaces.

Theory (T)-Solver. To check that current assignments in σ is feasible, the T-solver uses LP solving and polytope abstraction [8,18] to compute neuron bounds from the given precondition and σ, and checks the bounds are feasible with respect to the specified post-condition. Using LP solving and abstraction is standard in modern DNN verification [4–7,11,15,19]. However, the T-solver in NeuralSAT also implements *neuron stabilization* by creating and solving custom MILP constraints to determine if a neuron is stable (i.e., it is always active or inactive). If a neuron is stable, the T-solver does not need to guess its activation status, and thus reduces the search space.

3 Implementation, Features, and Limitations

NeuralSAT is implemented in Python, and uses Gurobi [8] for linear programming and the LiRPA library [18] for computing neuron bounds and other abstractions. Table 1 highlights the key implementation features.

Table 1. A neuralsat's features.

Feature	Supported
Network Type	Acyclic computation graphs, e.g., Feed-forward, Residual
Layer Type	FC, CNN, MaxPool, BatchNorm, Softmax
Activation Function	ReLU, Sigmoid, Tanh, Sign, Exp
Input	Pytorch, ONNX, VNN-LIB
Output	(sat, unsat, timeout), counter-examples
Property	Robustness, Safety
Search Algorithm	Parallel DPLL(T)
Abstract Domain	Polytope, Interval
Hardware	Multi-core CPU, GPU
Optimization	Adv. Attacks, Input splitting, Large Output Opt., MILP solving

3.1 Features

Here we discuss several design decisions and features of NeuralSAT that we believe are important for competition and practical use.

Fully Automatic, Yet Configurable. A key design decision was to make NeuralSAT fully automatic and *"just works"* for end users, even at some runtime cost. Invoking NeuralSAT is as simple as running a single command:

```
python3 main.py -net <n> -spec <p>
```

where <n> is an ONNX network file, and <p> is a VNNLIB specification file. During VNN-COMP, NeuralSAT was run on all benchmarks using a single default configuration, requiring no parameter tuning. Expert users can optionally adjust parameters such as the number of threads and timeout durations via command-line flags.

While NeuralSAT is fully automatic by default, it has a wide-range of configurable parameters, such as the number of threads, restart limits, and timeout durations. These options, which can be set via command-line flags or configuration files, allow expert users to fine-tune NeuralSAT's performance to suit their specific needs.

Engineering Optimizations. NeuralSAT integrates several practical optimizations to enhance verification speed and scalability. It employs adversarial attack strategies, such as derivative-free sampling and gradient-based [10] methods, to quickly identify counterexamples when properties are violated. The tool also includes preprocessing logic and automated heuristics to select suitable abstractions or reasoning algorithms according to the structure and dimensionality of the input network. For example, NeuralSAT prioritizes input range splitting for low-dimensional inputs and neuron splitting for high-dimensional cases. When working with networks with large output spaces or small ReLU-based fully connected layers, NeuralSAT adaptively adjusts abstraction granularity or applies MILP solving to improve efficiency. All of which contribute to its strong performance on diverse benchmarks, including VNN-COMP, motivating us to seek more challenging cases through our own research [16,17] and collaborations.

3.2 Limitations

NeuralSAT has several limitations. First, it does not support other architectures with cycles, such as graph neural networks (GNNs). Second, it only supports properties that can be expressed in the VNN-LIB format, which at current time mainly consists of safety and robustness properties. Third, NeuralSAT depends on high-performance hardware, such as multi-core CPUs and GPUs, and thus performs poorly on low-end machines like standard laptops or desktops. Finally, it relies on Gurobi, a proprietary, general-purpose LP solver that does not leverage GPUs, which are commonly used in DNN reasoning, and therefore can become the bottleneck when verifying large networks.

4 VNN-COMP Participation

We summarize the setup and configuration of NeuralSAT in VNN-COMP'24. The full details including runscripts and results are available in the official VNN-COMP Github repo [13,14] and report [1].

Benchmark Participation. NeuralSAT competes in all regular benchmark categories of VNN-COMP. For example, in VNN-COMP'24, it was evaluated on all 12 standard benchmarks [13], including ACAS Xu, cGAN, Cifar100, Collins Rul CNN, Cora, DistShift, LinearizeNN, MetaRoom, NN4Sys, SafeNLP, TinyImageNet, and TLLVerifyBench. These benchmarks cover a diverse set of neural networks, ranging from models with a single input (e.g., 1 for NN4Sys) to those with high-dimensional inputs (e.g., 9408 for TinyImageNet), and from small networks with only a few thousand parameters (e.g., 4K for SafeNLP) to large models with tens of millions of parameters (e.g., 68M for cGAN). In total, the regular track features 2,567 benchmark instances, where an instance is a pair of a network and a verification property.

Configuration. As described in Subsect. 3.1, NeuralSAT is designed to work out of the box. In VNN-COMP'24, NeuralSAT was run using a default configuration, with examples of major parameters set as follows:

```
-batch 1000            -max_hidden_visited_branches 20000
-attack_interval 10    -mip_tightening_topk  64
```

The option -batch specifies the number of branches to explore in parallel, -max_hidden_visited_branches indicates the maximum number of hidden-layer branches to explore before triggering a restart, -attack_interval specifies how often to apply adversarial attacks, and -mip_tightening_topk sets the number of neurons to stabilize during the verification process (set to the number of threads available on the CPU).

Results. Fig. 2 summarizes the results[1] of VNN-COMP'24 [1]. The table, which corresponds to Tab. 35 in Apdx. B of [1], presents the overall rankings and scores of participating tools. The cactus plot, corresponds Fig. 28 in Apdx. B of [1], shows performance of tools on all benchmark instances.

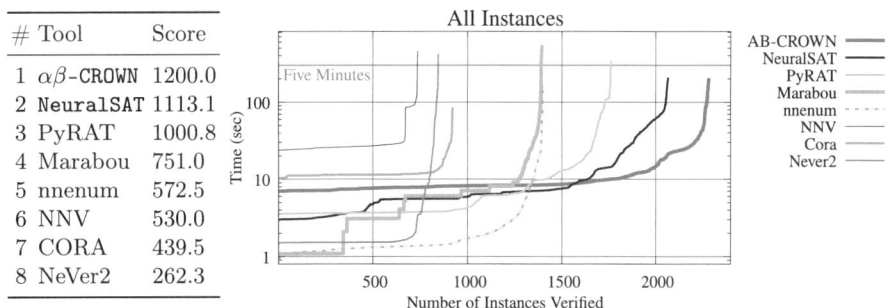

#	Tool	Score
1	$\alpha\beta$-CROWN	1200.0
2	NeuralSAT	1113.1
3	PyRAT	1000.8
4	Marabou	751.0
5	nnenum	572.5
6	NNV	530.0
7	CORA	439.5
8	NeVer2	262.3

Fig. 2. VNN-COMP'24 updated results [1].

---

[1] As is standard in VNN-COMP, after the initial results are released, authors are given the opportunity to review and report errors. In VNN-COMP'24, a problem with the competition's output parsing script resulted in NeuralSAT being incorrectly ranked last. After this issue, which also affected other tools, was identified and fixed within the designated review period, the official VNN-COMP results were updated, with NeuralSAT placed 2nd overall. The issues, corrections, and updated results are fully documented in the final VNN-COMP'24 report (e.g., see [1, Apdx. B]).

5 Conclusion and Ongoing Work

The DPLL-based `NeuralSAT` DNN verification tool demonstrated competitive performance in recent VNN-COMPs, achieving high scores across benchmark categories. The project is open source under the MIT license and available at https://github.com/dynaroars/neuralsat. We welcome contributions from the community and encourage users to report issues or suggest improvements via GitHub. Ongoing work includes new search strategies and engineering optimizations, e.g., compositional reasoning [12].

Acknowledgments. This material is based in part upon work supported by the National Science Foundation under grant numbers 2422036, 2319131, 2238133, and 2200621, and by an Amazon Research Award.

References

1. Brix, C., Bak, S., Johnson, T.T., Wu, H.: The Fifth International Verification of Neural Networks Competition (VNN-COMP 2024): Summary and Results. arXiv preprint arXiv:2412.19985 (2024). https://doi.org/10.48550/arXiv.2412.19985
2. Brix, C., Bak, S., Liu, C., Johnson, T.T.: The Fourth International Verification of Neural Networks Competition (VNN-COMP 2023): Summary and Results (2023). https://doi.org/10.48550/arXiv.2312.16760
3. Davis, M., Logemann, G., Loveland, D.: A machine program for theorem-proving. Commun. ACM **5**(7), 394–397 (1962). https://doi.org/10.1145/368273.368557
4. Duong, H., Nguyen, T., Dwyer, M.: A DPLL(T) Framework for Verifying Deep Neural Networks. arXiv preprint arXiv:2307.10266 (2024). https://doi.org/10.48550/arXiv.2307.10266
5. Duong, H., Nguyen, T., Dwyer, M.B.: NeuralSAT: a high-performance verification tool for deep neural networks. In: International Conference on Computer Aided Verification, p. to appear (2025)
6. Duong, H., Xu, D., Nguyen, T., Dwyer, M.B.: Harnessing neuron stability to improve dnn verification. Proc. ACM Softw. Eng. **1**(FSE), 859–881 (2024). https://doi.org/10.1145/3643765
7. Ferrari, C., Mueller, M.N., Jovanović, N., Vechev, M.: Complete Verification via multi-neuron relaxation guided branch-and-bound. In: International Conference on Learning Representations (2022). https://doi.org/10.48550/arXiv.2205.00263
8. Gurobi Optimization, LLC: Gurobi Optimizer Reference Manual (2022). https://www.gurobi.com
9. Kroening, D., Strichman, O.: Decision procedures. Springer (2008). https://dl.acm.org/doi/10.5555/1391237
10. Madry, A., Makelov, A., Schmidt, L., Tsipras, D., Vladu, A.: Towards deep learning models resistant to adversarial attacks. arXiv preprint arXiv:1706.06083 (2017). https://hdl.handle.net/1721.1/137496
11. PyRAT: A tool to analyze the robustness and safety of neural networks (2024). https://pyrat-analyzer.com/
12. Stark, E.W.: A proof technique for rely/guarantee properties. In: Maheshwari, S.N. (ed.) FSTTCS 1985. LNCS, vol. 206, pp. 369–391. Springer, Heidelberg (1985). https://doi.org/10.1007/3-540-16042-6_21

13. VNN-COMP 2024: VNN-COMP 2024 Regular Benchmarks (2024). https://github.com/ChristopherBrix/vnncomp2024_benchmarks
14. VNN-COMP 2024: VNN-COMP 2024 Results (2024). https://github.com/VNN-COMP/vnncomp2024_results
15. Wu, H., et al.: Marabou 2.0: a versatile formal analyzer of neural networks. In: International Conference on Computer Aided Verification, pp. 249–264. Springer (2024). https://doi.org/10.48550/arXiv.2401.14461
16. Xu, D., Mozumder, N.J., Duong, H., Dwyer, M.: Training for verification: increasing neuron stability to scale DNN verification. In: Tools and Algorithms for the Construction and Analysis of Systems - 30th International Conference, TACAS 2024, Held as Part of the European Joint Conferences on Theory and Practice of Software, ETAPS, p. to appear. Springer (2024). https://doi.org/10.1007/978-3-031-57256-2_2
17. Xu, D., Shriver, D., Dwyer, M.B., Elbaum, S.: Systematic generation of diverse benchmarks for DNN verification. In: International Conference on Computer Aided Verification, pp. 97–121. Springer (2020). https://doi.org/10.1007/978-3-030-53288-8_5
18. Xu, K., et al.: Automatic perturbation analysis for scalable certified robustness and beyond. Adv. Neural Inf. Process. Syst. **33**, 1129–1141 (2020). https://dl.acm.org/doi/10.5555/3495724.3495820
19. Zhou, D., Brix, C., Hanasusanto, G.A., Zhang, H.: Scalable neural network verification with branch-and-bound inferred cutting planes. arXiv preprint arXiv:2501.00200 (2024). https://doi.org/10.48550/arXiv.2501.00200

NNV: A Star Set Reachability Approach (Competition Contribution)

Diego Manzanas Lopez[✉], Samuel Sasaki, and Taylor T. Johnson

Vanderbilt University, Nashville, TN 37212, USA
{diego.manzanas.lopez,samuel.sasaki,taylor.johnson}@vanderbilt.edu

Abstract. We present the Neural Network Verification tool (NNV), a MATLAB-based software tool. This toolbox implements reachability methods for formally analyzing neural networks and control systems with neural network controllers in the area of autonomous cyber-physical systems (CPS). We describe the architecture of NNV, its core technology, and emphasize the approach and setup used for the Verification of Neural Networks Competition (VNN-COMP).

1 Introduction to NNV

The core technical approach of NNV is a collection of reachability algorithms that make use of star sets, although other convex set representations, such as zonotopes, are available as well. NNV supports both exact (sound and complete) and over-approximate (sound) reachability algorithms for verifying neural networks with piece-wise linear activation functions, and over-approximate for those containing nonlinearities. In addition, although outside of the scope of this competition, NNV also supports the verification of learning-enabled CPS, such as closed-loop control systems incorporating neural networks (Fig. 1).

NNV was first introduced in 2020 as a verification tool with a focus on feedforward neural networks and learning-enabled CPS [22], built on previously published algorithms [16,18,19]. Since the first tool publication, there have been several publications describing new approaches to improve scalability and support verification of novel deep learning architectures [3,9,15,21], as well as the use of NNV in case studies [6,12,23], and a more recent tool overview introduced as NNV 2.0 [8]. A full list of publications can be found on the project website.

Competition Approach

Our star-set-based algorithms are designed to run on CPU, and are naturally parallelizable, which allows NNV to perform efficiently on multi-core platforms. For this competition, we tailor the solver approach depending on the benchmark at hand, although all follow a similar flow, as depicted in Fig. 2. Initially, we import the neural network (ONNX) and specification (VNNLIB) into NNV. Secondly, we perform a simulation-guided search for counterexamples for a fixed number of samples, preset for the competition. If no counterexamples are found (i.e., demonstrate that the property is SAT), then we utilize an iterative refinement approach using reachability analysis to verify the property (UNSAT). This

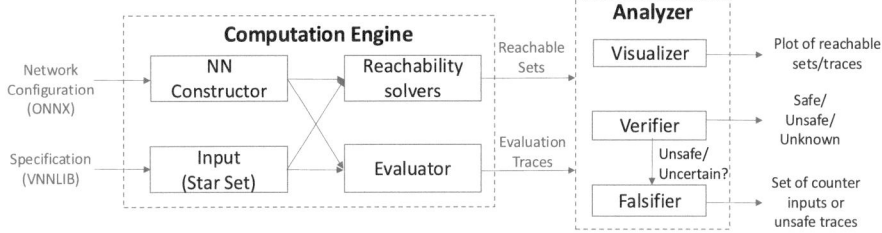

Fig. 1. Overview of our NNV architecture.

consists of performing more and more precise reachability analysis approaches until the specification is either verified or the time limit has been reached. Based on the benchmark to evaluate, the initial reachability analysis is selected based on the complexity of the benchmarks (size of network, input, etc.). The methods used can be divided into 3 main categories: "relax-star", "approx-star", and "exact-star" [19–21].

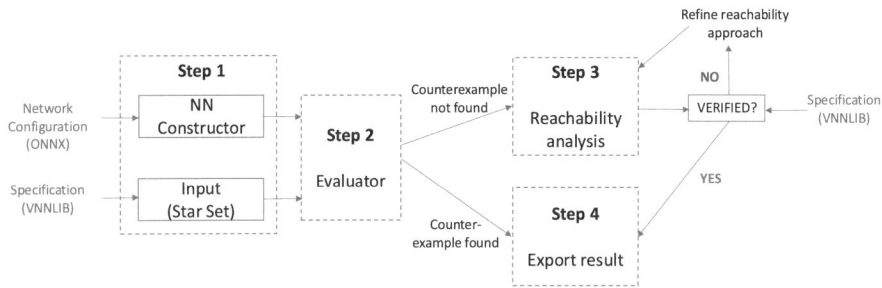

Fig. 2. Overview of our approach for the competition.

Similar to the 2024 approach, we participate in all the regular track benchmarks (except LinearizeNN) and as many of the extended track ones as our ONNX importer supports the conversion from. We illustrate Fig. 2 with one example computation of the *safeNLP* benchmark. **Step 1**, import the neural network ('Medical' or 'RUArobot') and specification (e.g., 'hyperrectangle_67) into NNV. **Step 2**, we search for a counterexample by doing a simulation-guided search for a maximum of N samples (In 2024, N=100 for all benchmarks). If no counterexample is found: **Step 3**, reachability analysis, otherwise, we skip this step and directly export the result as SAT, providing the counterexample and its computation time. For all *safeNLP* instances, we initially select a fast and over-approximate method, "relax-star" with a relax factor of 50% [21]. If the instance is not verified, then we would proceed to compute the reachable sets with the approximate reachability method ('approx-star') [20]. This may continue to refine until the "exact-star" method is used, which either proves the specification be SAT or UNSAT, no refinement possible. The other possible outcome is that the reachability computation does not end within the time allowed for the instance, for which the result is a *timeout*.

2 Tool Architecture

NNV is a verification tool written in MATLAB, and we make use of the following toolboxes:

- Computer Vision
- Control Systems
- Deep Learning
- Image Processing
- Optimization
- Parallel Computing
- Statistics and Machine Learning
- Symbolic Math
- System Identification

In addition to MATLAB's toolboxes, we built NNV using several open-source libraries, including CORA [1], used for reachability analysis of nonlinear ordinary differential equations, MPT toolbox [5] for polytope-based operations, YALMIP [7] to provide flexibility in choosing an optimization solver, as well as MATLAB's own optimization solver [14] and GLPK [10], the default solvers. NNV also makes use of MATLAB's Deep Learning toolbox to load the Open Neural Network Exchange (ONNX) format [11,13], and the Hybrid Systems Model Transformation and Translation tool (HyST) [2] for NNCS plant configuration. A parser for VNNLIB specifications was developed to allow import/export of neural network verification properties, and it is included in the repository alongside the core NNV operations.

3 Tool Setup and Configuration

NNV is available at our GitHub repository: https://github.com/verivital/nnv. Included in the repository is the **README** file detailing the instructions for installing and using the toolbox. For Ubuntu systems, after MATLAB is downloaded, it can be as simple as running the following commands:

```
$ git clone --recursive \url{https://github.com/verivital/nnv.git}
$ cd nnv
$ chmod +x install_ubuntu.sh
$ ./install_ubuntu.sh
```

Before running the tool for the first time, ensure you execute the *install.m* file to install MATLAB dependencies. From then onwards, users must run the *startup_nnv.m* to ensure the tool is added to MATLAB's path. To help get started with NNV, we provide a set of examples and tutorials [4,17] that include reachability analysis computation of several applications such as verification of semantic segmentation (UNet) of medical images, safety verification of NNCS, verification of MNIST classifiers, reachable set visualizations, and more. In addition, NNV can be executed online without installing MATLAB or other dependencies through CodeOcean[1]. For the competition, a sample script to reproduce an instance verification is as follows:

```
%% Sample script to verify VNNCOMP instance in NNV
% import ONNX network
net = importNetworkFromONNX('path-to-onnx-file');
% transform into NNV
net = matlab2nnv(net);
% Select property to verify
vnnlib_file = 'path-to-vnnlib-file';
% Define reachability parameters
reachOptions = struct;
reachOptions.reachMethod = 'reach-method'; % e.g.,
    'approx-star'
% Verify network
res = net.verify_vnnlib(vnnlib_file,reachOptions);
```

4 Software Project and Contributors

The NNV tool is an open-source project with an MIT License hosted on GitHub[2]. It is maintained by the VeriVITAL[3] group at Vanderbilt University, where the main developer (at time of publication) is Diego Manzanas Lopez.

Since its beginning almost a decade ago, there have been several contributors, directly (implementation, case studies) or indirectly (theory), including, in no particular order, Hoang-Dung Tran (original author and developer of NNV), Taylor T. Johnson, Neelanjana Pal, Xiaodong Yang, Samuel Sasaki, Sung Woo Choi, Patrick Musau, Anne Tumlin, Serena Serbinowska, Luan Viet Nguyen, Mykhailo Ivashchenko, Stanley Bak, Weiming Xiang, Kerianne Hobbs, Feiyang Cai, Xenofon Koutsoukos, Tomoya Yamaguchi, Bardh Hoxha, and Danil Prokhorov.

Acknowledgements. The material presented in this paper is based upon work supported by the National Science Foundation (NSF) through grant numbers 2220426 and 2220401 and the Defense Advanced Research Projects Agency (DARPA) under contract number FA8750-23-C-0518. Any opinions, findings, and conclusions or recommendations expressed in this paper are those of the authors and do not necessarily reflect the views of DARPA or NSF.

---

[1] NNV 2.0 CodeOcean capsule https://doi.org/10.24433/CO.0803700.v1.
[2] https://github.com/verivital/nnv.
[3] https://www.verivital.com/.

Data Availability Statement. As the 2025 event has not finished yet, we have not published the tool archive yet, but we will do so when it concludes. We will provide in a similar manner as we did for the 2024 edition, which can be found here: https://zenodo.org/records/6840546

References

1. Althoff, M.: An introduction to CORA 2015. In: Proceedings of the Workshop on Applied Verification for Continuous and Hybrid Systems (2015)
2. Bak, S., Bogomolov, S., Johnson, T.T.: Hyst: a source transformation and translation tool for hybrid automaton models. In: Proceedings of the 18th International Conference on Hybrid Systems: Computation and Control. p. 128–133. HSCC '15, Association for Computing Machinery, New York, NY, USA (2015). https://doi.org/10.1145/2728606.2728630
3. Ivashchenko, M., Choi, S.W., Nguyen, L.V., Tran, H.D.: Verifying binary neural networks on continuous input space using star reachability. In: 2023 IEEE/ACM 11th International Conference on Formal Methods in Software Engineering (FormaliSE), pp. 7–17 (2023). https://doi.org/10.1109/FormaliSE58978.2023.00009
4. Johnson, T.T., Lopez, D.M., Tran, H.D.: Tutorial: Safe, secure, and trustworthy artificial intelligence (ai) via formal verification of neural networks and autonomous cyber-physical systems (cps) with nnv. In: 2024 54th Annual IEEE/IFIP International Conference on Dependable Systems and Networks - Supplemental Volume (DSN-S), pp. 65–66 (2024). https://doi.org/10.1109/DSN-S60304.2024.00027
5. Kvasnica, M., Grieder, P., Baotić, M., Morari, M.: Multi-parametric toolbox (mpt). In: Alur, R., Pappas, G.J. (eds.) Hybrid Systems: Computation and Control, pp. 448–462. Springer, Berlin Heidelberg, Berlin, Heidelberg (2004)
6. Lopez, D.M., Johnson, T.T., Bak, S., Tran, H.D., Hobbs, K.: Evaluation of neural network verification methods for air to air collision avoidance. AIAA J. Air Transp. (JAT) (2022)
7. Löfberg, J.Y.: A toolbox for modeling and optimization in matlab. In: Proceedings of the CACSD Conference. Taipei, Taiwan (2004)
8. Manzanas Lopez, D., Choi, S.W., Tran, H.D., Johnson, T.T.: Nnv 2.0: The neural network verification tool. In: Enea, C., Lal, A. (eds.) Computer Aided Verification, pp. 397–412. Springer Nature Switzerland, Cham (2023)
9. Manzanas Lopez, D., Musau, P., Hamilton, N., Johnson, T.: Reachability analysis of a general class of neural ordinary differential equation. In: Proceedings of the 20th International Conference on Formal Modeling and Analysis of Timed Systems (FORMATS 2022), Co-Located with CONCUR, FMICS, and QEST as part of CONFEST 2022. Warsaw, Poland (September 2022)
10. Oki, E.: GLPK (gnu linear programming kit) (2012)
11. (ONNX), O.N.N.E.: https://github.com/onnx/
12. Robinette, P.K., Lopez, M.D., Serbinowska, S., Leach, K., Johnson, T.T.: Case study: neural network malware detection verification for feature and image datasets. In: Proceedings of the 2024 IEEE/ACM 12th International Conference on Formal Methods in Software Engineering (FormaliSE), pp. 127–137. FormaliSE '24, Association for Computing Machinery, New York, NY, USA (2024). https://doi.org/10.1145/3644033.3644372

13. The MathWorks, I.: Deep Learning Toolbox Converter for ONNX Model Format. Natick, Massachusetts, United State (2024). https://www.mathworks.com/matlabcentral/fileexchange/67296-deep-learning-toolbox-converter-for-onnx-model-format
14. The MathWorks, I.: Optimization Toolbox. Natick, Massachusetts, United State (2024). https://www.mathworks.com/products/optimization.html
15. Tran, H.D., Bak, S., Xiang, W., Johnson, T.T.: Verification of deep convolutional neural networks using imagestars. In: 32nd International Conference on Computer-Aided Verification (CAV). Springer (2020)
16. Tran, H.D., Cei, F., Lopez, D.M., Johnson, T.T., Koutsoukos, X.: Safety verification of cyber-physical systems with reinforcement learning control. In: ACM SIGBED International Conference on Embedded Software (EMSOFT'19). ACM (2019)
17. Tran, H.D., Manzanas Lopez, D., Johnson, T.: Tutorial: Neural network and autonomous cyber-physical systems formal verification for trustworthy AI and safe autonomy. In: Proceedings of the International Conference on Embedded Software, pp. 1–2. EMSOFT '23, Association for Computing Machinery, New York, NY, USA (2024). https://doi.org/10.1145/3607890.3608454
18. Tran, H.D., et al.: Parallelizable reachability analysis algorithms for feed-forward neural networks. In: Proceedings of the 7th International Workshop on Formal Methods in Software Engineering (FormaliSE'19), pp. 31–40. FormaliSE '19, IEEE Press, Piscataway, NJ, USA (2019). https://doi.org/10.1109/FormaliSE.2019.00012
19. Tran, H.D., et al.: Star-based reachability analysis for deep neural networks. In: 23rd International Symposium on Formal Methods (FM'19). Springer International Publishing (2019)
20. Tran, H.D.: Verification of piecewise deep neural networks: a star set approach with zonotope pre-filter. Form. Asp. Comput. **33**(4–5), 519–545 (2021). https://doi.org/10.1007/s00165-021-00553-4
21. Tran, H.-D., et al.: Robustness verification of semantic segmentation neural networks using relaxed reachability. In: Silva, A., Leino, K.R.M. (eds.) CAV 2021. LNCS, vol. 12759, pp. 263–286. Springer, Cham (2021). https://doi.org/10.1007/978-3-030-81685-8_12
22. Tran, H.D., et al.: NNV: The neural network verification tool for deep neural networks and learning-enabled cyber-physical systems. In: 32nd International Conference on Computer-Aided Verification (CAV) (2020)
23. Tumlin, A.M., et al.: The neural network verification tool for certifying fairness. In: Proceedings of the 5th ACM International Conference on AI in Finance, pp. 36–44. ICAIF '24, Association for Computing Machinery, New York, NY, USA (2024). https://doi.org/10.1145/3677052.3698677

PyRAT: Verifying Neural Networks with Abstract Interpretation (Competition Contribution)

Augustin Lemesle, Julien Lehmann, Tristan Le Gall[✉], and Zakaria Chihani

University Paris-Saclay, CEA, LIST, Orsay, France
tristan.le-gall@cea.fr

Abstract. PYRAT, a tool based on abstract interpretation to verify the safety and robustness of neural networks, is participating in VNN-Comp for the third time in a row. PYRAT uses multiple abstractions to find the reachable states of a neural network, starting from its input and propagating it through the layers in a fast and accurate analysis. It has been applied on public benchmarks as well as industrial use-cases.

1 Introduction

PYRAT (**Py**thon **R**eachability **A**ssessment **T**ool), a verification tool under development at CEA since 2019, relies on *Abstract Interpretation* techniques to prove safety properties on Neural Networks (NN). It has participated in the international neural network verification competition (VNN-Comp) in 2023 and 2024, achieving third and second place respectively [1,2], and is participating in 2025 as well.

Abstract Interpretation. The main idea is to abstract the set of inputs as an element of an *abstract domain* (such as a Zonotope or a Polytope) which is then passed along the NN; it yields an over-approximation of the output which is used to evaluate the property. The accuracy of an analysis by abstract interpretation heavily depends on the chosen abstract domain. If the result of the analysis is too imprecise, one way to improve the precision is to combine several abstract domains [5,10]. By default, the low-cost Box domain (relying on interval arithmetic), will always be used by PYRAT as it is exact on ReLU. Nevertheless, it cannot represent relations between different variables. Therefore, more precise domains are used, mainly (constrained) Zonotopes.

Zonotopes and Constrained Zonotopes. A *zonotope* is formally defined as the weighted *Minkwoski sum* over a set of m *noise symbols*. Initially, noise symbols are introduced to represent the variations of the inputs. More noise symbols are later introduced to overapproximate non-linear operations such as ReLU. Since the noise symbols are shared between variables of different dimensions, they implicitly define linear relations between variables. For the affine layers, PYRAT relies on affine arithmetic [4] to compute the layers' output.

In order to get more precise abstractions of non-linear functions, we add linear constraints shared over the dimensions of the *zonotope* [12]. Thus, *constrained zonotopes* are more precise, but their concretisation requires to solve a system of linear equations with linear inequality constraints. To efficiently solve these equations, PYRAT integrates an in-house linear solver that computes simple yet precise conservative bounds.

Correctness. At the end of its analysis, PYRAT obtains an over-approximation of the achievable outputs of the network on which it evaluates the given property. In that sense, PYRAT is **correct** but the abstraction may be too rough and the reachability analysis alone may not be able to conclude on the property.

2 Tool Architecture

2.1 Preprocessing

PYRAT first performs a simplification of the network by relying partly on the `onnx-simplifier` library to remove unneeded dynamical parts of an ONNX model. Further simplifications may include removing unneeded softmax, fusing matmul and add, etc. Some patterns from exported neural networks are also recognized and simplified, e.g. the SiLU ($x \mapsto x \times sigmoid(x)$) is treated as a unique *SiLU* layer. These operations remain conservative and do not alter the result of the network inference w.r.t. the property.

2.2 Reachability Analysis

After preprocessing, PYRAT performs its main analysis. As explained in the introduction, it is a reachability analysis based on abstract interpretation that mostly either proves the given property or does not conclude and, in rarer cases, disproves a violated property. When an analysis does not conclude, PYRAT can perform multiple analyses to provide more accurate results by partitioning the verification problem. This method is called *Branch and Bound* (BaB) [3]. PYRAT implements both BaB on inputs and BaB on ReLU nodes.

BaB on inputs. splits the input space of the property recursively until every subspace is proven safe or until one of the subspaces invalidates the property. To determine how to split the inputs, PYRAT implements multiple heuristics including its own: ReCIPH [6]. This BaB approach performs well on low dimensional inputs but struggles when the input space gets bigger, e.g. for images. Indeed, with higher dimensions, the number of divisions needed to achieve an increase in precision grows exponentially as inputs are often very interconnected. To resolve this issue, BaB on ReLU has been developed, directly dividing the intermediate network space.

BaB on ReLU. Initially presented in RELUPLEX [8], BaB on ReLU is also implemented in PYRAT. It forces the input of a specific ReLU to be either positive or negative which transforms the ReLU into a linear operation: the 0-function if the input is negative and the identity if the input is positive. On each branch, these constraints are enforced on the current abstract domains and are soundly handled by our solver. The *constrained zonotope* domain is by default the domain used in this case as it can natively support these constraints. Thus, using BaB on ReLU allows PYRAT to be **complete** given an infinite timeout for ReLU-only networks.

2.3 Counterexample Check

While the primary objective of PYRAT remains to prove that the property holds, it can happen that the property does not hold. Such cases tend to be hard to handle with abstract interpretation alone as it over-approximates the outputs. Thus, complementary to reachability analysis, PYRAT will look for a counterexample. Random points and adversarial attacks will be generated before the analysis to try to falsify the property through inferences on the model. If a counterexample is found, PYRAT will return it and conclude the analysis as the property is falsified. This counterexample search is optional and tunable with the adversarial attack parameters. Using the `foolbox` library on top of in-house adversarial attacks, PYRAT can use a large scope of attacks such as FGSM [7], PGD [9], DeepFool [11], etc.

3 Discussion

In this section, we discuss the results of PYRAT on the benchmarks of VNN-Comp. While writing this paper, new benchmarks were recently proposed for VNN-Comp 2025, but not yet officially selected. Therefore, we focus the discussion about the 2024 benchmarks.

3.1 Choice of Parameters

We first discuss some general strategies when choosing the parameters of an analysis with PYRAT depending on the type of benchmarks. While each benchmark presents its specificities and the parameter tuning might be very specific, we regroup them here according to general categories.

First are benchmarks with small size networks (`acasxu`, `linarizenn`, etc.), usually fully connected networks and low number of inputs. *zonotope*, combined with BaB on input to balance speed and precision, is often enough to prove most properties and more precise domains do not bring concrete improvements to the analysis. Multi processing can also be used to speed up the analyses. For larger size benchmarks, such as `cora` or `cgan`, with more inputs or more parameters in the network, the imprecision introduced when using the *zonotope* grows faster and thus we prefer to rely on more precise domains such as *constrained zonotope* and eventually BaB on ReLU nodes, if such exist. The gain of precision outweighs the additional costs of these methods. Additionally, in the case of ReLU-only networks, we can provide a complete approach. For more diverse activation functions (Sigmoid, Sin, Pow,...) that we can find in the VNN-Comp benchmarks (`ml4acopf`, `dist_shift`,...), the *constrained zonotope* domains may still bring some additional precision as compared to *zonotope* but PYRAT is not complete in these cases.

Finally, on large scale benchmarks like `cifar100` or `vggnet16` with a large number of parameters and inputs, on top of *constrained zonotope* and BaB on ReLU, PYRAT relies on GPU to speed up the analysis which would quickly timeout on CPUs. However, with this we loose soundness $w.r.t$ to real arithmetics.

On top of PYRAT's analysis, counterexamples search is tuned depending on the benchmark to allocate more or less time to this search.

3.2 Strengths

PYRAT performs particularly well on problems with small input spaces which can be explained by the cheapness of the *zonotope* domain combined with a well-calibrated BaB on input.

Additionally, the *constrained zonotope* domain in PYRAT provides an important increase in precision on many activation functions through the addition of constraints. The maximal number of allowed constraints can also be tuned to limit the overhead.

All domains and abstractions of PYRAT provide a correct over-approximation of the reachable states of a neural network, thus preventing false negatives or positives, as shown by [13] and the absence of penalties received in the VNN-Comp 2024. Contrary to many tools, PYRAT is also sound $w.r.t$ real arithmetic. This is done by ensuring, for each floating-point operator, that each possible rounding of its output is included in the abstraction of this operator, bringing an additional guarantee on the result of the analysis. Since selecting the rounding mode on a GPU is more complex, this guarantee is foregone when PYRAT runs on a GPU.

Finally, PYRAT supports a large number of layers such as the attention layers of transformers, trigonometric activation functions, etc. While some of this support remains limited, it was one of only two tools (with $\alpha, \beta-$CROWN) used on all benchmarks of the main and extended tracks in 2024.

3.3 Weaknesses

On larger problems requiring the use of BaB on ReLU like `tinyimagenet`, PYRAT still struggles to reach the performance of $\alpha, \beta-$CROWN and fails to prove some properties. Our BaB heuristics and techniques would thus benefit from more improvements to fully scale on large models. Moreover, the counterexample search in PYRAT is not very adapted to the BaB on ReLU yet, *i.e.* not taking the current fixed ReLU as inputs. Therefore, this results in lower performance in terms of the number of UNSAT results for some benchmarks, compared to other tools. The counterexample search will be improved in future work, including its automation based on the ongoing analysis, for example so that we do not spend too much time when the property is close to being proved.

In theory, methods based on Abstract Interpretation can deal with any layer of a NN. In practice, the abstract domains currently implemented in PYRAT do not fare well with any operator that involves the multiplication of two matrices. Therefore, PYRAT works poorly on benchmarks like vit. More generally some abstraction like Cos and Sin, due to their limited use in the use case encountered by PYRAT, remain quite imprecise and could be further improved.

4 Usage and Availability

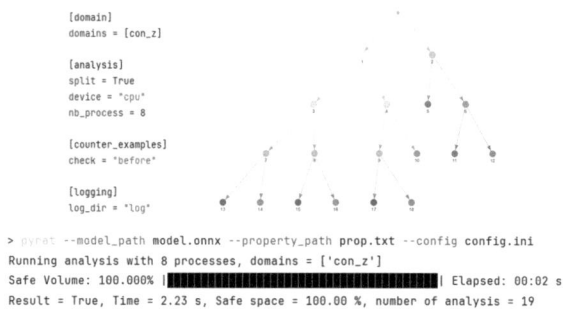

Fig. 1. Example of configuration file (top left), command line execution (bottom) and output split tree (top right).

As a Python module, PYRAT can be used directly in Python or from command line. Using `ConfigArgParse`, it can take arguments from the command line using specific keywords or with a configuration file containing the different parameters. This is the easiest way to run PYRAT on a new task, as shown in Fig. 1: write a small, rather simple configuration file and call PYRAT with the following command:

```
> pyrat -mp model.onnx -pp property.vnnlib -c config.ini
```

Using the *zonotope* domain is a good starting point for any task and depending on the input dimensionnality BaB on either input or ReLU can be used to improve the results.

During the analysis, PYRAT displays information such as the current time taken by the analysis along with the percentage of completion for BaB. Following an analysis, PYRAT will provide four possible outputs: "True", the property is verified; "False", the property is false and a counterexample is provided; "Unknown", it could not be verified nor falsified with the given options; "Timeout", the analysis stops when the (optional) timeout is reached.

Availability. While PYRAT is closed-source, it can be made freely available under an academic licence for research and teaching purposes. To obtain a license and a compiled version of the tool, please contact us through the PYRAT website, which is available at https://pyrat-analyzer.com/.

Main contributors. (current) Augustin Lemesle, Julien Lehmann, Tristan Le Gall; (past) Serge Durand, Samuel Akinwande.

References

1. Brix, C., Bak, S., Johnson, T.T., Wu, H.: The fifth international verification of neural networks competition (VNN-comp 2024): summary and results (2024). https://arxiv.org/abs/2412.19985
2. Brix, C., Bak, S., Liu, C., Johnson, T.T.: The fourth international verification of neural networks competition (VNN-comp 2023): Summary and results. arXiv preprint arXiv:2312.16760 (2023)
3. Bunel, R., Lu, J., Turkaslan, I., Torr, P.H., Kohli, P., Kumar, M.P.: Branch and bound for piecewise linear neural network verification. J. Mach. Learn. Res. **21**(42), 1–39 (2020)
4. Comba, J.L.D., Stol, J.: Affine arithmetic and its applications to computer graphics. In: Proceedings of VI SIBGRAPI (Brazilian Symposium on Computer Graphics and Image Processing), pp. 9–18 (1993)
5. Cousot, P.: Principles of abstract interpretation. MIT Press (2022)
6. Durand, S., Lemesle, A., Chihani, Z., Urban, C., Terrier, F.: Reciph: relational coefficients for input partitioning heuristic. In: 1st Workshop on Formal Verification of Machine Learning (WFVML 2022) (2022)
7. Goodfellow, I.J., Shlens, J., Szegedy, C.: Explaining and harnessing adversarial examples (2015). https://arxiv.org/abs/1412.6572
8. Katz, G., Barrett, C., Dill, D.L., Julian, K., Kochenderfer, M.J.: Reluplex: An Efficient SMT Solver for Verifying Deep Neural Networks. In: Majumdar, R., Kunčak, V. (eds.) CAV 2017. LNCS, vol. 10426, pp. 97–117. Springer, Cham (2017). https://doi.org/10.1007/978-3-319-63387-9_5
9. Madry, A., Makelov, A., Schmidt, L., Tsipras, D., Vladu, A.: Towards deep learning models resistant to adversarial attacks (2019). https://arxiv.org/abs/1706.06083
10. Mazzucato, D., Urban, C.: Reduced products of abstract domains for fairness certification of neural networks. In: Drăgoi, C., Mukherjee, S., Namjoshi, K. (eds.) Static Analysis, pp. 308–322. Springer International Publishing, Cham (2021)
11. Moosavi-Dezfooli, S.M., Fawzi, A., Frossard, P.: Deepfool: a simple and accurate method to fool deep neural networks (2016). https://arxiv.org/abs/1511.04599
12. Scott, J.K., Raimondo, D.M., Marseglia, G.R., Braatz, R.D.: Constrained zonotopes: a new tool for set-based estimation and fault detection. Automatica **69**, 126–136 (2016). https://doi.org/10.1016/j.automatica.2016.02.036, https://linkinghub.elsevier.com/retrieve/pii/S0005109816300772
13. Zhou, X., Xu, H., Xu, A., Shi, Z., Hsieh, C.J., Zhang, H.: Testing neural network verifiers: a soundness benchmark with hidden counterexamples (2024). https://arxiv.org/abs/2412.03154

SobolBox: Boxed Refinement of Sobol Sequence Samples for Neural Network Verification (Competition Contribution)

Sarthak Das[✉] [iD]

Indian Institute of Technology Gandhinagar, Gandhinagar, India
sarthak.das@iitgn.ac.in

Abstract. SobolBox is a Python tool for the detection of safety violations in neural networks by computing the bounds of the output variables, given the bounds of the input variables of the network. This is done using global extrema estimation via Sobol sequence sampling, and further refinement using L-BFGS-B for local optimization around the initial guess. This paper presents an overview of SobolBox, as well as our results for the ACAS Xu benchmarks.

Keywords: Neural Network Verification · Sobol Sequence · L-BFGS-B

1 Verification Approach

SobolBox takes as inputs a neural network given in an ONNX (Open Neural Network Exchange) format, and a safety specification given as a VNNLIB file. Thereafter, SobolBox verifies whether the given neural network satisfies the safety properties specified by the VNNLIB file.

It extracts input bounds for any given neural network directly from the VNNLIB file and generates a sample of input points using Sobol sequence sampling, which is a quasi-Monte Carlo method used to generate a low-discrepancy, deterministic sample of parameter values from a multidimensional distribution [8]. Sobol sequencing is scalable and requires fewer samples to achieve the same level of accuracy as uniform sampling. This makes it particularly useful in sensitivity analysis.

By computing the neural network outputs across these points, SobolBox identifies promising regions where global optima might be found. For each output variable, the arg min and arg max are chosen, and a limited-memory boxed BFGS (L-BFGS-B) optimization [2] is performed to quickly converge to a local optima around that region and refine the preliminary estimate obtained from Sobol. This ensures a good estimate of the output bounds.

Once these extrema estimates are obtained, they are fed into Microsoft Z3 Theorem Prover [4] along with the safety specification for analysis.

- If the analysis determines that a safety violation is not possible given the computed output bounds, the tool returns unsat. The output bounds computed by our algorithm are under-approximations. As such, unsat results are high confidence, but not absolute guarantees.
- If the analysis finds a Sobol sequence sample or an optima that is a valid safety violation, the tool returns sat along with the counterexample.
- If the tool encounters safety specifications with complex disjunctions on input variables (such as in property 6 of the ACAS Xu benchmarks) or neural networks of input size greater than 21021 (SobolBox uses SciPy for Sobol sequence sampling, and is therefore limited to a maximum input dimension of 21201 as noted in SciPy's documentation [7]), or if the analysis is inconclusive, the tool quits gracefully and returns unknown.

Detailed pseudocode for SobolBox's verification algorithm is presented in Algorithm 1 and a schematic for the algorithm pipeline is presented in Fig. 1.

Algorithm 1. SobolBox Verification Algorithm

Require: Neural network N (ONNX), safety specification S (VNNLIB)
Ensure: Verification result: unsat, sat (with counterexample CE) or unknown
1: $inputSize \leftarrow getInputSize(N)$
2: $Solver \leftarrow Z3Solver(S)$
3: **if** $complexDisjunction(Solver) \lor inputSize > 21201$ **then**
4:     **return** unknown
5: **end if**
6: $\mathcal{B} \leftarrow extractInputBounds(Solver)$
7: $n \leftarrow \min(8192, \max(2048, 2^{\lceil \log_2(20 \times inputSize) \rceil}))$
8: $X \leftarrow Sobol(n, \mathcal{B})$
9: $R \leftarrow extractOptima(N, X)$
10: $O \leftarrow L\_BFGS\_B(R)$
11: $Solver.add(boundaryConstraints(O))$
12: **if** $Solver.check() = unsat$ **then**
13:     **return** unsat
14: **end if**
15: **for** $r \in R \cup X$ **do**
16:     **if** $Solver.evaluate(r, N(r))$ **then**
17:         CE $\leftarrow Solver.model()$
18:         **return** sat, CE
19:     **end if**
20: **end for**
21: **return** unknown

SobolBox also implements caching of Sobol sequences as well as computed output bounds to reduce computational overheads over incremental runs.

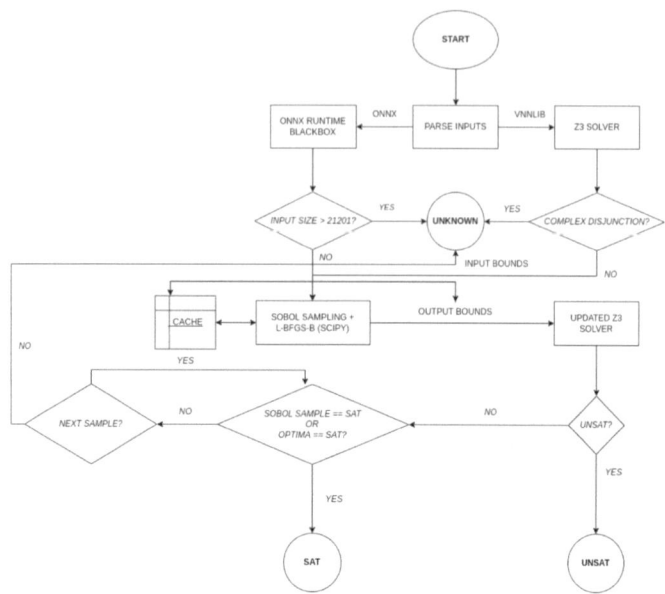

Fig. 1. A schematic of `SobolBox`'s verification algorithm.

2 Software Architecture

`SobolBox` is written in Python, and makes use of the following libraries:

- **Microsoft ONNX Runtime.** For ONNX parsing and computing neural network outputs.
- **SciPy.** For Sobol sampling and L-BFGS-B.
- **Microsoft Z3 Theorem Prover.** For SMT solving and VNNLIB parsing (a deliberate choice to minimize the number of libraries, given VNNLIB is written as a subset of the SMT-LIB2 standard [3]).

3 Discussion

`SobolBox` treats neural networks as non-convex, differentiable, multi-input multi-output (MIMO) black boxes. As such, its verification algorithm assumes limited resources (no GPU acceleration) and no domain-specific knowledge (no encoding of the neural network architecture) – meaning that the algorithm could potentially be extended to other such systems as well.

As Sobol sequencing is scalable and can be used in high-dimensional spaces, the tool is consequently scalable and – as our results show – able to detect counterexamples within reasonable time, providing safety certifications with high confidence but no absolute guarantees. Moreover, caching of Sobol sequences implies that given the number of input dimensions (regardless of network architecture), sampling is done only once – thus improving performance over incremental runs.

4 Tool Setup and Configuration

The source code is available at https://github.com/dassarthak18/SobolBox, licensed under the MIT license. All the prerequisites are in `requirements.txt`. Assuming Python 3.7+ and pip3 are already installed, install the tool by simply cloning the repository and running the `pip3 install -r requirements.txt` command. This process has been automated in `install_tool.sh` located in the `vnncomp_scripts` directory of the VNNCOMP-2025 branch.

SobolBox is designed for the safety verification of all non-convex, differentiable MIMO black boxes. As such, it intends to participate in all benchmark categories of the competition. The VNNCOMP-2025 branch has been finalized, and is configured for the competition. Thus, no additional configuration is required.

5 Experimental Evaluation

ACAS Xu is a family of 45 real-world deep neural networks (further classified into 5 groups of 9 networks each), developed as an early prototype for the next-generation airborne collision avoidance system for unmanned aircraft. All of these networks are fully connected, having 6 layers and 300 ReLU nodes each [6]. There are a total of 10 properties, with properties 1–4 to be verified for each network and properties 5–10 to be verified for a single network – amounting to a total of 186 benchmarks [1].

For the purposes of this paper, we evaluate SobolBox on all the 186 ACAS Xu benchmarks. The evaluation is done on a Google Colab notebook with Python 3 Google Compute Engine backend (with 2 vCPU cores and 12.7GB RAM) and takes a total of 250.872 s. We compare our results with the top 3 tools from VNNCOMP-2024 – namely α,β-CROWN [10], Marabou [9] and PyRAT [5] – in the same benchmarks. We observe that our tool generates only one false negative like Marabou (specifically on instance 1_3 for property 2, which is falsely marked unsat), and all our other sat and unsat results agree with the ground truth as established by α,β-CROWN (which boasts not only a 100% solvability but also a 100% accuracy). Our summarized results are presented in Table 1.

Table 1. Benchmark 2023-acasxu

Tool	unsat	sat	unknown	Penalty	Solved (%)
SobolBox	117	39	29	1	83.8%
Marabou	134	45	6	1	96.2%
PyRAT	137	47	2	0	98.9%
α,β-CROWN	139	47	0	0	100%

6 Conclusion

In this paper, we presented SobolBox – a Python tool for the safety verification of non-convex, differentiable MIMO black boxes such as neural networks. Future iterations of the tool will explore approaches for handling unknown instances and assuring soundness in unsat results via black box over-approximation techniques.

Acknowledgments. The author acknowledges Dr. Rajarshi Ray, Associate Professor at IACS Kolkata, Shubhajit Roy, Senior Research Fellow at IIT Gandhinagar, and Avishek Lahiri, Senior Research Fellow at IACS Kolkata for their valuable feedback. Last but not the least, the author would also like to thank his dear friend Katha Haldar, Research Assistant at Indiana University Indianapolis for her unwavering encouragement and support.

Disclosure of Interests. The author declares that he has no competing interests.

References

1. C. Brix, S. Bak, C. Liu, and T. T. Johnson, "The Fifth International Verification of Neural Networks Competition (VNN-COMP 2024): Summary and Results," arXiv preprint arXiv:2412.19985, 2024. https://doi.org/10.48550/arXiv.2412.19985
2. Byrd, R. H., Nocedal, P. Lu, J., Zhu, C.: "A limited memory algorithm for bound constrained optimization," SIAM Journal on Scientific Computing, vol. 16, no. 5, pp. 1190–1208, 1995. https://doi.org/10.1137/0916069
3. Demarchi, S., Guidotti, D., Pulina, L., Tacchella, A.: "Supporting standardization of neural networks verification with VNNLIB and CoCoNet," In: Proceedings of the 6th Workshop on Formal Methods for ML-Enabled Autonomous Systems, N. Narodytska, G. Amir, G. Katz, and O. Isac, Eds., ser. Kalpa Publications in Computing, vol. 16, EasyChair, 2023, pp. 47–58. https://doi.org/10.29007/5pdh
4. de Moura, L., Bjørner, N.: "Z3: an efficient smt solver," In: Tools and Algorithms for the Construction and Analysis of Systems, C. R. Ramakrishnan and J. Rehof, Eds., Berlin, Heidelberg: Springer Berlin Heidelberg, 2008, pp. 337–340, ISBN: 978-3-540-78800-3. https://doi.org/10.1007/978-3-540-78800-3_24
5. Lemesle, A., Lehmann, J., Le Gall, T.: "Neural network verification with PyRAT," arXiv preprint arXiv:2410.23903, 2024. https://doi.org/10.48550/arXiv.2410.23903
6. Owen, M.P., Panken, A., Moss, R., Alvarez, L., Leeper, C.: "ACAS Xu: integrated collision avoidance and detect and avoid capability for UAS,"In: IEEE/AIAA 38th Digital Avionics Systems Conference (DASC). San Diego, CA, USA **2019**, 1–10 (2019)
7. Oliphant, T., Jones, E., Peterson, P.:"SciPy documentation Version: 1.15.2", 2025. https://docs.scipy.org
8. Sobol, I.M.: "On the distribution of points in a cube and the approximate evaluation of integrals", USSR Computational Mathematics and Mathematical Physics, vol. 7, no. 4, 1967, pp. 86-112, ISSN 0041-5553. https://doi.org/10.1016/0041-5553(67)90144-9

9. H. Wu et al.: "Marabou 2.0: a versatile formal analyzer of neural networks," In. International Conference on Computer Aided Verification, Springer, 2024, pp. 249–264. https://doi.org/10.1007/978-3-031-65630-9_13
10. Zhang. H.: "α, β-CROWN (alpha-beta-CROWN): A Fast and Scalable Neural Network Verifier with Efficient Bound Propagation," GitHub, 2018. https://github.com/Verified-Intelligence/alpha-beta-CROWN

Author Index

A
Affeldt, Reynald 227
Agashe, Viraj 64
Alsmann, Eric 221
Alur, Rajeev 3

B
Barrett, Clark 64
Bosman, Annelot W. 29
Bruni, Alessandro 227

C
Capucci, Matteo 227
Casadio, Marco 180
Chakraborty, Saikat 64
Chihani, Zakaria 266
Chwiałkowski, Marcel 115
Clavière, Arthur 136
Cofer, Darren 136

D
Das, Sarthak 272
Dill, David 64
Duong, Hai 253

E
Elboher, Yizhak Yisrael 203

F
Flinkow, Thomas 180

G
Ghazel, Mohamed 97
Gopinath, Divya 3
Goubault, Eric 115

H
Hoos, Holger H. 29, 238

I
Isac, Omri 203

J
Johnson, Taylor T. 260

K
Katz, Guy 203
Kaulen, Konstantin 238
Kern, Philipp 156
Kessler, Colin 180
Khoo, Siau-Cheng 49
Kielhöfer, Lionel 29
Kirov, Dmitrii 136
Komendantskaya, Ekaterina 180, 227

L
Ladner, Tobias 203
Lahiri, Shuvendu K. 64
Lange, Martin 221
Le Gall, Tristan 266
Lehmann, Julien 266
Lemesle, Augustin 266
Lopez, Diego Manzanas 260

M
Malhotra, Alistair 180
Mangal, Ravi 3
Manino, Edoardo 156
Marchioni, Enrico 227
Marulanda-Giraldo, Jairo Miguel 227
McPherson, Robbie 180
Meyer, Pierre-Jean 97

N
Nguyen, ThanhVu 253

O
Othman, Albaraa Ammar 180

P
Păsăreanu, Corina S. 3
Putot, Sylvie 115

Q
Qiu, Xiaokang 64

S
Sasaki, Samuel 260
Sayed, Abdelrahman Sayed 97
Sinz, Carsten 156
Sun, Chuyue 64

T
Taneja, Jubi 64

V
van Rijn, Jan N. 29
Viola, Ignazio Maria 180

W
Watson, Christopher 3
Wu, Haoze 203

X
Xu, Hanping 49

Z
Zhi, Shaun Tan Zong 49
Zhong, Yuyi 49

MIX
Papier aus verantwortungsvollen Quellen
Paper from responsible sources
FSC® C105338

If you have any concerns about our products,
you can contact us on
ProductSafety@springernature.com

In case Publisher is established outside the EU,
the EU authorized representative is:
Springer Nature Customer Service Center GmbH
Europaplatz 3, 69115 Heidelberg, Germany

Printed by Libri Plureos GmbH
in Hamburg, Germany